POLITICS OF CONTROL

POLITICS OF CONTROL

Creating Red Culture in the
Early People's Republic of China

Chang-tai Hung

University of Hawai'i Press
Honolulu

26 25 24 23 22 21   6 5 4 3 2 1

Names: Hung, Chang-tai, author.
Title: Politics of control : creating red culture in the early People's
    Republic of China / Chang-tai Hung.
Description: Honolulu : University of Hawai'i Press, [2021] | Includes
    bibliographical references and index.
Identifiers: LCCN 2020043233 | ISBN 9780824884574 (cloth) | ISBN
    9780824886905 (pdf) | ISBN 9780824886912 (epub) | ISBN 9780824886929
    (kindle edition)
Subjects: LCSH: China—Politics and government—1949–1976. |
    China—Cultural policy.
Classification: LCC DS777.75 .H84 2021 | DDC 306.20951/09045—dc23
LC record available at https://lccn.loc.gov/2020043233

ISBN 978-0-8248-9260-9 (paperback)

Cover art: Tiananmen Gate, Beijing. The sign reads "Do not enter." Photo by Ming-mei Hung.

University of Hawai'i Press books are printed on
acid-free paper and meet the guidelines for permanence
and durability of the Council on Library Resources.

Illustrations

ACKNOWLEDGMENTS

A book that takes many years to write owes much to others. I gratefully acknowledge my intellectual debt to friends, colleagues, and scholars whose contributions are identified in the notes and bibliography.

This book is the result of many visits to the archives in the past fifteen years. I especially thank the staff at the Beijing Municipal Archives, the Shanghai Municipal Archives, the Academia Historica, and the Nationalist Party Archives for their valuable assistance.

Katy Meigs read the entire manuscript and offered trenchant comments and valuable advice on stylistic improvement. I am deeply indebted to Masako Ikeda at the University of Hawaiʻi Press who showed initial enthusiasm in this manuscript and prepared it for publication with meticulous care and efficacy. Managing editor Grace Wen wisely and gently guided me through the editorial process. I also thank Helen Glenn Court for copyediting the manuscript with great skill and a keen eye for detail.

On the personal side, I thank my daughter Ming-mei and my son Ming-yang for their help in preparing illustrations. My greatest debt is to my wife, Wai-han Mak, who read the manuscript many times and provided research input, incisive criticism, and editing support.

Several chapters of this book are revised versions of previously published journal articles. I thank the following publishers for their permission to reprint them here: "The Anti–Unity Sect Campaign and Mass Mobilization in the Early People's Republic of China," *China Quarterly* 202 (June 2010); "The Cultural Palace of Nationalities: Ethnicities under One Roof?" *Journal of Contemporary History* 47, no. 3 (July 2012); "A Political Park: The Working People's Cultural Palace in Beijing," *Journal of Contemporary History* 48, no. 3 (July 2013); "Inside a Chinese Communist Municipal Newspaper: Purges at the *Beijing Daily,*" *Journal of Contemporary History* 49, no. 2 (April 2014); and "Turning a Chinese Kid Red: Kindergartens in the Early People's Republic," *Journal of Contemporary China* 23, no. 89 (September 2014).

Note on Romanization

The book uses the pinyin system of transliteration. Exceptions, however, are the names of well-known persons, for example, Sun Yat-sen and Chiang Kai-shek, for which established spellings have long been familiar in the West.

Introduction

One night in January 1949, Tsinghua University professor Zhang Xiruo (1889–1973), accompanied by two People's Liberation Army (PLA) soldiers, paid a surprise visit to the renowned architecture scholar Liang Sicheng (1901–1972) at his home. The famed university, located in northwestern Beiping (renamed Beijing on October 1, 1949), had just fallen to the Red Army. For several weeks, Beiping had been under siege. This was a critical moment in the ongoing civil war (1946–1949) between the Nationalist Party, or Kuomintang (KMT), which controlled Beiping, and the Communists, and the Communists were unmistakably gaining an upper hand. The visitors came with a request. Liang's aide, recorded what happened:

> They said that the purpose of their visit was planning for a military assault on Beiping in case negotiations for a peaceful settlement with [KMT] commander General Fu Zuoyi [1895–1974] broke down. If the PLA was compelled to take the city by force, then [the Communists wanted] to take every measure to protect venerable architecture. These sites needed to be clearly identified. The soldiers then placed a military map on the table and asked Liang to mark down the locations of prized buildings.[1]

Liang Sicheng was deeply touched by this unexpected request, which was so unlike the usual behavior of local KMT authorities, who, according to Liang, showed little respect for China's historic buildings. He had been frustrated when these officials ignored his repeated requests for the preservation of old buildings and temples. In Liang's eyes, the Communists were true protectors of Chinese culture. Liang happily complied with the request.[2] He did not realize that the visit of the PLA soldiers was part of an overall city takeover plan of Mao Zedong (1893–1976) and the Chinese Communist Party (CCP) senior leadership. Capturing Beiping peacefully would mean that numerous lives and treasured buildings would be spared, which would be a major political victory for the CCP. The Communists could project themselves as protectors of the city, which was home to magnificent palaces and memorable buildings.

1

Liang badly misinterpreted the situation. A few years later, in the mid-1950s, he would come into bitter conflict with the Communist rulers, who ordered the demolition of Beijing's age-old city walls and buildings to develop a new industrial center.[3] He also would become a target of criticism for his alleged support of "traditional revivalism," "bourgeois idealism," and "formalism" in preserving dead relics and squandering money on constructing lavish ancient-style buildings. In 1956, the architect was forced to openly confess his "erroneous" views, admitting to being "a technological scientist who had committed serious mistakes in my work." He concluded, "I wholeheartedly thank the Party. After curing my physical illness, it also cured my intellectual disease." He would, he vowed, "never again deviate one step away from our Party."[4] Liang was a victim of what the political theorist Isaiah Berlin called coercive institutional force, which Marxists exercised when consolidating power.[5] The architect was definitely not the only intellectual or artist forced to repent under the new regime's dogmatic policy, especially during the Anti-Rightist Campaign of 1957 (purging "rightists" who were critical of the regime).[6] His censuring by an increasingly dictatorial CCP was typical of the Party's monopolistic control over people's cultural activities and thoughts.

When the People's Republic of China (PRC) was officially founded on October 1, 1949, the most critical issue was controlling culture and people's minds. Mao and senior Party leaders were determined to institute a new ideology and new values. This entailed refashioning traditional norms and archaic institutions by forcefully introducing nationalistic ideas and socialist aspirations.

The process of cultural control in China started long before the Communists actually came to power in 1949. The desire to change the country according to a new socialist image had its historical roots in the Yan'an era (1936–1947) in Shaanxi Province in a movement known as the Rectification Campaign. Mao, in his famous 1942 "Talks at the Yan'an Forum on Literature and Art," one of the principal documents of the movement, contended, "to defeat the enemy we must rely primarily on the army with guns. But this army alone is not enough; we must also have a cultural army, which is absolutely indispensable for uniting our own ranks and defeating the enemy."[7] The cultural army implied a new generation of writers, artists, and intellectuals who would write in Marxist language, uphold Party doctrines, and make every effort to serve the revolutionary cause. The Yan'an Talks laid the foundation for the Communists' future cultural control of the nation in that it set up the iron perimeter of what could or could not be penned or painted.

The founding of the PRC offered the Communists a novel opportunity to map out a comprehensive plan for consolidating their hold on power. This political control—what I call "the politics of control"—has defined the fundamental nature of the PRC since 1949. After the takeover, the CCP created a new political landscape in which a Communist or "red" culture could take control of people's lives and thinking. The creation and use of this red culture is fully evident in the uncompromising way in which the Communists consolidated their power by inhibiting cultural activities and restricting freedom of thought, especially in books, newspapers, religious activities, and ethnic minority affairs.

Mao's Yan'an Talks marked the beginning of the CCP's plan for political control of cultural activities. These ideas became official policy when the Party initiated a formal cultural control mechanism on the eve of the founding of the PRC. In early January 1949, when Beiping was on the verge of capitulating to Communist troops, PLA headquarters created a special agency, the Beiping Military Control Commission (Beipingshi junshi guanzhi weiyuanhui; BMCC), to oversee the takeover of the city. The Culture Takeover Committee (Wenhua jieguan weiyuanhui; CTC) was set up under this commission as the frontline organization for regulating Beiping's cultural activities.[8] One of its instructions was to "take over all cultural and educational institutions and cultural relics that belong to the nation."[9] Censorship became one of its primary tools of control. This dual military-cultural structure subsequently became standard in key cities (such as Nanjing, Shanghai, and Lanzhou) that fell to the Communists in the final phase of the civil war, thus fulfilling Mao's directive issued in the Yan'an Talks that battles must be won on both military and cultural fronts.[10] The patterns for establishing state cultural control were regularized after the founding of the PRC, expanding far beyond the perimeter of the temporary Culture Takeover Committee. From the beginning, the two most important branches of the party-state in charge of dispensing ideological and cultural guidelines were the Propaganda Department of the CCP Central Committee and the Ministry of Culture.[11] They came to penetrate almost every aspect of people's lives by controlling cultural activities, including print culture, mass media, education, religion, parks, and ethnic minority museums. How this system of cultural control was created and evolved, and what methods were devised to implement the party-state's decisions in this area, is the subject of this book.

The New Scholarship

This book covers the early years of the People's Republic of China, from 1949 to 1966, just before the Cultural Revolution (1966–1976). Interest in the critical transitional period of the early years of the PRC among China scholars has been increasing,[12] prompted partly by the reconsideration of 1949 as the watershed of modern Chinese history and partly by a renewed curiosity about how the party-state's systems of control began.[13] The question of origins of political control is important because it places historical events in a larger perspective and presents a clear timeline for the twists and turns of critical historical events. This has resulted in a host of excellent scholarly publications that cover a wide range of topics, including the military takeover of urban cities and the peripheral areas (Tibet and Xinjiang) in the early 1950s,[14] political campaigns,[15] the transformation of the family,[16] ethnic rivalries,[17] religious societies,[18] urban planning,[19] propaganda networks,[20] educational reforms,[21] book publishing,[22] newspaper reporting,[23] museums,[24] and socialist literature, art, and architecture.[25]

In addition, inquiry into the everyday lives of ordinary citizens of this period is yielding significant results.[26] Inspired partly by the sociologist Michel de Certeau's theory of "the practice of everyday life" and the political scientist James Scott's notion of "weapons of the weak," and drawing fruitfully from provincial and county archives,[27] this new study challenges high politics and state-centered approaches. It views "history from below" (borrowing a famous phrase from E. P. Thompson)[28] to explore how common people carved out an autonomous space for themselves, mounted resistance to the state's control, and made their own decisions.

Inspiring as they are, however, most of these new works cast light on isolated subjects of early PRC history. A more comprehensive and coherent understanding of this period is needed. In this book, I look at the party-state's attempt to create and control the everyday culture of people's lives and thoughts.

This book has four distinct characteristics. First, I am not as concerned with individual trees as with the forest, where an assortment of flora inhabit the same ecosystem. In other words, rather than focus on a specific area of cultural activity, I examine whole areas of culture to arrive at a more comprehensive picture of the CCP's policies.

Second, my approach is cultural-institutional; I analyze how high officials at state and municipal levels charted the course of cultural programs geared toward the general public through institutional approaches and discuss the difficulties they encountered in enacting those programs.

Third, I am concerned with the origins of these patterns of cultural control. Government policies are never born in a void. They are the unique products of particular historical, political, and cultural circumstances. By focusing on the Communist state in the early 1950s—the time of critical nation-building and a pressing need for party consolidation—to the mid-1960s before the Cultural Revolution, the origin and evolution of myriad cultural control mechanisms are revealed. During these early years, essential ideas, policies, systems, and methods of control were first systematically formulated and tested. This was never an easy task, and the Party (especially the members of the immensely powerful CCP Politburo Standing Committee) undertook it with a great deal of urgency, vigilance, and decisiveness. Mao and senior Communist leaders, fearful of foreign hostility and domestic chaos, adopted harsh measures to consolidate the new regime, evident in the Campaign to Suppress Counterrevolutionaries (Zhenya fangeming yundong, or the Zhenfan campaign) in the early 1950s, during which more than seven hundred thousand people were executed, including remnants of the KMT, suspected spies, and landlords.[29] Geopolitical exigencies compelled senior Party leaders to take stringent measures in cultural policies. These measures continued to evolve and be modified in the ensuing periods.

Fourth, archival materials are critical to our understanding of contemporary Chinese politics. China scholars have discovered, however, that conducting research in China's archives is a frustrating task because many sensitive topics, such as ethnicity and religion, remain closed to outside researchers. Fortunately, some recently opened archives (perhaps deemed less sensitive by the authorities) yield valuable information concerning how a decision may have been made. For instance, the *Beijing Daily* (*Beijing ribao*) files, stored in the Beijing Municipal Archives, cast light on what went on in editorial meetings. Contrary to the newspaper's pronouncements of unity and harmony, the minutes of the editorial board meetings often reveal a complex decision-making process behind closed doors. The sources show not only the newspaper's byzantine internal workings, the multiple layers of censorship, and the expediency of policy planners, they also reveal the infighting and political posturing among editors who navigated treacherous water in their attempt to follow the shifting ideology coming from the top (see chapter 2). These documents thus provide a hitherto unknown picture of the who (policy-makers), the what (types of policies), the when (the time when decisions were made), and the how (actual implementation) of these decisions.

By presenting case studies in a variety of cultural areas, I demonstrate that the CCP's political control of culture had a clear objective, namely, strengthening the power base of the Party and enhancing its legitimacy.

Key Concepts

A deeper understanding of the term "politics of control" is needed. It means here a systematic effort mounted by the party-state to create, implement, and monitor cultural activities of citizens' lives. "Cultural activities" is a notoriously difficult term to define. Although I agree with the historian Peter Burke's view that culture lacks "a fixed identity,"[30] I argue that it can be broadly defined as comprising ideas, values, habits, and symbols, as cultural historians such as François Furet and anthropologists such as Clifford Geertz suggest.[31] Cultural enterprises thus intersect with a wide range of fields, including not only history but also collective attitudes (what the French call *mentalités*), not only canonical doctrines but also popular religious trends, not only literary classics but also architectural space, and not only formal government institutions but also political symbolism and rituals. Along the lines that Jacob Burckhardt proposed in *The Civilization of the Renaissance in Italy*, I view cultural activities as entailing many facets of people's lives, including art, media, education, religion, and architecture.[32]

The term "control" requires even more elaboration. I use it to refer to the political expansion of state power into societal and cultural sectors and people's lives. As a result, the relationship between state and society is fundamentally altered to the disadvantage of the latter. The 1950s saw the relentless expansion of the state, including mass campaigns to suppress religion and intellectual freedom. By the time of the Cultural Revolution, the CCP controlled almost every facet of people's lives.

The politics of control is a phenomenon commonly associated with the idea of the totalitarian state. In her seminal work, *The Origins of Totalitarianism* (1951), Hannah Arendt argues that totalitarianism is a modern form of government different from traditional tyranny in that it uses terror to dominate private life. In tyranny, Arendt contends, "the whole sphere of private life with the capacities for experience, fabrication and thought are left intact." But totalitarian rulers are different because their use of "total terror leaves no space for such private life and that the self-coercion of totalitarian logic destroys man's capacity for experience and thought just as certainly as his capacity for action."[33] According to Arendt, totalitarian states—Stalinist Russia and Nazi Germany are her two prime examples—eradicate the boundary between public and private, attack plurality, atomize individuals, and demand complicity of their subjects. A totalitarian regime possesses two closely related and equally effective tools: propaganda and terror. The former spreads the regime's doctrines; the latter frightens people into submission.

The explanatory power of the concept of totalitarianism, however, has limitations when applied to the study of political control in China. First, if the term is defined narrowly by assuming the state's total control of people's lives, then realistically it has never existed in China or indeed anywhere because feuding factions, varied coalitions, and different voices have always been present. Second, the model presupposes that policies are initiated at the top (the Politburo). In reality, various levels of decision-making agencies are inevitably involved, although the Central Committee of the CCP has indeed always taken the decisive lead. Third, it assumes that decisions are made in a unilateral, undisputed fashion without compromises and adjustments. In practice, policies target a variety of areas and are constantly revised and adjusted in accordance with various needs. Fourth, it is a mechanistic view of how policies are imposed that disregards regional traditions and time differences in execution. Fifth, it ignores the reality that people on the receiving end are neither passive nor mindless. The recipients often negotiate, compromise, appropriate, or even distort policies to fit their needs, thus modifying or even subverting the original intentions of the central orders. Finally, Arendt's top-down approach ignores, as Sheila Fitzpatrick's criticism of the Soviet totalitarian model demonstrates, the role of social forces and ordinary people in shaping history. It sees society as an undifferentiated whole and ignores that it is driven by elements with diverse motives.[34]

Despites its many flaws, however, the concept of totalitarianism remains useful, not because any regime has ever succeeded in total control of its populace but because of the general questions it raises about authoritarian politics, namely, coercion, invasion of private life, and the extreme power wielded by a one-party state. I find these general concepts beneficial when analyzing Chinese politics during the Maoist era. Since the late 1970s, although the CCP has retreated in the economic realm under Deng Xiaoping's (1904–1997) market reforms, it steadfastly continues to hold on to one-party rule and retains a significant control of speech, flow of information, religious practices, and ethnicity policies. China's one-party rule means a CCP dictatorship. It implies top-down policymaking and the supreme authority of the Party.

I use the term "party-state" here to encompass both the CCP and the state. In China, similar to the former Soviet Union, the ideological and organizational functions of the Communist Party and the state were closely intertwined, like conjoined twins. This distinct feature of a communist state renders the concept of separation of powers meaningless.

The grassroots approach pursued by some of the younger historians of China challenges the conventional state-centered paradigm. These studies of local experiences and multiple tensions between officials and the popular sector undermine to some degree the totalitarian model.[35] Rewarding as it is, the grassroots approach has its drawbacks. It often stresses everyday life and social events at the expense of politics. It also ignores the importance of multilayered institutional networks in carrying out government programs. Moreover, it tends to underestimate the power of political leaders and key bureaucrats acting through seemingly impersonal rules (as both Karl Marx and Max Weber pointed out) to instigate large-scale plans that significantly affect people's lives. In reality, because of the ubiquitous presence of the party-state, most aspects of everyday life have never been truly free of state intervention. The government, as the ultimate allocator of resources and power, has enjoyed enormous leverage over the populace. Finally, grassroots interpretations often overstate the strength and results of mass resistance.

I use the cultural-institutional approach in this book because of its suitability for its objective—analysis of cultural policies initiated at the top. Three important aspects of this top-down approach should be mentioned. First, the CCP has never been a monolithic entity and its leaders have seldom spoken with one voice. Policies relating to cultural control, even those emanating from the Politburo, are the results of compromise among top leaders and at various agencies. Second, to argue that the CCP devised a comprehensive cultural plan does not mean that every policy originated from a master blueprint. Many programs were long in development and underwent much trial and error in implementation. Finally, policy was never merely imposed from the top, even under an authoritarian government. It was and is a two-way street between officials and citizens. In real life, policymaking is a long process of interacting, negotiating, and compromising undertaken by policymakers and recipients of policies, though leaders' decisions do finally prevail. Although I adopt a cultural-institutional approach in this book, I also investigate, as thoroughly as I can with the information currently available, grassroots reactions to governmental cultural policies.

Seven Areas of Control

The first chapter concerns censorship, which is a central characteristic of any authoritarian regime. In his book about censorship in Bourbon France, British India, and Communist East Germany, the historian Robert Darnton argues, convincingly in my opinion, that censorship is "a story of the struggle between freedom of expression and the attempts to repress it by political and religious authorities."[36] Like the Communist Party in the former Soviet Union, the CCP strictly enforces censorship as an essential component of its network of political control.[37] Throughout its history, especially since the Yan'an era in the 1930s and 1940s, the CCP has exercised stringent control over art and print culture (books, newspapers, magazines, and so on).[38] The pace of control was swiftly institutionalized and intensified after 1949.

The Beiping Military Control Commission created in January 1949 quickly moved to suppress KMT publications and close down foreign news offices.[39] The founding of the PRC shortly thereafter officially ended whatever limited pluralistic society existed before 1949, including a relatively free press, a bribery-ridden parliament, and a nascent civil society.

The CCP, as a Leninist party, was never interested in pluralism. Despite his call "to serve the people," Mao, like Lenin, had little faith in the untutored masses. He believed in firm discipline and the unification of thought, guided by dedicated professional revolutionaries.

Controlling print culture, especially book publishing, became the Party's top priority. At the top of its three-tiered system, the Propaganda Department of the

CCP Central Committee formulated general guidelines and provided ideological supervision. It was supported by the General Administration of Publications (Zhongyang renmin zhengfu chuban zongshu; GAP) in the central government, which mapped out strategies and put them into practice. At the municipal level, the Beijing Press and Publications Office (Beijingshi renmin zhengfu xinwen chubanchu) became the frontline organization overseeing the book industry.

Policing books in Beijing covered the entire life of a book, from approval to reaching the hands of a reader. This entailed a series of processes, including registration of bookstores, sending censors into the streets to locate and weed out undesirable publications (including books related to the KMT and the United States), vetting proposed books and periodicals, monitoring printing houses, overseeing the publishing process, and controlling the distribution network.

Archival sources reveal an intriguing behind-the-scenes story of censorship, which would begin with the compilation of a simple review sheet by the censors. These normally one-page reports document the daily tasks of censors: how a book was vetted and on what criteria, short comments by the censors, and a final verdict on whether a submitted item was approved for publication. The vetting process was elaborate, closely following the Party line. Sometimes, according to their superiors, censors made bad decisions. These stemmed partly from unclear central government instructions and partly from censors' inexperience. The censors were particularly concerned with private bookstores, which were deemed politically unreliable. In the mid-1950s, these bookstores were nationalized to eliminate the potential threat.

Chapter 2 addresses another kind of print media and its form of control: an internal censorship system built into the running of the *Beijing Daily* (founded in 1952), the flagship newspaper of the Beijing Municipal Party. In the West, although few believe that true objectivity in journalism is possible, the notion of objectivity nonetheless remains "at the heart of what journalism has meant in this country [the US]," according to the sociologist Michael Schudson.[40]

Chinese Communist newspapers have followed a different path, one influenced by the Soviets. Immediately after the October Revolution in 1917, the Bolsheviks issued the "Decree on the Press," signed by Lenin, which closed down newspapers that opposed the worker-peasant government.[41] For the Bolsheviks, newspapers needed to speak the Marxist language. The Chinese Communists followed this model closely. During the Yan'an era, Party newspapers such as the *Liberation Daily* (*Jiefang ribao*) were launched to promote the socialist cause. After 1949, the *Beijing Daily* inherited this tradition. As in book publishing, the newspaper was closely supervised by top officials tasked with propagating state policies.

Newly available archival sources reveal a depressing and disturbing story behind the façade of enthusiastic reporting. Control of editorial management, stringent censorship, skillful manipulation of news, and carefully selected read-ers' letters praising the Communist regime were the norm. In the early 1960s, senior editorial staff were trapped, like other officials, in the life-and-death ideo-logical infighting between radical Maoists and pragmatists led by Liu Shaoqi (1898–1969). The editorial staff used a variety of techniques—double-talk, fence-sitting, lip service to official lines, and self-criticism—to navigate their way through the perilous political shoals. Despite such efforts, they were eventually purged by the Maoists during the Cultural Revolution for siding with the prag-matists. Chinese journalists, including the *Beijing Daily* staff who worked in the system, lived a precarious life under an Orwellian government.

Chapter 3 explores control of religion. Marx once famously wrote, "Religion is the opium of the people."[42] Lenin voiced a crude Russianized version: "Reli-gion is a kind of spiritual vodka in which the slaves of capital drown their human shape."[43] Stalin's war on religion in the 1920s was brutal. Through the League of the Militant Godless, he closed down churches and arrested priests in an all-out attack on religious institutions in the countryside, although he met stubborn re-sistance from the peasants.[44]

Similar to the rulers of the former Soviet Union, the Chinese Communists, as self-proclaimed atheists, have long held a deep suspicion of religious activities in China because of their pervasive influence in people's lives. Scholars of Chinese religion such as John Lagerwey call China "a religious state," arguing that "Chi-nese society is a religious society."[45] For the Chinese Communists, religion, both domestic and foreign, was never simply a spiritual pursuit of believers; it was a highly sensitive political issue that needed urgent attention. Officials were par-ticularly concerned about foreign churches, which, in their eyes, were closely tied to foreign imperialist interests. After 1949, foreign missionaries were expelled and Christian publications were banned. Prominent Chinese Christians were asked to write a declaration in September 1950 stating that Chinese religious communities had begun to "sever ties to the important political movements as-sociated with imperialism." They promised that they would conduct their own religious services, independent of foreign churches.[46] Domestic religions set off even greater alarms. In addition to the five established institutions—Buddhism, Daoism, Islam, Roman Catholicism, and Protestant Christianity—they also in-cluded folk religions. Folk religions especially invited the suspicion of officials because of their unorthodox practices and menacing presence.

Folk religion has an age-old history in China. It is deeply rooted in Daoism and Buddhism and covers a colorful mix of complex, mystic, and existential spir-itual terrains.[47] Its millennial yearning for the divine and salvation had proved remarkably resilient over the centuries. Occasional eruptions of popular religious uprisings frightened imperial rulers, who suppressed them with ruth-lessness.[48] The White Lotus Rebellion (1796–1804), a major religious uprising in central China that called for the overthrow of the Qing dynasty, is such a case.[49] The rebellion contributed to the decline of the Manchu regime.

The tension between the Chinese Communists and popular religions was particularly acute in the early days of the PRC. The Party perceived these unpre-dictable sects as a threat to the new regime at a time when political stability was the uppermost priority. Officials mounted a mass campaign to root them out, targeting especially the most powerful one: Yiguandao (Unity Sect), which was active in North China, especially in the countryside. In his address to a gathering of labor unions in August 1949, Mao warned, "Superficially, the Kuomintang has been crushed, but in reality they have not been completely annihilated. They [continue to] organize secret societies and superstitious sects like Yiguandao. In Anhui and Henan Provinces, the sects number one hundred thousand."[50] Mao lumped Yiguandao with evil elements such as bandits, local despots, and spies. He believed that together they formed a major conspiracy to derail the new gov-ernment. He ordered swift action to annihilate them as evil groups.[51]

From 1949 to 1953, Chinese officials conducted a nationwide anti-Yiguandao campaign. Through a host of propaganda channels, including media attacks and public trials, they crippled the sect. But the campaign was not an isolated inci-dent; it was instead a precursor to the Zhenfan campaign in the early 1950s, which was an even bigger mobilization to suppress reactionaries.[52] Mao called this effort "a great struggle."[53] The campaign turned many citizens into support-ers and agents of the government, and its tactics were soon repeated in other mass political movements, including the 1999 suppression of Falun Gong, a heal-ing movement that blends Buddhist practices with breathing exercises.

Chapter 4 investigates cultural centers (wenhuaguan), local agencies launched in cities in the early days of the PRC to advance the government's social policies and to carry out political indoctrination. Different from the Propaganda Depart-ment of the CCP Central Committee, which set general policies at the top, cul-tural centers were lower-level propaganda stations designed to work closely with ordinary people. This device was inspired by the mass line Mao proposed during the Yan'an days,[54] calling on intellectuals and writers to go "among the masses" to work with them and learn from them.[55] Launched in 1949, the centers had the mandate of constructing a bridge between state and society while working to improve the lives of the people. In the beginning, staff at cultural centers set up local libraries and opened newspaper reading rooms as part of an endeavor known as the Eradicating Illiteracy movement. They also conducted rural hy-giene classes and held talks on production techniques. But these grassroots centers were soon turned into small political propaganda units to promote government policies through mass mobilizations, including land reform, the Zhenfan campaign, and the Resist America, Aid Korea Campaign. Politics soon took center stage. The pace of politicization of the centers quickened beginning in the mid-1950s, when the Party launched its sweeping campaigns such as the Anti-Rightist Movement (1957–1958) and the Great Leap Forward (1958–1960, a radical modernization of China's industry and agriculture).

Documents from this period show that it was mostly through these municipal-level cultural centers, rather than the Propaganda Department, that the Party was able to interact with the common people. In practice, the cultural centers did not always follow high-level directives, which could be general or vague. Cultural centers were down-to-earth in practice, adjusting to local needs and showing a large degree of ingenuity and flexibility in coming up with pragmatic solutions to unique situations. The history of the cultural centers thus belies the conventional view of a preconceived, unilateral, and all-embracing propaganda scheme emanating from the top and put into practice at the grassroots.

Chapter 5 focuses on education, which was another crucial field that the Chinese Communists seized immediate control of when they took power. For Mao and other top Party officials, education was by definition political and class oriented. Senior Party officials took control of higher institutions such as Tsinghua University and Peking University in early 1949. But they also had a longer view of how the entire educational realm should be run under socialism. They believed education was best addressed at the fundamental level: kindergarten. Their goal was to nurture a new generation that, unburdened by feudalism, would be free of religious dogmatism, champions of socialist ideals, and, most important, patriots devoted to China's independence.

The concept of the "new man" had its roots in the European Enlightenment, which encompassed the idea of the autonomy of reason and the infinite malleability of human beings. Such ideas were prevalent in the Soviet Union in the 1930s, where they were commonly related to the idea of reeducation through labor for juvenile delinquents and criminals.[56] A similar kind of reeducation was introduced during the Yan'an years in 1942, when Mao initiated the Rectification Campaign to bring unity of thought to intellectuals, writers, and artists. The purpose of the campaign could be summed up in Mao's slogans: "Cure the sickness to save the patient" and "Learn from past mistakes to avoid future ones." The way of doing this, according to Mao, was to engage in criticism and self-criticism to eliminate "subjectivism, sectarianism and stereotyped Party writing."[57] But curing the sickness can never get to the root of the problem, only preventing the disease can. Education was thus the best answer. How to turn a young Chinese child "red" and patriotic became the top priority of Chinese educators.

After 1949, under the strong influence of Soviet advisers, the Chinese Communists launched a series of kindergarten education reforms. Through a variety of methods (games, singing, storytelling, site visits), children were taught the nobility of labor, the sacrifices of soldiers, the wise leadership of Chairman Mao, and the evilness of imperialist powers. However, contrary to the conventional view, Chinese kindergarten teachers never blindly followed Soviet educational models. They appropriated Moscow's techniques to suit their domestic needs, which included promoting nationalist feelings. Ultimately, kindergartners were turned into CCP loyalists, not admirers of a foreign socialist model. Although the Party encountered difficulties in recruiting reliable teachers to implement its policies, it was able to impose pedagogical and political control over the education of Chinese kindergartners.

Chapter 6 looks at the Party's control of public parks. In the early years of the PRC, to provide recreational activities for local residents, the government created many public parks in cities across the nation. These parks were created not only for leisure, but also for mass demonstrations. This chapter traces the transformation of the Working People's Cultural Palace (Laodong renmin wenhuagong; WPCP), a former imperial temple in Beijing, into an urban park where political rallies could be staged. This metamorphosis of an age-old temple into a political park signaled the reach and intrusion of the CCP into people's leisure time and private lives.

The WPCP, near Tiananmen Square in the heart of the capital, became one of the best known urban parks in China. This formerly closed sacred ground, where emperors of the Ming (1368–1644) and Qing (1644–1911) dynasties offered sacrifices to their ancestors, became in 1950 an open urban amenity where citizens could enjoy reading newspapers, playing chess, and dancing. Its creation seemed to embody the Epicurean philosophy of the ancient Greeks as well as the serene life cultivated by the poet Tao Yuanming (365–427) of the Six Dynasties period, that is, apoliticism.

But this "people's park," as the government labeled it, had an ambiguous identity from the start. On the one hand, it was a municipal park belonging to ordinary citizens, welcoming visitors from all walks of life. On the other, it was supervised by a particular class, given that it was put under the management of the Beijing Federation of Trade Unions (Beijingshi zonggonghui). The workers had political significance from the beginning because, as Marx emphatically argued, the working class was "the class to which the future belongs."[58] Workers take the lead in overthrowing capitalism and establishing a socialist system. This view was held by the new Communist rulers. According to the Common

Program—an interim constitution adopted at the Chinese People's Political Consultative Conference in September 1949, a few days before the official founding of the PRC—the new nation would be "led by the working class, based on the alliance of workers and peasants."[59] The workers' leading role was reaffirmed in the first constitution of the PRC in 1954.[60]

Thus, the Party never had the intention of creating a pure urban amenity in the WPCP. It and other major parks in China were soon turned into political arenas. Officials transformed them into platforms to honor labor heroes, launch large-scale political campaigns, promote government agendas, and advance international diplomacy. This politicization of urban parks occurred during the first decades of the PRC, when Mao mounted massive gatherings to mobilize people to denounce bureaucratism and capitalists (such as the Three-Antis and Five-Antis Campaigns of 1951 and 1952) and to attack American imperialists (such as the Resist America, Aid Korea Campaign of 1950–1953). During the Cultural Revolution, the WPCP became a strategic site for radical Maoists to denounce the "capitalist-roaders" led by Liu Shaoqi.

Clearly, urban parks were convenient spaces for realizing the political objectives of the Party. The parks were no longer "public," belonging to the people. Instead, they were turned into "private" political theaters managed by the CCP to promote its single-party agendas. This monopolization of power delimited citizens' living space, blurred the distinction between state and society, and forced the government's agenda on its citizens.

Chapter 7 concerns museum architecture and how the Party used Beijing's Cultural Palace of Nationalities (Minzu wenhuagong; CPN), a key government building, to promote ethnic harmony. Throughout history, architecture has been the most visible form of public art. It is also a powerful representation of politics. Political events never take place in a spatial vacuum; they occur in specific landscapes and buildings. Key governmental buildings are invested with rich symbolism and compelling meanings, signifying state authority, majesty, and ambition. The National Mall in Washington, D.C., marked by the Washington Monument at the center and with the White House, the Capitol, and the memorials to Thomas Jefferson and Abraham Lincoln as its connecting points—is a celebration of the triumph of democracy. The seven skyscrapers in Moscow (especially the Ministry of Foreign Affairs), designed in the Stalinist style and built at the intersections of the capital's main radial roads, were meant to symbolize the victorious power of the Soviet regime.

The CCP understood the polemical value of architecture. Party leaders carefully exploited the built environment when redesigning city landscapes and regulating people's life. The Cultural Palace of Nationalities is such an example. It was designed to impose its monopolistic discourse on three areas: public architecture, ethnicity, and museums.

The CPN, one of the "ten monumental buildings" in Beijing, was built in 1959 to celebrate the tenth anniversary of the founding of the PRC. Located in the heart of the capital on the celebrated main boulevard, Chang'an Avenue in Xidan, the CPN symbolized the central priority the Party gave to the welfare of ethnic minority communities. Its austere and imposing presence was intended to inspire and impress, invoking a sense of national pride.

The CPN, as its name implied, also addressed the urgent, sensitive ethnic issues of the formative years of the PRC, when uncertainty concerning ethnic minorities' loyalty to the new regime was considerable. It was built primarily to project the ideal image of harmony among China's fifty-six designated ethnic groups. Mao summed up this ideal well by his command: "Ethnic groups of China, Unite!" which is inscribed in marble near the entrance of the building.[61]

The CPN was quintessentially a museum that chronicled the successes of the CCP's ethnic policies. Exhibition halls displayed artifacts, photographs, charts, and illustrations that impressed visitors with the CCP's respect for ethnic minority communities. They could see how minorities were provided with new schools and hospitals in greatly improved economic situations. Not allowed in the displays, however, were native voices (especially from Tibet and Xinjiang) who feared for the survival of their traditions, which were crumbling under the pressure of massive Han migration, rapid economic change, and harsh government measures.[62] The CPN was designed to be both a cultural symbol and an ideological instrument for legitimizing the CCP's right to rule over ethnic minority territories.

The relationship between the party-state and the ethnic minority regions nevertheless remains volatile. A close look at the CPN reveals two major unsettling problems: the CCP's manipulation of official images of national minorities and its difficulty in dealing with ethnic nationalism, regional separatism, and local identity. These issues remain a major headache for the Chinese government and continue to threaten China as a unified country.

Five Approaches

Seventy years after the founding of the PRC, China remains a paradox: free-market dynamism functions alongside stringent state controls, and global interests exist alongside nationalistic fervor. I use five approaches to investigate the political control of culture in the formative years of the PRC to understand how this is possible.

First, I explore a wide variety of topics. Each chapter can be read as a separate subject; nevertheless, these chapters have a unity in that each describes one aspect of the Party's cultural activities, and when viewed together they provide a more holistic understanding of China's complex policies. Second, all of the chapters are historical-empirical studies rather than theoretical expositions. Unencumbered by theoretical preconceptions, the different mechanisms of control can be examined historically, situating them in China's political, social, and cultural contexts. Third, I investigate the genesis of how political control came into being, especially during the early years of the PRC, when basic patterns of control were first officially formulated and implemented. Not all of these were new: many had their roots in the Yan'an era, if not earlier. But they acquired an official (hence legitimate) status after 1949 and continued to evolve. Many of these strategies remain more or less intact today, such as the Propaganda Department of the CCP Central Committee. Fourth, these case studies are grounded in a close reading of primary sources: unpublished archival materials, official documents, newspapers, periodicals, interviews, memoirs, and published reminiscences of the people involved. Archives that have been made available to scholars in China in the last two decades have allowed me to trace the continuities and discontinuities of some of the methods of control. These materials provide a rare glimpse into the world of political manipulations that took place behind the scenes. Finally, I use an interdisciplinary approach. A subject as complex as political control calls for more than one way of looking at it. Hence, to better understand CCP methods of cultural control since 1949, I use historical, cultural, religious, and anthropological approaches.

This is not a comprehensive study of the political control of all cultural activities in China. I limit my exploration to seven key areas and aim to identify patterns of party-state control in Chinese politics. My area of focus is the capital, Beijing. I do not pretend to address all regions in China—no single book could. I use Beijing as representative because it is at the heart of China's politics. It is in Beijing's Zhongnanhai—the headquarters of the CCP and the State Council—where top officials set the national agenda and decide on policies that other areas must follow. My discussion, nevertheless, is not confined to the capital. Whenever possible, I draw on regional and parallel examples to demonstrate the impact of national policies in local areas. In the case of book censorship (chapter 1), for example, I show that censorship was systematically and relentlessly pursued not only in the capital but also in other cities, such as Shanghai, Tianjin, and Guangzhou. This technique of censorship, directed by multilayers of government control agencies in the capital, was effective and pervasive. Its practice continues to have relevance today.

CHAPTER 1

Policing Books in Beijing

The Kuomintang [KMT] bandit troops in the four surrounding suburbs of Beiping [Beijing] will soon be annihilated, and the city will soon be liberated. To protect the life and property of the people, maintain social stability, and establish revolutionary order, the four suburbs—east to Tongzhou, west to Huangcun, southwest to Changxindian, and north to Shahe—are now placed under control of the Beiping Military Control Commission, a division of the Beiping-Tianjin Frontline Headquarters of the Chinese People's Liberation Army. This commission will serve as the center of power of this region during the period of military control and will be responsible for the military and civilian administration of the entire area. It will be incorporated into Beiping as soon as the city is liberated. Ye Jianying is now appointed as the director of the Beiping Military Control Commission.

> —"Proclamation of the Establishment of the Beiping Military Control Commission" by the Headquarters of the Chinese People's Liberation Army, January 1, 1949

The creation of the Beiping Military Control Commission (BMCC) under General Ye Jianying (1897–1986) in early January 1949 was a momentous event in the history of modern China.[1] Under the command of Kuomintang General Fu Zuoyi, Beiping was on the verge of capitulating to the encircling People's Liberation Army. The fabled city fell on January 31. The victorious Red Army made its official grand entry into the city on February 3, transformed symbolically from an army of liberation into an army of reconstruction. Chairman Mao and senior Chinese Communist Party (CCP) leaders began to immediately plan for creating a new city and, by implication, a new China.

The Communists dubbed the nonviolent liberation of Beiping the "Beiping model" (Beiping *fangshi*) and widely hailed it as a brilliant strategy for preserving life and cultural relics.[2] This strategy, according to Ye Jianying, would serve as a "touchstone" (*shijinshi*) for other yet-to-be-conquered cities, including

Nanjing (the Kuomintang capital), Shanghai, Wuhan, and Guangzhou.[3] It indeed proved useful in the final phase of the Communists' consolidation of power at the end of the civil war. By June 1949, the new authorities declared the military occupation of Beiping "a resounding success."[4] Ye Jianying jubilantly proclaimed, "The peaceful liberation of Beiping was a great contribution of General Fu Zuoyi. We must cherish the circumstance that this ancient city was unscathed. We must take care of every tree and every blade of grass. We must work together to heal the wounds of the war and to put the nation in order."[5] The Communists thus touted themselves as the protectors, not the destroyers, of China's culture. The new government, however, quickly evolved into a regime that curtailed cultural activities and imposed censorship on books and speech, becoming one of the most authoritarian governments in modern history.

After the founding of the PRC on October 1, the Communists moved swiftly to restore peace in the war-ravaged country, a herculean task. It is generally believed that in the next few years, from 1949 to before the announcement of the First Five-Year Plan in 1953, the Communists took a gradual approach to establishing political and social order, winning widespread approval from a war-weary population who credited them with bringing peace and independence to the nation. Mao promised a gentle path to transforming China into a socialist state. In his famous 1949 article "On the People's Democratic Dictatorship," he called for the new nation to be governed by a broad union of Chinese people under the leadership of the workers, peasants, petite bourgeoisie, and national bourgeoisie, with the CCP at the forefront.[6] In his study of the Communist takeover of Hangzhou in May 1949, the historian James Gao writes, "At first glance, the PRC appears in its early years to have pursued a gradualist approach to revolution: it executed a series of well-designed political campaigns—each solving a specific problem and one following another—to reach the final goal of a fundamental reconstruction of China's society."[7] But "gradualist" and "peaceful" are relative terms. China scholars have underestimated the swiftness of the CCP's consolidation of power and the harsh measures that went into accomplishing it. This is particularly evident in the two general policies put into place immediately after 1949: coercive force and censorship of publications. The most obvious example of coercion was the Campaign to Suppress Counterrevolutionaries (the Zhenfan campaign) from 1950 to 1953. The Party launched this to eliminate enemies both real and imagined, including KMT secret agents, local tyrants, bandit leaders, and members of clandestine sects. It is estimated that more than seven hundred thousand "class enemies" were executed.[8] But a more important policy than the Zhenfan campaign was the unleashed censorship of print media, especially of books. Its wider and longer lasting impact remains a relatively unexplored field.

The literature on the history of books in the late imperial and Republican periods—from printing houses, bookstores, book markets, commercial publishing, to best sellers—is extensive.[9] But, with the exception of a few studies,[10] little scholarly attention has been paid to book publishing after 1949; fewer still are studies of the government's book-publishing policies and censorship. Here I examine how book censorship began and the decisions behind the party-state's move to control print media in general and book publishing in particular.

Contrary to the common assumption of a gradual CCP approach, the Party moved expeditiously to control practically all realms of cultural activity. The Bolsheviks, on seizing power in Russia in 1917, issued a decree signed by Lenin taking control of publications and news media and suppressing rivals.[11] The Chinese Communists followed the same pattern. Their first action after entering Beiping was to build a system of control over printed (books), visual (art), and broadcast (radio) media. To that end, it devised a systematic organizational network. This system of censorship, conceived and constructed in the 1950s, became a general model that was followed in the ensuing years. It continues to thrive today in the age of the internet.

Historical Precedents

I define censorship essentially as a form of political power wielded by the state that judges what can and cannot be put into print.[12] I use the noun "censor" to refer to two types of people: senior cultural bureaucrats who formulate general policies at the top, and junior officials or cadres who serve as field investigators at the street level and in their offices vetting books and periodicals.

The urge to censor seems to be a natural response to political disagreements. In *The Republic,* Plato, not a liberal thinker, famously says, "We must begin then, it seems, by a censorship over our storymakers, and what they do well we must pass and what not, reject."[13] When a state unleashes this power, it generates an unstoppable force and has grave consequences. Censorship has appeared in different forms throughout human history. In Enlightenment France, the king outlawed the writings of Voltaire and Rousseau, and censors were sent to Diderot's headquarters to confiscate all the papers of his *Encylopédie.*[14] In 1937 in Nazi Germany, Adolf Hitler and Joseph Goebbels notoriously banned "degenerate art."[15] In tsarist Russia, the revolutionary movement of 1848 virtually halted intellectual freedom because government departments had the right to place restrictions on written material, including even that of the famed writer Gogol. The tsarist government was also determined to keep out the pernicious influence of the West.[16] During the Soviet period, censorship of literature turned out to be even more repressive and pervasive, especially under Stalin.[17]

China's history of book censorship goes as far back as the third century BCE, when the first emperor of Qin ordered the burning of books deemed detrimental to his rule.[18] Closer to the modern era, the eighteenth-century Qing emperors (especially Emperor Qianlong), banned books and eliminated any anti-Manchu references.[19] In the Republican era (1912–1949), the KMT tightly controlled publications. Chiang Kai-shek (1887–1975) outlawed literary and scholarly works he thought harmful to social morals and subversive to the Nanjing regime.[20] The Chinese Communists followed the same pattern, with renewed energy. They had practiced systematic censorship since the Yan'an era, especially of books and newspapers.[21] This appeared in three ways. First, in April 1937, the New China Bookstore (Xinhua shudian) was established in the caves of Mount Qingliang in Yan'an as the principal government unit to select, screen, and publish books and journals in line with Party polices.[22] Second, two years later, the CCP Central Committee established the Publication and Distribution Department (Zhongyang chuban faxingbu) to coordinate the distribution of printed information. In late 1941, the department was renamed the Central Publishing Bureau (Zhongyang chubanju). The new bureau had more weight because it was headed by the senior leader Bo Gu (Qin Bangxian, 1907–1946) and supervised by the Propaganda Department of the CCP Central Committee. Third, in April 1942, the Central Committee issued the important "Circular on the Unification of Publishing Work in Yan'an," which instructed the Central Publishing Bureau to "unify the task of guiding, planning, and organizing the general work of editorial, publishing, and distribution in various departments in all of Yan'an."[23] To "unify" meant to centralize under the direction of the Party; the trend was toward a complete merging of editing, production, and distribution of printed materials in Communist-controlled territories.[24]

When Mao launched the Rectification Campaign with his famous 1942 "Talks at the Yan'an Forum on Literature and Art," he demanded unequivocally that literature and art must serve political goals and that the Party was the arbiter of what could or could not be written and published.[25] The slogan "Let the entire Chinese Communist Party run the newspaper" (quandang banbao), popular at the time, epitomized this idea.[26]

The book industry grew after the founding of the PRC, but political control over literature and art grew even faster. In 1950, the first year when national publication data became available in socialist China, 6,689 new titles were published and 275,000,000 copies printed nationwide. Two years later, the corresponding numbers were 7,940 new titles and 786,000,000 printed copies.[27]

The new regime saw book publishing as a valuable tool for propagating state policies. But it also saw it as a potential threat because print was a powerful medium of communication that could also carry subversive content. Officially, Party censorship started with the BMCC in January 1949 and soon developed into a well-coordinated interlocking network of control. Building on the Yan'an experience, and given unlimited resources, this system of censorship had three distinct characteristics: first, a multilayered organizational framework that set general policies and issued specific directives for regulating the book trade; second, a review system at the municipal level in Beijing that oversaw the screening of books; and, finally, supervision of printing and distribution to keep undesirable books from the market and potential readers. This operation should not be trivialized as a mere censuring of printed materials by a bureaucratic office. Rather, it was an extensive network of cultural control that bound Party officials, cultural bureaucrats, censors, authors, publishers, booksellers, peddlers, and readers together, reaching deep into the people's cultural life. In these beginnings, one sees the ever-expanding power of the state to control book publishing (and hence people's minds) and absolutely no sign of slowing down in today's internet age.

Organization

In his influential work *What Is to Be Done?* (1902), Lenin contended that the socialist revolution could be led only by a vanguard party staffed by professional revolutionaries.[28] This was a major amendment to Marx, who believed that workers were capable of leading themselves in revolution. The CCP, as a Leninist party, built a tightly knit organization that demanded absolute obedience from Party members. The goal of a tight organization was manifest in the creation of the BMCC, which saw restoring order in the nation as its top priority. It was charged with four missions: to eliminate every reactionary oppositional force, to take over enemy properties, to establish order for the newly created municipal government, and to educate the masses.[29] Although the Common Program, an interim constitution promulgated in September 1949 before the founding of the PRC, guaranteed that the people should enjoy "freedom of thought, speech, [and] publication" (Article 5),[30] the BMCC had already denied these rights to people labeled as "counterrevolutionaries" in March of the same year.[31]

Lenin had a good understanding of the importance of the Communist Party newspaper (*Iskra*) to reach out to the masses; he called it "an excellently organized all-Russia newspaper."[32] Radio could play an equally important role. According to Anne Applebaum, during the Soviet occupation of Eastern Europe after World War II, one of the first measures that the Red Army took was to take control of the radio stations.[33] The CCP also saw books, newspapers, and media as effective ways of disseminating official policies and propaganda.

Immediately after taking over Beiping, the BMCC closed down the KMT-run news agencies and radio stations. On the night of January 31, 1949, the day of the KMT's surrender, Fan Changjiang (1909–1970), the celebrated former *Dagong bao* (*L'Impartial*) reporter and now a Communist Party member, was sent to seize control of the Central News Agency (Zhongyang tongxunshe), the KMT's flagship news agency. He put sixty-nine members of the staff under Party direction, denouncing them as "bad elements" (*huaifenzi*).[34] The sign "Central News Agency, Beiping Branch" was taken down and replaced with "Beiping Branch of the New China News Agency."[35] The Communists also put religious newspapers such as the noted Catholic *Yishi bao* (Social Welfare) under their control and sealed off "reactionary books" in the National Beiping Library.[36]

Although the primary function of the BMCC was to formulate general policies and oversee the takeover operation, the Culture Takeover Committee (CTC)—one of the four departments created by the BMCC—was the frontline organization for monitoring Beijing's cultural activities.[37] Censorship became one of its primary tools of control.

The CTC was conceived early in December 1948 in Liangxiang, south of Beijing, when the city was still under siege. The committee comprised four administrative sections: education, literature and art, cultural relics, and news and publications. Its directive was to "take over all cultural and educational institutions and cultural relics that belong to the nation."[38] To facilitate the work and add credibility, the CTC recruited the best talents to the organization. The scholar Qian Junrui (1908–1985) headed the committee. (He later assumed the post of vice minister of education.) A veteran CCP member who joined the Party in 1935, an economist by training, and a dedicated educator, Qian was determined, as he wrote in his autobiography, "to carry out the Party's educational and literary and art policies."[39] He was assisted in the committee by other veteran Communists, including the dramatist Sha Kefu (1903–1961) and the poet Ai Qing (1910–1996). In February 1949, other left-wing luminaries—such as the playwright Tian Han (1898–1968), the publisher Hu Yuzhi (1896–1986), and the historian Wu Han (1909–1969)—also joined the team.[40] By late March 1949, the committee had seized a total of sixty-one educational and cultural units, including Peking University, Tsinghua University, and the Palace Museum. It also shut down all foreign news agencies and banned reporting by foreign correspondents as well.[41]

In the officials' words, the BMCC had gone through three successful phases: "well-planned preparation, early stages of takeover, and full-scale occupation."

This resulted in the "ancient cultural capital Beiping's returning to the hands of the Chinese people, completely intact."[42] Both the BMCC and the CTC were temporary setups. Their work was taken over by more formal institutions, such as the Beijing Municipal Government, after the founding of the PRC.

After October 1949, the mechanism of cultural control continued in an office known as the General Administration of Publications of the Central People's Government (GAP), which drew its inspiration from the earlier Yan'an Central Publishing Bureau. It was created in November 1949 and placed directly under the Government Administration Council (renamed the State Council in 1954). It took over national administration of the publishing industry and news media.[43] Hu Yuzhi, a former member of the CTC, became its director. Perhaps no one was better suited to head this office than Hu Yuzhi, who had joined the CCP in 1933 as an underground member.[44] In public, however, he was known as one of the founders of the National Salvation Association. The association was a left-leaning patriotic organization whose seven members Chiang Kai-shek had jailed temporarily in July 1936 for their criticism of the KMT leader's appeasement policy toward Japan. Hu was also vice chairman of the Democratic League, a liberal party in the Republican era. He was most widely known, however, as a seasoned publisher, a senior editor at the respected Commercial Press before 1949. After the founding of the PRC, Premier Zhou Enlai (1898–1976) asked Hu, "Are you an open CCP member or still an underground member?" Hu replied that his membership remained a secret. Zhou's instruction was, "As an underground member, it is better for you to continue to work inside the democratic parties."[45] Hu Yuzhi was careful not to appear "communistic," particularly in the early 1950s, when Mao was courting members of democratic parties to build a broader base of support for the new Communist regime.

The GAP worked closely with a lower-level bureau in the Beijing Municipal Government known as the Press and Publications Office (BPPO).[46] The office was created in April 1949 under the BMCC and veteran journalist Zhou You (1915–1995) appointed as its head. A committed Communist, Zhou was a graduate of the journalism department at Yenching University. He worked as a journalist in the Jin-Cha-Ji (Shanxi-Chaher-Hebei) Communist Border Region during the War of Resistance against Japan (1937–1945). When Beiping fell to the Communists, he helped Fan Changjiang take control of the KMT's news agencies. Zhou was a hard-liner. His principal responsibility was centralizing news reporting.[47]

The guiding office was the powerful Propaganda Department, which Mao had considered the ideological beacon of the Party since the Yan'an era.[48] It was primarily responsible for indoctrination and mass mobilization in the nation, similar to the Department for Agitation and Propaganda in the Soviet Union.

It supervised two state agencies, the Ministry of Culture and the Ministry of Education, in coordinating major cultural activities.[49] The Propaganda Department's director, Lu Dingyi (1906–1996), and vice director, Hu Qiaomu (1912–1992), firmly laid out general policy regarding publications.[50] Hu Qiaomu was particularly active in dispensing advice to editors and publishers. A chief aid to Mao from the Yan'an days, Hu oversaw the New China News Agency and the *People's Daily* (*Renmin ribao*) after the founding of the PRC. His mission was to make sure that literature and art never strayed from the Party line.

Sometimes other municipal departments were also involved in decision making on censorship, especially when dealing with foreign books. In mid-November 1950, a meeting was called to discuss regulating imported books and magazines. Nine departments took part, among them the BPPO (represented by Zhou You), the Public Security Bureau, the Customs Service, the Bureau of Foreign Trade, the Postal Service, and the International Bookstore.[51] This was an especially important meeting because mishandling the issue of foreign publications could bring trouble to the new regime, which was surrounded by a host of hostile foreign powers, especially the United States. This meeting ended in agreement to devise a system that would protect China from pernicious Western influences.

The multilayered system of control increased bureaucratization and hampered decision making. But it also reflected the importance that the party-state gave to devising an effective system of censorship. Censorship was essential to keeping the country unified behind a single doctrine. After 1949, the Party placed the New China Bookstore in charge of book publishing nationwide.[52] This decision was made, in a late September 1949 directive of the Propaganda Department, "to ensure that the publication of official documents and speeches made by comrades are absolutely correct in their wording" to "prevent distortion of the original meaning."[53] A few days later, on October 3, 1949, a national conference on the work of the New China Bookstore was convened to map a nationwide publication strategy. Hu Yuzhi, who delivered the opening address, emphasized the importance of centralizing publishing.[54] To underscore the importance of the conference, Mao threw his weight behind centralization with his own writings: "Carry out the publishing work conscientiously!"[55] At the conclusion of the meeting, he welcomed the delegates and supporting staff to Zhongnanhai, the central headquarters of the CCP and the Government Administration Council, for a celebratory gathering that was attended by Lu Dingyi and Hu Yuzhi.[56] In September 1950, the government convened an even bigger conference, the First National Conference on Publishing, in Beijing to lay down more detailed policies and rules on publications.[57] This eleven-day meeting was a testimony to the Party's emphasis on unifying ideas throughout the country.

Archival sources I have consulted are mostly silent on the issue of how many junior employees were involved in the day-to-day operation of the government agencies related to censorship. The limited available information indicates that in the early phase of the BPPO, twelve people were hired to run this municipal office.[58] They were mostly inexperienced. The workload kept expanding as the years went by, and the shortage of personnel prompted the office to request additional help.[59] The Beijing Municipal Party's immediate remedy was to hurriedly put together five training classes between March 1949 and March 1950 to prepare 4,133 new cadres to work in various agencies of the municipal government. It is unclear, however, how many were eventually assigned to the BPPO.[60] Although the size of the staff in each agency responsible for book publishing remains unclear, the censors seemed to go to work with gusto. They started at the most basic level of control: registration of publishers.

Registration

Registration here means gathering information about every aspect of a publishing entity, collecting basic facts and figures about who, which, where, and in what form. It is a process of identifying what is most fundamental while paying painstaking attention to details. The process is extremely tedious, but it would be a mistake to trivialize it. The importance of registration lies exactly in its tediousness and simplicity, for the process allowed the authorities to separate friends from foes and define boundaries between the legal and the illegal.

On March 10, 1949, the BMCC issued an important announcement titled "On Temporary Registration Methods of Newspapers, Periodicals, and News Agencies in Beiping."

(1) To protect the freedom of speech and publication of the people, but to strip the counterrevolutionaries of these rights, all newspapers, periodicals, and news agencies (in operation or soon to be in operation) in the city should register at the commission according to these rules.

(2) When registering, newspapers, periodicals, and news agencies must fill out a form and provide the following information, truthfully and in detail:
(a) The name of the newspaper, magazine, or news agency;
(b) The address of the person in charge with their past and present occupations, past and present political stands, career in politics and affiliation with any political parties and organizations;

(c) The organizational structure of the newspaper;

(d) The name, address, past and present occupations, past and present political stands, career in politics and affiliation with any political parties and organizations of the editor in chief;

(e) The period of the publication (daily, weekly, or monthly, etc.), the word count of each issue, the number of copies published per issue, and area of distribution;

(f) Financial source and economic conditions and information concerning all shareholders;

(g) Any concurrent business of the applicant;

(h) The name and address of the publisher and distributor.[61]

The details demanded enabled the government to keep track of every book or periodical seeking to publish in a comprehensive way. They also set the parameters within which an individual publishing company could operate. Most important, the registration information created a chart that allowed the censors to gain a sense of the applicants' political stand and ideological disposition. On the surface, the BMCC promulgated freedom of speech and writing, but, as Frederic Wakeman comments in regard to a similar instruction issued by the Shanghai Military Control Commission when the Communist troops captured the city in May 1949, it was in reality "designed to curtail it."[62]

The registration process became even more demanding as time went on, developing in response to different types of publications, publishers, and bookstores.[63] Interestingly, the process was not confined to non-Communist publications. In November 1949, the Beijing Municipal Party, following an order of the BMCC, issued the following instruction: all CCP publications, including newspapers, periodicals, readings for cadres, and public pronouncements must be registered at the Municipal Government Office so they can be screened by the Municipal Propaganda Bureau "before being published."[64] The registration system was comprehensive. No one was overlooked—even someone who was a longtime Communist had to fill out an application.[65] The veteran Communist journalist Zhao Yimin (1904–2002), editor of the *Beiping Liberation Daily* (*Beiping jiefangbao*), filed an application, as required. In the space for "past profession," he filled out "professional revolutionary," and under "past political stand," he wrote, "My political stand is the one always in line with the Chinese Communist Party."[66]

In a CTC report in March 1949, the committee blamed staff for not acting more quickly and effectively, stating that they "do not understand that the [registration] process is a weapon of class struggle, which is a part of [establishing] the regime." As a result, "many reactionary publications were not banned in time, allowing them to seize the opportunity to distort facts."[67] This included KMT-related newspapers such as the *World Daily* (*Shijie ribao*), which was not closed down during the initial takeover. In essence, the report reflects the senior leaders' pressing desire to establish a stable new regime as quickly as possible. Putting literature and art under Party control was part of the overall plan.

Censors and Censorship

We do not know how the censors made their decisions or their criteria for approving or rejecting a book. The inside story of censorship behind the façade of bureaucratic rhetoric is not available because the censors' personnel files are closed to outside researchers. Fortunately, the censors' voices can be partially recovered in three post-1949 archival sources: the minutes of internal meetings of the GAP, official pronouncements bearing cultural bureaucrats' names, and—most important—reports that censors filed after scrutinizing a book. Although brief, these reports provide a rare window into censors' closed-door activities and the inner workings of the censorship system. We can gain precious information about the decision-making process by examining censors' reasons for approval or denial of a book for publication. Most of the time, censors attached their names in their reports. Occasionally, two censors—one superior, the other subordinate—were involved when a case was disputed. Predictably, the superior had the final say on the eventual fate of the publication. It is their comments that make the reports so revealing and valuable. Through these venues, we can discern a number of patterns and criteria censors used in arriving at a judgment.

The official Marxist rhetoric—"Does the book hold any class viewpoint?"—was theoretically the point of reference.[68] In reality, however, the censors often acted more like nationalists imbued with pride that China had won its independence from foreign imperialists. China had "risen up" (as Mao famously said) and was on its way to reclaiming its national greatness.

Censors were told by their superiors, such as Hu Yuzhi and Zhou You, to pay special attention to four unacceptable topics: the KMT (especially Chiang Kai-shek and Wang Jingwei [1883–1944]), anti-Communism, anti-Soviet Union, and propagating fascist and Trotskyite ideas.[69] Pre-1949 titles were of special concern. Zhou You called these publications "existing old reactionary books" that needed immediate attention because they were still circulating widely.[70] Many of these old texts, as another report pointed out, were "taking the stand of the exploiting class to spread unhealthy thoughts."[71]

In the early 1950s, the BPPO sent censors out as cultural police to inspect bookstores. The capital was divided into three regions for this work: South City (centering on Liulichang, a bustling book and antique market since imperial times), East City (centering on the Dong'an markets and Dongdan), and the Xidan markets in the west. The staff were instructed, "Never expose your identity and the purposes of your visit. The principal goal is to find out the basic situation concerning reactionary and reprinted books. We need to know their distribution, quantity, sales figures, years of publication, and the bookstores that carry them." Staff were required to accomplish their mission by early July 1954.[72] Initially, the censors targeted one hundred thirty-eight bookstores (sixty-three in Liulichang, forty in Dong'an, and thirty-five in Xidan).[73] Private bookstores were the prime areas of investigation. Communists, by definition, have an intrinsic distrust of things private. But these private bookstores were of major concern, not only because they were regarded as "capitalistic," but also because they were well entrenched in the publishing industry with a large volume of trade. Yichang Bookstore, for instance, had 664,000 titles in its inventory in 1953.[74]

In another investigation launched in 1953 headed by the chief censor, Su Xinqun, two other well-known bookstores were targeted: Baowentang, founded in the late Qing dynasty (1869), which specialized in popular books, and the Fifties Publishing House (Wushi niandai chubanshe), a major commercial bookstore. The inspectors were asked to help these old stores to transform into new socialist ones. More important, the field investigators were asked to "find ways to strengthen [the government's] ability to supervise the private publishing industry."[75] When problematic bookstores were identified, they were put under close watch. For example, a certain Gao Qingfeng, owner of Industrial and Commercial Publishing House (Gongshang chubanshe) in Dongdan, was uncovered as a former member of the KMT. He was criticized for publishing "counterrevolutionary books" and immediately put under surveillance. Subsequently, his bookstore was closed down.[76]

I have yet to find a full inventory report enumerating how many censors were sent and how many site visits were conducted. However, one of the preliminary surveys done by the BPPO in 1951 reported that many "reactionary books published before the Liberation" were still in print: "From January to May 1951, we discovered and confiscated twenty-four kinds [of these books], a total of forty-two copies. Seven kinds were foreign books, a total of twenty-one copies. At the time of confiscation, we also educated the booksellers about the proper conduct of book selling."[77]

Back at their desks at municipal government offices, the censors vetted books, producing two types of reviews: first, a standard sheet of short spaces where they filled in answers, and, second, a longer report that could amount to a few pages.[78] The standard form, more commonly used, included spaces for the title of the book, the author or editor, the publisher, edition, number of copies to be published, price, publication date, main contents, merits and demerits of the book, whether it was recommended or denied, and remarks.[79] A slightly different review sheet added a new space: "Intended readership: workers, students, general public?"[80] At first glance, these reports seem flat and businesslike. Yet they contain intriguing information about the books under appraisal. Among the eleven spaces to be filled in, the last four—main contents, merits and demerits, recommended or denied, and remarks—are the most pertinent for researchers. In the space for "merits or demerits," for example, the censors were required to indicate their opinions concerning "shortcomings [of the book], including political or technical errors." To be sure, the former weighed heavier as an offense. On closer examination, we can discern patterns in the censors' decision making.

From the beginning, the censors tried to ferret out subversive books, especially those that were blacklisted in the four unacceptable topics mentioned earlier. These books were denounced as "extremely reactionary" (jiduan fandong),[81] and, in the words of Qian Junrui, "causing poisonous effects, especially on the youth."[82] Zhou You called for their immediate elimination.[83]

The banning started with books related to the Kuomintang. Zhongguo Kuomintang shi (History of the Kuomintang), published by the Commercial Press, was immediately removed from bookstores.[84] A children's book with an airplane displaying the KMT party emblem was condemned as celebrating the "Kuomintang bandits." Publishing such a book was "a grave mistake," the censor commented.[85] A dictionary that contained "Double-Ten Festival" (October 10), the national day of the Nanjing regime, was banned.[86] Books on the New Life Movement, an anti-Communist ideological campaign that included a mix of Confucian morals and military discipline launched by Chiang Kai-shek in 1934, were also prohibited.

Books affiliated with the Nanjing regime or written by liberal thinkers (thus upholding bourgeoisie values) were barred from circulation. Among them was Zhongguo zhengzhi sixiangshi (History of Chinese political thought) by Tao Xisheng (1899–1988), an economic historian who for many years served as Chiang Kai-shek's adviser. Tao was denounced by the censors as a "war criminal" (zhanfan).[87] In June 1950, Liangyou Bookstore and Yimin Bookstore, both located in Liulichang, were found selling books about the New Life Movement. Zhou You mounted an investigation. At the end, he reported to his superior Hu Yuzhi that the incident had a happy ending. The bookstore owners "admitted their mistake" and "were willing to hand over the reactionary books to the

People's Government. They promised that they would never sell them again." Zhou concluded, "They thanked the People's Government for treating them with leniency."[88]

The BPPO confiscated many "undesirable" books. The list was long, including *Jiluan wencun* (The collected writings of Zhang Jiluan), whose author Zhang Jiluan (1888–1941), the famous editor in chief of *Dagong bao,* was chastised as a pro-Kuomintang journalist.[89] Books by liberal scholars and writers were also banned. On the list were Hu Shi's (1891–1962) *Changshiji* (A collection of experiments) and Lin Yutang's (1895–1976) humorous writings.[90] A national campaign against Hu Shi was launched in 1954 on the basis of his alleged "petit-bourgeois ideas" and pro-Western stands. He was denigrated as a "cultural comprador" and an "accomplice in the slaughter of our cultural and intellectual elements."[91]

Zhou You was a vocal proponent of banning foreign books, many of which he described as carrying "reactionary political views."[92] On top of his list were those favorable to the United States, and his staff at the BPPO were asked to be watchful on this subject. Such a view of course was shaped by Mao's pro-Soviet theory of "leaning to one side" in the early years of the PRC. Mao saw the postwar international system as divided into the Soviet-led socialist camp and the American-led imperialist camp. "Sitting on the fence will not do, nor is there a third road," Mao said.[93] This Manichaean Cold War view of light versus darkness, good versus evil was reinforced in June 1950 when the United States intervened in Korea and the Seventh Fleet entered the Taiwan Strait. Mao's long-standing policy of condemning what he viewed as US imperialism was clearly reflected in the censors' decisions. A case in point was a supplementary grade school textbook printed in 1950. The book was jointly published by a group of five private bookstores, among them the famous Baowentang. It posed a question: "Why are we still hostile to the United States?" The author gives two reasons: the American invasion of Korea during the Korean War and America's "occupation of Taiwan." The censors at the BPPO judged these responses inadequate because they failed to put the US invasion in a larger historical and political time frame. The correct answer, according to the censors, was "because the US has been constantly invading China for the past hundred years."[94] In other words, the Korean War and the Taiwan issue were merely recent evil deeds, part of the Western encroachment that had begun in the nineteenth century, in the late Qing dynasty.

In the censors' minds, books that did not expose the evil nature of the American imperialists were superficial, which was sufficient grounds for rejection. When the picture book *Zhanzheng fanzi* (Warmonger) about General George C. Marshall's peace mission to China during the civil war between the Kuomintang and the Communists was submitted to the BPPO for approval, the censor Su Xinqun rejected it. His reason was that the book failed to expose the "real intention" of Marshall's "mediation," which was to safeguard Washington's interests in China. His final verdict was "Not recommended for publication."[95]

Conversely, books about US aggression and exploitation in China were readily approved. The pictorial book *Zhongguo renmin de sidi* (The deadly enemy of the Chinese People) by the artist Zhang Wenyuan (1910–1992) received high marks from the censor Jiang Xuezhu. Jiang wrote, "[This is a book about] the numerous methods used by the American imperialists to invade China, including colluding with the Manchu court, making an alliance with Chiang Kai-shek the bandit to suppress the Communist revolution and slaughtering people, and supplying ammunition to aid Japan in the Marco Polo Bridge incident against China." Jiang's conclusion was that the book would be good reading "for workers, students, and the general public."[96]

Titles that praised Chinese heroes who stood up against foreign aggression were lauded. A case in point was *Da yeshou* (Hunt down wild animals) by the popular writer Wang Yaping (1905–1983), about a woman soldier who fights gallantly against US troops during the Korean War. The theme was timely, conforming to the official line. In the space for "merits and demerits," the censor Liang Zhengjiang wrote approvingly that the book was "delightfully written and deeply moving, especially about the heroine." He concluded, "It should be widely promoted in cities and in villages alike."[97]

If American imperialists were the villains, then Russians were upheld as staunch friends who came to China's help in time of need. In the 1950s, the heyday of Mao's policy of "leaning to one side," an abundance of books were published that lavishly praised Moscow's achievements and friendship with China. The 1952 book *Shi shui zhansheng le Riben qinlüezhe?* (Who defeated the Japanese aggressors?) was quickly approved. The censor Zhou Yining listed a number of its merits: it showed that the Soviet Army made a great contribution to defeating "Japanese fascism" and that Moscow was China's "faithful friend." In conclusion, Zhou did not fail to add a familiar remark that, unlike the friendly Soviet Union, America was China's "mortal enemy."[98]

It is unclear how many books about the Soviet Union were screened by the BPPO, as a complete list is unavailable. But from the archival sources that I was able to review, themes related to the Soviet Union were of an overwhelmingly appreciative nature, ranging from the success of the Sino-Soviet alliance, the excellence of the Soviet educational system, happy children growing up in Soviet families, the bravery of the Soviet Red Army in liberating Berlin, and Russian folklore.[99] All these attested to a slogan popular in China in the 1950s: "The Soviet Union's today is China's tomorrow."[100]

With the exception of books on Russia, foreign books and periodicals were generally suspect. The Chinese translations of Trotsky's *The Russian Revolution* and Hitler's *Mein Kampf* were banned because they were, in the censors' words, "filled with poison."[101] Imported publications were heavily screened, especially those coming from Hong Kong, a British colony.[102] The review system was elaborate. Normally, the first inspection of foreign books and periodicals took place in Shanghai, Tianjin, or Guangzhou, cities that had much international trade. A second inspection in Beijing was necessary for some items.[103] Rejected items included *Time* and *Newsweek,* which were classified as "the most reactionary magazines in the United States."[104] *US News & World Report* belonged on the same list, but one copy was allowed to be acquired by the *People's Daily* after the flagship government newspaper requested that it needed the news magazine for reference purposes.[105] Even academic books for university libraries required heavy scrutiny. In mid-1952, Yenching University Library submitted a purchase request to the BPPO for a copy of E. M. Forster's *A Passage to India.* After a series of meetings by the censors, they finally agreed to allow it, commenting that "although the book contains [a number of] incorrect viewpoints, it holds no obvious reactionary ideas."[106] This Christian university, however, was closed down by the Communists later that year.

Another primary task of the censors was to vet proposed domestic titles. The framework they adopted was predictably Mao's concept of history. Mao viewed China's imperial history as a detestable past ruled by feudal lords and the exploitative Confucian literati class. The incursion of foreign capitalists beginning in the nineteenth century brought further disaster to an already battered and demoralized land.[107] Understandably, books on the imperial past and rulers often drew heavy criticism from the censors.

Photos of Empress Dowager Cixi (1835–1908) of the late Qing dynasty were banned. In the scathing words of a censor, Cixi "was one of the representatives of the feudal ruling class and a foreign slave who repeatedly knelt down obsequiously in front of the imperialists to cede lands for peace. In reality, she was a tool used by the imperialists to plunder and exploit the Chinese people." In conclusion, the censor noted, "She surely won't be missed by the vast Chinese laboring people."[108]

The censors were also alarmed to find that pornographic periodicals, nude pictures, and fantasy martial arts books circulated widely in Beijing and Shanghai. They moved quickly to ban them.[109] Another dubious genre was the old almanac, which had a long history in China. Almanacs enjoyed great popularity among the common people because they contained a wealth of what was regarded as practical information, including planting calendars, selection of auspicious days, divination, and magic charms. In 1951, it was estimated that twenty-one bookstores in Beijing published and distributed almanacs. Knowing the popularity of almanacs, the censors were cautious about removing them. They therefore did not ban almanacs immediately. Instead, they went to the publishers and demanded that those parts that they deemed "seriously hurting people's lives, such as recommendations for talisman healing" be taken out.[110]

The censors used another tactic to address a type of publication generally known as "popular readings" (*tongsu duwu*), which included folk songs, New Year prints, comic dialogues (*xiangsheng*), and serial picture books (*lianhuanhua*). Mao had long viewed these popular cultural forms as a creation of the folk that genuinely reflected their lives. Their widespread influence also allowed Communist propagandists to use them to disseminate socialist messages during the Yan'an era.[111] But these traditional popular forms were not without problems. They were filled with religious materials, archaic images of feudal lords, and stories about outdated historical personages, which needed to be transformed into new stories with socialist values (beloved leaders, labor heroes, and bumper harvests under socialism) in a process known as "filling new wine into old bottles."[112] The censors used a combination of approaches to deal with this kind of publication. First, existing titles were purchased and removed in a buy-back strategy. Zhou You was active in promoting this move.[113] Second, old books were exchanged for reformed books, a method first implemented in Shanghai, Beijing following suit.[114] Third, publishers were encouraged to join the government in designing new publications with fresh socialist content.[115] Finally, the state eventually bought out private publishing houses, ending the printing of old-style books. From the beginning, in the words of the officials, the plan was to place this popular reading medium "step by step under the supervision of the government." They were "too important a propaganda tool" to be left uncontrolled, the officials added.[116]

A closer examination of the review sheets makes it clear that the vetting process was laborious. Although their comments were usually terse and standardized, the censors adhered closely to the approved line. They took their jobs seriously, making sure that the books passing across their desks were ideologically safe, even to the extent of filtering out taboo words and inaccurate descriptions. A case in point was *Xin xiangsheng* (New comic dialogues), a book edited by Lao She (1899–1966) and two assistants, which was submitted to the BPPO for approval in July 1951. Lao She was the celebrated author of *Luotuo Xiangzi* (translated as *Rickshaw Boy*, 1945), a story about the tragic life of a rickshaw puller in Beijing. Lao She returned to China from the United States in late 1949 to embrace the new regime. He was an avid promoter of folk culture in line with

Mao's policy of reaching out to the masses. He became the vice president of the Research Institute of Chinese Folk Literature and Art and edited the periodical *Shuoshuo changchang* (Storytelling and singing) to promote this goal.[117] He sympathized with the Communist cause and was an influential voice that senior leaders (especially Zhou Enlai) wanted to court.[118] One therefore would expect that the proposed book would sail through the screening process.

But this was not the case. The censor Shen Yu found two inaccurate descriptions in the text. In the end, he recommended against publishing it. The first error, according to Shen, was the description: "July 1 is the festival of the Chinese Communist Party." The correct wording, Shen wrote, should be "July 1 is the birthday of the Chinese Communist Party." The second error was the description that "The first Congress of Representatives of the Chinese Communist Party was held in Shanghai on July 1, 1927." The correct answer, according to Shen, should be "The first National Congress of Representatives of the Chinese Communist Party was held in Shanghai on July 1, 1921." These two did not seem to be serious errors, although Lao She and his assistants did get the year of the first Party Congress wrong and leave out the word "national," which could be easily corrected, but Shen was adamant in his decision.

Luckily, Shen Yu's superior, Su Xinqun, overruled this negative decision. After revisiting the case (perhaps due to Lao She's reputation), Su decided that the factual errors were minor oversights and reversed the verdict, suggesting that "we should explain to Lao She and the other two editors about their mistakes and encourage them to revise them."[119] The book was finally approved for publication. That a book by a famous pro-Communist author could be almost refused publication because of a few minor errors indicates the stringent standards that the censors used in making their judgments. It was possible that the censors made strict decisions in order to be safe from possibly making a mistake and deviating from the approved line.

What, then, were considered safe titles by the officials? In June 1951, the Beijing Municipal Government published "A List of Excellent Popular Books Recommended by the City." On it were titles such as *Renmin datuanjie* (The great unity of the people), which announced the dawning of a new era under communism, and *Xiongmei kaihuang* (Brother and sister clear the wasteland), which praised the glory of labor, using Yan'an as its backdrop.[120]

Publishing and Distribution

The question of distribution of publications had been of concern since the Yan'an era and continued to be an important issue after 1949. Censorship was not confined to registration, vetting procedures, on-site visits, and reviews of application; it also involved publishing and distribution. The party-state continued to expand its influence in these last two areas. Thus the censors came to control the entire life of a book from its conception until it landed in the hands of a reader. Through this sequencing, the CCP kept books under close control.

In a meeting on censorship held at the Ministry of Culture in November 1954, officials proposed that one way to stop reactionary books and pornographic materials from circulating was to make it illegal to publish undesirable books. "If they were to secretly print them," officials warned, "they would be punishable according to law."[121] The idea of controlling publishers began with censors in Chinese imperial courts and continued with the Kuomintang regime. But it was also promoted by the throngs of Soviet experts who arrived in China in the 1950s.[122] In a meeting held in August 1952, Soviet publishers proudly told their Chinese admirers that publishing houses in their country were "under the direct control of the central government."[123] In an authoritarian regime, the centralization of power is inevitable. By adopting this method to control publishers, the Chinese Communists simplified the job of the censors down the line.

The situation was particularly worrisome in regard to private bookselling, which was permitted in the early years of the "People's democratic dictatorship" when a modicum of political tolerance was still in place.[124] Because private bookstores maintained a well-established distribution network, officials realized that they could not "completely replace them at the moment" and therefore tried not to antagonize them. But their policy was to "steadily reform them," the intention being to eventually limit all private ownership of bookstores and publishing houses.[125]

Among senior cultural bureaucrats, Hu Yuzhi was the first to point out the importance of book distribution. No nationwide book distribution network had existed before 1949, so Hu proposed an "overall coordination" that would place the different facets of book publishing under one umbrella.[126] This would, he believed, greatly facilitate the flow of books (and hence information), an essential ingredient in building a strong socialist state. Hu suggested that the first step should be to make the New China Bookstore, already the most important government-run bookstore, the center of national book publishing and distribution.[127] The senior leaders agreed. By October 1949, seven hundred branches of the New China Bookstore had been launched and the number kept expanding.[128] Controlling the flow of information by controlling book distribution made the state the arbiter of what the Chinese people could or could not read.

The municipal government cooperated in this goal by gradually terminating the right of private bookstores to distribute books. In September 1954, the BPPO issued an order declaring that all private publishing companies must "both directly and indirectly distribute books through the government's channels." The measure was intended "to sever the ties between publishers, distributors, and retailers."[129] In early 1956, the process was completed when major private bookstores were forced into a public-private partnership with the government.[130]

The censors targeted not only big private bookstores (such as Baowentang), they also took aim at peddlers, the small fry at the bottom of the book trade. In June 1951, when some informants wrote the municipal government that dangerous books such as Hitler's *Mein Kampf* were available in small bookstalls in Dong'an and Xidan markets, Minister of Culture Shen Yanbing (1896–1981), a well-known novelist under the name of Mao Dun, suggested that "we could advise them to remove the books."[131] Although we do not know what actually transpired with the sellers, it is reasonable to assume that peddlers could ill afford to ignore this advice.

Letters to the Editor were seen as voices coming from the people in whose name the revolution was carried out, in accord with Mao's celebrated mass line. But they also served indirectly as another pretext for the state to enforce censorship. Such letters of complaint touched on a wide array of subjects.[132] For example, in December 1950, the BPPO received a letter from a worker, Zhang Beiye, who complained that old-style almanacs left out "all memorial days of world Communism as well as those of the Chinese People's Government." Zhang concluded, "I believe that these almanacs are the reactionaries' propaganda materials" and suggested banning them.[133] Another reader wrote that he disliked the book *Zenyang tiao jiaojiwu* (How to do ballroom dancing) because it taught readers social dances, including the waltz, which, in his view, "promotes merely decadent bourgeoisie values" in order to "mislead young cadres."[134] In November 1951, the *People's Daily* printed a suggestion from a reader in Changsha, Hunan Province, calling for the government to eliminate certain serial picture books that, in his words, "spread imperialist ideas."[135] It is unclear how these letters were selected, but Hu Qiaomu praised them highly, and they were regularly reprinted in official newspapers. He viewed them as a way not only of demonstrating that the masses supported the government's censorship policy but also of showing that the Party cared about their views.[136]

Problems Encountered

Sailing was not always smooth for censors. They faced many obstacles, some political and some structural. The first problem was the unclear division of power between the Party and the state. The parallel bureaucratic structure—that of the Party (the Propaganda Department), on the one hand, and the state (the GAP) on the other—bore a close resemblance to bureaucratic organization in the Soviet Union. In the Soviet Union, the supremacy of the Communist Party of the Soviet Union resulted in its domination over the state.[137] This dual system had three consequences: the overlapping jurisdictions of the parallel Party and state authorities, the growing concentration of power in the Party, and the Party's continuous infiltration into governmental departments. China's censorship system resulted in what the journalist Deng Tuo (1912–1966) called "twofold leadership" (*shuangchong lingdao*). The BPPO had to take orders from two different superior units: the GAP and the Propaganda Department, causing confusion and generating conflict between the two organizations.[138] In the end, as Deng Tuo noted, the Propaganda Department would always take the leading role.[139] Moreover, the distinction between a Party member and a government official was often blurred, causing unavoidable role conflict. In the case of some prominent Party members, their political identity was even more complicated. Hu Yuzhi is a case in point. He was a government bureaucrat as director of GAP, a Democratic League leader, and an underground activist ultimately loyal to the CCP. Blurred differentiation of functions occurred at the state level when censorship decisions were made. In addition to the BPPO, other government departments such as the Public Security Bureau and the Customs Service also had a say. Some had their own screening units.[140] This resulted in confusion over censorship decisions.

Another problem came from the policy itself. The GAP instructions on publication were largely phrased in general terms.[141] Hu Yuzhi, as GAP director, often gave talks that were long on theory but short on practicality, which made it difficult for junior censors to make decisions. Hu stressed the importance of "the people's publishing enterprise" in building a new China. In his major speech at the First National Conference on Publishing in 1950, for instance, he stated that the general direction of the GAP was to become "nationalistic, scientific, and popular."[142] This was a reiteration of Mao's speech as enshrined in the Common Program of 1949. Such general policy guidelines, however, proved not particularly useful for frontline censors when reviewing a book. They often had to use their judgment and discretion.

As the workload increased, the GAP was confronted with two immediate challenges: a shortage of manpower and the inexperience of the censors. For instance, the Public Security Bureau had only one censor in charge of inspecting foreign periodicals and magazines and, according to one report, "his English is mediocre at best."[143] Hu Yuzhi proposed a remedy in 1951—launching a training program in Beijing. He required provincial officials to send a number of selected candidates to the capital. They needed to be "politically reliable" and have at least "a junior high school education." The initial quota was set at 120. The main purpose of the training, according to Hu, was to "raise the cadres' political and vocational levels."[144] But the limited number of trainees proved far from adequate to meet the growing demand for censors.

Most of the censors were young cadres. "I was twenty-two when I joined the BPPO," censor Zhou Yingpeng commented in an article.[145] Luckily, his superior, Zhou You took him and his colleague Shen Yu under his wing. His inexperience, however, caused uneven assessments. Standards, in reality, varied greatly from one censor to another because the censors had few specific rules to follow. Decisions were made based largely on individuals' personal knowledge, experience, and interpretation of the rules. Discrepancies of judgment therefore occurred, as was evident in the case of Lao She's new comic dialogues. Different places produced differing judgments. *Jin Ping Mei* (The plum in the golden vase), a famous Ming dynasty novel with uninhibited erotic scenes, is a case in point. In 1954, the book was banned in Shanghai but not in Beijing. The two cities differed because the novel was deemed lewd in Shanghai, but the Beijing censors concluded that it enjoyed "a considerable standing in the history of Chinese literature" and "we do not consider it a pornographic book."[146] This difference reflected more than a regional difference of judgment; it reflected a lack of clear guidelines from the top.

Hu Yuzhi hoped that, with some training, young censors would eventually become "specialized" (*zhuanyehua*).[147] It is hard to know what Hu meant by specialization in the field of censorship. In reality, the job called more for political reliability than technical virtuosity. In a July 1952 review document, senior GAP bureaucrats reported that they were appalled to find that many books were mistakenly banned, based often on questionable and even faulty grounds. The office issued a harsh criticism: "We have reviewed the banned books and documents in the first half of this year and discovered that quite a number of them were improperly done. They should be immediately corrected." Why had such errors occurred? The office admitted that it was "because up until now we still do not have precise standards for reviewing books and periodicals. We tend to judge a case based on personal likes or dislikes, using [personal] sentiments to replace policies." The report continued, "We can, and of course we should, use Marxist viewpoints to evaluate newly published books. But it does not mean that we should ban all non-Marxists titles. We cannot substitute banning [*chajin*] for criticism [*piping*]."[148] But the document never spells out what those "policies" were and how they could be objectively applied in practice.

Censorship is a political tool the state wields to safeguard its legitimacy by excising printed words and visual images that pose a challenge to the regime. In his influential chronicle of the history of Marxism, the philosopher Leszek Kołakowski called attention to two of the most prominent ideological features of the Soviet totalitarian regime, which were deeply embedded in Leninist dogmas: "the progressive destruction of civil society and absorption of all forms of social life by the state."[149] Indeed, Soviet censorship was pervasive and overpowering, imposed not only on its own people but in its heyday on Eastern European countries as well.[150] The Chinese Communists used even more draconian tactics to ensure that no dissenting voices were heard.

Even before capturing Beiping in late January 1949, the Chinese Communists had mapped out a cultural strategy to put books and media under their control. In Beijing, censorship was accomplished by creating a three-tier interlocking organizational structure made up of the Propaganda Department of the CCP Central Committee, the General Administration of Publications of the Central People's Government under the State Council, and, at a lower level, the Press and Publications Office of the Beijing Municipal Government. This three-agency combination inevitably resulted in confused decision making, but also became a formidable apparatus for solidifying the Party power. To say that the Chinese Communists devised an effective censorship system does not mean that they planned it perfectly, but they were persistent in their efforts to control books and periodicals in accord with state-approved ideology that sought to guard against capitalist infection and imperialist penetration.

Both senior cultural bureaucrats such as Hu Yuzhi and Zhou You, who formulated general policies at the top; and junior cadres such as Su Xinqun and Zhou Yingpeng, who worked at their office desks—were essential in the process. Hu Yuzhi was surely one of the best enforcers of censorship. Through his long career, he set basic policies and deftly oversaw the development of a sophisticated network of party-state publication houses. Although secretly a veteran Communist, Hu appeared in public as a leader of the Democratic League so as to gain the trust of liberal intellectuals and broaden the support base for Mao Zedong and Zhou Enlai. When Hu died in 1986 at the age of ninety, he was eulogized by his colleagues as "a pioneer" and a man who "devoted his entire life to news publishing."[151] His widow remembered him as "a good student of Comrade Zhou Enlai."[152]

Starting in the early days of the PRC, the CCP gradually built a comprehensive censorship system that oversaw the entire life of a book. The Party developed tight control of what was available in print through its system of registration, publishing, and distribution. This start-to-end process was more pervasive than in any other country, including the Soviet Union and East Germany. In the Soviet Union, samizdat—a type of government-suppressed underground litera-ture—could still evade the imposed censorship and circulate clandestinely from reader to reader.[153] Even in the German Democratic Republic, authors who felt unjustifiably banned could send letters of protest to the Ministry of Culture.[154] China's censorship was harsher. True, underground journals have been in circu-lation, especially during the Cultural Revolution, and some have appeared in re-cent years.[155] Under China's severe surveillance system, however, journal editors can be easily identified and imprisoned.

Despite market reforms Chinese leaders have promoted vigorously since the Deng Xiaoping era in the late 1970s, the party-state has not relaxed its grip on print culture. On July 6, 1987, the State Council issued the "Notice of the State Council on Severely Striking Down Illegal Publishing Activities." It laid down a set of new rules:

> First. With the exception of state-approved publishers, no unit or indi-vidual is permitted to publish and distribute books, newspapers and peri-odicals, and audiovisual materials. Violators are considered to be committing illegal publication activities.

> Second. No state-owned, collective, or individual publisher (including bookbinding factory) is permitted to print illegal publications.

> Third. No state-owned, collective, individual distribution unit, or indi-vidual is permitted to sell illegal publications.[156]

Thorough as it is, the directive does not explain what these "illegal publications" are. The vagueness of this document made the already frightened literary and scholarly communities shudder. In addition to being ambiguous, it placed more arbitrary power in the hands of the censors, whose stances (hence judgments) were constantly changing in response to shifting political winds.

China remains an authoritarian state where freedom of the press and writing exists only on paper. The internet has only advanced the state's ability to control what is disseminated because Beijing has built a cybersurveillance system unpar-alleled in the world. The CCP has elevated its monopoly on communication by adding a heightened level of sophistication. The history of Chinese censorship in the 1950s makes it clear how censorship became such a deeply rooted Chinese Communist tradition.

CHAPTER 2

Censorship and Purges at a Municipal Newspaper

The Case of the *Beijing Daily*

One day in September 1952, Mao Zedong, in response to a request by the editors, wrote the four Chinese characters—*Bei jing ri bao* (*Beijing daily*) (figure 1)—on People's Revolutionary Committee stationery to be used on the masthead of the soon-to-be-published official voice of the Beijing Municipal Party.[1] Chairman Mao's rare endorsement, through bestowing his calligraphy, was a great honor that endowed this new city newspaper, inaugurated on October 1, 1952, with enormous political weight. But Mao's approval was also a double-edged sword, for in giving approval he also unmistakably claimed political control of the newspaper for the Chinese Communist Party (CCP), and, by implication, asserted control of all newspapers in China.

Like Lenin, who regarded the press as "our strongest weapon" in the success of the October revolution,[2] Mao had long considered newspapers an indispensable tool for advancing the CCP's political goals. Back in the Yan'an era, the most crucial period in the history of the CCP before 1949, Mao used the Party's *Liberation Daily* to set a new national agenda, sinicize Marxism, and disseminate socialist ideas to the people.[3] Immediately after the People's Liberation Army's takeover of Beiping in late January 1949, the Beiping Military Control Commission moved to close down Kuomintang (KMT) newspapers and expel foreign journalists, exercising control similar to that over the book publishing industry. In the early 1950s, the government also forcefully uprooted *Dagong bao,* the pre-1949 liberal newspaper, relocating it to the capital from Tianjin. Party members were placed in senior management, and the newspaper was placed under the supervision of the General Administration of Publications of the Central People's Government. The liberal newspaper thus became another mouthpiece of the party-state.[4] The government also kept a close eye on its own Party newspapers.

In this chapter, which relies primarily on archival sources from the *Beijing Daily* found in the Beijing Municipal Archives, including minutes of editorial committee meetings and Party Branch forums, I analyze the Party's inner

Figure 1. Front page of the inaugural issue of the *Beijing Daily*, October 1, 1952. At the top is Mao's calligraphy, at the bottom, the inaugural editorial.

workings and its control of this important municipal publication. I examine the *Beijing Daily*'s multilayered decision-making processes, feature articles, editorials, readers' letters, and, most important, debates among the staff in the face of the ideological split between Party Chairman Mao Zedong and head of state Liu Shaoqi in the early 1960s. The *Beijing Daily* editors' ties to Liu eventually brought them down in the Cultural Revolution that followed.

A New Municipal Newspaper

After the founding of the People's Republic of China (PRC), the Beijing Municipal Party, under the leadership of its first secretary and mayor Peng Zhen (1902–1997), a member of the powerful CCP Politburo, entertained the notion of publishing a city newspaper in the capital. The *Beijing Daily* would produce reportage along the lines of what the historian Jeffrey Brooks observed in regard to *Pravda,* that is, they would be interpretive (stories that carried ideological messages), interactive (opinions of sympathetic readers), and informative (news for the general public).[5] This new Beijing newspaper also added something more: an educational unit that served as a training ground for junior staff and future propagandists.

When the *Beijing Daily* was officially launched on October 1, 1952, to coincide, by design, with the third anniversary of the founding of the PRC, it spelled out its purpose in an internal document titled the "Rules of Publication":

> The *Beijing Daily* is the official newspaper of the Beijing Municipal Party; it is a paper belonging to the people of Beijing. It is an effective weapon of the Municipal Party and the citizens of Beijing to conduct the socialist revolution, to advance socialist construction, and to fight against enemies. The newspaper forms a bridge between the Municipal Party and the community. It is the eyes and ears as well as the mouthpiece of the Municipal Party.[6]

Such purpose resembled that of its predecessor, Yan'an's *Liberation Daily,* as well as its more influential contemporary, the *People's Daily.*[7] But Mayor Peng Zhen quickly added that the *Beijing Daily* would focus on the local needs of Beijing's residents.[8] The new municipal paper must serve, as stated in one internal circular, the "organic unity among the Municipal Party, the people, and their locales."[9]

The *Beijing Daily*'s role as the eyes and ears of the government was markedly different from the goal of objectivity espoused by Western journalists. It was clear that the *Beijing Daily* would not play an independent role but instead follow the Municipal Party's orders. A popular Yan'an slogan, as mentioned in chapter

1, was "Let the entire Chinese Communist Party run the newspaper."[10] In its inaugural issue, the *Beijing Daily* added a new slogan: "Let the entire city run the newspaper" (*quanshi banbao*).[11] Of course, few Western journalists believe that newspapers can be truly independent. Yet objectivity in reporting—impartiality as well as separating facts from values—continues to be a cardinal value that most Western reporters embrace.[12] The *Beijing Daily*, being an official promoter of CCP policies and socialist values, eschewed these rules.

To contrast the *Beijing Daily* with Western newspapers is easy given that they operate from two sets of social values, one monolithic and the other pluralistic. But Chinese newspapers have also been quite different from their Soviet counterparts in terms of historical development. When Lenin and the Bolsheviks took power in Russia in 1917, newspapers there enjoyed a short period of openness, especially during the New Economic Policy period (1921–1928). Intra-Party debates such as disputes over economic policy between Trotsky and three other Bolshevik leaders—Stalin, Zinoviev, and Kamenev—were reported in *Pravda*, the official press of the Soviet Communist Party. The relative openness of this first decade came to an end when Stalin assumed control of the Party in the mid-1920s and began to clamp down on his rivals, notably Trotsky and Kamenev.[13] The press in China after 1949 had a different trajectory: Mao and his associates exercised tight control of the media soon after they seized power in 1949 and from the beginning merely paid lip service to the virtues of a free press.

Soviet Influence

In the early years of the PRC, under Mao's pro-Soviet policy—"leaning to one side"—Chinese journalists closely followed the Moscow line. Journalists, like other Chinese delegations, were sent to the Soviet Union to learn from the first socialist country in the world. In April 1950, a Chinese delegation, headed by Zhou Yang (1908–1989), deputy director of the Propaganda Department of the CCP, spent more than three weeks in Moscow on a study trip, visiting *Pravda* and other major news agencies. Hu Jiwei (1916–2012), a member of the delegation and a veteran journalist dating back to the Yan'an days, recalled in his memoirs, "Like primary school students . . . we wanted to know everything. . . . We reached a unanimous conclusion at that time: 'The Soviet Union's today is China's tomorrow' and '*Pravda* is the most ideal model for us (Chinese press).'"[14]

Soviet editors divided their newspapers into several sections. *Pravda*'s front page resembled a Party circular, long reports on Party plenums detailing the names of senior leaders with long-winded titles. Important international news also occupied the front pages. The rest of the paper was divided into specific sections addressing different aspects of life. Party Life, for example, reported on the political activities of Communist Party members.[15] Chinese newspapers followed this model quite closely, even borrowing directly from the Soviets, as was the case with the *Beijing Daily,* which used Party Life (Dang de shenghuo) as the name of one of its sections.[16]

To target a variety of audiences, *Pravda* divided its editorial staff into various branches, including an industrial branch and an agricultural branch. This type of differentiation was quickly copied by the Chinese press, terming it "specialization."[17] Soviet journalists' emphasis on economic development and industrialization also influenced their Chinese followers because it matched the practical interests of a young nation in need of fast development. "Centering on economic construction" soon became a buzz phrase in the Chinese press.[18] Both the Soviet and Chinese Communist newspapers were filled with spirited reporting on the marvelous achievements of their respective regimes, uplifting stories of model workers, and vignettes of the happy life of the people.

Since Lenin's days, the Soviet press had emphasized reaching the grassroots. The popular Letters to the Editor section in Russian newspapers was designed so that the people's voice could be heard. The Chinese had no difficulty in following this practice, for it accorded with Mao's idea of the "mass line" developed in the Yan'an days when the Chairman called on cadres and intellectuals to learn from the masses.[19] Soviet newspapers also served as ombudsmen, forwarding readers' complaints to appropriate government agencies and following up on the cases to make sure agencies were responding to people's concerns.[20] Letters to the Editor (Duzhe laixin) also became a popular section in both the *People's Daily* and the *Beijing Daily.* Chinese newspapers also played the role of ombudsman by relaying readers' complaints to appropriate departments, though this role was less developed than it was in the Soviet Union. To a large extent, these letters to the editor were akin to readers' letters of complaint sent to book censors. The major difference was that letters to the editor could be either positive or negative, whereas book readers' complaints were mostly accusations against authors they thought were straying from the Party line.

Contents

From the beginning, the Municipal Party, which oversaw the operation of the *Beijing Daily,* made it clear that the newspaper needed to be placed in the hands of "those comrades who were politically most reliable."[21] Two Municipal Party members with strong backgrounds in journalism were entrusted with this important task: Fan Jin (1919–2009) and Zhou You. Fan Jin, the daughter of a landlord, joined the CCP in January 1938 and worked as a reporter for the influential *Jin-Cha-Ji Daily* (*Jin-Cha-Ji ribao*) in the 1940s, under the tutelage of Deng Tuo, the paper's chief editor and one of the most prominent journalists in modern China.[22] Fan was vice director of the Propaganda Department of the Beijing municipal government when she became the director of the *Beijing Daily*. Zhou You, the former head of the Press and Publications Office of the Beijing municipal government, became the newspaper's associate director and the editor in chief.[23] Zhou's experience before 1949 as a journalist in the Jin-Cha-Ji Border region and after 1949 in overseeing the capital's book publishing industry made him an ideal person to run the day-to-day operation of the new press. Initially, Fan and Zhou led a newspaper staff of 296. The exact size of the Editorial Department is unknown, however.[24] The number of staff was increased to 409 in 1960, of whom 120 were involved in the Editorial Department.[25]

The *Beijing Daily* started out with a four-page issue. The opening headline read "Celebrating the Third Anniversary of the Founding of the People's Republic of China" and featured photos of Sun Yat-sen and Mao Zedong placed next to each other (see figure 1). Thereafter, a six-page edition would be issued on special occasions, such as Chinese National Day. As a rule, the front page covered major issues and key trends, both domestic and international. Sections in the subsequent pages included Party Life and Letters to the Editor, showing the clear influence of the Soviet press.[26]

Similar to the advice given by Lenin to Soviet journalists, when he cautioned that half of the Russian population was illiterate and thus newspaper language must be simple and direct,[27] one of the guidelines of the *Beijing Daily* was that the language used must be "easily understood and succinct in style, clearly comprehensible to the laboring people."[28] The articles were usually short to keep readers' attention. Moreover, to reach a wider audience and to relieve monotony, the *Beijing Daily*, like the *People's Daily*, deftly incorporated photographs, cartoons, and serial picture stories. Many came from the hands of established artists, as in the case of the woodcut artist Li Hua's (1907–1994) serial Combating Conservative Thought.[29] The Chinese use of pictorial representations proved more sophisticated and innovative than the Soviets' in form and content.

As a Municipal Party newspaper, the *Beijing Daily* served both as an interpreter of government policies and an information center on their implementation, functions similar to what Jeffrey Brooks describes for the Soviet press. The paper duly reported on the proclamation of China's first constitution in June 1954,[30] the Rectification Campaign of 1957,[31] and the launch of the Three Red Banners—the General Line of Socialist Construction, the Great Leap Forward, and the People's Commune—Mao's rapid modernization programs in 1958.[32]

The *Beijing Daily*'s foreign news reporting was not as extensive as that of the *People's Daily*; it was nonetheless a way for the Municipal Party to disseminate stories about Beijing to the world. Predictably, much front-page space was devoted to the remarkable achievements of the Soviet Union, especially during the celebration of the anniversary of the October Revolution.[33] Stalin was eulogized by the newspaper after his death in early March 1953 as "the greatest genius in the contemporary world and the great teacher of the world's Communist movement."[34] The state visit of North Korean leader Kim Il-sung on November 22, 1958, was also front-page news, demonstrating the close ties between these two Asian socialist countries.[35] Denunciations of US imperialism were plentiful, especially of its aggression against Arab countries in the Middle East.[36]

As its name implied, the *Beijing Daily* devoted the majority of its pages to city events. One salient feature was the continuous reporting on the achievements of the Shijingshan Steel Plant, one of China's major steelmakers and located in western Beijing. Coverage of it became even more intense after the initiation of the First Five-Year Plan in 1953, it being a sign that China was moving full speed ahead in industrialization.[37] Fan Jin and Zhou You also realized that to draw in Beijing readers, their newspaper had to speak a familiar cultural and social language that residents could affectionately relate to. To that end, sections that promoted regional identity were developed, among them Beijing Salespersons, Beijing Women, and Beijing Children.[38]

The layout of the *Beijing Daily* underwent a transformation in early 1956: local news was given even greater priority in the first two pages and international events were pushed back to page four. Special sections such as Popular Science and Physical Training and Sports were added.[39] These changes no doubt appealed more directly to local interests.

The *Beijing Daily* drew a warm response from readers. The newspaper was priced at 6 fen per issue in 1952 and 5 fen in 1957.[40] This amounted to less than 2 yuan per month, whereas the monthly salary of a junior-level construction worker in Beijing in the mid-1950s was 33.66 yuan.[41] The *Beijing Daily*'s circulation doubled from the original twenty-seven thousand in 1952 to fifty-six thousand by the end of 1953.[42] By the late 1950s, it reached more than a hundred thousand.[43] In 1962, it increased to 149,284, slightly lower than the *People's Daily*, which had a local circulation of 159,009.[44] Like Soviet newspapers, the *Beijing Daily* conducted occasional surveys to assess its role and to solicit public opinion. A survey by the newspaper indicated that the *People's Daily* was read mostly by officials and teachers, whereas the *Beijing Daily* was usually read by workers and clerks.[45] But behind the rising sales lay a clear Party hand. A 1958 internal Municipal Party memo instructed, "Besides individual subscriptions, every Party

Branch must subscribe to at least one copy of the *People's Daily* and one of the *Beijing Daily,* paid for by the Party or labor union funds."[46]

In March 1958, a sister newspaper, *Beijing Evening News* (*Beijing wanbao*), was launched to "reach the grassroots, and make up the insufficiency of the daily press," according to municipal officials.[47] More than the daily, the *Beijing Evening News* concentrated almost exclusively on local events.[48] In the late 1950s, a third newspaper, *Beijing Peasant News* (*Beijing nongminbao*), was published, aimed specifically at rural readers and addressing agricultural matters.[49]

An Interlocking System of Control

What were the daily routines at the *Beijing Daily*? How did the editorial committee run the paper? What was the link between the newspaper and the government? These questions lie at the heart of understanding the control of the press in socialist China. Indeed, the *Beijing Daily* seemed to be carrying out what was expected of it as an official Municipal Party mouthpiece: disseminating government news in accordance with approved procedures. But behind the outward façade of unity and loyalty to the Party, the inner workings of the press, as revealed in internal sources, were far from harmonious. Communist officials developed a system of tight control, similar to that of book publishing, over what could or could not be printed in the *Beijing Daily*. This system included horizontal and vertical checks on editorial policies. They conducted internal purges, exercised censorship, and selected readers' letters that supported the CCP regime.

At the horizontal level, the *Beijing Daily* was publicly run by its editorial office, headed by Fan Jin and Zhou You. Fan and Zhou met regularly with editorial committee members to discuss key issues. Whenever major CCP policies were involved, the editorial committee called what was known as the "enlarged editorial committee meeting," to which they invited people in high positions at the press outside the editorial committee to join in a collective decision. Overseeing the ideological operation of the newspaper was the *Beijing Daily* Party Branch (Dangzhibu), which represented the CCP's interest at the paper. "The Party Branch must provide leadership in [political] learning [at the newspaper]," stressed one Municipal Party circular.[50] Liu Ren (1909–1973), the second secretary of the Municipal Party, reminded his colleagues at the paper that "if we give up control of the newspaper's Party Branch, then the CCP's guiding principles, policies, and advocacies will be obstructed, and many tasks will not be accomplished in the end."[51]

This horizontal check was reinforced with a vertical form of supervision imposed by senior Party leaders. In her study of the *People's Daily*, Patricia Stranahan found that the CCP Central Committee exercised enormous control over the newspaper even though "no Central Committee members served on the newspaper's staff."[52] This was also the case at the *Beijing Daily*. The Party had an overpowering influence on the newspaper at both central and municipal levels. This control was evident at three levels. Sitting immediately above the editorial committee was Zheng Tianxiang (1914–2013), a key member of the Municipal Party in charge of propaganda work. Archival sources indicate that Zheng, who as a rule did not participate in editorial committee meetings, nevertheless gave regular instructions on how essential official matters should be underscored in the paper. Zheng corrected editorials or feature articles placed on his desk for approval. He was often critical of what he perceived as substandard pieces. For instance, in 1963 he lashed out against a report in the *Beijing Evening News* for what he considered a gross exaggeration of cotton production in China.[53] Director Fan Jin consulted with him on a regular basis to make sure that she did not deviate from approved views.[54] Powerful as he was, however, Zheng Tianxiang served under the direction of Beijing Mayor Peng Zhen. Peng paid close attention to the *Beijing Daily*. He seldom dealt with specifics but frequently gave general "instructions" (*zhishi*) to the senior editors on the overall direction of the newspaper.[55] Fan Jin recalled years later that the mayor often telephoned to remind them that it was imperative to publish the CCP's pronouncements in a timely fashion.[56] The third vertical line of supervision came from an even higher source of authority outside the Municipal Party office—the all-powerful Propaganda Department of the CCP Central Committee. Frequently Fan Jin would communicate the CCP's decisions, passed along to the Municipal Party by the Propaganda Department, to the editorial committee, a procedure known in the press office as "transmitting an order" (*chuanda*). This was the most authoritative way a decision was conveyed by the central leadership to the newspaper. The editorial committee seldom acted independently. When important matters arose, it often requested guidance from their various superiors—a process known in the press office as "asking for instructions" (*qingshi*).[57] These three vertical levels of supervision—from Zheng Tianxiang, Mayor Peng Zhen, and the Propaganda Department—ensured that the *Beijing Daily* spoke with one voice. This combined system of horizontal and vertical supervision resulted in much tighter control than the system in place in the Soviet Union with *Pravda, Izvestia,* and other newspapers.[58]

Training and Purges

In addition to journalists' interpretive, interactive, and informational reporting, the *Beijing Daily*'s senior editors, unlike their Soviet counterparts, also trained junior reporters, turning the press office into a mini-school for future professional cadres and propagandists. This mission was spelled out in the *Beijing Daily Office Guide,* which stated that one of the purposes of the newspaper was to conduct "cadre training" because "raising the standard of cadres [in journalism] is an important reason" for the success of the newspaper.[59]

The training took two forms, one professional and the other ideological. The newspaper ran intermittent "journalism training class" for junior editors and reporters, which taught editorial styles and advanced reporting techniques.[60] At the conclusion of a 1961 training session, it was noted that of the twenty-eight trainees, twelve (43 percent) were regarded as "demonstrating better political conviction and with higher vocational aptitude" than others, thirteen (46 percent) were found to be mediocre, and "three (11 percent) were politically inferior and professionally incompetent, unsuitable for journalistic work."[61]

Even more important was ideological training. Supervised primarily by the Party Branch, the press organized periodic study sessions for reporters and every year sent a number of them away for short-term study.[62] In reality, the two programs were hardly distinguishable because participants in both categories were immersed in political indoctrination by senior Municipal Party members. During the training sessions, for instance, participants were required to absorb Mao Zedong's celebrated writings such as "On Contradiction" and "On Practice."[63] A 1960 report gave the following good news: "[All participants] recognized that to be a good journalist, [he or she] must care about politics, seriously study the CCP's policies and obey the Party directives."[64]

An equally important task of the Party Branch was to weed out undesirable elements inside the Municipal Party organization, an unending campaign since the founding of the newspaper. Normally, a young aspirant joined the CCP as a probationary member, which lasted for a year. To become a full-fledged member, he or she needed to go through a process known as the "becoming a full member" (*zhuanzheng*) exercise, during which the applicant's past history and current performance were closely scrutinized by Party Branch officials.[65] The process was rigorous, and it was important symbolically because it showed who was in charge. Archival sources indicate that senior review officials often dispensed arbitrary and disparaging comments in individual cases. In an August 1953 review session, reviewers deliberated on an application submitted by a certain probationary member Wu; the following decision was finally reached: "[Wu] is reasonably capable, but he retains certain element of petit-bourgeois ideology. He is not modest, works erratically. [We need to further] test his loyalty to the CCP before we can approve his application. This case should be deferred for another year."[66] The minutes provide no information about the background of Comrade Wu, so it is unclear why he was chastised as politically problematic. But there is no question about who wielded the ultimate authority both at the newspaper and in the Municipal Party to decide a staff member's fate.

The Municipal Party's control system made its strongest presence felt in the purges of suspected enemies in the press office. In July 1955, when the CCP Central Committee launched the nationwide campaign called Purging Hidden Counterrevolutionaries to ferret out and remove concealed enemies, the *Beijing Daily* responded enthusiastically with an internal investigation.[67] Such a campaign was not unheard of: one had been conducted during the Yan'an years when the CCP eliminated Party members suspected of spying for the KMT inside the Communist-controlled Shaan-Gan-Ning (Shaanxi-Gansu-Ningxia) Border Region.[68] This time, however, it was carried out after the founding of the PRC. Director Fan Jin warned that "the political background of the cadres at the *Beijing Daily* was enormously complicated; an extreme degree of impurity existed." She confessed to her superiors that the newspaper management team did not carry out a thorough background check before hiring these people, and she herself was largely responsible for this negligence.[69] What the Party Branch officers eventually found during the investigation was alarming. Of the 247 cadres hired at the newspaper, twenty-eight had "committed serious political offenses." Of these twenty-eight, twenty-three were associated with the editorial office, the most important of all the departments at the paper. Of the twenty-three, five were "former spies," five were "former Kuomintang agents," two were "counterrevolutionaries," one was a "betrayer of the Chinese Communist Party," one was a "Trotskyite," and nine were still under investigation.[70] These disclosures were chilling: even years after the founding of the new republic, "enemies" continued to conceal their identity and could wreak havoc when opportunities arose. Unfortunately, the report gave no names, nor did it indicate why and how these problematic figures were unmasked six years after the founding of the PRC. Fan Jin only mentioned that these people "work passively . . . and adopt a hostile attitude toward the populace."[71] The vague denunciatory charges and the confusing conditions under which the investigations took place make one suspect that, like the earlier Yan'an practice, many of these uncovered "enemies" were wrongly accused or victims of political vengeance motivated by malice.

The launching of the Rectification Campaign in 1957, followed by the Anti-Rightist Movement, gave impetus to another round of purges at the *Beijing Daily*. Predictably, the newspaper's managerial team followed the central government's order to conduct a quick investigation. After a thorough investigation a total of seven "rightists" were exposed in 1958 and were soon "expelled from the CCP."[72] Again, Fan Jin and her associates publicly went through another round of customary "self-criticism," admitting that they had committed errors because they themselves still wrongly held on to "bourgeois ideas." The purges this time, as earlier, offered another chance for the newspaper to declare its unwavering loyalty to the CCP. "The bourgeois rightists caused chaos and stirred up turmoil during the Rectification Campaign; meanwhile, the political stand of our newspaper is crystal clear: we steadfastly follow socialism," declared the paper's report to the Municipal Party.[73]

In the early 1960s, the Anti-Revisionist campaign, launched by the Maoists, caused further panic. By then, the ideological split between the radical Maoists and the pragmatists led by Liu Shaoqi had intensified. Under a directive of the CCP Central Committee, which Mao controlled, Fan Jin mounted an internal investigation to remove "revisionists" (*xiuzhengzhuyi fenzi*) from the office. Three troublesome groups were identified. Sixteen were listed as "having political problems," including "serious past misdeeds, revisionism, and right-leaning tendency" and were purged. Ten were listed as needing "to be assigned to manual labor." Twelve were listed as being "not suitable for staying on the job." This time, names were given, indicating the severity of the charges and the senior editors' determination to expose and remove these individuals from their jobs. The successive purges in these political movements resulted in there being too few qualified journalists at the newspaper to perform even routine tasks. A 1960 internal memo revealed that "only seventy-nine editors and reporters now remain at the *Beijing Daily* and twenty-one at the *Beijing Evening News*." Because the number of the qualified reporters and editors was declining, Fan Jin sent an urgent request to her superiors asking for "replenishing the newspaper with a reasonable number of comrades who are politically sophisticated and skilled in writing."[74]

Internal Censorship

What news was fit to print? This seemingly simple question is difficult to answer when examining the *Beijing Daily*. As mentioned, the Municipal Party demanded that the *Beijing Daily* be managed by the politically most trusted. From the beginning, the Municipal Party instructed the editorial committee to set up "a review system" to assess every article carefully. Before a piece could be considered for publication, its author's "political background" (*zhengzhi mianmu*) needed to be carefully scrutinized.[75] The editors guarded against not only outside submissions from undependable sources but also articles from within the newspaper.

Fan Jin and Zhou You believed that guidelines should also be in place for editors and reporters. In an editorial committee memo, they recommended that "To avoid political and technical errors and to coordinate the working sequence, a set of review rules must be established." The publication rules specified a careful monitoring system for reviewing articles. For major pieces, a system of "first internal and then external" regulation was set up, meaning that editorials and key articles needed to be reviewed by chief editors before they were sent to Municipal Party leaders, including Peng Zhen and Liu Ren, for final approval. But the rules also covered basic details, including which people and which departments had the authority to send an approved article to the typesetting room.[76] Without question, the Municipal Party, not the editorial committee, set the agenda as to what kinds of articles could appear in print.

To ensure that the paper followed the approved path, Fan Jin and Zhou You made up an internal list of dos and don'ts titled "The Limits of Criticism" (*Piping jiexian*). These fell roughly into three categories: "not to be published" (*bufa*), "minimally reported" (*shaodeng*), and "can be published" (*kefa*). "Not to be published" included criticism of China's economic and social system, divulging the conditions of the state market supply, discussion of the quality of industrial products, and mention of China's backwardness. "Minimally reported" were topics that were not prohibited but should be avoided if possible, namely, stories about disastrous fires, industrial failures, gas poisoning incidents, and rising commodity prices. "Can be published" were pieces about everyday life such as the public's demand for more choices of products and better customer service in stores.[77] Clearly, what eventually appeared in the paper were articles that would not embarrass the government. When it came to reporting on sensitive political subjects, such as government corruption, religious activities, and ethnic troubles, the *Beijing Daily* had major blind spots.

The dos and don'ts on the list, however, were not always specific and often caused confusing and trepidation in the newspaper office. Some of the subjects discussed in print were later considered to be too politically and militarily sensitive. In a 1960 internal memo titled "An Account of the Review of the Confidential Nature of Reporting," the *Beijing Daily* was criticized by its superiors in the Municipal Party for printing articles on forbidden topics, including a piece on electronic engineering research at Beijing's universities. This was an error because it exposed "the confidential addresses of three Beijing companies that produced wireless electronic equipment,"[78] a subject that had become off-limits because of national security.

The list of permissible topics did not remain static in the shifting political tide. As veteran Communists, Fan Jin and Zhou You showed a knack for navigating the treacherous political waters. Occasionally, however, some editors objected. In an editorial meeting held on May 14, 1962, for example, associate editor-in-chief Luo Lin (1919–1992), grumbled, "How to publish a quality newspaper in a new historical era is our fundamental principle . . . [but right now] some topics are off-limits, and we cannot report on some things that were formerly permitted."[79] Luo Lin's rare complaint points to the harsh reality that Chinese journalists were walking on a tightrope. They needed to constantly remind themselves not to go beyond the officially sanctioned boundaries of publication.

Letters to the Editor

Like the Soviet press, the *Beijing Daily* was, in the publisher's words, determined to "reflect public opinion and the demands of the masses" and to "divulge and criticize the shortcomings and mistakes in different departments in the Beijing Municipal Government."[80] The masses were defined as "workers, peasants, cadres working in the government and industry, teachers, and students."[81] The editors and writers took this task seriously. Having a Letters to the Editor section beginning in the very first issue was designed to address this need.[82] But the *Beijing Daily* went a step further than its Soviet counterparts. Taking into consideration that many readers could barely read or, in the words of the editors, "found writing inconvenient," the paper suggested that readers could visit their office "to have a chat,"[83] further breaking down the barrier between publisher and reader.[84] This creative move buttressed the image at least of the *Beijing Daily* as truly belonging to the people.

The Letters to the Editor section appeared regularly and quickly became one of the most popular sections in the paper. The *Beijing Daily* received a total of 2,855 letters in 1952.[85] In 1953, a record 29,355 letters were received.[86] By 1959, the total amount decreased to 18,492, for reasons unknown.[87] In the first three quarters of 1962, readers' letters totaled 12,175.[88] The press office also received 188 reader visits in 1952, the first year that such records were kept.[89] In 1959, 475 readers came to the newspaper office.[90] In the first three quarters of 1962, 283 readers arrived for a visit.[91]

Among the 29,355 letters received in 1953, 9,481 were reportedly "letters of criticism"—but how critical were they and of what?[92] What conversation took place between the press staff and the readers when readers knocked at the door of the press office? Did these letters and visitors really reflect "public opinion and the demands of the masses"? Did any of them "criticize the shortcomings and mistakes in different departments in the Beijing Municipal Government" as the newspaper claimed?

In her study of readers' letters sent to *Krest'ianskaia Gazeta* (The peasant newspaper), a paper founded by the Soviet authorities in 1923 for a broad peasant audience, Sheila Fitzpatrick finds that they covered a wide range of topics, including denunciation of local officials for their abuse of power, unfair distribution of kolkhoz income, having private plots, and even job seeking. Many denunciation letters directed against kolkhoz chairmen and rural soviet leaders appealed to higher authorities to conduct an investigation and to correct their wrongdoings.[93] Unfortunately, the Beijing Daily files at the Beijing Municipal Archives contain no actual letters, only statistics about them. The only available letters in existence are excerpts printed in the newspaper. It is reasonable to assume, because they are extracts, that many of them were carefully edited and perhaps even rewritten by the newspaper staff to make them more presentable. Any assessment of them at this stage can therefore only be preliminary.

The editors broke down the 2,855 readers' letters received in 1952 into three categories: 830 on financial matters, 1,187 on legal issues, and 838 on culture.[94] The 18,492 letters received in 1959 fell into somewhat different classifications: 40 percent were on industry, infrastructure of the city, finance, and agriculture; 25.3 percent on culture, education, and hygiene; and 31.7 percent on administrative and legal issues.[95] The editors did not explain how and why these classifications were made. A closer look at the published letters reveals that they covered a wide array of topics. For instance, a certain labor hero, Liu, wrote a letter to the editor in praise of the central government's Increase Production, Practice Economy campaign.[96] The majority of the letters, however, concerned people's everyday lives. For example, an elementary school teacher in Dongdan, east of Tiananmen Square, pledged to do her best to teach her students with all her heart on International Working Women's Day.[97] A woman in Haidian, in the northwestern part of the city, fought for her right to arrange her own marriage in opposition to her conservative parents, who frowned on her choice of spouse, a right guaranteed by the new marriage law proclaimed in March 1950.[98] Some letters can be categorized as a sort of denunciation. They included one deploring an unlawful capitalist in Xuanwu district, southwest to the city center, who stole state property to benefit his enamel factory.[99] The Shijingshan Steel Plant Hospital was criticized for negligence in failing to treat a worker's child who had carbon monoxide poisoning, causing the child's death.[100]

As mentioned earlier, under the influence of Soviet newspapers, the Chinese press played the role of ombudsman, eager to address readers' concerns and channel their complaints to appropriate government departments. This service yielded some results. In response to a reader's criticism of their abruptly stopping the water supply without prior notice, the Beijing Waterworks Company wrote to apologize for their negligence when installing new waterpipes.[101] Similarly, after a reader complained about the poor quality of meals served for workers at a major machine shop, the company responded by promising immediate improvement.[102] Such an interactive process created a laudable image for the Beijing Daily as a newspaper genuinely serving the interests of its readers. But a closer look reveals that despite the variety, the "opinion" letters in general resembled government pronouncements, only transmitted in the name of the people. On the whole, the letters were filled with optimism, mostly endorsing state policies and affirming the CCP's rule. Few, if any, offered what the newspaper originally suggested: criticism of the government's "shortcomings and mistakes."

These letters were apolitical in that they revolved mostly around people's everyday lives. Nevertheless, they can also be read as extremely political in that they were written by enthusiastic supporters of the CCP, reporting mostly good news and exaggerating the achievements of the government. In March 1953, the *Beijing Daily* printed a letter from a North Korean soldier who wrote to "express gratitude for the aid given to his country" by the Chinese during the Korean War.[103] On June 9, 1957, a different type of letter appeared in support of the government's censure of liberalism in China. The letter writer condemned Chu Anping (1909–1966), the editor in chief of the intellectuals' newspaper, the *Enlightenment Daily* (*Guangming ribao*), for his open criticism of the CCP as a dictatorial "party empire" (*dang tianxia*)—a well-known episode in the early phase of the Hundred Flowers Campaign in 1957. "Chu Anping's denigration [of the Communist Party]," in the words of the letter writer, was "totally unfounded." The writer concluded, "Our nation is taking the socialist road, and following the leadership of the CCP is one important reason we can be assured that we are on this bright path."[104] Chu was soon openly condemned in the government-controlled press.

On the surface, these "opinion" letters can be regarded as "public" in that they were seen as an expression of public opinion. In reality, however, they were a convenient way for the CCP to gauge and assess popular sentiment, especially when major political campaigns were mounted, as in the Hundred Flowers period. True, occasional letters complained about minor abuses of power by local agencies or wrongdoings at individual industrial plants, but rarely did they constitute open criticism of the CCP. If such letters were written, they were unlikely to be printed. Julian Chang correctly observes that one distinct feature of both the Chinese and Soviet propaganda systems was their "lack of any open expressions of cynicism toward the masses."[105] This does not mean, however, that the Communists trusted the masses either, as demonstrated in the readers' letters sent to the *Beijing Daily*. The "people's voices" had to be carefully monitored and channeled in such a way as to benefit the socialist revolution.

The Looming Crisis

Like the Soviet Union's high politics concealed behind a façade of comradeship, differences among senior CCP leaders rarely came into the open. This changed in the late 1950s when a major ideological split occurred at the highest leadership level between Mao, who advocated continuous class struggle ("putting politics in command") and rapid collectivization under the Three Red Banners, and Liu Shaoqi, who opted for a more pragmatic approach in economic planning that allowed for private agricultural plots and more room for free markets. Mao saw in Liu an ominous reemergence of the capitalist spirit, warning in September 1959 that "bourgeois elements" had infiltrated the CCP.[106] This story is now familiar to many. We also know that in this conflict, Mayor Peng Zhen and key members of the Beijing Municipal Party as well as the senior editors and managers of the *Beijing Daily* took Liu's side. They were therefore subsequently purged by the Maoists in the early days of the Cultural Revolution. Conventional argument holds that Fan Jin and Zhou You were solidly behind Liu Shaoqi in this power struggle. Such an interpretation, however, ignores a far more complicated world that saw heated debates, raucous infighting, and uncertainty inside the press office.

To be sure, the *Beijing Daily* eventually favored Liu Shaoqi's pragmatism, but this was an evolutionary process. At least in the late 1950s and early 1960s, the newspaper continued to report on Mao's Three Red Banners with enthusiasm. The news about the triumphant results (later found out to be overblown) of Mao's radical economic programs gained prominent headlines in the paper. For example, on October 2, 1958, an article titled "Hail the General Line! Sing in Praise of Great Harvest!" occupied the front page.[107] Likewise, on August 30, 1959, a lead article praised the achievements of Jianmin Commune, a model people's commune in Hebei Province.[108]

Such glowing reports, however, did not sit well with senior Municipal Party officials. According to an official biography of Liu Ren produced by the Beijing Municipal Party, Second Secretary Liu was furious when he learned that the *Beijing Daily* had published an article titled "With One Stroke, Production of the Backyard Steel Furnaces in Chaoyang District Surpasses That of Two Steel Plants" in late October 1958. The story reported that the total steel output in Chaoyang District in eastern Beijing reached 265 tons in a single day, far exceeding the combined output of the two major steel plants Beijing Special Steel Mill and Shijingshan Steel Plant. Liu lambasted the editors for publishing a shoddy and grossly inflated report.[109] Liu Ren's views were endorsed by Peng Zhen, who was critical of the Great Leap Forward. Minutes of the editorial committee meetings at the *Beijing Daily* also show deep concern about countless reports that included "exaggerated" (*fukua*) production figures resulting from Mao's mass mobilization programs.[110] Deng Tuo, the former editor in chief of the *People's Daily*, joined the Municipal Party in 1958 as the head of the Propaganda

Department. Beginning in March 1961, he contributed a series of short articles to the Five-Colored Soil (Wusetu) section of the *Beijing Evening News* (later collectively known as "Evening Chats at Yanshan") that lampooned Mao's unrealistic industrial goals and his frenetic Great Leap Forward.[111] At the beginning of the Cultural Revolution, Deng was denounced by the Maoists as a "big poisonous weed" who was "anti-Party and anti-socialism."[112]

Inside the press office not everything was serene. To avoid political trouble, Communist officials tended to speak a deliberately vague and elusive language. They included Mayor Peng Zhen. As early as November 1958, in an article written for the inaugural issue of *Qianxian (Frontline)*—a Municipal Party theoretical journal, edited by Deng Tuo—Peng reminded his colleagues to do things "according to objective laws," a clear disapproval of Mao's frantic industrialization programs. But then Peng immediately asserted in safe Maoist political rhetoric that "the Municipal Party is steadfastly following Comrade Mao Zedong and the Central Committee."[113] It was indeed this kind of double-talk and ambiguity from the Municipal Party that befuddled the editors of the *Beijing Daily*.

Initially, Fan Jin and her colleagues adopted an understandably cautious approach by holding editorial committee meetings and conducting study sessions to discuss the conflicting policy decisions from top levels. The meetings were held with greater frequency and took longer to complete in the early 1960s than previously, an indication that sensitive issues were mounting and that collective decisions were harder to reach. For example, on July 8, 1961, an important meeting that included the editorial staff of the *Beijing Daily,* the *Beijing Evening News,* and *Frontline* was held in Beihai Park to map out a correct publishing strategy, but no clear resolution was reached except on lofty general principles.[114] One such principle was what Fan Jin and Zhou You called the newspaper's "directions" (*fangxiangxing*), which, participants agreed, should adhere to "major CCP policies that would [allow us to] solve the key current contradictions."[115] But the term "direction" is mercurial and ill defined, and the language used to delineate it was too abstract to tie it to any concrete situations. This highly formulaic language, often intentionally employed, seemed the safest way to work around a politically difficult situation in an era of uncertainty.

Confusion and frustration thus filled the press office. True, Mao was the supreme leader of the CCP, and his words were considered sacred, but the editors complained that his instructions were often difficult to follow. In an editorial committee meeting held on October 22, 1963, to discuss "anti-bureaucratism," the eight members who attended, including Fan Jin, Zhou You, Luo Lin, and He Guang (1920–2015), were unable to decide on what action the newspaper should take:

Fan Jin: It's not easy to resolve the problem of the Red Line [referring to Mao's vision of socialist revolution and his Three Red Banners]. We have not yet used our collective strength to do it, but we can find out what this line is all about if we try hard. [At present] we have an inadequate understanding of class education. . . .

Luo Lin: This is first and foremost an ideological problem. Often [major policies at the top] have been tersely proclaimed and are rather imprecise. If our editorial committee members cannot figure these out ourselves, how can we expect our subordinates to follow? There is a big chance that this will result in taking blind action. . . .

He Guang: We are dismissing things we need to pay attention to, while clinging to things we should let go of.[116]

Although this discussion was laconically, and at times vaguely, recorded in the minutes, there is no question that an air of anxiety and uncertainty prevailed in the room. Few of the editors understood clearly the policies of the CCP Central Committee, given that the policies seemed to conflict and change all the time. He Guang lamented at another editorial committee meeting held on January 6, 1964, that "implementing the Chairman's thoughts is by no means easy."[117]

Editorial committee meetings often turned into a confessional gathering, a platform for participants to criticize themselves—and others as well—for perceived deviation from the central Party line. Such a device, dating back to the Yan'an days, was established to allow Party members to admit their mistakes, declare their allegiance to the Party, and renew their commitment to the revolutionary cause. In 1950, the CCP Central Committee had issued an important document insisting that "criticism and self-criticism should be conducted in the newspapers," thus reviving an old Yan'an practice.[118] In implementing Mao's belief in "putting politics in command," Fan Jin confessed that "[we] did not emphasize enough the importance of politics; and we paid insufficient attention to ideology and were inadequate in promoting the thought of Mao Zedong."[119] Editor Li Ye (1922–2012) criticized himself in an editorial meeting held on March 23, 1964, saying, "In the past few years I did not seriously study Chairman Mao's writings, nor did I understand the Party policy. I was detached from realities over a long period of time. My standard for myself was not high enough, and I was satisfied with the status quo and intellectually lazy."[120]

To avoid stepping into a political minefield, many journalists wrote gingerly. Some employed two defensive measures: fence-sitting and expressing others' views without stating their own. The first technique was ridiculed by critics as "*qiangtoucao*," meaning "grass on the top of a wall that sways shamelessly with wind."[121] Fan Jin also mocked those in the second group: "Even copying [from others] will not prove safe." A culture of fear increasingly engulfed the office of the *Beijing Daily*. This prompted Fan Jin, with irritation, to call on her colleagues to "stop being afraid."[122] But such counsel was ignored as fear quickly frightened people into obedience.

Sensing that Mao was beginning to reassert his unparalleled authority, many found it wise to openly pledge loyalty to him. Major Maoist themes appeared in great frequency at the editorial meetings. First, in an expanded editorial committee meeting held in January 1965, the slogan "Class struggle is the key link" and Mao's theory of ceaseless contradictions reoccupied the center stage. Considerable time was spent on how to reemphasize the importance of class struggle in the nation's economic development.[123]

Second, the supreme importance of studying the thought of Mao Zedong was highlighted. In a March 1964 meeting, Fan Jin, relaying Zheng Tianxiang's instruction, called on others to "[restore] the revolutionary spirit, raise the banner of Mao Zedong, hold high the General Line, and never waver from beginning to end."[124] Studying the writings of Chairman Mao now became a top priority for the editors.[125]

Third, the battle against revisionism was a major theme at the meetings. The call for "the struggle between the two lines" was raised, underscoring what the radicals called a confrontation between Mao's "proletarian revolutionary line" and the "bourgeois reactionary line" associated with Liu Shaoqi.[126] Terms favored by the pragmatists such as "private plots" were ridiculed and denounced.[127]

Fourth, "Learn from the People's Liberation Army" became a key topic of discussion, a sign that the Maoist radicals were increasingly counting on the support of the military, especially Minister of Defense Lin Biao (1907–1971), in their fight against the "revisionists."[128] Two documents—Mao's January 1964 directive to the *People's Daily* that instructed journalists to learn from the People's Liberation Army and Lin Biao's article on the importance of studying the thought of Mao Zedong published in the *Liberation Army Daily* (*Jiefangjun bao*)—became required reading for editors and reporters alike.[129]

Mayor Peng Zhen, however, continued to call for a different reading of Mao's policies. He used veiled language when he advised the editorial staff not to learn Mao's writings mechanically. In a 1965 speech, for example, he said,

We should not exploit revolutionary fervor. Indeed, there are already too many meetings [spent on studying Chairman Mao's writings]. . . . People are fed up, even if they don't say it openly. . . . [These] meetings have become too many, too big, too long, too weighty, and are utterly lacking in substance.

Once again, he criticized the reckless exaggeration of fulfilled production quotas, which, he warned, could eventually "spell trouble."[130] Peng's disagreement with Mao's mass mobilization programs eventually brought him to ruin. He became one of the most senior officials to be purged at the beginning of the Cultural Revolution. The Beijing Municipal Party, which Mao had long condemned as a fortress tenaciously resisting his policies, came under fire as well. It was completely reorganized in June 1966, Mao swiftly replacing Peng with Li Xuefeng (1907–2003), an early supporter of his radical policies, as the first secretary of the Municipal Party.[131] Senior editor and journalist Deng Tuo committed suicide in May 1966. Other purges quickly followed: Liu Ren was incarcerated in July 1966; Fan Jin and Zhou You were humiliated and subsequently purged, dubbed "counterrevolutionary revisionists." Fan's "landlord" family background no doubt was on the list of her evildoings.[132] Further, it is now widely known that those who were closely associated with the Beijing municipal government were also purged, among them Deputy Mayor Wu Han, whose 1960 historical play *Hai Rui Dismissed from Office* (*Hai Rui baguan*) was charged by the radicals with being an indirect attack on Mao's dismissal of Marshal Peng Dehuai (1898–1974) during the Lushan Conference in 1959.[133]

Scholars have argued that Chinese Communist newspapers since the Yan'an days functioned as textbooks, given that their primary task was to promote official policies.[134] The *Beijing Daily* functioned essentially as an arm of the Beijing Municipal Party. Its purpose was not to report objectively but instead to propagate the great achievements of the CCP. Despite the newspaper's exuberant reports of the PRC's myriad achievements, however, archival sources reveal the disturbing reality of a tight system of editorial control, stringent censorship, skillful manipulation of news, carefully selected readers' letters, and anxious journalists caught in a vise between two powerful Communist Party factions.

The *Beijing Daily* exhibited two significant features that had been inadequately understood because of the lack of reliable sources. First, an interlocking system of CCP editorial control, both inside and outside the office, was firmly in place from the inception of the newspaper in October 1952. To cement its rule, the Party mounted a series of investigations to weed out "hidden counterrevolutionaries" in the press. Although influenced by the operation of the Soviet press, the control system in the *Beijing Daily* was far tighter than its Soviet counterpart, as evident in the manipulative production of Letters to the Editor.

Second, contrary to the conventional view that Fan Jin, Zhou You, and other senior members of the newspaper sided clearly with Liu Shaoqi and his more realistic approach rather than with Mao and his radical line, a far more complicated picture of the contradictions at the newspaper is revealed: senior editors did try to adhere to the Maoist policy of high-speed economic advance and to reaffirm loyalty to him, but at the same time, they called for an objective law of industrial development. In general, editors and reporters lived in a world of uncertainty and fear, notwithstanding their role as of the voice of the Municipal Party. Double-talk, fence-sitting, doing nothing, paying lip service to the official lines, and conducting numerous rounds of self-criticism as an effort at self-preservation were some of the techniques the journalists used to try to navigate the perilous political and ideological shoals.

The *Beijing Daily* was forced by Maoist radicals to close down in September 1966, at the beginning of the Cultural Revolution.[135] It resumed publication in April 1967 under the control of the radicals. Fan Jin, Zhou You, and their senior associates in the Municipal Party, such as Peng Zhen and Liu Ren, were purged for taking the wrong side in the political struggle. Their tragic stories expose a disturbing reality in the history of the modern Chinese press: that freedom of the press never really existed in China after 1949, and that Chinese journalists, including those working inside the system, lived precarious lives and easily became victims of the factional fights raging at the top.

After the end of the Cultural Revolution, Fan Jin and Zhou You were politically rehabilitated. Fan was appointed vice chair of the Beijing Municipal People's Congress.[136] Zhou became active in literary circles as a writer. Today, the *Beijing Daily* is still the most important municipal daily in the capital. In 1993, the first post–Cultural Revolution year for which reliable statistics are available, its daily circulation was 523,600 and its staff numbered 753.[137] The *Beijing Daily* continues to be the mouthpiece of the Municipal Party, working strictly within the ideological boundaries established by the CCP.

The *Beijing Daily*, of course, is not the only municipal newspaper that the central government keeps a close eye on; all official media are considered to be under the same umbrella. The primary task of journalism in China, according to an authoritative three-volume reference work on journalism in the PRC, is "to promote socialist modernization."[138] Sun Xupei, a journalism scholar and once a reporter for the *People's Daily*, observes that two slogans have guided news coverage in China since the late 1980s: news reports must be "primarily for positive publicity" (*yi zhengmian xuanchuan weizhu*) and must uphold the principle of "stability overriding everything" (*wending yadao yiqie*). When major incidents occurred, Sun writes, the government would immediately impose restrictive orders, demanding that "these incidents must be positively reported and that with the exception of the official press release from the authoritative departments, there must be no new report and commentary."[139] Under the leadership of President Xi Jinping (b. 1953), harsh censorship of journalism has been imposed, especially on politically sensitive subjects such as ethnicity and religion. These restrictions are unlikely to go away anytime soon.

CHAPTER 3

The Attack on a Popular Religious Sect

Yiguandao and Mass Mobilization

On January 4, 1949, in the face of imminent takeover of Beiping by the People's Liberation Army, the North China People's Government, which had been established by the Chinese Communist Party (CCP), announced a ban on the activities of popular sects and secret societies:

> Secret societies and superstitious sects [*huimen daomen*] are not only feudal, superstitious organizations; they are also frequently controlled by reactionaries to conduct various counterrevolutionary activities. During the War of Resistance against Japan and the current War of Liberation, they caused great harm, for example, spying for enemies, gathering military intelligence, spreading rumors, misleading people, even staging armed uprisings, seriously disrupting the social order. . . . Starting today, all secret societies and superstitious sects will be disbanded and no further activities allowed.[1]

With this pronouncement, the CCP declared war on what it saw as two pernicious forces in traditional Chinese society: "secret societies and superstitious sects." In the past, these groups were often closely associated to the point of being indistinguishable. The attack was launched with a great deal of urgency because these groups were considered hostile to Chinese Communists. After the founding of the People's Republic of China (PRC) in October 1949, the attack became even more intense. On September 25, 1950, the CCP Northwest Bureau issued a specific directive against "the activities of Yiguandao (Unity Sect)," one of the most influential sects in North China.[2]

Confrontation between state and religion has been a recurrent theme throughout Chinese history. From the late Qing dynasty to the Republican era, this conflict was seen in the state's campaign against religion in the name of building a modern secular society. The late Qing reformers of the early twentieth century and the Kuomintang (KMT) activists in Nanjing from the late 1920s to the early 1930s dismantled Daoist temples, confiscated temple properties, and used the resources to build village schools.[3] But the PRC's attack on religion was unrelenting and undertaken on a much larger scale with more coordination. As an atheistic state, Communist China, like the Soviet Union, showed little tolerance for religion, which Marx derisively called "the opium of the people."[4] The CCP's war on religions, which replicated the methods Moscow used in the 1920s,[5] is well documented.[6]

Scholarly interest in the party-state's assault on organized religions in the 1950s, the early years of Communist rule, is growing. This has resulted in many excellent publications, including a 2016 article about the confiscation of Buddhist properties and the systematic destruction of monasteries and temples in Suzhou.[7] Holmes Welch calls this process the "decimation of the Sangha" in his pioneering work *Buddhism under Mao* (1972).[8] A 2011 monograph addresses the early 1950s Communist crackdown on Shanghai's Catholic Church, which the party-state saw as a tool of the imperialists. The history of the Shanghai suppression included the seizure of Church assets, imprisonment of Church leaders, and the expulsion of foreign missionaries by the new regime, but it is also a fascinating story of how Church leaders mounted a courageous (though ultimately futile) resistance against the state's encroachment.[9] The story of the government's suppression of popular religious sects, however, especially the attack on Yiguandao, is less well known. Although the anti-Yiguandao campaign has drawn occasional scholarly attention, as in Kenneth Lieberthal's 1980 investigation of the Communists' takeover of Tianjin, a commercial center in North China, in late 1949,[10] the exact meaning and implementation of that campaign has seldom been explored. The nature of Chinese popular sects, the political implications of these sects and how they have been treated in socialist China is a crucial topic that needs to be addressed.

The official assault against popular religious groups, commonly referred to as "sectarian" and "heterodox" groups or "redemptive societies" (the latter referring to similar groups that thrived during the Republican China) was by no means new.[11] It is well known that religious sects thrived in traditional China, especially in times of dynastic change and social upheaval.[12] These popular religious groups are part of what the sociologist C. K. Yang calls the "diffused religion," a fixture of China's religious landscape, where such groups have traditionally been at the core of villagers' social life and moral universe.[13] These religious sects—particularly those espousing millenarian ideologies and messianic promises aimed at setting up a new political order—were sometimes called "evil cults" (*xiejiao*) by the authorities, who feared them as subversive and sometimes military opponents of the established political structure. The famous White Lotus Rebellion during the Qing dynasty is one example of a sectarian movement that challenged the established order.[14]

When the Chinese Communists came to power, they viewed Yiguandao and other popular religions with suspicion and trepidation. Mao and top Party leaders considered these sects even more dangerous than organized religions (such as Buddhism and Roman Catholicism) because of their pervasive influence in rural areas, especially in North China, and therefore wasted no time in banning them.

The Common Program, adopted by the Chinese People's Political Consultative Conference in September 1949, officially raised the issue of the counterrevolutionaries: "The People's Republic of China shall suppress all counterrevolutionary activities, severely punish all Kuomintang counterrevolutionary war criminals and other incorrigible counterrevolutionary elements who collaborate with imperialism, commit treason against the fatherland, and oppose the cause of the people's democracy."[15] However, the concept of counterrevolution (*fangeming*) remains a nebulous catch-all for all the Party's adversaries, including unauthorized religious groups.[16]

On October 10, 1950, the CCP Central Committee issued its Directive on the Suppression of Counterrevolutionary Activities (the Double-Ten Directive), which banned Yiguandao and other religious sects.[17] This directive is significant in the history of the PRC because it defined the CCP's policy toward religion, in general, and popular sects, in particular. It resulted in a swift expansion of state power over people's religious lives.

The attack on popular religions that began in 1949 paved the way for the even more violent Zhenfan campaign that was officially announced in July 1950 by the Government Administration Council (forerunner of the State Council) and the Supreme People's Court.[18] The campaign, which was conducted through a series of propaganda devices, was a violent mass mobilization movement that also had the purpose of consolidating Party rule. Mao Zedong threw his weight behind the Zhenfan campaign when he wrote in 1951, "The campaign is a great struggle. Our political power cannot be consolidated until this crusade is completed satisfactorily."[19] He viewed the earlier war against religious sects as part of this bigger campaign against counterrevolutionaries. Similar techniques of mass mobilization were applied in political movements as in the case of the Resist America, Aid Korea Campaign (1950–1953).

The Threat

Yiguandao was founded by Wang Jueyi during the late Qing dynasty,[20] though he claimed that its doctrines were passed down secretly from earlier times, especially after the Ming dynasty.[21] A complex and syncretic religion, distinctive in its esoteric teachings, the sect incorporates doctrines from Confucianism, Daoism, and Buddhism, but shows influences from Christianity and Islam. Although espousing extremely diverse doctrines, the sect's core teachings, as David Jordan and Daniel Overmyer point out, center on the Buddhist mythology of the Eternal Mother–Maitreya.[22] This doctrine holds that the world will soon descend into chaos as the last phase of the three kalpas—past, present, and future—approaches. As the supreme deity of boundless compassion, the Eternal Mother sends Maitreya, the Buddha of the Future, and other saints to rescue people in crisis and persuade them to join Yiguandao to avoid disaster.[23]

The sect gained wide acceptance in the early decades of the twentieth century, when its charismatic leader, Zhang Guangbi, also known as Zhang Tianran, taught extensively in North China, especially in the Tianjin area. During the War of Resistance against Japan, Zhang managed to carry on with the blessing of the Japanese occupiers. He even once held a low-level position in Wang Jingwei's puppet government in Nanjing and attracted a number of high officials in Wang's administration to join the sect.[24] Zhang was arrested after the war for collaborating with the enemy,[25] which greatly tarnished his reputation.[26] He died in 1947. In 1946, after the victory over Japan, the Nationalist government banned all secret societies. Taking advantage of Yiguandao's popularity, however, the government converted it into a charitable organization known as the China Moral Philanthropic Association (Zhonghua daode cishanhui) and maintained a tie with it. This connection later prompted the Communists to accuse the sect of falling "completely under the control of the KMT spy network."[27] Facing the impending victory of the Communists toward the close of China's civil war, the sect warned of the coming of the last kalpa. Many of its leaders fled the country, taking refuge especially in Taiwan and Hong Kong.[28]

The new regime was deeply worried about the mysterious and popular Yiguandao sect for six reasons in particular.

First, the sect's exaltation of spiritual authority over the secular order—a common element of folk religions in imperial China—ran counter to the materialist historical philosophy of the new state.

Second, the sect's great popularity made it an unpredictable social force that could challenge the Communists' legitimacy to rule. A 1950 New China News Agency internal circular announced that the sect was entrenched in northern provinces such as Gansu.[29] In Suiyuan, about three hundred thousand people, 11 percent of the population, were sect members.[30] The situation was more acute in Hebei, especially in the vicinity of Beijing, where 15 percent of the rural population were found to be involved in various sects, mostly affiliated with Yiguandao.[31]

Third, the sect's rapid spread, especially after the Communist takeover in 1949, was consistent with the tendency of sects to thrive during dynastic transitions and sociopolitical uncertainty in traditional times. In September 1950, the Northwest Bureau issued a report warning that Yiguandao was "spreading fast in Shaanxi, Gansu, and Ningxia Provinces." In some locations, "everyone in the village was a sect member."[32]

Fourth, Yiguandao's esoteric practices often made members difficult to detect. Feng Jiping (1911–1983), Beijing's vice mayor and Public Security Bureau chief, referred to them as "invisible enemies."[33]

Fifth, the government discovered that many comrades, including local Party chiefs and members of youth leagues, "had joined the sect," seriously destabilizing the Party.[34] In one Beijing district alone, 23 percent of the police force were discovered to be Yiguandao members.[35] Even more alarming, an internal security check uncovered that "about 1,100 members of Beijing's Public Security Bureau had joined the sect."[36]

Finally, the sect was anti-Communist. According to the officials, the sect fabricated rumors that the arrival of the Red Army meant there would be "sharing of property and wives" (*gongchan gongqi*), which grossly distorted the ideal of collectivism.[37] The sect also undermined the Communists' land reform programs.[38] It had also forged close ties with antigovernment forces. Hangzhou's Public Security Bureau concluded that Yiguandao was controlled by US imperialists and the KMT.[39] On the outbreak of the Korean War in 1950, Chinese Communists charged Yiguandao leaders with spreading rumors of an approaching third world war in which the CCP would lose control over China. Thus the sect was maliciously undermining the nation's stability and creating an "America-phobia mentality" (*kong Mei xinli*) among the populace.[40] In 1950, the Ministry of Public Security described Yiguandao as "the biggest counterrevolutionary organization" in the nation, which needed to be crushed.[41] Luo Ruiqing (1906–1978), minister of public security, insisted that the anti-sect drive was at the core of the Zhenfan campaign. "Doing everything right against these reactionary sects," he said, "led to the complete success of the campaign."[42]

The Suppression

The Zhenfan campaign was launched systematically. First the government investigated Yiguandao. Mao commended local administrators in Shanxi Province for conducting a survey of the activities of Yiguandao from 1949 to 1950 before they moved against sect leaders.[43] Within a few days, key sect organizers in

Shanxi were arrested and incarcerated. The Beijing municipal authorities also conducted clandestine, systematic surveys of the sect's activities in villages near the capital, collecting, in the words of the officials, "criminal operation records" to "get the situation under control." The number of sect members in this region was reported to be at a staggering one hundred thousand, which included 2,432 core members.[44]

Originally, the official policy was to "prosecute the leaders, ask no questions about the followers, and reward those who render service," a strategy combining suppression with leniency according to the general principles laid down in the Common Program.[45] Security forces arrested senior leaders ranking from grand master (shizun) to mid-level senior instructors (dianchuanshi) in a sect hierarchy of nine ranks.[46] They registered the junior leaders and encouraged rank-and-file followers to withdraw from the sect, a process commonly known as tuidao (sect withdrawal). Efforts were also made by local police to dismantle the sect's networks. In only a few months, from late 1950 to early 1951, more than ninety thousand sect members in the Beijing area left the organization.[47] The government promised that once members relinquished their ties with the sect, abandoned their religious practices, and halted unauthorized gatherings, no further questions would be asked. In addition, ordinary followers were asked to unmask and denounce their leaders, "revealing their deceitful acts and reclaiming money and belongings that had been improperly taken."[48]

In the early phase of the campaign, from 1949 to the mid-1950s, although key sect leaders were arrested, severe measures such as capital punishment were rarely taken. Mao warned that "excessive killing . . . would not only lose society's trust [of the regime], it would also reduce the labor force."[49] In the summer of 1950, however, after the outbreak of the Korean War, the government adopted a harsher stand. The armed confrontation with the United States was an opportunity to rally people to support the new regime and silence dissent. "We must hit the counterrevolutionaries with firmness, precision, and ruthlessness," Mao announced in December 1950.[50]

The early actions against the sect were now criticized as too lenient, inconsistent, and ineffective, a "rightist-leaning error" that underestimated the serious threat posed by the sect. The government now warned against the danger of "limitless indulgence" (kuanda wubian) in regard to the religious sects. The Shanghai Municipal Party called it a "paralysis disease," caused by judging the enemy too lightly.[51] "To be lenient to counterrevolutionaries is to be cruel to the Chinese people," stated an editorial in the People's Daily.[52] Luo Ruiqing criticized officials' misjudgment of the widespread influence of Yiguandao, citing Sichuan Province as an example: "Though officials calculated the number of sect leaders in all of Sichuan to be 1,077, it turned out that there were actually 6,559 in one city alone."[53] Making matters even more difficult, the leaders of Yiguandao continually changed the name of the sect to avoid detection. It was discovered that among 217 newly identified sects in the southwest, 146 (about 67 percent) were actually Yiguandao.[54]

The anti-sect campaign went into high gear in the second half of 1950. The Beijing Municipal Party struck on the night of December 18, 1950, the eve of the city's major official announcement of the banning of Yiguandao. A score of sect leaders were rounded up, the sect's papers seized, and its property confiscated.[55] To demonstrate its firm control, the authorities executed a number of Yiguandao leaders amid much publicity. Those put to death in January 1951 included two elderly organizers: Liu Xieyuan, allegedly a Japanese spy who later served under the KMT, and Liu Xiangting, who also worked under the Japanese occupation authorities during the War of Resistance.[56] On its front page on January 19, 1951, the *People's Daily* carried the headline "Liu Xieyuan and Other Reactionary Sect Leaders Executed!"[57]

The executions continued, with great fanfare. On February 18, 1951, the authorities sentenced another thirty-one sect leaders to death, along with twenty-seven KMT spies. "On the same day they were tied up, sent to the locations where their crimes were committed, and then shot," reported the *Enlightenment Daily*.[58] In March 1951, another 199 counterrevolutionaries were shot, including a certain Wang Tingshu. According to the government, Wang, a Yiguandao leader, was "a despotic landlord" nicknamed "South Overlord" (*nanbatian*) and "King of Hell" (*yanwangye*), who once arrested dozens of patriotic students and was also responsible for the suicides of many destitute peasants. After the founding of the PRC in 1949, the unrepentant Wang continued to secretly organize his followers, and "repeatedly disseminated counterrevolutionary tracts and spread seditious rumors."[59] At the same time, some erstwhile sect members became informers. In Xi'an, in the summer of 1951, 113 counterrevolutionaries and spies, as well as 159 Yiguandao "accomplices," were identified and reported to the authorities by former sect followers.[60]

The state-run media began to do its work, too. To be effective, propaganda had to be accompanied by known faces, the Party realized, making the evildoers concrete and visible. Photographs of key sect leaders were prominently printed in the newspapers ("guilty of the most heinous crimes"),[61] as were the lists of those executed.[62] In an important editorial in the *People's Daily* titled "Determined to Eliminate Yiguandao," published in December 1950, the authorities called on the Chinese people to eliminate this evil sect once and for all: "This work is important to consolidate the people's democratic dictatorship."[63]

This later phase of the anti-sect campaign was better coordinated and more violently executed. Localities spearheaded the campaign by setting up "anti-sect suppression offices."[64] In September 1952, during celebrations of the third anniversary of the founding of the PRC, Luo Ruiqing announced "the great achievements" of the Zhenfan campaign. "In the past three years," he said, the government "has dealt a devastating blow to a large number of remaining KMT forces in China, namely, bandits, local despots, spies, counterrevolutionary associations, and reactionary sects."[65] At the critical Fifth National Conference on Public Security, held in October 1952, it was decided that suppression methods must vary according to different locales and social contexts.[66] In 1953, four and a half years after the initiation of the anti-Yiguandao campaign, the government declared it a huge success.[67]

The exact number of people executed during the course of the Zhenfan campaign remains in dispute, although some scholars place it at more than 710,000.[68] Of this total, the number associated with Yiguandao is even harder to gauge. Luo Ruiqing, in a report to the Government Administration Council in August 1951, stated that among those counterrevolutionaries executed, 7.7 percent were "leaders of the antirevolutionary sects and reactionary political parties."[69] The final number of sect leaders executed will not be known until more archives are opened in China. Nevertheless, the Party's violent suppression was decisive and effective.

Mobilizing the Masses

The significance of the anti-Yiguandao campaign cannot be fully comprehended without understanding its basic nature. The Communists called the Zhenfan campaign one of the three "greatest mass mobilization movements" (*weida de qunzhong yundong*) in the early 1950s. The others were the land reform movement and the Resist America, Aid Korea Campaign.[70] The anti-Yiguandao campaign was never simply antireligious; essentially it was a crusade to politicize the masses, as Luo Ruiqing pointed out. He called the movement a crushing attack against reactionary forces in China and said that "through this fierce struggle, we gave the masses an effective political and class education."[71] It was this latter aspect of the movement that made the suppression of Yiguandao a model for subsequent political movements.

Certainly, government-sponsored mass mobilizations to advance official policies and augment state power are common in modern history, as in Stalin's Stakhanovite movement in the mid-1930s.[72] What distinguished CCP mass movements from others, Julia Strauss contends, was the Party's "genuine desire for popular participation."[73] To ensure success, though, a mass mobilization campaign requires close cooperation between the initiator, in this case, the PRC government, and enthusiastic crowds that actively join in the process. It would be simplistic to view the PRC, even in its early years, as a police state that imposed its will dictatorially from above. In reality, to execute its policies the regime required plenty of help from below. In the anti-Yiguandao campaign, the agitated populace played an enthusiastic role in helping realize the CCP's goals.

Many Party leaders recognized that a successful mass mobilization campaign depended on the skillful use of propaganda. Mao ordered a massive operation to drive home the government's messages to "every household" in both urban and rural areas.[74] Liu Shaoqi, in his directive to the Northwest Bureau concerning the threat of Yiguandao, was even more specific when in October 1950 he ordered that "mass propaganda education" be used to counter the cult.[75]

The CCP used two common propaganda tactics from the outset: portraying Yiguandao as a politically subversive element and associating it with the exploitative class. The first strategy linked Yiguandao with remnant KMT forces within China. In a score of Muslim riots in Gansu Province in June 1950, allegedly involving sect members, the official media asserted that the violence was largely instigated by "[KMT] spies and bandits."[76] A Yiguandao leader in western Beijing, Zhao Ziguang, was exposed as a KMT secret agent who had brutally stifled patriotic student demonstrations in the past and now was organizing a network to gather intelligence for subversive operations.[77]

The second strategy labeled many sect rebels as actually people with "bad class backgrounds."[78] Yiguandao leaders were "mostly landlords, rich peasants, and capitalists," according to a Beijing Municipal Party report.[79] These class enemies deceived people, stole money from their followers, raped hapless female disciples, and spread rumors of pandemonium, the official media charged.[80] Clearly, the Communists' strategy was to convince the Chinese people that their two key enemies—the KMT and landlords—were conspiring to bring chaos and suffering to the masses. The alleged link between Yiguandao and these groups spurred the people to be vigilant and expose this reprehensible conspiracy.

It appears that Communist propagandists carried out the mobilization along three fronts: organization, media, and public trials. In terms of organization, the government's immediate task was to train enough trusted cadres to eradicate the sect. From the beginning, the campaign faced a serious shortage of manpower, which was a major obstacle in Communist efforts to control Beijing immediately after defeating the KMT in 1949.[81] Beijing's Public Security Bureau had no choice but to hastily train a large security force, which it called, hyperbolically, "a

Yiguandao smashing army."[82] Other major cities did the same. In Shanghai, for example, in the early 1950s, the municipal government assembled 7,280 people to form what it termed "a propaganda network."[83] The numbers proved woefully inadequate, however, given that the propagandists were dealing with a national problem of enormous magnitude.

In 1951, Beijing's Public Security Bureau also called on cadres at different levels to organize and mobilize "under the leadership of the Beijing Municipal Government" to "resolutely suppress Yiguandao." Citizens in the capital were encouraged to "assist the government in reporting (*jianju*) the sect's activities."[84] Mayor Peng Zhen, a vocal advocate of active citizen participations in the Zhenfan campaign, argued that, "to suppress so many counterrevolutionaries, relying merely on our public security forces, is unimaginable. . . . We must mobilize the masses so that thousands of eyes and hands can greatly strengthen the public security forces and thereby reduce counterrevolutionary activities."[85]

In addition to training security forces, recruiting propagandists, and actively involving various government agencies in the anti-sect campaign, the government used the powerful state-sponsored media to raise political consciousness among the masses. In this effort, aural and visual methods such as *yangge* dance, cartoons and serial picture stories, and radio broadcasting were vital. The Party was well aware of the importance of couching their message in simple terms. Targeting rural audiences, the propagandists engaged *yangge*, a familiar folk art, as a tool. "New *yangge*"—a reformed rural dance extolling the achievements of Communist rule—and its accompanying short plays (known as *yanggeju*), popular since the Yan'an era, channeled anti-sect messages to the villagers.[86] In Beijing in the early days of the PRC, a *yangge* company of nine hundred folk dancers, divided into four groups, was sent to villages near the city to disseminate government policies.[87] This use of *yangge* indicated the propagandists' intention to adapt their techniques to their audience. A government document contended that "in the outlying areas, the target audience is quite different from that of the city. The principal audience there is peasants."[88] The hope was that a well-liked, lively folk dance or play would draw many enthusiastic viewers, who would in turn respond positively to the official policy portrayed.

The attack against Yiguandao was also carried out using visual methods. Since the Yan'an days, especially after Mao's famous Yan'an Talks, Communist artists used art and literature to serve political goals.[89] In 1952, the film *Yiguan hairendao* (A reactionary sect) was produced by the government-run Central Film Bureau to expose the crimes of Yiguandao.[90] A cartoon in the *People's Daily* by staff cartoonist Fang Cheng (1918–2018) portrayed Chiang Kai-shek as a Yiguandao instructor, preaching the Canon of Destruction to rapt religious devotees. The sinister image in this cartoon implies a politico-religious conspiracy to undermine the peace and social order of the new regime.[91]

Serial picture stories were another familiar form for communicating a Party theme. This format had earlier enjoyed great popularity among poorly educated urban audiences, especially in Shanghai and Tianjin. After 1949, predictably, serial picture stories became another method for creating agreement with government views. Tian Zuoliang's (1921–1997) series, *The Class of the Immortals* (*Xianban*) is a case in point. Appearing in the *People's Daily* in May 1951, it told the fictional story of the depraved career of Yiguandao instructor Zhang Falun, an unmarried landlord claiming to be the Maitreya Buddha who has descended to the world to save mankind. Zhang assembles his followers in secret locations and preaches seditious ideas. In reality, Zhang misleads people, beats his followers, and defrauds them of their money and belongings. Although he advocates abstinence from sex, he is actually a sex maniac and frequently molests young, attractive female converts. After 1949, Zhang is arrested by the police, and a search of his house unearths evidence that he has surreptitiously hidden anti-Communist tracts. In the end, Zhang grudgingly confesses his "counterrevolutionary crimes."[92]

Radio broadcasts were also used to spread propaganda. In the early 1950s, the Propaganda Department of the Shanghai Municipal Government instructed the propagandists to design special anti-sect radio programs to encourage "factory workers, local residents, to tune in."[93] To promulgate the public trials of sect leaders, officials relied heavily on radio. In a mass trial of counterrevolutionaries in Shenyang in May 1951, for example, more than one million people reportedly listened to it on the radio.[94]

The Communists also called on religious leaders sympathetic to socialist causes to openly support this campaign, essentially using one religion to attack another. The renowned Buddhist monk Juzan (1908–1984) was said to have enthusiastically endorsed the policy. "Yiguandao has no theories or canons," he stated, "but is only a feudal, reactionary organization intent on cheating and harming people."[95] We cannot know, of course, whether Juzan genuinely supported the policy or his statement was merely a ploy to ensure his safety. In either case, the CCP received much needed backing when the new regime's policy was endorsed by an influential religious leader who was also a member of the People's Political Consultative Conference.

Chinese officials generally portrayed the followers of Yiguandao as illiterate and naïve folk who had been coaxed into joining the cult. But officials realized that maximum impact could only be generated among the populace if the victims of the cult were given a face and a voice. The best strategy was to highlight the ordeals of individual sect members, who were often carefully selected and screened by the authorities. One former member, Geng Zhizhong, a vendor in Beijing, came forward with the story of his regrettable encounter with the sect:

> Three years ago, our only son died of an illness. It was a grave blow to a fifty-year-old man like me. Losing our beloved son was unbearable. It was at this time that Yiguandao entered the picture and persuaded me to join the sect. I was told that, if I joined, I would be released of hundreds of predestined disasters and would also see my departed child again. I was a bit superstitious, so when they encouraged me I joined. . . . Since I had no money to contribute, the sect leader suggested that, instead, I could clean the worship hall every day. . . . I was [also] asked to persuade others to join. . . . The sect leader told me, "Recruiting a rich convert is a thousand times better than recruiting countless commoners." Why rich people are so superior that even deities would favor them escapes me.[96]

In the end, Geng was rescued by "a worker" (someone with the right class background) clever enough to spot the shadowy side of the religious organization. "The sect leaders have done every bad thing imaginable," Geng said, but "now the people are the masters, and we definitely will not permit them to inflict damage again."[97]

For its propaganda to be effective, the government had to have physical evidence to support its charges against the condemned sect. It gathered and openly displayed this evidence and held public trials. Of course, public displays were not new in the history of the CCP. During the Yan'an era, many exhibitions, such as factory production displays, were held in Communist-controlled border region.[98] Unlike those exhibitions, which focused on the Communists' accomplishments, the anti-Yiguandao exhibits showcased the transgressions of an evil cult. The post-1949 exhibitions were held in accessible locations such as popular parks or the streets.

An ideal location was the popular Zhongshan Park near Beijing's Tiananmen Square. In mid-January 1951, the city's Security Bureau mounted an exhibition of the criminal evidence of "the evil deeds of Yiguandao leaders and the schemes they used to deceive the people."[99] Several exhibition rooms were set up in the park and filled with four types of evidence, reportedly confiscated from sect leaders. The first category was precious items, including jewels and gold bracelets that the masters allegedly took from their followers. Some of the treasure was said to be discovered in the possession of the patriarch Zhang Tianran, who, the exhibition organizers maintained, had amassed a hefty amount of gold extorted from his followers. The second category was evidence of treason, including certificates of appointment issued to sect leaders by the KMT as well as pictures of the leaders taken alongside warlords and Chinese who had worked with the Japanese occupation forces. Even American flags were on display, confirming, officials said, the disturbing connections between the sect and foreign imperialists. The third category was illustrations of sect leaders' decadent lifestyle, and included pictures of their luxurious household furnishings and pornographic paintings they secretly collected. Last was a display of ritual texts and planchette writings that the leaders used to trick novices to join.[100] By juxtaposing these various pieces of evidence, the government showed not only that the sect masters lived a debauched lifestyle but also that their political ties with the KMT and foreign imperialists made them extremely dangerous. The exhibition brought in big crowds, according to the *People's Daily,* "with long queues lined up every day outside the park to see the show."[101] Shanghai held similar exhibitions including movable street displays.[102] In Guisui (now Hohhot), Suiyuan Province, one anti-Yiguandao exhibit drew one hundred seventy thousand viewers in a single month.[103] Local governments were responsible for ensuring that the exhibitions were a success.

Perhaps the most problematic attacks against Yiguandao were the public trials (figure 2). These raucous gatherings were largely staged by the authorities, but they also involved enthusiastic crowd participation. These assemblies were loosely known as "public trials" (*gongshenhui*), "accusation meetings" (*kongsuhui*), "mass gatherings" (*qunzhong dahui*), "mobilization meetings" (*dongyuan dahui*), or simply "the grand meeting" (*dahui*).[104] Like Soviet show trials of the 1920s and 1930s,[105] Chinese public trials were arranged to expose the offenses of a targeted group to the public. The authorities chose a format that was both politicizing and entertaining in order to arouse community interest. The goal was to elicit positive responses from the attendees and encourage them to participate in the official anti-sect movement.

Predictably, Beijing and Shanghai were the leading centers in staging public trials.[106] In the early 1950s, the Shanghai Municipal Party asked various districts to organize accusation gatherings to "deplore the reactionary sects that have inflicted great harm on the people."[107] By June 1951, the city reported that between seven and eight hundred thousand people had participated.[108] Public trials also appeared in other major cities such as Tianjin. For instance, a banner hoisted in Wande Village near Tianjin announced the nature of the gathering as an "accusation meeting of the residents of Wande Village."[109]

The accusation meetings could be held in practically any setting with space large enough to accommodate the crowds, including, as noted, public parks (Zhongshan Park in Beijing), ritual sites (the capital's Temple of Heaven), open

控訴一貫道罪惡

Figure 2. A public trial against Yiguandao in the early 1950s (location unknown). The banner reads, "Denouncing the crimes of Yiguandao." Source: http://dangshi.people.com.cn/BIG5/n /2014/0608/c85037-25118652.html (assessed February 28, 2020).

county grounds, and school dining halls.[110] Typically, they began with local officials assembling the viewer-participants. Makeshift stages were built. The accused would either be led to the stage or taken to the center of the public space and told to kneel, which newspapers described as "kneeling before the people."[111] The accuser or accusers would stand and berate the accused, elaborating on his or her crimes, particularly those that took place before the Communist takeover in 1949. The audience generally shouted in unison with rage, demanding severe punishment. The meeting often ended with the ritual incantation of thanking Chairman Mao and the CCP for finally bringing justice to the nation.[112]

In an accusation meeting held in Beijing on May 20, 1951, a certain Hou Yongchang stood up to denounce Zhang Yonghai, a local despot as well as a Yiguandao leader. Nicknamed "Local Tiger," Zhang was also identified as a KMT spy. He was accused of bullying and killing people without mercy. It was said that after his village was liberated by the Communist troops, he secretly called on KMT remnant forces to retake the village, but the People's Liberation Army defeated them. In this meeting, enraged citizen Hou ran up to the accused, who was kneeling on the stage. Hou first detailed Zhang's past evil deeds, and then, with tears in his eyes, "turned around, faced the portrait of Chairman Mao, bowed deeply, and shouted, 'Long Live Chairman Mao! Long Live the Chinese Communist Party!'" The audience responded as one, shouting, "Shoot the spy! Shoot Zhang Yonghai!" Two days later Zhang was sentenced to death.[113]

Like Pavlik Morozov, the Soviet Young Pioneer who openly denounced his own father for cheating the state by hoarding grain,[114] many junior Chinese family members informed on elder family members in these public meetings. Cases were numerous of sons scolding their fathers, nephews humiliating their uncles, and wives berating their husbands for blindly following Yiguandao and causing unspeakable damage to their kin and neighbors.[115] "These [denunciations] were touching scenes," the state media commented approvingly.[116] When Yiguandao leader Yu Yiqing was arrested in Shanghai, his son, according to official sources, came forward and bitterly denounced his father, shouting, "It is true he is my father, but in terms of his [political] stand, he is my adversary!"[117] Like Morozov, the junior Yu was extolled by the official media as an exemplar of the virtuous citizen who selflessly puts public interest above family allegiance.[118]

Perhaps the most notorious of these denunciations was when Feng Shaoqian accused his grandfather of multiple crimes associated with his membership in Longhua, an influential sect in North China:

> My grandfather's name is Feng Jinxiu, a native of Feng Village of Ba County, Hebei Province. In the past he was the Buddhist Longhua leader in Mount Miaofeng. During the Japanese occupation, he worked under Okamura Yasuji [Japanese Army commander-in-chief in China] and the major collaborator Wang Yitang.
>
> Fifteen years ago, he sucked people's blood in Ba County. I was still young then and cannot remember the exact details. But I recall that people lost everything because they put their faith in the sect. In order to give money to my grandfather—the living Buddha—they had to sell their children....

I never knew that my grandfather's hands were tainted with blood or that he was such a sinister and shameless person. He forced my father to cruelly beat my mother. . . . My mother lived a life of great suffering because of him; she later died at the hands of this thug. So nine years ago I became a motherless child. . . .

I now know that my grandfather is an absolute villain and should not be pardoned. I reported him to the local police station. Three or four days later he was arrested. I was so elated that I became speechless. I hope the government quickly shoots him, avenging the folks of Ba County, my mother, and all the people he hurt. . . .

I wanted to take part in his public trial. . . . I cannot allow this enemy of the people to continue to live. . . . I wanted to see with my own eyes that he dies in front of the people![119]

In public trials, the accused were made to appear inhuman. Accusation meetings often reached a pitch of hysteria in the participants' hunt for sect leaders and other counterrevolutionaries, especially in a mass gathering, when crowds were inflamed by suspicion, hatred, and rage. Like Stalinist show trials of the 1930s, Chinese anti-sect trials were designed to arouse massive emotion and form opinion.

But public trials are complex political texts. Denunciatory language is customarily blunt, emotional, and often inflammatory, but it is also extremely hard to read because it uses stereotypical rhetoric and official discourse that can easily drown authentic voices. Because it is formulaic and controlled, it forbids unauthorized opinions and disallows unpredictable views.

On the surface, denunciation meetings were spontaneous gatherings, but in actuality were carefully scripted by officials. That the government called these occasions "mobilization meetings" explains a great deal, if not all.[120] The denouncers were not necessarily motivated by a sense of justice and could be prompted by malice or a desire to settle a personal score. Such a frenzied event was also an ideal occasion for declaring one's loyalty to the new regime, especially during the revolutionary euphoria in the early days of the PRC.

Public trials can be understood as theatrical performances incorporating tense situations, agitated crowds, public reproof, and, to some extent, entertainment. They combined education with suppressive measures. As such, they resembled both schools and law courts. Strictly speaking, public trials did not have to follow justice or legality, and often the line between private and public was blurred. They were public forums of intimidation and shaming, the state clearly trying to direct every move in the process.

The results of the meetings were predictable: the accused was convicted by consensus and justice seemed to have been served. Such an outcome was said to be possible only because of the superiority and correctness of the new CCP government. Although the precise impact of these trials is difficult to assess, they clearly helped create a network of loyal, voluntary agents ready to offer their services to the new government. Overall, a new culture of surveillance and mutual suspicion was being shaped to permeate society.

Problems Encountered

The government declared a triumphant conclusion to the anti-Yiguandao campaign by mid-1953. Archival sources and internal circulars, however, reveal a campaign beset with difficulties. The first problem was finding enough propagandists to undertake the assignment. Even among those who had been trained, many were found to be unqualified to serve. To their chagrin, officials discovered that many propagandists had actually come from dubious class backgrounds. In a county in Hubei Province, for instance, among the 105 propagandists, "thirteen were either landlords or rich peasants, thirty-two were hooligans and local ruffians, and only twenty-five met the required criteria."[121] This discovery revealed the difficulties in recruiting and training frontline cadres for the campaign.

Identifying Yiguandao leaders posed an even greater problem. Two key criteria were used for identifying leaders as counterrevolutionaries: either they were political foes who collaborated with the KMT and in some cases even served under the Japanese during the occupation, or they were class enemies—landlords, rich peasants, and capitalists. The sect leaders' alleged association with the KMT and foreign imperialists was not always provable. In addition, asserting that sect leaders were landlords and capitalists was sometimes based on flimsy evidence. Public trials were controlled spectacles based more on the emotions of the crowd than on reaching a verdict through established legal procedures. Very often they were political exercises following an official script. True, Mao earlier had warned against "excessive killing" of counterrevolutionaries, but because "counterrevolutionary" was more a term of political denigration rather than a legal verdict, reckless executions were not uncommon in the Zhenfan campaign, especially when a frenzied crowd had assembled.[122]

Another major problem for the government was the infiltration of Yiguandao members into local militias, rural administrations, and Party apparatuses. Some even gained important government posts, so that unmasking them became very difficult.[123] In implementing suppression policies, the party-state also encountered resistance from local law enforcers. Some security forces, as one source revealed, "were reluctant to take action against sect leaders," no doubt because of complicated social networks and personal ties.[124]

In general, the mass mobilizations worked better in urban areas than in the countryside.[125] Some local officials complained that even after meetings were held, "the majority of the people still had no clue about the nature of the event."[126] In other words, public trials did not always end as organizers anticipated. Local officials complained that many of these gatherings were hurriedly staged and poorly organized. In addition, some of them, instead of being solemn political events, turned into boisterous circuses that, according to one Tianjin report, "failed to arouse citizens' hatred against reactionaries."[127]

The anti-Yiguandao drive, as part of the Zhenfan campaign, was a complex politico-religious event that took place in the early days of the PRC. It went beyond the conventional confrontation between state and religion that prevailed in China's imperial past; it was an all-out assault on peasant religious tradition aimed at supplanting it with atheism. It was also a violent suppression of a particular popular sect that was perceived as a special threat to the new regime. Rooting it out was considered necessary for building the new nation. The campaign was also considered significant for fully implementing Mao's mass line, which held that building a socialist country required citizens to be fervent popular supporters, not merely passive observers. As mentioned, Beijing Mayor Peng Zhen called for the active participation of citizens in wiping out counterrevolutionaries. The willing involvement of the audience was a sign of grassroots approval of the government's policy. Public trials of sect leaders were regarded by officials as an effective form of mass mobilization because they were emotionally charged political spectacles that appealed to a mostly illiterate populace, and they involved revolutionary justice against sect leaders who had committed grave crimes. The anti-Yiguandao drive clearly was a mobilization on a grand scale.

Without a doubt, mass mobilization was a salient political tool. According to one official account, from the early years of the PRC until the eve of the Cultural Revolution, forty-four mass mobilization movements were launched by the CCP Central Committee and the Beijing Municipal Party. These included large nationwide campaigns such as the Zhenfan movement and the Resist America, Aid Korea Campaign in the early 1950s, the Anti-Waste Movement in 1963, and the Campaign to Creatively Study and Apply Chairman Mao's Writings in 1965.[128] This saga of popular mass mobilizations reveals a number of unusual, if not unique, traits of the Maoist conception of the new China. First, it was a utopian vision that viewed mass campaigns as necessary for helping construct a socialist paradise. Second, it was a belief that economic and social progress would not be possible until the population's political consciousness was fully raised and mobilized. Third, these movements were seen as an antidote to capitalistic-revival trends that Mao saw as reemerging in the Party as well as in the government. Finally, it was considered perfect political theater for training a new generation of revolutionary leaders, such as the Red Guards during the Cultural Revolution. Mass movements, as in the case of the anti-Yiguandao campaign, were a full realization of the Maoist mass line.

Yiguandao never completely faded away even after the successful conclusion of the Zhenfan campaign was officially declared in 1953. In all likelihood, the sect went underground. It and other similar religious groups resurfaced from time to time and continued to cause the government frustration and pain.[129] In the 1980s, for instance, Yiguandao reappeared in Henan and Yunnan Provinces.[130]

Yiguandao was banned in mainland China but enjoyed some freedom in Taiwan even though it was at first outlawed there. The sect was legalized in the mid-1980s when Chiang Ching-kuo (1910–1988) began to loosen the KMT grip on the political system. The sect, which has undergone reform through incorporating Christian teachings, is now thriving on the island.[131] Some of its members are prominent business leaders. The sect has also been active in charity work, including establishing meal programs that provide inexpensive vegetarian meals to poor rural students on university campuses.[132]

By attacking Yiguandao simply as an evil cult, the Chinese Communists ignored its importance in the history of Chinese religion.[133] Scholars of Chinese religions have argued that popular religions draw large followings because of their rituals and beliefs that pertain to the well-being of the living. The Buddhist message of universal deliverance from suffering, which lies at the core of Yiguandao as well as many other popular religions, has special appeal. This "salvational proposition"—as C. K. Yang calls it—has proven particularly popular in times of crisis because it promises to bring not only otherworldly rewards but also solutions for social ills and human suffering.[134] In today's China, many religious sects are making a comeback in the countryside.[135] Although the reasons for this resurgence remain unclear, some scholars believe that it may stem from Deng Xiaoping's opening of the economy in the late 1970s. Under Deng's market-oriented reforms, China has become more open and dynamic than in the Maoist days of rigid Marxist centralized planning. But economic success has also brought such ills as rampant corruption, widening income inequality, a deteriorating environment, and many displaced rural people. The nation is currently seeing a spirit of exorbitant consumption and crass materialism. Rapid changes and social distress have brought insecurity and uncertainty about the future, creating what many in China call "a crisis of faith" (*xinyang weiji*).[136] Anxiety and unhappiness feed the religious revival. When distressed people can no longer find answers in the once-revered Maoist creed or today's crass materialism, they begin to turn to religion to fill the void.

The return of these religious sects poses a challenge for the PRC. As Pitman Potter argues, the post-Mao government confronts the problem of granting more freedom of religious practice in order to present a new image of religious tolerance while maintaining the Party's grip on power by stifling perceived religious challenges to its authority.[137] In reality, the government continues to keep a close eye on religious activities, and does not hesitate to use force to crush dissent, much as it did in the 1950s.

The suppression of the Falun Gong sect is an example. The government's current national campaign against Falun Gong, a healing sect blending Buddhist folk practices and *qigong* (breathing exercises), closely resembles the anti-Yiguandao campaign of half a century ago in terms of its rationale, targets, and strategies. In April 1999, Falun Gong's massive, peaceful protest in front of Zhongnanhai, the leadership compound in Beijing, shocked the Party. Like Yiguandao in the 1950s, Falun Gong had drawn a large following in China, and, like Yiguandao, had also included in its membership many Party officials and bureaucrats.[138] Also, again like its predecessor, Falun Gong is perceived by the authorities not just as a religious congregation but, more important, as a subversive association that needs to be swiftly stifled by any method necessary. The widely publicized arrest of its leaders and the mass mobilization mounted by the authorities to discredit the sect are familiar tactics. China continues to view unauthorized organized religious groups as a threat to the Party's political supremacy. They must be placed under tight control, and all the resources of the state are put into service to that end.

CHAPTER 4

Building Cultural Centers
at the Grassroots

The Chinese Communist Party's (CCP) politics of control can be read as an unending story of propaganda. One chapter in this saga concerns the construction of cultural centers (*wenhuaguan*), grassroots propaganda stations first established by the party-state in 1949 to disseminate socialist ideas among the populace. These centers were, according to Chinese officials, an essential component of "mass culture" (*qunzhong wenhua*) and "an organic part" of the Party's mass educational network.[1]

Peter Kenez describes the former Soviet Union as "a propaganda state."[2] This description is equally applicable to the People's Republic of China (PRC). Over the past two decades, scholars have studied a wide range of topics about propaganda, from its institutional structures, networks, communication methods, to key policymakers.[3] Most of this focus, though, has been on the state and provincial levels; few works have examined systematically how propaganda operates at the grassroots and its impact on everyday life.

In this chapter, I examine cultural centers at the community level. A close look at the CCP's propaganda system reveals that it was mostly through these municipal-level cultural centers and their subordinate organizations that the party-state reached ordinary citizens. I also examine the use of a variety of popular devices (such as folk art and traveling libraries) used early on to disseminate socialist messages as well as the difficulties the staff at the centers encountered. The centers' activities reveal a large degree of complexity, ingenuity, and, most important, flexibility, which challenges the conventional view of an all-embracing propaganda program directed from the top. The flexibility that cultural centers had in devising ways of spreading propaganda made these centers one of the CCP's most effective tools for advancing its political goals.

Cultural centers are a perennial presence in China's major cities. But today's centers are quite different from those in the early decades of the People's Republic. When I visited Beijing's Western District Cultural Center (Xichengqu wenhua zhongxin or Xichengqu wenhuaguan) (figure 3) on a rainy day in the summer

Figure 3. Western District Cultural Center, Beijing. Source: Photo by author, July 8, 2013.

of 2013, I was struck by its rich array of activities and their nonpolitical nature. Located just above the Xinjiekou subway station near Xizhimen in the western part of Beijing, the building is elegant and multistoried, planned by the Ministry of Culture to be a "first grade cultural center." It is akin to a Western urban civic and recreational club, its tenants include the Western District Dancers' Association, and it offers a Chinese painting class for children and a photography class for the adults, among many other activities. On that day, the sole sign of politics was a play titled *My Father Li Dazhao* (*Fuqin, Li Dazhao*), about the heroic life of the legendary cofounder of the CCP. The current center looks nothing like centers in the early decades of the PRC, when they often were just a street platform for frenzied political campaigns. Perhaps, though, it serves similar functions.

Two Precedents

Cultural centers in the early People's Republic had two roots in the pre-1949 past. They can be traced back to the late Qing dynasty, when the declining Manchu court launched a series of "new policies"—an array of educational, military, and administrative reforms—in an attempt to save the nation from collapse. By then, combating illiteracy and educating the masses was considered by even the most conservative officials essential to strengthening the nation against the encroachment of foreign powers.[4] Lecture halls, libraries, and literacy classes began to spring up all over China.[5] These local centers received formal recognition during the ensuing Republican era, when, in 1928, the Kuomintang (KMT) used the term "popular education center" (minzhong jiaoyuguan) for their movement.[6] The number of lecture centers reached its zenith in 1936—on the eve of the official outbreak of the Sino-Japanese War—a total of 1,509.[7] To mobilize the Chinese people against the Japanese invaders, the KMT turned the education centers into stations for stirring up patriotism.[8] During the civil war between the KMT and the CCP in the late 1940s, however, these centers declined.

Chinese Communist cultural centers also had roots in the Soviet Union. Lenin saw illiteracy as a major impediment to building a strong socialist state. Many agencies were established by the People's Commissariat of Enlightenment to combat illiteracy and to spread socialism in the Soviet Union.[9] Soviet officials also created "cultural palaces" (dvorets kultury) and workers' clubs in the cities as frontline organizations for political indoctrination. Tens of thousands of agitators, armed with very specific instructional manuals, were sent to various parts of the country to spread the word about Bolshevism. Agitators were advised to "avoid pomposity and speak directly" and instructed that "they should make sure they had had plenty of sleep and avoid eating anything that might challenge their digestion before taking to the platform."[10] Reading rooms, known as red corners (krasnyi ugol), were set up in factories, offices, and villages nationwide.[11] The term "red corner" originally referred to a sacred corner in peasant homes where religious icons were located. These corners were transformed during the Soviet era into rooms decorated with portraits of Soviet leaders and filled with propaganda materials. In these areas, ideologically festive events were held, including administering loyalty oaths and accepting children as Young Pioneers.

The Soviets used a variety of methods to reach out to the masses, including posters, films, and "living newspapers" (zhivaya gazeta, a form of agitprop theater), to spread their socialist messages.[12] These methods were gradually introduced to the Chinese Communists during the Yan'an era, if not earlier.[13] The Chinese Communist media regularly gave coverage to Soviet mass mobilization activities. In February 1949, for example, eight months before the founding of the PRC, the People's Daily reported with great enthusiasm on the popularity of village clubs in the Soviet Union: "The educational network in rural Soviet Union continues to grow. In 1948, close to 150,000 village clubs were established. . . .

Their primary goals are to spread progressive thoughts and to meet the cultural needs of the collectivized peasants."[14] Under Mao's "leaning to one side" policy in the early years of the PRC, a large number of literary and art teams were dispatched to the Soviet Union to study Russian propaganda techniques.[15] The Chinese, however, did not blindly follow Soviet models but instead developed something of their own.

Development

At the time of the Communist takeover in January 1949, Beiping was home to six KMT-sponsored education centers—two within the city, the First and Second Popular Education Centers, and four in the outlying districts of Mentougou, Changxindian, Nanyuan, and Gaobeidian.[16] The Beijing Municipal Party quickly reshaped the old centers into something new. They changed the name from "popular education centers" to "people's education centers" (renmin jiaoyuguan), and soon to "people's cultural centers" (renmin wenhuaguan).[17] Using the word renmin (people) signaled the new era, echoing the core value pronounced by Mao Zedong in his celebrated 1949 essay "On the People's Democratic Dictatorship." The new "People's Republic," Mao declared, would be run by four types of new "people": "the working class, the peasantry, the urban petite bourgeoisie, and the national bourgeoisie," the first group taking the lead.[18]

The KMT system of education centers was condemned as serving only the avaricious interests of the capitalists and US imperialists with their "anti-Communist" stance and to promote American interest in China.[19] These centers were said to be run by "the reactionary ruling class for the purpose of controlling and deceiving the laboring masses,"[20] and their libraries contained "portraits of reactionary men of the feudal, reactionary past."[21]

In 1952 the minister of education, Ma Xulun (1885–1970), said of the new Communist cultural centers that "the primary purposes are to spread literacy, conduct political propaganda, promote recreational activities, and popularize scientific knowledge."[22] Indeed, Communist officials saw great advantages in this grassroots organization because the centers would be located in familiar settings, programs would be conducted in a language intelligible to the masses, and face-to-face dialogue could be held between officials and local folks. The lowest strata of the social ladder would be met with an attitude of compassion that inspired trust. Ideally, when fully implemented, these centers would form a close bridge between the government and the person in the street.

The number of cultural centers gradually increased. By the end of 1956, nineteen were operating in Beijing. Those in Xidan and Qianmen in the inner city were considered exemplary.[23] To best allocate limited resources and flexibly respond to local needs, smaller-scale cultural stations (*wenhuazhan*) were also established under the supervision of the major centers. These stations included reading rooms with newspapers and popular books. They also distributed government pronouncements. The Beijing Municipal Party suggested that each county should, ideally, set up at least one cultural center and three cultural stations, but this was easier said than done because of inadequate resources, insufficient space, and, most important, an acute shortage of trained personnel to run them. By the end of 1959, twenty-six cultural centers had been launched in the greater Beijing area, which included the city's thirteen districts and four counties. All together the count was fifty-eight cultural centers and cultural stations.[24]

As in the Soviet Union, "village clubs" (*nongcun julebu*) were established in China's rural districts. These were modest recreational houses run by peasant enthusiasts for their communities, performing functions similar to those of the urban cultural centers and cultural stations but on a much smaller scale. Those in Changping District (north of the capital) and Daxing District (south of the capital) were representative examples. Table 1 shows the development of this three-tier division of cultural centers in the first decade of the PRC in Changping District.[25]

Table 1. Cultural centers, cultural stations, and village clubs in Beijing's Changping District in the first decade of the PRC

	1949	1950	1951	1952	1953	1954	1955	1956	1957	1958	1959
Cultural centers	2	2	2	2	1	1	1	1	1	4	1
Cultural stations	0	0	0	5	3	3	3	3	3	24	2
Village clubs	0	0	0	0	6	13	15	66	66	143	113

Source: "Beijing de wenhuaguan" (Beijing's cultural centers), BMA, 1–12-870.

Cultural centers sprang up all over China, including in minority nationality regions.[26] In 1955, the Ministry of Culture issued a special order to create cultural centers in Inner Mongolia, Gansu, and Heilongjiang. Mobile cultural service teams were established in Inner Mongolia, catering to the nomadic population.[27] The total number of cultural centers in the entire nation in the first decade of the PRC is not clear, but most of them were hastily constructed and small scale. According to the *People's Daily,* many were privately funded by local enthusiasts and built in "one or two days' time," as in the case of the cultural centers in Yongxiu County and Duchang County of Jiangxi Province, where the centers contained only "two or three hundred popular books and half a dozen magazines, plus a few recreational tools."[28] Together, these three types of grassroots organization—cultural centers, cultural stations, and village clubs—became "a powerful cultural center network" crisscrossing the nation.[29] This multilayered approach added organizational structure and hence control to a community institution that had been more loosely organized under the KMT.

Tasks of the Cultural Centers

Just as Lenin understood the importance of "bringing enlightenment to the masses,"[30] Communist leaders in China saw how spreading knowledge to the populace could build a strong socialist state. Thus, Education Minister Ma Xulun made raising literacy the top priority for cultural centers. The Eradicating Illiteracy movement became the concern of every official.[31] The centers contained libraries and newspaper reading rooms, and hosted book clubs, much like the reading rooms the Soviet set up in the countryside in the 1920s.[32] Soon Chinese officials could boast that "all of a sudden, there were no more urchins on the streets." Presumably, children were now hunkering down in neighborhood libraries.[33]

Beyond literacy, new cultural centers were also intent on "bringing education to the people" (song jiaoyu shangmen) and "bringing activities to the people" (song huodong shangmen).[34] Large audiences were drawn to the centers' slide shows, song and dance troupes, and recreational clubs.[35] Promoting hygiene was another key task of the cultural centers. During the Patriotic Hygiene campaign in 1952—a nationwide movement to control infectious diseases—the cultural centers organized communal meetings, mounted street exhibitions, and made public media announcements on the importance of sanitation. Basic hygiene was taught; neighborhoods were tidied up; potholes and manure pits were filled in; and pests were eradicated. The Xidan District Cultural Center prided itself on being at the forefront of this campaign. From May to July 1952, it "set up mobile street exhibitions and organized twenty-three mass gatherings that drew a total of 41,000 participants."[36] In Nanyuan District, south of the capital, "a total of 2,274,000 flies and 123,000 mosquitoes were exterminated."[37] The inclusion of these precise statistics in the report was no doubt intended to buttress its credibility.

The cultural centers also held regular talks on factory production techniques, staged operas performed by amateur actors, and showed popular films.[38] In an interview with a Russian reporter from *Pravda* in 1952, Beijing municipal officials proudly presented a list of cultural activities sponsored largely by the cultural centers that included 1,074 slide shows on current affairs, 186 science talks, and more than 110 science exhibitions.[39]

From the beginning, cultural center activities, including the literacy and hygiene campaigns, were not launched in isolation. Municipal officials before 1953 called on cultural center staff to "closely coordinate with major political movements, including Land Reform, the Zhenfan campaign, and the Resist America, Aid Korea Campaign."[40] The dominance of politics also extended to the countryside, where village clubs were instructed to put together programs according to state policies. The most noticeable examples in the early 1950s were the drive to wipe out the Yiguandao sect and to hold anti-American rallies.

In 1953, when the government launched its first Five-Year Plan, the cultural centers took a sharp turn to become much more politicized.[41] In December, the Ministry of Culture published new guidelines for cultural centers titled "Instructions on Reforming and Strengthening Cultural Centers and Cultural Stations." The government insisted that from then on the centers would have to follow the "general line of socialism by disseminating the official policies, organizing people to eradicate illiteracy, helping to develop amateur art troupes, and spreading knowledge about industrial and agricultural production."[42] The move stemmed from municipal officials' being displeased with what the cultural centers had done in their first three years. The officials criticized the centers for reaching mostly urbanites. A survey had found that 75 percent of the visitors to the cultural center libraries were students and that few workers or peasants had come.[43] They wanted to know the whereabouts of the workers and peasants who, according to the Common Program, were the main pillars of the new socialist nation.[44] The officials charged that staff misunderstood their mission by treating the eradication of illiteracy as "the centers' only task," thus turning them into a mere "educational institution" and "administrative agency."[45] The mistakes, the report charged, were the result of a lack of "ideological guidance" from the top.[46]

Municipal officials also criticized cultural centers for their poor management. The Beijing Municipal Cultural Department (Wenhuachu) officially was in charge of overseeing the cultural centers' operations, but in reality the community district offices did. The centers' budgets and personnel appointments were an administrative nightmare that required quick remedy.[47] A new Popular Culture Department (Qunzhong wenhuachu) was created in the municipal office to manage the cultural centers.[48] Such a restructuring was more than just an act of administrative streamlining; it was an exercise of political centralization that gave the Party a firmer hand in directing the cultural centers and, as a result, greater involvement in the cultural life of ordinary citizens. The Beijing Municipal Party now demanded that the cultural centers practice what it called "the fundamental principle of serving workers, peasants, and the masses, and not simply serving the urban petite bourgeoisie."[49]

The 1953 policy brought several changes. First, the cultural centers would no longer function as units for eradicating illiteracy—that task would be taken over by the Eliminating Illiteracy Office, another municipal agency, and the centers would play only a supporting role by maintaining libraries.[50] Second, the target audience was now clearly understood to be workers and peasants, not citizens in general. Finally, and perhaps most important of all, cultural centers would serve a larger political goal designed by the Party.[51]

In January 1956, when the CCP Politburo announced the National Program for Agricultural Development, 1956–1957, it affirmed the Maoist vision of transforming rural China by setting up cooperatives and enhancing agricultural production through mass peasant mobilization. A widespread "agricultural cultural network," according to the proclamation, would include establishing "cultural stations, libraries, and drama troupes."[52] The spread of this network became even more pronounced after the Eighth Party Congress in 1958 when the CCP officially endorsed Mao's Great Leap Forward. Cultural centers were again placed at the frontline to vigorously implement this vastly ambitious mass movement.

In Changping District, the number of peasant clubs jumped from sixty-six in 1956 to 143 in 1958, and remained quite high at 113 in the following year (table 1). New village clubs appeared in nearby districts as well.[53] The Mentougou Cultural Center, for example, responded to the government's call by gaily declaring, "In 1958, following the policy of the Great Leap Forward, the two cultural centers in our district channeled their major energy toward the villages, concentrating on the People's Commune and organizing cadres to be sent to the countryside . . . to aid the production teams and conduct propaganda work."[54] Students were also encouraged to merge with the masses and assist in production.[55] Students from the history department of Beijing Normal University, for instance, were praised for spending considerable time at the mines in Mentougou, "eating, living, and working together with the coal miners" and faithfully recording their life histories. In the words of Beijing municipal officials, the ultimate goal was to make the students realize that "only the laboring people are the real masters of history."[56]

How Did They Do It?

The cultural centers adopted flexible strategies in conducting their propaganda drive. This array of practices took into consideration location (both urban and rural), expediency, practicality, and timing. In the end, the Beijing Municipal

Party was able to create a relatively systematic "propaganda network" (*xuan-chuanwang*) in the capital and its outlying areas.[57] But archival sources indicate that the propaganda drive also encountered many difficulties that were not reported in the official media.

Programs

The cultural centers used both "stationary" and "mobile" methods to draw in more users. Stationary methods (*zhendi*, literally "a military position"), were carried out primarily within the physical compound of the center or in its close vicinity. A detailed 1960 report titled *Beijing's Cultural Centers* (*Beijing de wenhuaguan*), compiled by the Library Department of Peking University under the direction of the Beijing Municipal Party's Propaganda Department, includes a list of stationary cultural facilities set up in the first decade of the PRC. They included theaters, libraries, reading rooms, and recreation corners. According to the report, by 1952, Beijing's cultural centers owned forty-eight slide projectors (and 485 sets of slides), forty-eight radios, 2,421 photos, 2,872 newsboards, nine pieces of wired broadcasting equipment, 208 musical instruments, 174,275 books (54,064 classified as "popular"), 637 magazines, and 179 newspapers. These numbers mean little without understanding how they were used. In their daily operations, the centers welcomed visitors and readers, staged theater performances, and held talks on sanitation and current affairs. These were practical and straightforward programs. The rural Nanyuan Cultural Center, for example, conducted a series of talks on a new cotton-planting technique. Talks on preventing infectious diseases through practicing good hygiene were held at the Fengtai Cultural Center. One Fengtai participant said with gratitude, "Previously, I did not have basic knowledge of sanitation and regularly drank unboiled water. Now I realize that this is dangerous for my health." Topics such as how to raise ducks were also popular with peasants. The centers also provided several basic services. One of the favorites was a free letter-writing service for the illiterate, a project that many local people found helpful.[58]

After 1953, these stationary programs came increasingly under fire from senior officials in the Beijing Municipal Party. They considered such activities to be passive, pedantic, bureaucratic, and out of touch with realities on the ground.[59] Cultural centers were instructed to move beyond the comfort of physical sites and into factories, farms, and fields to bring programs into the actual daily life of the workers and peasants.

This shift from station to mobile field unit became even more pronounced during the Great Leap Forward. The Eastern District Cultural Center, for example, followed the Party's call to organize "down-to-the-factory teams" (*xiachangzu*) and to send "cultural carts to the villages" (*wenhuache xiaxiang*). At Miyun Cultural Center, northeast of Beijing, staff were instructed to go "deep into the mountains to serve the peasants," which would enable them to "participate directly in agricultural production."[60]

Theater troupes traveled from one location to another. Bookmobiles were sent to distant villages. Performers and staff were instructed to acquaint villagers with current government policies and information. The results seemed encouraging. For instance, when the Changxindian Cultural Center in the southwest of the city got mobile libraries going, the number of readers using its library services each day increased from seventy to two hundred—a significant jump.[61] Obviously, this new strategy was more than a technical adjustment but an intrinsically political move that was publicized as an enthusiastic response to Mao's call to "Serve the people!"

Bulletin Boards

Early on, the propagandists accorded great importance to bulletin boards (*heibanbao*, literally "blackboard news"). These were small, easily moved, rectangular newsboards written on in chalk that promulgated public announcements, performance records, and criticisms of workers' misdeeds, and aided communications among workers. The boards displayed uplifting slogans, short essays written in simple language by the workers, and simple drawings on current affairs or production.[62] They exhibited what the officials called three of the most essential ingredients needed for agitprop—"mobility, dexterity, and timeliness."[63]

Reportedly, staff at the cultural centers were enthusiastic. The Chongwen Cultural Center in central Beijing used the boards to great effect for spreading knowledge of popular science.[64] In outlying areas where material resources were scarce, such as Mentougou, west of Beijing, staff often used bulletin boards for teaching the villagers and miners. The Mentougou Cultural Center produced 1,406 bulletin boards in 1958.[65]

Cultural center staff realized that they could not create bulletin boards all by themselves. They needed help from the public so that creating them became an interactive grassroots project. Staff at better-funded cultural centers taught workers how to make them, partly to train new recruits and partly to encourage spontaneous action from the people.[66] In 1955, the Chaoyang Cultural Center, east of Beijing, sent staff to Beijing Weaving and Dyeing Mill to teach novices how to prepare newsboards. The center also ran short courses on this communication tool, and graduates were sent back to their units after completing the course.[67]

Bulletin boards appeared in factories in abundance. They were primarily of two types: "red registers" (*hongbang*) and "black registers" (*heibang*). The former, also known as "honor rolls" (*guangrongpai*), promoted exemplary deeds of model workers; the latter did the opposite, recording poor performances or singling out those who violated production rules.[68] Shijingshan Steel Plant, a major factory located in western Beijing, was known for its many honor rolls. In the first four months of 1956, forty-eight bulletin boards were produced there.[69] Criticism of workers was not uncommon; however, the demerits often had an exhortatory rather than a harsh tone. In 1954, an essay by a model worker named Wu Jifu was posted on a newsboard at the People's Printing House: he confessed that his team violated the socialist spirit of collectivism by failing to work with other teams. This resulted in delays in the completion of assigned jobs. Wu vowed to correct the mistake. Subsequently, according to the newsboard, "the thought of collectivism has been strengthened, and the targets were being met on a daily basis."[70] Clearly, newsboards were more than record-keeping devices about production figures; they were a public pronouncement of workers' devotion to a collective socialist goal.

Folk Art Forms

A variety of folk arts was also used to promote government programs. This was inspired by two traditions: the earlier Yan'an practice, which drew inspiration from village visual art forms, and the long-standing rural performative culture, which elicited excited audience participation in singing and dancing. The Communist attitude toward folk arts in China differed substantially from how these traditions were treated in the Soviet Union. Early Soviet leaders had a low opinion of the oral traditions and folk culture of the peasantry. Lenin's disdain of *lubok* (popular prints) was famous. Although later Soviet propaganda artists (such as Dmitri Moor and Viktor Deni) drew inspiration from folk art during World War II, Russian intellectuals by and large dismissed folk songs, religious tales, and tales of saints' lives as trivial.[71]

Unlike their Russian counterparts, Chinese Communist leaders were early on attracted to traditional art forms, including folk songs, dances, and storytelling, calling them "familiar and beloved" (*xiwen lejian*).[72] Mao was a fervent advocate of these rustic forms, which he praised in his 1942 Yan'an Talks.[73] He did not view them as independent art genres but as a faithful historical record of the people's determined struggle against oppressive landlords and capitalists. These natural forms, he believed, could be reshaped into a socialist weapon to combat injustice.

Building on the Yan'an legacy, staff at cultural centers added more folk forms in their outreach, including *yangge* (rice-sprout dances), *yaogu* (waist drums), *kuaiban* (storytelling with a clapper), and *xiangsheng* (comic dialogues).[74] These were performed by musical teams, song and dance troupes, and theater groups sponsored by the cultural centers. In Mentougou, from December 1953 to February 1954, the cultural center organized fifteen performances that included folk dances, clapper talks, and comic dialogues, drawing in 18,350 viewers, according to one report.[75]

These reformed theatrical pieces were not the original voices of the people but designed by Communist artists. The dance patterns of the *yangge* may have been time honored, but the contents were definitely new. The new *yangge* plays reflected not the original world of the peasants—a landscape dominated by deities and ancient customs—but a new world of socialist workers, hardworking peasants, and heroic soldiers. This transformation, known as "filling old bottles with new wine" (*jiuping zhuang xinjiu*), was in full sway during the Great Leap Forward. In 1958, when Mao called for a nationwide new folk song movement that would support industrial and agricultural production, staff at cultural centers responded enthusiastically.[76] They encouraged peasants to compose their own songs with their own lyrics. In Changxindian District, one report noted, peasants produced 73,550 new compositions in 1958, mainly folk songs.[77] In Fengtai District, a ten-year old boy, Chen Junlan, was said to have written an inspiring new poem about the determination of the younger generation:

> Senior citizens can compete with Huang Zhong [an elderly hero of the
>   old days],
> Young fellows are as good as Luo Cheng [a legendary young warrior],
> We children will never fall behind,
> Heroes are what we are striving to become.[78]

A woman named Liu Shuzhen and nicknamed "Muddleheaded" wrote what the officials lauded as "a philosophical song about picking corn":

> I plant corn in the spring,
> I snap the corn cobs in the fall,
> If you ask me how many I can harvest,
> Not even the gods can foretell.[79]

FESTIVALS

Cultural centers made ingenious use of festivals and holidays—both traditional and modern, domestic and foreign—to advance the Communist Party agenda. Scholars have long argued that festivals are more than a magical time for a society to create itself anew; they are also extraordinary moments for national leaders to display pomp and power, thus advancing their political ambitions.[80] The propagandists realized that their activities could generate maximum impact if they coincided with major festivals and holidays. In its 1954 directive, "Strengthening Cultural and Artistic Activities in Villages during the Spring Festival," the Ministry of Culture proposed, "We could impart patriotic and socialistic education to the broad masses of the peasantry through a series of celebratory activities during this festive period."[81] The Beijing Municipal Party followed this lead by calling on cultural centers to make the most of "New Year's Day, the Spring Festival, May Day, the First of July anniversary of the founding of the Chinese Communist Party, and National Day [to] eulogize the heroic work of the laboring people and their struggle, and to publicize the socialist construction and the People's Commune Movement."[82] Staff at the Changxindian Cultural Center quickly stated, "Recreational activities for the masses are to be coordinated primarily with political movements; we go all out to do this during festivals such as the Spring Festival."[83] During the 1956 Spring Festival, the activities organized by cultural centers in Beijing's outlying villages were said to have drawn enthusiastic crowds totaling 723,000 people.[84]

In addition to the Spring Festival, another time-honored folk gathering exploited by the cultural centers was the temple fair (miaohui)—a colorful community event held on special days that traditionally combined deity worship, entertainment, and business. The Zhoukoudian Cultural Center, for instance, proudly declared its presentations at temple fairs (including newsboards and folk dances) a spectacular propaganda success.[85]

Foreign socialist holidays were viewed as another opportunity to attract crowds. These holidays went beyond stimulating only nationalist spirit to include the importance of socialist alliances and international friendship. The anniversaries of the October Revolution and the 1950 signing of the Sino-Soviet Treaty of Friendship, Alliance, and Mutual Assistance were considered the most significant.[86] These festivities, however, were never as popular as the native ones.

Visual Images

Although the early Bolshevik leaders disdained folk forms, they understood the effectiveness of visual images in connecting with the masses, especially the peasants. Nadezhda Krupskaia, Lenin's wife, famously observed, "For the present and the near future, a peasant can learn to improve his production only if he is taught by visual example."[87] Chinese Communist artists, likewise, had an early appreciation of the power of pictorial representations in disseminating political messages. As early as 1927, Mao, in his influential "Report on an Investigation of the Peasant Movement in Hunan" called on cultural agitators to use "simple slogans, cartoons and speeches" to produce "a widespread and speedy effect among the peasants

[so] that every one of them seems to have been through a political school."[88] These tools were put into systematic use during the Yan'an era. Artists such as the noted cartoonist Hua Junwu (1915–2010) and the woodcut artist Gu Yuan (1919–1996) created memorable images: Hua ridiculed Chiang Kai-shek as a bloodthirsty killer and Gu portrayed a blissful rural society under the wise rule of the CCP.[89]

Cultural centers built on this Yan'an tradition by continuing to exploit visual images. Amateur artists used a variety of visual tools to communicate with workers and peasants. Of these, cartoons were regarded as one of "the most popular and mass-oriented tools of propaganda, full of combative spirit."[90] The cartoons can be roughly divided into two groups. The first were down-to-earth images aimed at workers and peasants on the subject of such things as agricultural technology, food production, hygiene, and how to prevent plant diseases and eradicate pests.[91] Factory workers at the Shijingshan Power Plant, in summer 1951, were encouraged to create their own cartoons. They drew caricatures that emphasized plant safety and the importance of reducing the consumption of coal. One cartoon depicted a robust man boarding an airplane, which signified workers' resolve to reach a higher production target. Another portrayed a handicapped fellow riding a slow train, which was meant to ridicule indolent workers who failed to fulfill their quotas.[92]

The second group of cartoons was full of "combative spirit," that is, political cartoons touching on current affairs and Party policies and aimed at transforming popular attitudes. These cartoons were a prominent visual presence in all of the mass movements in the first decade of the PRC, such as the Resist America, Aid Korean Campaign.

In addition to cartoons, "propaganda pictorials" (xuanchuanhua), sometimes known as "wall pictures" (bihua), were also popular. These were simple political drawings pasted on factory and street walls. In 1958, the Beijing Municipal Cultural Bureau estimated the city's production of wall pictures alone at 516,000.[93] In reality, the line between propaganda pictorials and cartoons was not clear, and propagandists often used the two terms interchangeably. If one thing separated them, it was that the wall pictures provided what the sociologist Victoria Bonnell has called "the visual syntax" of drawing, which moored the images to a specific social and political context.[94] In 1954, a propaganda pictorial printed by the People's Printing House depicted a dialogue between an oilcan and a worker in a factory. The oilcan is saying, "This machine needs to take a break to add oil," reminding workers that time must be taken for maintenance and that failure to do so will disrupt the entire production process.[95]

Serial picture stories were a third type of visual image. Traditionally, serial picture stories were a favorite with both urbanites and villagers, especially youngsters. But, like *yangge*, they underwent thorough transformation to get rid of what officials described as "feudalistic," "capitalistic," and "supernatural" contents. Serial stories such as "The Workers Have Power" and "America Is a Paper Tiger" topped the new list of favorites.[96] The Nanyuan Cultural Center set up seven temporary libraries, providing serial picture books for local lending.[97] In 1959, during the Great Leap Forward, the promotion of serial picture stories became even more intense. Cultural center staff were urged to take pictorial booklets directly to the fields and "deliver them into the hands of People's Commune members."[98]

BROADCASTING

From the early 1920s onward, Russian propagandists and journalists used radio as a convenient way to reach out to workplaces and communal flats, teaching people, in the words of the historian Stephen Lovell, "exactly how to 'speak Bolshevik.'"[99] The CCP followed suit. When People's Liberation Army troops seized Beiping in late January 1949, they closed the KMT-controlled radio stations and promptly renamed the Beiping Broadcasting Station, one of the most important radio stations in the city, the New China Broadcasting Station. It was renamed the Beiping People's Radio Station two months later. The new station wasted no time in airing programs attacking Chiang Kai-shek and US imperialists.[100] By the end of the 1950s, the Beijing People's Radio Station had four channels, which were devoted to politics, art and literature, education, and a "comprehensive station." The political channel was aimed at the countryside.[101] Communist radio broadcasting made a big leap in early 1956 when the first wired rural broadcasting station—Red Star Collective Farm Broadcasting Station—was established in Nanyuan. By the end of the year, more than thirty small stations had sprung up in Beijing's outlying districts, and 6,447 loudspeakers were installed, blasting out information continually in the open fields.[102] A year later, the number of stations had risen to forty-seven, and loudspeakers exceeded fifteen thousand.[103] By 1959, the tenth anniversary of the founding of the PRC, the number of stations had risen to 219.[104] The Beijing Municipal Propaganda Department proudly proclaimed that the unprecedented development of this "communication network" (*tongxunwang*) had "greatly benefited farm production," among other things.[105]

The cultural centers had neither the personnel nor the funding to run their own stations but put radio communication technology to good use. In the 1950s, each center was generally equipped with a radio, and larger ones in the inner city had two.[106] By working with local broadcasting stations, the radios were used to relay to visitors at the centers the news produced by the Central Broadcasting

Station (which was targeted at a nationwide audience) and the Beijing People's Radio Station (which aimed at the local population). During the Great Leap Forward, information on drought-relief measures, irrigation, and crop experiments were served up with a heavy dose of the superiority of the People's Communes.[107] These broadcasts were primarily political in that they closely followed Mao's plan for transforming China rapidly from a backward agrarian state to a modern society through collectivization and industrialization. In the words of the municipal officials, the main purpose of the radio stations was to disseminate propaganda "centering on the principal tasks of the CCP."[108]

Loudspeakers were used in the countryside. This was called "homegrown broadcasting" (tuguangbo), which required close cooperation between rural cultural centers and local wired broadcasting stations. The Gaobeidian Cultural Center, for example, set up public loudspeakers on rooftops to broadcast radio programs to the peasants. Radio programs were quite diverse. In addition to information on farming techniques and crop selection, entertainment programs were aired, offering peasants temporary respite from their endless chores. During the Great Leap Forward in particular, the air was filled with officials proudly exclaiming about high production. For instance, in this period, the staff at the Haidian Cultural Center used "four radio broadcasting stations and fifty-five loudspeakers" to transmit "round the clock . . . the [marvelous] deeds of model workers."[109] These enthusiastic pronouncements, however, are hard to verify because few independent sources are available.

Telephones were another important tool. Liu Ren, the powerful second secretary of the Beijing Municipal Party, was an avid promoter of this technology.[110] Lack of resources at first hampered the extensive installation of telephone lines. Changping County, due to its relatively backward conditions, was the last to be finally linked by telephones in December 1956. "Normally it took two days to travel from here to there; now we can solve the problem in a few minutes," officials exclaimed.[111]

In addition to radios and telephones, other methods of communicating state policies to large numbers of people were also in practice, including slide shows, which were popular and easy to put on, and films, which required more sophisticated equipment and technical knowledge to show.[112]

Flexibility

In 1953, senior officials, recognizing the problem of limited resources and lack of trained personnel, called for merging and restructuring the centers to create more uniform stations. As a case in point, the Guanxiang Cultural Center and the

Gaobeidian Cultural Center were combined into the Chaoyang Cultural Center. But disparities continued. Large venues such as the Dongdan Cultural Center could easily mount a big exhibit in 1954 to celebrate the "Great Achievements of Our Motherland," which drew more than twelve thousand spectators, but remote rural ones such as the Changping Cultural Center were concerned with mere survival. When the Changping center was established in 1949, it was difficult even to find it a home. Eventually, it was housed in the local drum tower in the center of town, a mere two hundred square meters. The tiny place had only two desks and two hundred books, donated by local enthusiasts, in its library. The Pinggu Cultural Center had its own problems. This backward rural county had been devastated by Japanese invaders during the War of Resistance against Japan, so it had to start from scratch. The staff used a local Christian church and barely managed to provide minimum services, offering only a combined reading room and exhibition corner.[113]

Flexible strategies included targeting diverse audiences in different ways. Rural cultural centers served primarily peasants who were largely illiterate; hence, their programs had to take this into consideration. Methods of delivery had to be simple, accessible, and easily comprehensible. Folk art was a convenient choice. The staff of such rural centers also put a strong emphasis on developing mobile libraries. This was the case at the Gaobeidian Cultural Center, which served an area with a population that was 80 percent peasant.[114]

In a more industrialized part of the capital, the strategy was quite different. In the early 1950s, Chaoyang District had a population of more than seven hundred thousand. Because it also had more than two hundred major industrial plants (including Beijing Weaving and Dyeing Mill, mentioned earlier), it had a large concentration of industrial workers. Accordingly, newsboards were actively promoted at its center. In 1959, before National Day, two large honor rolls were erected to pay tribute to local and national model workers.[115]

Obstacles

Government publications, especially the official *Beijing's Cultural Centers,* were full of reports of the magnificent accomplishments of the cultural centers.[116] But can these reports be trusted? Internal sources reveal a different picture: from the outset, the cultural centers were beset with problems, large and small, technical and social. Some programs were harder to implement than others, and results were uneven. Radio is a case in point. Given the limited number of broadcasting stations and radios, covering a vast territory posed a formidable challenge to cultural center staff, especially in the rural areas where people were less educated and widely scattered.

Social problems proved equally difficult to overcome. The first trouble was the low status of the cultural centers. It may sound surprising, but, despite repeated government endorsements, many officials, including those high in the Ministry of Culture, did not take these grassroots organizations seriously. An internal report was critical of some district leaders for their condescending attitude toward the centers, complaining that "district leaders do not attach great importance to the centers; one piece of evidence is that they randomly transfer cadres [from one place to another]."[117] This was partly because the center staff were considered low-level employees.[118] The widespread impression among senior officials was that the centers were merely places for entertainment.[119] Among cultural agencies under the direction of the city's Cultural Bureau, the cultural centers were considered inferior to other departments such as the No. 1 Art Department, which supervised various groups, including the Beijing Opera.[120] Officials' low opinion of the cultural centers resulted in rapid turnover of staff, especially in the first few years, which hampered daily operations. In 1954, in the Oxen Street Cultural Center, which was in the southwestern part of the city where a large number of Muslims were concentrated, three cadres were replaced within six months.[121] Local cultural centers catered to the well-being of the people in whose name the Party ruled. This discrepancy between the public significance attached to the cultural centers and the negligence of the bureaucrats raises doubts about how sincere the Communist propagandists were concerning these street-level sites.

The entire project from the start encountered problems of limited funding and manpower shortages. In the mid-1950s, the operating budget for the smaller Mentougou Cultural Center was 90 yuan a month, or 1,080 yuan a year, whereas the annual budget for larger cultural centers such as the Guanxiang Cultural Center was 2,300 yuan.[122] Inadequate funding certainly limited the cultural centers' activities, which makes the high usage figures in official reports suspect.

Previous studies have pointed out that in the 1949 Communist takeover of major cities (such as Hangzhou) the shortage of reliable cadres who could maintain law and order was acute.[123] The cultural centers faced a similar manpower problem. Archival sources show that even a well-run cultural center usually had no more than four or five staff members to oversee the entire operation.[124] Normally, the staff consisted of one director and several cadres who ran education classes, managed a small library, and scheduled outreach functions. The dearth of staff was so serious that in 1952 four cultural centers in Beijing operated without a director. For those sites lucky enough to get one, the director often had a myriad of chores and, apparently, received minimal help from the municipal government. For instance, the head of the Xidan Cultural Center in western

Beijing had eighteen distinct responsibilities to fulfill in 1952.[125] The shortage of staff naturally impeded normal operations. A case in point was the reading room of the Nanyuan Cultural Center, which was closed for a month in 1952 because staff were not available to run it.[126]

One attempted remedy for the personnel shortage was to recruit what the municipal officials called "activists" (*jijifenzi*) or "core members" (*guganfenzi*)— that is, non-CCP individuals who had strong local ties and who were sympathetic to the Communist cause—and demanded that this recruitment should be done on a regular basis.[127] In a 1954 circular issued by the Beijing Municipal Party, city officials instructed the cultural centers to "gather together activists and train them" so that they could "play a leadership role in various activities" within a short period.[128] Such a practice bore a close resemblance to that of the Bolsheviks when they recruited local agitators to conduct propaganda work.[129] But the officials soon discovered that local recruits were not always reliable politically because their histories and dubious class backgrounds (such as having been landlords) could be concealed. Hence, the safest route continued to be setting up short training courses to teach their own cadres.[130]

The quality of the staff was another concern. Most staff members had, at most, a middle school education; very few had a college degree.[131] Some centers had worse personnel problems. Although the Changpingdian Cultural Center had a director who was a Communist Youth League member deemed politically reliable, most of the staff in the 1950s were men of dubious background, described in one internal report as "complicated, with despicable behavior." Some were said to have joined the centers with ulterior motives, such as having a chance to visit movie theaters, tour parks, and develop "improper relationships with women members."[132]

Many staff members were unenthusiastic about their work, especially those who were sent out to the villages. Sources indicate this was a perennial problem; many artists and writers who worked for the cultural centers refused to go out into the countryside. Quite a large number thought there was "no future for agricultural labor."[133] Those who did go to the villages were often criticized for having condescending attitudes toward the peasants.[134] Many, especially students, insisted on "wearing a mask when collecting night soil, considering it filthy." A large number of young cadres eventually confessed that they went to the villages "under pressure" and wished to be transferred out as soon as possible.[135] Officials sarcastically noted that these cultural workers showed no gratitude to those who labored in the fields. They "could not even distinguish the difference between the five major grains" and definitely had no idea "where their food came from."[136]

Another challenge was finding suitable materials for filling center libraries and reading rooms. The earlier promising report that "all of a sudden, urchins on the streets disappeared" turned out not to be the complete picture. Those who came to the libraries to read did not always pick books on government pronouncements or agricultural technology, which many found boring or beyond their reading ability.[137] The majority of readers read only newspapers or comic books.[138] Cultural center staff found it difficult to strike a proper balance between political coaching and pleasure reading.

The fast tempo of the Great Leap Forward produced some adverse results, and many projects were later found to be completely unrealistic. In one instance, the Supply and Marketing Cooperative asked rural cultural stations to distribute 4.08 million copies of books and magazines to people in various districts near Beijing within a short time, amounting to seven or eight books per person. This proved to be an impossible task and was later criticized as "unduly hasty."[139] The problem reflected a serious flaw prevalent during the Great Leap Forward, when, under pressure from high Party officials, local subordinates often grossly inflated their results. The cultural centers were no exception. An internal report complained,

> The leaders paid little attention to the views of the people; they made plans [arbitrarily] without taking into consideration local specificities and original plans. They knew only how to use administrative means [to solve problems] and were in pursuit of high [production] figures. [As a result], they built a structure without a foundation [kongjiazi].[140]

The principle behind the introduction of the cultural centers was the Maoist mass line. The centers were designed to be interactive, bridging the gap between the government and the people. Policymakers did not intend for citizens to be merely passive recipients of state policies. Willing participation and enthusiastic support from the grassroots, however, was not always easy to accomplish. Many peasants perceived the centers' activities as meddling, destroying their way of life, and, most important, interrupting their work in the fields. One complained, "[The staff] made no distinction between the busy farming season and the slack period," which hampered farm production.[141] The situation was particularly bad during the Great Leap Forward, when long and tedious meetings were frequently called to settle disputes and followed with the writing of long and dreary reports.[142] Many complained that the lengthy meetings were "truly unbearable"; some peasant women opted for the strategy of resistance by "locking the doors and leaving home" or "turning out the lights [and pretending that they were] going to bed early."[143] It is unclear whether these personal strategies worked, given that group pressure must have been immense. Without a doubt, the centers encountered many reluctant audiences.

How to bring socialist messages to a largely illiterate population was a top concern for both Soviet and Chinese Communist leaders in the early days of their respective regimes. Governing in the name of the people, leaders in both countries realized that power consolidation and nation building would require massive popular support for their policies. To that end, both Communist Parties created a variety of propaganda tools to win over the hearts and minds of the public. The Soviets built workers' clubs and red corners. Chinese Communists established grassroots cultural centers.

Chinese cultural centers underwent changes from when they were first established in 1949. At first they were largely used to combat illiteracy. In 1953, however, they metamorphosed into a political machine to support the Party's mass movements and programs. Increasingly, the cultural centers became, in the words of officials, "a docile propaganda tool" (*xunfu de xuanchuan gongju*).[144] Cultural center activities came to an abrupt halt during the tumultuous Cultural Revolution, but exactly why or how this happened remains unclear for now because few reliable documents are available.

I am not aware of any in-depth studies on cultural centers in locations other than Beijing. It is unclear how much these other cultural centers differed from those in Beijing, but future research will surely reveal that variations did exist between locations. The capital nevertheless served as a model for other major cities such as Shanghai.[145]

Did the cultural centers reach the populace, especially the peasants, and serve as a useful bridge between the CCP and the common people? The question has no simple answers. As might be expected, the official media of the time was full of glowing reports about the remarkable achievements of the centers.[146] At least one *People's Daily* reader from Hebei Province sent a letter to the editor in 1950, praising a local cultural center:

> Coming from an impoverished family, [as a teenager] I had no choice but to work in a shop as an apprentice. I was so depressed then that I thought I had no future at all. But I found an excellent place to learn after the People's Government established this Cultural Center for the People. The cadres there assisted me patiently to study. So whenever I had time I went there; not only my educational level was raised but so was my political consciousness. It solidified my outlook on life and revolution. I am now determined to devote my life wholeheartedly to the construction of a new democratic China and to the liberation of the entire human race.[147]

As we see in chapter 2, readers' letters to the editor, certainly at the *Beijing Daily*, were carefully selected for use as propaganda tools, so their content must be understood in that context. It is also difficult to separate the impact of the cultural centers from other more visible local propaganda tools such as the *Beijing Daily*. Historians must deal with a scarcity of independent sources, of sources other than government reports and official documents. Although their impact in Beijing is difficult to measure, we can assume that, despite the many problems, such as inadequate funding and manpower shortages, cultural centers played a considerable role in advancing the Communists' policies among the populace in the capital and its outlying areas. They found a direct and down-to-earth way to approach a variety of people, providing much-appreciated cultural entertainment to a wide audience. Community libraries and reading rooms quite likely helped raise the literacy level; imparting simple knowledge of hygiene presumably did raise the level of public health.[148] Talks on farm machinery and new planting techniques may have improved agricultural production. The flexibility of the centers' strategies meant they could adjust approaches to meet local needs. As time went on, the centers helped promote the CCP's political agenda in the party's mass mobilization movements. This effectiveness stemmed not just from the activities that the centers initiated but also from being part of large political campaigns (such as the Land Reform Movement in the early 1950s). In a closed society, the Party was able to control the information the people received. When a piece of government news was repeatedly broadcast on the radio, it became accepted as absolute truth. As the sociologist Jacques Ellul argues, the effectiveness of propaganda, lies in its "continuous repetition."[149]

Cultural centers, which were closed during the Cultural Revolution, reappeared in the early 1980s under the leadership of Deng Xiaoping. Today they are a fixture in local communities across China.[150] But problems persist, including staff shortages, young people viewing work there as undesirable because of the modest pay and low social standing.[151] One Wenzhou Cultural Center staff member in Zhejiang Province noted in a 2016 report that the average age of staff members in the center was over fifty. "Those under thirty-five are extremely rare," he wrote, causing "serious disruption in terms of the talent supply."[152]

Despite these ongoing problems, the centers remain one of the most important basic communication units between the party-state and the public. So long as the central government continues to promote the notion of a harmonious society that cares about the well-being of people's lives, these centers will be ideal locations for fostering a spirit of social unity. They function in today's era of market reform and opening up as popular entertainment centers with stages for live performances and movie theaters. They also offer calligraphy lessons and dance classes. All this implies that the government wants its citizens to enjoy a rich cultural life.

When I visited Beijing's First Eastern District Cultural Center (Dongchengqu diyi wenhuaguan), a sister institution of the Western District Cultural Center, on a weekend in January 2014, I noticed the seemingly apolitical nature of its myriad cultural programs. In the spacious theater, I enjoyed an act of *The Butterfly Dream,* a popular opera based on the traditional story of star-crossed lovers Liang Shanbo and Zhu Yingtai (figure 4). But the audiences could not have missed the words continuously flashed across the screen above the stage, "Chinese Dream. My Dream. Happy Dream" (figure 5), which referenced not only the opera but, more important, President Xi Jinping's now famous call to revive the nation by fulfilling its century-old dream of becoming a strong and independent country. As government-funded institutions, cultural centers can never enjoy total artistic autonomy. Given that the CCP continues to control the cultural and intellectual media, the words above the stage served to remind audiences that the Party has never left the hall. It stands nearby and always wants to make its presence known.

Figure 4. The Chinese opera *The Butterfly Dream.* Source: Photo by author, January 11, 2014.

Figure 5. The words flashed above the stage read, "Chinese Dream. My Dream. Happy Dream." Source: Photo by author, January 11, 2014.

In January 2016, a new opera titled *One Belt, One Road* was staged at the First Eastern District Cultural Center. This musical production, as stated in the center's official announcement, was designed to "reflect the nation's strategic initiative."[153] There is no question that the opera was organized to support Xi Jinping's newest initiative of the same name—the Silk Road Economic Belt and the Twenty-first Century Maritime Silk Road, commonly known as the New Silk Road. Announced in late 2013, this New Silk Road initiative is an ambitious intercontinental trade and infrastructure project that aims at fostering closer economic ties between the PRC and many countries along the land and sea-based routes of Eurasia, including several resource-rich Central Asian countries. This initiative will no doubt uplift the national pride of the Chinese people, which in turn will further cement the one-party rule of the CCP.

In late December 2018, the staff of the Guangzhou Cultural Center gathered in Shaoguan, north of Guangzhou, to attend a conference. Their aim was to study "the spirit of a series of important speeches made by General Secretary Xi

Jinping" during the Chinese leader's visit to this southern province in October to reaffirm his commitment to Deng Xiaoping's market reform.[154] This conference was part of the staff's routine political study program. Such a meeting is a clear reminder that a primary responsibility of the staff of the cultural centers is to propagate the Party line.

CHAPTER 5

Turning Chinese Children Red

Redesigning Kindergarten Education

A children's song appeared in a kindergarten textbook put together by teachers and printed in Beijing in 1950, barely a year after the founding of the People's Republic of China (PRC) in October 1949.

The Five Star Red Flags are fluttering in the wind;
The thunderous sound of gong and drum fills the air;
"What day is today?" I ask;
"It's October 1, National Day!"[1]

On the surface, the song sounds innocuous and exuberant, but deep down it is highly political, representing a marked change in China's education system in general, kindergarten in particular. Once the Chinese Communist Party (CCP) took power, the role education should play in effectively transforming children into eager contributors to the development of the new socialist state became a major concern.

To that end, leaders moved swiftly to introduce a radically reformed education system based heavily on the Soviet model. For the Soviet revolutionaries, children were the hope of the future.[2] Chinese Communists held the same belief, perhaps with even greater urgency. They were inspired by one of the missions of the May Fourth intellectuals in the early twentieth century, which was to raise children in a new radically different way from the conventional method. When Lu Xun (1881–1936) wrote his 1918 influential short story "Diary of a Madman," he ended it with an appeal to "save the children." This had a strong impact on reform-minded Chinese intellectuals, who believed that a new China could only be built when children were brought up free of the pernicious influence of antiquated traditions, especially dogmatic Confucian moral teachings.[3]

Since the 1980s, our understanding of education in socialist China has greatly advanced, inspired by the pioneering works of Gu Mingyuan, Suzanne Pepper, and Ruth Hayhoe.[4] In the past, scholarly attention had focused on universities and middle schools, but today interest in kindergarten education is growing.[5] Inspiring as these contemporary scholars are, systematic efforts to place children's education within a close analysis of the wider political sweep of the period are still inadequate. In this chapter, I examine the intertwined relationship between kindergartens (*youzhiyuan* or *youeryuan*)—where children from three to seven make their transition from home to school—and politics in the newly established PRC.[6] Contrary to the conventional view that the kindergartens in socialist China were a faithful imitation of the Russian model, however, Chinese nationalism, not Soviet ideology, dominated the new curriculum.[7] Children were taught that the CCP saved China by bringing independence and peace to a land long ravaged by war, social turmoil, and foreign invasions. Focusing on Beijing, I present a close analysis of the kindergarten curriculum and examine the centrality of political purpose behind the reshaping of children's education in the 1950s. I also evaluate the influence of Soviet educational advisers, which is a subject often not adequately addressed.[8]

Unlike the Soviet Union's, the PRC's approach to this period in a child's life was motivated by a strong sociopolitical agenda from the beginning of the new regime. In Russia, after the Bolshevik Revolution of 1917, the proper education of proletarian children sparked heated debates among top policymakers.[9] In her book about Soviet kindergartens, Lisa Kirschenbaum shows that during the first fifteen years of Soviet rule, officials viewed kindergartens as a way of freeing children from "authoritarian constraints of school and family."[10] Such a view paralleled Bolshevik leaders' early vision of constructing child-centered education that focused on personal development and creating legislation to protect children from having their labor exploited. As ideological winds shifted, however, indoctrination in how to behave like proper Communists took priority over personal development, as evident in the Commissariat of Enlightenment's increasingly centralized curricula and control of teaching methods in the mid-1920s.[11] By the time Stalin introduced the First Five-Year Plan (1928–1932), kindergartens had become a form of childcare that liberated mothers to work as part of an ambitious drive to achieve high industrial production.[12]

The initial PRC childhood education policy departed from this Soviet trajectory. Mao and his associates were pragmatists who at the outset saw education as a top ideological priority and quickly seized control of the content of kindergarten education. Children should be taught from the beginning to advance socialist goals. This generation would grow up to become socialist "new men," the first generation to be free from feudal ills and bourgeois materialism and, even more important, become patriots who would build a strong new China.[13] A model child would have to be both obedient and devoted to the state.

Modern political scientists and educational psychologists have found that children tend to learn uncritically and that this learning takes place at a time when a child's basic personality is being molded.[14] Mao and senior leaders saw it this way, viewing children as "blank slates" on which to inscribe socialist ideals. The state should thus take the commanding role in the shaping of children's minds in multiple ways.

The Pre-1949 Educational Setting

The newly established PRC inherited three educational models from its immediate past: the general school system of the Republican era, the Maoist principles and practices formulated during the Yan'an era in the 1930s and 1940s, and the Russian influence in Communist-controlled Northeast China in the late 1940s. Each model had its distinct characteristics, but they were soon fused by the government into a more or less coherent whole under the close supervision of the CCP.

Education in Republican China had been an amalgamation of traditional training—which emphasized morality, deference to authority, hard work—and Deweyan-inspired progressive education.[15] Traditional training, in association with Sun Yat-sen's (1866–1925) Three People's Principles, was actively promoted by Kuomintang (KMT) officials, especially the minister of education, Chen Lifu (1900–2001), during the War of Resistance against Japan.[16]

The CCP's early education policy was developed in the Jiangxi Soviet period (1931–1934), and it became more systematic in the ensuing Yan'an era. This educational policy, which espoused the principle of the mass line and practicality, stressed production and close attention to people's immediate needs.[17] It tied schooling to the harsh realities of rural China in northern Shaanxi Province, where Yan'an was located, and underscored the importance of uniting theoretical learning with practical applications.

Russian Soviet-style education was the most recently introduced. Its primary aim was to foster a generation of "new socialist men" committed to the revolution.[18] In 1948, Soviet educational systems were slowly introduced into Northeast China, which was under Chinese Communist control. For instance, in Lüshun (Port Arthur), which had a sizable Russian population, Soviet pedagogical methods were employed at places such as Lüshun Middle School.[19] This Soviet trend soon took center stage after the establishment of the PRC in 1949 and merged with the Maoist model to form the basis of post-1949 education.

Mao and senior Party leaders considered China's pre-1949 educational system deeply flawed. In their eyes, it was elitist and urban oriented, influenced by Confucian philosophy and bourgeois Western models that instilled a snobbish disdain for manual labor. After 1949, the Yan'an idea of a mass line in education, coupled with the Soviet model, was introduced to remedy prerevolutionary educational wrongs.

As discussed, after the Red Army seized Beiping, the Communists proceeded to take control of all major cultural institutions, including universities and schools throughout the capital. The process was largely completed by May 1949.[20] The new education system was officially described in the Common Program, proclaimed officially in September 1949 by the Chinese People's Political Consultative Conference:

> The culture and education of the People's Republic of China shall be New Democratic—national, scientific, and popular. The main tasks of the People's Government in cultural and educational work shall be the raising of the cultural level of the people, the training of personnel for national construction work, the eradicating of feudal, comprador and fascist ideology and the developing of the ideology of service to the people.[21]

Following this command, the newly formed Kindergarten Division of the Beijing Municipal Education Bureau stated that from now on education at all levels would be available to "the masses," especially "the workers and peasants."[22] These municipal pronouncements reiterated Mao Zedong's insistence in his famous 1940 essay "On New Democracy" that culture under the new socialist regime should primarily be "national, scientific, and popular."[23] Of these three, Chinese kindergarten teachers prioritized "national" in their curriculum because it served two important immediate objectives: it was the most natural and practical way to teach children by using materials directly related to their own country, and, even more important, it was convenient for the CCP in advancing its political goals.

Facing the gargantuan tasks of state building, national security, economic recovery, and military tensions in Korea, the government admitted that it had "severely limited" resources to devote to education.[24] For this reason, it first put its greatest emphasis on higher education because the new nation required a large number of experts in the critical fields of industry, economy, and the military for the pressing needs of nation building. The government thus called the university system its "focal point" (zhongdian) in its overall educational strategy. But it also realized that in the long run, education must start from "the foundation" (jichu), which meant kindergartens and primary schools.[25]

A New Beginning

The earliest official nationwide statistics on the number of kindergartners in the PRC was one hundred forty thousand in 1950, of whom eighty-eight thousand were enrolled in government-sponsored schools and fifty-two thousand in private institutions.[26] The Beijing Municipal Government reported that the number of kindergartners in the capital in 1949 was 2,255 and by 1951 was 3,144.[27] The Committee on Culture and Education, which was set up in 1951 by the municipal government under the supervision of the Government Administration Council, gave a smaller total figure in another report in 1952 and broke the numbers down. Beijing had twenty kindergartens, including three that were state run, five that were municipal, and twelve that were private, taught by 103 teachers, with a total enrollment of 2,645 children in 1952.[28] The reliability of these figures is hard to ascertain, but both seem to be too small considering that Beijing's urban population in the early years of the PRC was 1.4 million. It is very likely that many young children did not go to regular schools, given that they were traditionally kept at home and taught by private tutors. In any case, the number in schools increased dramatically shortly thereafter.

The first important national directive on kindergartens, "Temporary Rules for Kindergartens," was issued by the Ministry of Education in 1951. It laid down a general framework for educating children "from three to seven years" of age. Kindergartens would be staffed by "kindergarten teachers" (*jiaoyangyuan*), whose responsibilities were to

> enhance the health of the children, develop their intelligence, nourish their moral responsibility, and cultivate their initial aesthetic talents so that they can be developed in full. This lays the foundation for their primary school education, and, simultaneously, eases a mother's burden of childcare, allowing her to participate freely in the new political, economic, cultural, and social life.[29]

In the beginning, the government's policy toward kindergarten was flexible and not overwhelmingly imposing, for several reasons. Mao's New Democracy theory called for a tolerant approach toward education. Weng Dujian (1906–1986), the head of the Beijing Municipal Education Bureau, issued a directive in 1954 declaring that "at a time of transition," private kindergartens could still be run by local communities.[30] For example, "street kindergartens" (*jiedao youeryuan*), which were nominally placed under the direction of the government, were actually run by local neighborhood committees and regional women's associations.[31] The Communists' lack of experience in this area also made them cautious about making decisions too hastily. This decentralized policy afforded a degree of flexibility in the way private kindergartens were run. But not for long.

Although I have not yet found reliable information concerning the institutional background and financial support of Beijing's kindergartens in the early days of the PRC, I have assembled information from archival sources about the agencies that were funding private primary schools. Many of these schools in Beijing were church affiliated and therefore viewed with suspicion by the new Communist rulers. A municipal government document shows that of the 171 registered private primary schools in the capital in 1950, the majority were private secular schools, but more than fifty others were linked to Catholic, Protestant, Muslim, or Buddhist organizations; and among these, Catholic and Muslim schools were the most numerous, fifteen schools each.[32] This was alarming because, as one official warned, they could be "used by the reactionaries for spying activities and to disseminate antigovernment publications and propaganda materials."[33] Other officials viewed the flexible education policy as a sign that the Party lacked toughness, which needed correcting.

In actuality, the municipal government began to tighten its control over education in 1952. The first action they took was to begin bringing religious schools, as well as other private schools, under official supervision, a process known as "taking over control [of the school]" (*jieban*), which the Beijing Municipal Government commenced in the fall of 1952.[34] Private textbook companies were forced to shut down. In 1953, the municipal government closed twenty-one private companies, half of the total number then in operation. A year later, the government went a step further to declare that school textbooks could only be published by approved publishers.[35] The content of textbooks needed to be carefully "guided from above."[36]

On another front, Chinese Communist officials launched a scathing verbal attack on the KMT, which had retreated to Taiwan. Education under Chiang Kai-shek's government, according to Qian Junrui, the PRC's vice minister of education, was nothing more than "reactionary education" that served the interests of "imperialism, feudalism, and bureaucratism" and had never had the well-being of the "workers and peasants" in mind.[37] As we have seen, Qian was a staunch believer in Chinese Communist values, and earlier had been active in overseeing book censorship in his role as director of the Culture Takeover Committee. The American educational system, especially the progressive Deweyan method that was a component of the Kuomintang's education programs, was also denounced by the Communists as "reactionary" and "shallow." Dewey, according to the education critic Cao Fu (1911–1968), taught the principles of individualism and promoted an exploitative capitalist economy.[38] Dewey's students in China, notably the renowned early childhood educator Chen Heqin (1892–1982), were criticized for implementing Dewey's erroneous "comprador bourgeoisie" ideas in Chinese kindergartens.[39] Chen was forced to make a public self-criticism.[40]

As the influence of the American education model declined during the first decade of the PRC, the Soviet model grew in importance under Mao's pro-Soviet policy.[41] Soviet influence was manifested in at least three areas. First, an abundance of Soviet books on education were translated into Chinese. Second, Chinese teachers, who were searching for methods to replace the old-style of teaching and the American model, eagerly studied Soviet pedagogical theories and systems.[42] Finally, exchanges and dialogues between Chinese and Russian educators intensified after 1949 (later extended to include Eastern Bloc countries). In the 1950s, more than eighteen thousand Soviet advisers were sent to China, including military experts, engineers, city planners, and educators to help the Chinese modernize along the lines of the Soviet model.[43]

Russian publications, including I. A. Kairov's *Pedagogika* (Educational pedagogy), which was translated into Chinese in 1948, became must reads for Chinese teachers.[44] In this influential book, Kairov, president of the USSR Academy of Pedagogical Sciences, underscored the importance of political education as the main goal for schools. The purpose of the school under socialism, according to Kairov, was "to turn it into a weapon for Communism to transform society." Pupils must be taught the communist view of society and the importance of labor. It was only under the "socialist system," Kairov asserted, "that man's full potential can be fully developed."[45] Kairov's ideas were also directly transmitted by Soviet experts sent to China to help establish kindergarten programs. Of these, perhaps the most influential was Galina,[46] a kindergarten education expert hired by the Ministry of Education and one of eighteen Soviet educators sent to the Beijing Normal University, a premier institution for training future teachers.[47] She was a popular teacher because of her enthusiastic dedication to working, holding training sessions, and giving direct instructions on how kindergarten classes should be conducted. Galina's views soon became authoritative in the training of kindergarten teachers in China.[48] But Chinese kindergarten teachers were never completely comfortable with the Soviet educational programs. Instead, they introduced a strong measure of nationalism into the curriculum, reiterating Mao's call that Chinese culture should become "national, scientific, and popular."

Methods

In "Temporary Rules for Kindergartens," published in 1951, the Ministry of Education furnished two specific guidelines for teachers: they must compile their own instruction materials because no textbooks were available from the authorities; and "no textbooks should be used" by students because these were deemed unnecessary and impractical at this early stage of children's education.[49] Teachers soon devised a variety of original teaching aids and programs. Among them, games, singing, storytelling, and site visits were the most salient.[50] These undoubtedly reflected the strong Soviet influence, given that they bore a close resemblance to those suggested by Galina.[51] Galina's "Working Guidelines for Kindergarten Teachers" were systematically discussed in her influential book *Sulian youer jiaoyu jiangzuo* (Lectures on kindergarten education in the Soviet Union), which was translated into Chinese in 1953 and became an essential guide for kindergarten teachers.[52]

Among the teaching tools in the 1950s, games were considered one of the most fundamental. This view is similar to that of modern Western kindergarten teachers, who believe that children, while playing games either in unison (such as clapping hands together or riding little trains) or in small groups (such as building models with blocks), are interacting in a lively and fruitful fashion.[53] Games are also widely recognized as a way to teach kindergartners how to balance study and relaxation at a very young age. Games thus provide children with a sense of togetherness and prepare them socially to become supportive citizens in the future. In the 1950s, passing a ball around in a circle was a favorite game in Chinese kindergartens.[54]

Engaging in simple games in kindergartens was hardly exclusive to post-1949 China. They were widely played in schools in the Republican era.[55] After 1949, however, a strong dose of politics was decidedly introduced. Here, Soviet influence was again strong. Soviet advisers, including Galina, stressed that games were not only essential for training kindergartners to interact with one another but also needed to reflect "the salient aspects of contemporary society."[56] Galina pointed out that kindergartners were especially fond of games related to transportation and travel, given that they happily imagined themselves as the drivers of a train or car, or as airplane pilots going on a tour. However, these games, Galina insisted, should never be conducted only for the sake of fun. They needed instead to focus on "historicity, nationality, and [the concept of] class." Hence Russian children were taught to play games associated with "factories" and "collective farms" and even wars (as in the Great Patriotic War against the Axis powers), instilling in them ideas of class and nationalism.[57] This notion was picked up by her Chinese followers. In addition to popular, conventional games such as Cats Catch Mice, new games like My Beloved People's Liberation Army (PLA) Soldiers were introduced. In My Beloved PLA Soldiers, kindergartners were taught to play the role of soldiers. They took terms throwing balls (representing artillery shells) at toy blocks placed in a circle (representing Taiwan). "Those who knock down the blocks win collective applause," a teacher reported.[58]

A second popular method used in the classroom was singing, which was inseparable from games, and they were often done together to achieve the best results.[59] Educators have long looked at the benefit of using singing for teaching kindergartners, believing that a child's ability to sing and dance is "an indication of intelligence and potential in other cognitive domains."[60] In the 1950s, Chinese kindergartens were filled with songs. Here, the Soviet influence was again apparent.[61] Like many Soviet songs, which were heavily political, the newly composed Chinese children songs were used to express group solidarity as well as to communicate political values, as in "The Friendship between China and the Soviet Union" and "July 1," the latter referring to the founding date of the Chinese Communist Party in 1921. In "July 1," children were taught to sing "It is because of the wise leadership of the CCP that the entire population has now been liberated."[62]

In addition to games and singing, Galina stressed the value of storytelling.[63] This method was also eagerly adopted in Chinese kindergartens. In China, storytelling appeared in a variety of forms, including traditional folktales, fables, and fairy tales.[64] Chinese teachers realized that narrative stories usually are told chronologically, thus furnishing a natural sequence and coherent pattern that kindergartners could follow. A Beijing teachers' handbook advised that stories must include "rich contents, [be] full of common sense, and [be told] in a lively style."[65] But, it quickly added, they must be delivered in close association with "current Chinese affairs," as in stories about "the triumph of the People's Liberation Army and the Chinese People's Volunteer Army in the Korean War."[66] Here, the emphasis of the story was never on a past foreign conflict, such as the Great Patriotic War the Russians fought against the Axis powers, but on the ongoing war on the Korean Peninsula where Chinese soldiers were helping a socialist neighbor to repel American aggressors. Thus, invoking nationalism was not a celebration of China's past glory but rather of the CCP's contemporary moral strength and military might in standing up to a ruthless foreign invader. Other pedagogical methods included using picture books and films, all of which "made a deep impact on the children."[67]

In addition to classroom teaching, extracurricular activities were actively promoted by Chinese teachers following the example of their Soviet counterparts. Both Kairov and Galina underscored the value of site visits.[68] "Visits and travels can greatly broaden children's worldviews," opined Galina.[69] She added that field trips should not be taken purely for amusement but should have a clear political purpose. In the Soviet Union, students' visits to famous national sites, especially Red Square, where Lenin's tomb was located, were considered reward-ing learning experiences.[70] Such activities were especially meaningful when un-dertaken on national days. "To celebrate the great October Socialist Revolution," Galina counseled, "teachers should pay special attention to arouse the joyful an-ticipation of the kindergartners for this great day, especially seeing the portraits of Lenin and Stalin."[71] Thus children's outings were another opportunity for po-litical education.

Chinese teachers followed the Russian model but added an indigenous touch. In Beijing, a field trip to a park, a museum, or an exhibition hall celebrating labor heroes was happily enjoyed by kindergartners.[72] But perhaps no single event was more important and exhilarating than making a trip to Tiananmen Square, the sacred site where the new nation was founded in 1949. The vastness of the space (hence the greatness of the country), the red flags, and the giant portrait of Chairman Mao at the front of Tiananmen Gate made a spectacular sight. Teach-ers timed the trip painstakingly, often planning for it to coincide with the May Day or the National Day parades to experience the high drama of this memorial occasion.[73] This kind of site visit, one teacher asserted, "provided a good chance to conduct patriotic education."[74]

Curriculum

A close examination of the teacher-prepared kindergarten textbooks and the school reports submitted to the Beijing Municipal Education Bureau reveals the many "political lessons" (*zhengzhike*) that teachers were required to teach.[75] The principal topics were the importance of labor, with a special tribute to Chinese workers; stories of national heroes, especially soldiers; Tiananmen Square; Chairman Mao Zedong; and criticism of Chiang Kai-shek and Ameri-can imperialists.

THE NOBILITY OF LABOR

Laodong (labor) was one of the key terms repeatedly mentioned in the teacher-prepared textbooks in the 1950s. This was inspired by the Soviets. In *Pedagogika*, Kairov devoted an entire chapter to highlighting the importance of labor in edu-cating Soviet kindergartners.[76] This view was echoed by Galina, who believed that a top priority for kindergarten teachers was to teach children to respect pro-duction, hard work, and workers—the heart of Marxist philosophy.[77] Teachers in China thus taught kindergartners to "know their environment" (*renshi huan-jing*), a nebulous term referring to their daily routines, social setting, and learn-ing milieu, with a special emphasis on actual experience and work.[78]

To emphasize the importance of labor was to pay special tribute to the workers, the leading force in the socialist revolution, a point clearly stated in the Common Program adopted in 1949. A textbook suggested that the best way to teach it to kindergartners was to start out with the basics:

Children are taught to wash their faces and hands, and learn how to put on their own clothes. . . . In places where schools are bigger, teachers can teach them how to plant trees and raise small animals. Through this, the kids learn how to take an interest in labor activities.[79]

Such training in routines was considered just the beginning, not the essence of early childhood education. The real emphasis, the teachers added, was on teaching children to properly respect the value of "work" and "the working people," and learning "how to serve the workers."[80] To underscore the importance of real labor, children were brought to nearby dairy farms to observe firsthand how farmers worked in the fields and milked the cows. Harvesting peanuts became part of the curriculum for older school children.[81]

In the emphasis on "the working people," a subtle shift in the new curriculum is apparent. In the pre-1949 textbooks published in the Shaan-Gan-Ning Border Region and Jin-Cha-Ji Border Region, two rural bases controlled by the Chinese Communists, great weight was placed on the peasants; "workers" were barely mentioned.[82] This situation changed soon after the founding of the PRC, workers now occupying center stage in the curriculum. Affectionately called "uncle workers" (*gongren shushu*) by children, they were praised for producing everything that the country needed, including building the new capital and reconstructing Tiananmen Square as well as helping those in need.[83] "Without them, we would have nothing to eat and no clothes to put on," one textbook proclaimed.[84] Kindergartners were encouraged to embrace the spirit of the workers, who worked as a group and were said to be selfless and hard-working, just like bees. One song goes:

Little bees, little bees,
Buzzing all around;
You are truly little labor heroes,
Making sweet honey for us all.
We will be as united as you, little bees.[85]

Those working in heavy industry received the highest accolades, reflecting the nation's need for rapid industrialization. For instance, in a 1950 children's song, coal miners were lauded for their valuable contribution:

> Our great country,
> Rich in coal,
> Abundant and inexhaustible;
> Our miners are working day and night to extract it.[86]

Everyone in jobs formerly considered inferior (not just coal miners) was accorded respect in the symbolic gesture that the new regime considered all jobs equally valuable. For example, kindergartners were taught to sing a song in praise of night-soil collectors:

> How wonderful are the night-soil collectors;
> What a superb job you have done.[87]

The children were brought to Model Workers exhibits, held in such important places as the former Forbidden City, to learn from their heroes.[88] Xu Jianchun (b. 1935), a female peasant from Shandong Province and a mutual-aid team leader, was singled out as a model for kindergartners.[89] Model workers included peasants, from whom the Maoist revolution drew its most critical support before 1949. One must, a textbook emphasized, recognize the great role "the peasants and the villages" played.[90]

HEROIC SOLDIERS

In addition to model workers and the nobility of labor, heroic soldiers received ample attention in teacher-compiled kindergarten textbooks. Child psychologists have argued that young children are cognitively incapable of thinking in abstract terms and that identification with a distinguished group of people will help them to develop their identity.[91] In the 1950s, Chinese children's identification with heroic soldiers was clearly political: it was conforming to a group who had made great sacrifice for their country.

Similar to the Soviet educators who taught Russian children to pay respect to the valiant Red Army soldiers who "sacrificed their lives to save their motherland,"[92] Chinese teachers taught kindergartners about the courageous and selfless PLA soldiers, whom they should emulate. "Letters from Your Friendly PLA Soldiers" was a favorite topic in class.[93] The exercise went beyond showing respect and paying tribute to soldiers; it had a practical intention. For example, in the game My Beloved PLA Soldiers, mentioned earlier, children played soldiers who were attempting to liberate Taiwan from Kuomintang rule. The Chinese People's Volunteer Army that was sent to the front during the Korean War also received profuse praise, but the main target now was the American imperialists.

In a story read to the children titled "The Post Office," the surgeon father of the six-year-old boy Mingming is sent to assist in the war effort in Korea. One day the child receives a letter from his father at the front. He quickly hands it to his mother to read:

> "What exactly is in the letter, Mom? Please tell me now," Mingming asks impatiently.

> His mother reads the letter: "Your father says, 'Our Volunteer Army soldiers have crushed the American devils after they entered Korea. Many Americans surrendered without even a fight.'"

> "I am so happy. I want to look for my father, and join other uncles to fight against the devils," Mingming begs.

> "You are still a child. When you grow up, without a doubt, I will let you enlist," replies his mother.[94]

In a 1950 song about the Volunteer Army, a child aspires to the same goal:

> Riding a wooden horse,
> Putting on swords and wearing guns;
> I am a small soldier in the Volunteer Army.
> I am going to the battlefield.
> Why did you set off?
> Bang, bang, bang,
> I want to smash the American imperialists.[95]

TIANANMEN SQUARE

The government was open about wanting to implement "patriotic education" (*aiguozhuyi jiaoyu*) in the kindergarten. "Patriotic education" was a recurrent term used in official communications and in teachers' textbooks in the 1950s.[96] To that end, Tiananmen Square and Chairman Mao Zedong were two of the most familiar symbols used to engender children's pride in their nation, thus reinforcing the story of the great success of the new Communist regime. Tiananmen Square was a ubiquitous symbol of the new China. Children were taught to sing such songs as

> Oh, how great is Tiananmen!
> With its red walls and glazed tiles,
> And Chairman Mao's portrait, hanging high above;
> We all dearly love him![97]

Just as Moscow's Red Square was a pilgrimage site for Soviet students, Tiananmen Square was for their Chinese counterparts. The vast square at the center of the capital became a favorite destination for kindergartners, who arrived by rickshaws or streetcars.[98] One teacher's account of a trip conveyed joy and excitement:

> The trip was a golden opportunity for patriotic education. On May 5 we brought more than 240 children to visit Tiananmen Square. They were brought to the site by streetcars and saw the portrait of Chairman Mao and the majestic vast space. We told them that this grand site was the result of the hard work of our uncle workers. It is also a place where Chairman Mao inspects the parades. We also let them know that Moscow's Red Square is not as big as ours. This way we arouse their fervent love for this capital of the people and for their motherland. The children sang in jubilation and chanted slogans. More than four hundred little eyes sparkled with an innocent but sincere glow.[99]

The myriad symbolic sights on the square, including Tiananmen Gate, the *huabiao* (ornamental columns) in front of the gate, the stone lions, and the vast space were a most impressive sight for visitors.[100] This revered site, the teachers reminded their students, was the product of the "great strength of the Chinese laboring people."[101] The careful assertion that Tiananmen Square surpassed Red Square in size was no doubt intended to instill nationalistic pride in the children; this was done even at a time when the Chinese government was officially proclaiming that "the Soviet Union's today is China's tomorrow." A tribute to Tiananmen Square was more than a declaration of national pride; it was also an assertion that nationalism is even more important than socialism.

A field trip to Tiananmen Square was considered best done during national festivals, especially the October 1 anniversary of the founding of the People's Republic and on May Day, so as to generate maximum impact, the celebrations and thunderous cheers easily stirring patriotic fervor among participants.[102] "Through these special events," one school report noted, "teachers led the way by putting on new dresses" and teaching the children "how to decorate their classrooms" in a process known as "beautifying the environment." Such activities became an annual ritual for the children.[103]

To be sure, since the Enlightenment, rulers and politicians in the West have used national festivities as a way to propagandize the grand achievements of their regimes. The anthropologist Clifford Geertz calls this "the theatrical state," in which flags, songs, and majestic parades held in a nation's capital during major holidays combine to invoke images of optimism that are ideal for forging a shared national identity.[104] Likewise, spectacles and images were often more important than China's reality, being carefully choreographed to instill pride in China's greatness. This was certainly influenced by Soviet methods.

MAO ZEDONG

Soviet children were taught to love Lenin and Stalin. Lisa Kirschenbaum tells us that heroic stories of Lenin (kindergartners calling him a "good uncle") and revolutionary holidays, particularly May Day and the commemoration of the October Revolution, were central to Russian kindergarten education.[105] Likewise, Chinese kindergartners were educated to grow up as children of Mao, who was celebrated in the teacher-prepared textbooks as the emblematic figure of the new China and the incarnation of its ideals. The story of Mao's life was a favorite tale told by the teachers, with special emphasis on stories of his childhood.[106]

In the early 1950s, Mao was praised not only as the great leader but even as a savior. A children's song invokes stars:

There are two sparkling stars;
One shines in the West, the other in the East;
One is Stalin, the other is Mao Zedong;
They are the great saviors of the people;
Because of these two stars,
People are now standing up!
People are now standing up![107]

Of the two bright stars, Mao outshone his Soviet counterpart, which is clear in his being extolled by name in so many children's songs and stories. Although in the mid-1950s, several additional important Russian political events, such as the commemoration of the death of Stalin, were included in the Chinese kindergarten curriculum to promote communist internationalism, at heart it was their own country that Chinese children were taught to celebrate, not a distant foreign model.[108]

Teachers told the kindergartners that one goal in visiting Tiananmen Square was to possibly catch a glimpse of the great chairman who led the revolution. One teacher-prepared textbook imagined such an encounter as happening between a peace dove and the Five Star National Flag in the square on National Day:

"Where is our dear Chairman Mao?" asked one peace dove;
"Standing at Tiananmen Gate," answered the national flag;
"Let's salute him, quick!" urged the dove.[109]

Another textbook imagined conversations by kindergartners:

> Chen Hongye says, "Our teacher writes a letter to Chairman Mao, saying we should not put our fingers into our mouths. The fingernails are dirty, can spread infectious disease, [so we listen]."
>
> Zhao Changhai says, "Teacher, please bring us to Tiananmen Gate on National Day to see Chairman Mao. I can walk, no matter how far it is."
>
> Zhang Shuzhao says, "I want to be Chairman Mao's child, so that I can see him every day!"[110]

When arriving at Tiananmen Square, teachers were asked to tell the children that "Chairman Mao is waving at us," which was intended, as the handbook suggested, to "allow the children to think 'Chairman Mao must have seen me.'"[111] Mao thus served not only as a national leader and wise teacher, but also as a family elder who cared about his family members, China in essence being one large socialist family. "Listen to the words of Chairman Mao and become a good child of his" was told repeatedly to children so they would aspire to his goal of building a strong nation.[112]

The CCP, of course, was not the only political party to indoctrinate children by eulogizing its leaders. In his study of the political socialization of children in Taiwan in the 1950s and 1960s, Richard Wilson observes that children there, under the KMT-controlled curriculum, were taught early to admire and identify with their national leaders, in particular Sun Yat-sen and Chiang Kai-shek.[113] Taiwan's practice, however, was never overwhelming and ceased when the KMT loosened its control of the island after the mid-1980s, whereas in China the practice has remained strong. In a 2001 first-grade reader, a lesson titled "Grandpa Deng Xiaoping Plants a Tree" tells the children that China's Tree-Planting Day on March 12, 1985, was indeed significant because on that day Deng Xiaoping came to the Park of the Temple of Heaven in Beijing to perform a memorable task: "With a shovel and in high spirits, he digs and digs a hole to plant a cypress sapling. He refuses to take a rest even when he is streaming with sweat." The story continues, "Today this Xiaoping Tree is one of the most beautiful sights in the park."[114] In the accompanying *Teachers' Handbook,* kindergarten instructors are reminded to stress Deng's saying that "Planting trees and greening our motherland are great enterprises that will build socialism and bring much benefit to future generations."[115]

ENEMIES

Political education, however, did not concentrate only on the accomplishments of the CCP; it simultaneously exposed the dark sides of China's enemies, both domestic and abroad. An easily comprehensible Manichean demarcation of black-and-white, right-and-wrong pitted the good Communists against the bad forces, which delivered the necessary political message of patriotism to the children.

In the early 1950s, teachers were asked to explain to their students about major political efforts, including the Zhenfan campaign, the Three-Antis Campaign (launched in the fall of 1951 to fight corruption, waste, and bureaucracy), and the Five-Antis Campaign (initiated in January 1952 to criticize the vices of the bourgeoisie, including bribery and tax evasion).[116] Kindergartners were taught to distinguish between the rapacious bourgeoisie and labor heroes and heroic soldiers.

External foes were considered as dangerous as domestic ones. Kindergartners were told that Chiang Kai-shek in Taiwan and the Americans were two evil forces that looked for every possible means, including conspiring with insidious domestic groups, to undermine the new socialist regime. Chiang Kai-shek was depicted as an arch villain in stories, songs, and games. Although Taiwan was described as an island of great abundance, full of "sugarcane and banana trees," the defeated KMT leader was ridiculed for shamelessly obeying his imperialist masters.[117]

American politicians were similarly condemned. They were compared to flies and mosquitoes and denounced as pests. Children were asked to draw small dots to represent these bugs, which, their instructors said, "can spread germs." The goal of this kind of education, the teachers said, was "to enhance the children's hatred of American imperialists!"[118] The following imagined conversation was noted in a report:

"I will ask my mother to buy a gun because I want to kill the enemies too."
"Who are our enemies?"
"American imperialists," the children shouted in unison.
"Who are the bad guys?"
"Truman is a dreadful man! He dares to bully us," the children responded.[119]

Kindergartners were told that imperialists used various reprehensible methods to advance their exploitative interests in China. Among them, Christianity was one of the most deplorable.[120] In a 1953 textbook, the Resist America, Aid Korea Campaign and the "atrocities of the American imperialists" were taught in a storytelling format.[121] The children were told that when the Korean War was in full swing, the Americans schemed to rearm Japan.[122] Children were also taught that in the Korean War the American imperialists did not "allow us to have a happy life. They invaded our neighbor North Korea and destroyed its kindergartners. They killed parents of the North Korean children and were ready to invade China." As a result, when the children were taught to shout slogans such as "Long live our beloved Chinese People's Volunteer Army!," which was sent to the Korean front, "their emotion was genuine and forceful" (*ganqing shi zhenshi er youlide*).[123] Kindergartners were encouraged to write letters of sympathy to North Korean children, and sent gift bags to the soldiers to show their appreciation.[124]

Problems Encountered

By 1957, China had a record 1.08 million kindergartners, 8.3 times more than the 130,000 recorded in 1946, the highest figure known before 1949.[125] Can we assess the impact of political indoctrination in kindergartens in the early PRC? Did the children know what they sang when they extolled the wise leadership of Chairman Mao or, conversely, condemned Chiang Kai-shek and the American imperialists? What effect, if any, did this type of political socialization have on their behavior when they grew up? Reliable information is hard to come by, and what there is is often impressionistic and fragmentary.[126] Contrary to the reports of the Beijing Municipal Education Bureau touting its myriad achievements in kindergarten education, available archival sources thus far reveal a far different picture, one of a shortage of teachers and those poorly prepared for fulfilling the new tasks the Party assigned.

The rapid change of education systems and the new socialist curriculum in the early 1950s meant that teachers needed to be retrained in a hurry to comprehend the new pedagogical language. This was a difficult task, given that people were generally afraid of abrupt changes, and it seemed natural for them to hold on to the familiar and conventional. What worried officials most was finding teachers with high "political consciousness." Many kindergarten teachers were considered unsuitable because, according to the Municipal Education Bureau, they clung stubbornly to their pre-1949 bourgeois ideas and lifestyle or they carried seriously flawed historical "burdens" (*baofu*).[127] Those who had ties to religious groups before 1949 were deemed politically suspicious, and many of them were demoted or dismissed.[128] School principals and senior administrators were also found to be lacking "ideological leadership," which meant that their ability to understand and implement the Party's line was in doubt.[129]

The Beijing municipal government took immediate steps to address the problem by requiring kindergarten teachers to undergo intensive retraining sessions. This was done partly by the Committee on Culture and Education,[130] which held mandatory "ideological retraining" sessions on Marxist doctrines and international situations. These included current political movements such as the Resist America, Aid Korea Campaign, so that teachers could "communicate hatred of imperialism" to kindergartners.[131]

Teachers' meetings were not confined to the study of current affairs or state policies; they were also used for teachers to undergo "self-criticism," a process that encouraged them to confess their past dubious political thoughts and to express willingness to be reformed following the Party line.[132] Many teachers grumbled about these training and self-criticism meetings. The sessions were downright boring. "Each time the topic was more or less the same," one teacher complained.[133] The meetings were often long and tedious, at least five sessions per week, just on the concept of labor. Some were held even on Sundays, resulting in "no rest on that day."[134]

The new bureaucratic methods were also tiresome. As officials increased their hold on the education sector, more and more instructions were issued to schools. At the same time, officials also demanded more reports on the progress the schools were making. A considerable amount of teachers' time had to be spent on writing reports and entertaining frequent inspectors sent by the Education Bureau.[135] "We were asked to write the summary reports; I suspected that the officials did not read them," one teacher remarked, "because we received no response from them."[136]

Textbooks also were a thorny issue for teachers. Compiling their own textbooks became a major concern for many because they were unsure of what the new government wanted and were naturally afraid of running afoul of the Party. The teachers felt that they were walking a tightrope that required self-censorship. The safest route for them was, as one teacher advised, to "seek help from their leaders."[137] But the problem was not resolved at the next higher level, given that school principals and directors were unsure of things themselves. This heightened uncertainty and dampened teachers' spirits.

Predictably, official publications reported that children embraced the new curriculum with great enthusiasm. Stories about Tiananmen Square and Chairman Mao and games such as "Little Volunteer Army Soldiers" were reportedly among the most popular in class.[138] In government publications, upbeat statements told of how "children knew nothing about politics [in the past]; but now they know who our leaders, our friends, or our enemies are."[139] "They are sensitive," said one, "they know that they have a deep hatred of the American imperialists; [but] they all love their motherland, their people, their own army, and they also love North Korea and the Soviet Union."[140] So it seemed the politicized curriculum was a resounding success.

In reality, highly abstract patriotic ideas (paying tribute to Chairman Mao and saluting the national flag) and Marxist doctrines could not be comprehended by children whose cognitive ability, according to psychologists and educators, was still at a primitive stage.[141] Archival sources reveal that teachers repeatedly complained about this almost impossible task. "The meaning of a national flag is too difficult for kindergartners to comprehend," one teacher confessed. "It generates little interest among them, especially when no games were involved."[142] The black-and-white opposition—North Korea and the Soviet Union good, Americans bad—seemed, as one report stated, "rigid and forced." "Many [stories] were too sensational," one teacher remarked, referring to the descriptions of "the brutalities of the American imperialists," and hence they were unsuitable for such young children.[143]

It is likely, however, that the new socialist curriculum had substantial impact on the children simply because it was the only content available and was repeated and reinforced in a variety of ways. The Party made sure this was the case, gradually monopolizing teacher training after 1952. There were no alternatives. We can also assume that the method was effective because it involved not only the children but also the educators and the entire school system. Kindergarten education became wedded to a rigid authoritarian socialist ideology that taught children what the Party wanted them to know.

Kindergarten education in China in the early 1950s was transformed in a way that went beyond a mere pedagogical change. Several prominent features emerged in the process: increased control by the government over a formerly diffused system, a strong Soviet influence, rapid politicization of the curriculum with socialist and nationalist themes, and teachers retrained to become transmitters of Party values. The national kindergarten program was redesigned to tighten the connection between education and politics. Increasingly, the CCP dictated the nation's entire educational agenda from kindergartens to universities.

Predictably, under Mao's pro-Soviet policy of the 1950s, Soviet kindergartens were lauded as a model China should emulate. The official media routinely heaped praise on Soviet educators who were sent to China to help. Galina—described as "strict, serious, and conscientious"—is a case in point. She was said to be both a devoted teacher in the classroom and a tireless mentor to her many young followers. According to one report, she was so dedicated to her work that after a short rest and relaxation trip ordered by Moscow, she hurried back to Beijing because "she kept thinking about the kids in China."[144]

Despite the influence of the Soviet education system, Chinese kindergartens in the early days of the PRC were not just Soviet replicas. In her study of secondary school and higher education reforms in post-1949 China, Suzanne Pepper argues that Soviet models were used "selectively by the Chinese."[145] As we have seen, this observation is equally applicable to kindergartens. Although the veneration of Mao in children's songs was partially inspired by the Soviet model, the real hero was always Chairman Mao, not Comrade Stalin. Nationalism took priority over proletarian solidarity and socialist internationalism.

The CCP continuously exploited patriotic passions to justify its legitimacy; this was particularly evident during the early days of the PRC, when the new regime sought every viable way to underscore its right to rule. Mao and other senior leaders realized that routing the Nationalist troops militarily was but one step toward the control of China and that winning the support of the entire Chinese people would be a far harder and longer struggle. To achieve their goals, perhaps nothing was more important than raising a new generation of patriotic children to become faithful supporters of the new regime.

Kindergarten education freed mothers to work, and thus women could serve the nation's immediate need for a large workforce to bring about rapid industrialization. But the officials' interest in establishing kindergartens was more than economical—it was primarily political. As we have seen, multiple methods— games, singing, storytelling, drawing, and site visits—were systematically used to socialize children politically to serve the Communist revolution.

Few countries have pursued political socialization of children as rigorously, thoroughly, and as long as the CCP has since it took power in 1949. Unlike in the United States, where politics, as Fred Greenstein has argued, is regarded as "one of those sordid aspects of adult existence from which it is thought that young children are best shielded,"[146] children in China have been subjected to continuous political indoctrination.

It would be a mistake, of course, to assume that China is the only country that has conducted a tight political socialization program for kindergartners. Its archrival, Taiwan, as indicated earlier, adopted a similar policy but with a pro-Kuomintang, anti-Communist agenda in the 1960s and 1970s. The KMT pursued an educational goal that included national recovery, resisting the Russians, and destroying the Communist regime in mainland China. Taiwan kindergartners were taught such epithets as "despicable Communist bandits" while they learned to love the KMT government and its leader Chiang Kai-shek, calling him "the people's savior."[147] What distinguished Taiwan's program from mainland China's, however, was that it was less organized, less rigid, and much more decentralized. Political authoritarianism dissipated in Taiwan in the 1980s, especially after the lifting of martial law in 1987.

Kindergarten education in China has changed since Deng Xiaoping's market-oriented economic reforms in the 1980s. The Maoist legacy of continuous class struggle and incessant mass movements is no longer the order of the day. Chinese scholars and teachers are now calling for more plurality in kindergarten curricula, with an emphasis on cultivating children's independent thinking, to acknowledge the importance of what some educators call children's "subjectivity" (*zhutixing*).[148] Ironically, Chen Heqin's Deweyan theory of child-centered learning, condemned as depraved bourgeois thinking in the early 1950s, has regained popularity in China. In 1992, a kindergarten in the city of Shangyu, Zhejiang Province, was even named Heqin Kindergarten after the early childhood educator, recognizing him as a pioneering reformer of "noble character."[149] Thus, the trend toward granting more autonomy to kindergartens seems to be gaining momentum. The government appears to endorse this development with some enthusiasm. In July 2001, the Ministry of Education issued its *Essential Guide to Kindergarten Education,* which calls for respecting children's "personality and rights." In 2006, at a conference on the K–12 curriculum reform program, then President Hu Jintao (b. 1942) repeatedly said that more focus should be placed on cultivating students' innovation, creativity, and critical thinking.[150] This guideline was widely applauded by kindergarten teachers as a much-hoped-for improvement on conventional rote learning methods.[151] Despite this new attitude toward instruction, teachers have always been reminded that kindergartners must be taught to love "collectivity, their hometown, and their motherland."[152]

Since 1949, Communist leaders have upheld the idea that education is a critical ideological arena that they must control. This principle was reaffirmed in a major directive, "Opinions on Strengthening and Improving Ideological and Political Work in Higher Education Institutions under New Circumstances," jointly issued by the CCP Central Committee and the State Council in February 2017. The directive stipulates that universities and colleges must adhere firmly to "the correct political orientation and carry out to the full all Party guidelines on education for cultivating first-class talent." A major goal for university students is to build successfully in China "socialism with Chinese characteristics."[153] Clearly, the directive does not confine itself to university students; it applies to all levels, kindergartners included. Children need to be taught, under the leadership of the CCP, to become "successors" to a strong country and to eventually fulfill the "Chinese Dream," meaning "the great rejuvenation of the Chinese nation," in the catch phrase of the current leader Xi Jinping.[154]

CHAPTER 6

A Political Park

Public Space as Propaganda Theater

Beijing's Working People's Cultural Palace (Laodong renmin wenhuagong; WPCP) is a celebrated city park—a "people's park" (*renmin gongyuan*), as it was commonly called in socialist China[1]—as well as a major political landmark in Beijing (figure 6). Located immediately east of Tiananmen Gate, the WPCP's front wall is marked with a plaque that reads, "A key protected national cultural relic: The Imperial Ancestral Temple" (Taimiao), as well as a sign proclaiming, "Beijing's First-Rank Municipal Park."[2] The fusion of the historic WPCP and a modern urban park into a single space in May 1950, only months after the founding of the People's Republic of China (PRC) in October 1949, typifies the political strategy of the Chinese Communist Party (CCP) to turn popular urban recreational spaces into convenient sites for political rallies and for promoting the state's labor policies and international diplomacy. This appropriation of urban spaces created a conflict between the government's use of parks for political purposes and the city dwellers' desire to use them for recreation.

From the outset, the WPCP was created primarily to serve the specific interests of the Party. Chinese Communist leaders generally were suspicious of large open spaces, particularly popular recreational parks in the capital because they could be readily used for protest assemblies by unauthorized groups. They believed that such areas needed careful monitoring and control. At the same time, these were ideal locations for holding large-scale official functions. Cultural and recreational activities in the parks, therefore, were often pushed aside in favor of government uses. Activities there were blurred and eventually erased the line between the political agenda and private lives. The story of the WPCP thus encapsulates the state's move into people's private activities.

Renaming an Old Temple

The Imperial Ancestral Temple was built in 1420 in the early Ming dynasty (1368–1644) as a shrine where emperors offered sacrifices to their ancestors on

Figure 6. The main hall of the Working People's Cultural Palace, the former Taimiao. Source: Photo by Ming-mei Hung, March 5, 2010.

special occasions. During the Ming and the ensuing Qing dynasty (1644–1911), for example, emperors performed sacrificial rituals to their forebears on New Year's Eve and on the occasion of the Qingming Festival, when respect is paid to ancestors.[3] A rectangular building complex occupying an area of 197,000 square meters, the temple includes three grand halls and is surrounded by ancient cypresses. The front hall, which is the main hall (known as Xiangdian), is the largest of the three and is where grand sacrifices formerly took place; the middle hall (Qindian) held the memorial tablets of the immediate ancestors; and the rear hall (Tiaodian) housed distant ancestors' tablets. During the sacrifices, considered one of the most sacred of all imperial rituals, the ancestral tablets from the middle and rear halls would be assembled in the main hall. They would be restored to their original locations at the conclusion of the ceremony.

In 1950, soon after the founding of the PRC, the central government renamed the Imperial Ancestral Temple the Working People's Cultural Palace and placed it under the supervision of the Beijing Federation of Trade Unions (Beijingshi zonggonghui; BFTU). The renaming, according to the government, was to enhance the "cultural and recreational activities of Beijing's workers."[4] Chairman Mao honored the rechristened building with his calligraphy on the sign over the front-gate entrance. The name change was significant in that it symbolized the end of what the Communists called the lengthy feudal era ruled by despotic emperors and oppressive lords, and it also brought to the fore the role of the "working people" in new socialist China. The act reaffirmed the government's pronouncement, in the Common Program in 1949 and in the subsequent First Constitution of 1954, that the new PRC was a socialist state led by "the working class and based on the alliance of workers and peasants."[5]

At the rededication ceremony, held appropriately on Labor Day in 1950, labor leaders assembled to announce a new chapter in the history of Chinese workers. As reported in the official *Enlightenment Daily*, "With red flags fluttering and giant portraits of Chairman Mao and Marshal Stalin hanging on two sides of the front hall, this was a special day of jubilation."[6] The vice chairman of the BFTU, Xiao Ming (1896–1959), proudly declared, "This centuries-old temple, originally built with workers' blood and sweat, was always forcibly occupied by reactionary rulers. Not until the Liberation of Beijing and the leadership of the Chinese Communist Party and Chairman Mao was the temple finally returned to the working people."[7]

From the beginning, the WPCP was hailed by the official press as a "paradise of the working people in the capital." It was an ideal location for recreational activities for common folks and fulfilled a promise that socialism would bring abundance to the working people, including a richer cultural life.[8] In the early People's Republic, the term "working people" had three somewhat different but interrelated meanings. First, it referred specifically to the traditional Marxist designation of "the proletariat." In public discourse, it seemed natural for the Chinese Communists to accord the leading role of the revolution to the proletariat, for this agreed with conventional Marxist ideology. Second, it embraced not only industrial workers but also peasants, in keeping with the spirit of the 1949 Common Program and the 1954 Constitution. Finally, in an even broader sense, it meant anyone who performed manual labor. The last definition is the one that officials often meant when they spoke of the WPCP as a place for Beijing's working people.[9] A socialist worker was supposed to know the rules governing Chinese workplaces, to be technically competent as well as informed about domestic issues and international affairs.

The BFTU staff fully remodeled the hall of the main temple, converting it into a grand auditorium suitable for holding major gatherings. The rear hall was turned into a library, offering popular books and magazines that catered to the general public. Adjacent halls in the compound were refashioned into newspaper reading rooms, entertainment rooms, a drama theater, and music rooms.[10] Special chambers were also created to teach technical skills such as electrical work and "advanced production experience."[11] Occasionally, science exhibitions were featured in the main hall. A film division was created in 1953 to cater to public interest in movies.[12] The same year, an outdoor dance floor, said to be "the biggest in the city" by the *People's Daily*, was built inside the compound.[13] The WPCP, according to BFTU officials, was geared "to the needs of grassroots units and the masses."[14] Other leisure activities for common people included classes in reading, dancing, playing music, and various vocational skills. The popular Mid-Autumn Festival was also celebrated here, citizens gathering to enjoy moon cakes and delicious fruit as well as to engage in moon-gazing. "These festive activities had never occurred [in a place like this] before the Liberation," one park-goer gleefully said.[15] In a very short time, the former Imperial Ancestral Temple had seemingly been transformed into a place truly belonging to the people. The new park provided a relaxed setting where people could interact with one another in an open and pleasant atmosphere away from their generally noisy, crowded urban environment.

The WPCP was not the only cultural palace in Beijing. By the early 1960s, the capital saw the creation of more than 1,300 cultural palaces and workers' clubs, both large and small.[16] The idea spread to other parts of China, including Shanghai, Nanjing, Tianjin, Guangzhou, and Chongqing.[17] Among the new facilities was the Shanghai Workers' Cultural Palace, a vast complex of more than ten thousand square meters in the eastern part of the city, where major industries were concentrated.[18] Other workers' clubs were set up in different parts of Shanghai, for example, in the old Jing'an District.[19] Chongqing in Sichuan Province was especially known for its multiple park facilities, including a library, a football field, and a skating rink.[20]

But were the WPCP and similar sites truly geared "to the needs of grassroots units and the masses," as the government claimed? A closer look reveals a more complicated story. In fact, the WPCP was never simply a recreational area but was actually more of a political park designed by the Party to conduct diverse state activities for the advancement of socialist policies. Its location at the heart of the capital made it even more subject to political uses than other similar parks elsewhere in China. The complexity and real nature of the WPCP are evident in a number of manifestations: Soviet influence, state funerals, the championing of labor policies, political campaigns, and the contrast between the WPCP and public parks in the West.

Soviet Influence

Chinese Communists had several sources of inspiration when creating public parks. The concept of the garden (*yuanlin*) dates back to the Western Han dynasty (206 BCE–8 CE) in China, if not earlier.[21] But Chinese gardens were primarily private spaces reserved for the personal entertainment of officials and gentry. A notable example is Suzhou's Humble Administrator's Garden (Zhuozheng yuan), famous since Ming and Qing times. In the modern era, however, public recreational parks began to emerge in treaty ports to meet the needs of the growing urban population. Major influences were Western parks such as Hyde Park in England and Central Park in the United States. In Shanghai, parks managed by foreigners appeared in the Bund in the nineteenth century. Gradually, private parks owned by rich merchants began to open their gates to the public. Perhaps the best known of these is Zhang Garden (Zhang yuan), owned by a rich merchant named Zhang Shuhe.[22] In 1914, during the early Republican era, the name Central Park was given to a new public park that had once been Beijing's Altar of Earth and Grain (Shejitan), to the immediate west of Tiananmen Gate, where emperors had offered sacrifices to the God of Earth and prayed for good harvests. In 1928, the park was redesignated Zhongshan Park, in memory of Dr. Sun Yat-sen, China's most prominent revolutionary leader in the modern era.

Public recreational parks in China, especially the WPCP, were influenced more by the Soviets than by the West. This was to be expected because Mao Zedong and senior Party leaders had taken an unequivocal pro-Soviet stance in the early phase of the PRC. Given that China was internationally isolated and threatened by hostile foreign powers such as the United States, Mao's decision to seek help from a socialist ally was understandable. The influence of the Soviets on the WPCP became evident in the name and political nature of the park. First, the Chinese name *wenhuagong* (cultural palace) was clearly a direct translation of the Russian term *dvorets kultury*. The Russian Communist Party, after the October Revolution and under the drive to develop a proletarian culture (*Proletkult*) and transform the masses along socialist lines, founded many workers' clubs (see chapter 4). These clubs had their origins in the nineteenth-century Russian philanthropic "people's house" (*narodnye doma*), which provided a communal space for workers and their families to socialize and relax.[23]

The modern-day workers' clubs—or in their more grandiloquent designation as "palaces of culture"[24]—appeared in profusion in the 1920s and 1930s. Touted by the Soviet authorities as ideal locations for workers to enjoy their leisure time, they testified to the growing prosperity and improved quality of life in Soviet society. The clubs were established mostly in areas where workers were concentrated. For instance, the Palace of Culture, designed by the architects Leonid, Victor, and Alexander Vesnin, three brothers, rose up in the Proletarian District (until April 1929, the Rogozhsko-Simonovskii District), home to the Sickle and Hammer (Serp i molot) metallurgical factory, one of Moscow's flagship enterprises.[25] Among these clubs, the Constructivist architect Konstantin Mel-nikov's Rusakov Club was perhaps the most well known.[26] Workers' clubs sprang up in other East European countries and included the Palace of Culture and Science in Warsaw.

Even more important, the inspiration for the WPCP as a public park was the Soviet "parks of culture and leisure" movement in the 1920s. Historically, Russian parks were patterned after those in the West. Tsar Peter the Great was impressed by Western parks during his European tour, and so enlisted leading gardeners from Germany and France to create magnificent gardens in Russia, such as the park at Peterhof. Catherine the Great followed suit, creating great parks resembling those in Europe (such as the garden at Tsarskoe Selo).[27] In the Soviet era, however, a different kind of urban park emerged. In a move similar to the establishment of the workers' clubs, Stalin in the 1920s created "parks of culture and leisure" (*park kultury i otdykha*) in line with Marx's notion that rest and leisure are important elements of a worker's life. Although Marx did not produce a systematic analysis of leisure, he wrote about it intermittently and considered it important. In *The Grundrisse,* for example, he associated leisure with enjoyment. He argued that "free time—which includes leisure time as well as time for higher activities—naturally transforms anyone who enjoys it into a different person, and it is this different person who then enters the direct process of production."[28] Marx's "higher activities" included education "in the arts, sciences, etc." that people practice in their free time.[29] This leisure time, according to Marx, is important to ensure workers' personal development and ultimately to enhance their productivity.

The model for Stalin's "parks of culture and leisure" was Moscow's Gorky Park (formally known as Gorky Park of Culture and Leisure). Built in 1928, the park extends along the banks of the Moscow River and contains many popular attractions, including outdoor fairs, a Ferris wheel, bowling alleys, dance floors, and newspaper reading rooms. Like similar parks built at the time, however, Gorky Park was never simply an entertainment site but was also meant to be a political arena to propagate official doctrine. In a 1932 Soviet poster, a public park was identified as a "proletarian park of culture and leisure."[30] In 1935, Stalin's famous slogan "Life has become better; life has become more cheerful" was hung for a time across the gates of many parks. In the 1930s, posters calling for the elimination of kulaks were found everywhere in the parks, and loudspeakers broadcast Soviet leaders' speeches and Radio Moscow's official programs.[31]

Gorky Park also became a favorite place to visit for Chinese delegates on official trips to the Soviet capital. When the Chinese novelist Shen Yanbing—the future minister of culture—visited the park in December 1946 to see the exhibition of the Red Army's war trophies, he lavishly praised the Soviets for the large number of captured German tanks and cannons, commenting that "the defeat of the German Army showed the greatness of the Soviet military industry. Yet the most important reason for the Soviet victory lay not in its weaponry but in the superiority of the Soviet political, economic, and social systems."[32]

In the early 1950s, the Russian term *kultury i otdykha* was directly translated into Chinese as *wenhua yu xiuxi* (culture and rest) and widely used throughout the country.[33] Because of its inexperience in managing large parks, the Beijing Municipal Bureau of Parks (Beijingshi yuanlinju; BMBP) invited Soviet experts to come to Beijing to offer their advice. "Their suggestions made a significant impact on our work," acknowledged the bureau officials.[34] Indeed, China's parks, in general, and Beijing's Working People's Cultural Palace, in particular, resembled their Soviet counterparts in that they were both recreational centers and propaganda platforms. But the WPCP was unique: as a workers' cultural palace and a park of culture and rest, it combined the two Soviet institutions and was thus more forceful and versatile than its Soviet counterparts in serving the Party's interest.

Ren Bishi's Funeral

The first sign that the WPCP was to become a vehicle for the Party's political purposes came in October 1950, when the CCP turned this newly rechristened public park into a place for the body of Ren Bishi (1904–1950) to temporarily lie in state, a clear indication that the state's political agenda was taking over the social functions of public urban spaces. Ren, a member of the powerful CCP's Central Secretariat and one of Mao's closest comrades since the Yan'an era, died of a cerebral hemorrhage after a long illness at the age of forty-six on October 27, 1950. The CCP central leadership immediately formed a commission, headed by Mao, to organize Ren's funeral. It was decided that a state funeral for Ren would be held in the WPCP, returning the newly converted cultural palace to its former role as a memorial hall for honoring the dead.

Ren's death was announced in an obituary in the press by the CCP's Central Committee and the Central Committee of the Chinese New Democratic Youth Corps, the latter of which Ren had served as honorary chairman.[35] On the morning of October 28, a deeply saddened Mao, together with the three remaining members of the Central Secretariat—Liu Shaoqi, Zhou Enlai, and Zhu De (1886–1976)—visited Ren's residence in Beijing to bid farewell. The casket, draped with a Party flag, was then moved to the WPCP.[36]

In front of the main hall a long black-and-white banner was hung, inscribed with the words "The Mourning Hall of Comrade Ren Bishi." Ren's casket, guarded by four soldiers and four members of the Chinese New Democratic

Youth Corps, was placed in the center of the hall, where in bygone days the emperors performed sacred sacrifices to their forebears. A huge PRC flag on the central wall and a large photograph of Ren gave the room a solemn air. Thousands of mourners filed past the casket to pay their final tribute to the deceased leader.

A memorial service was held on October 30 in an open court in front of the main hall. Led by Mayor Peng Zhen and with senior Party leaders present, including Liu Shaoqi, Zhou Enlai, and Chen Yun (1905–1995), the service was also attended by forty thousand solemn mourners.[37] After the service, Ren's body was laid to rest in the Babaoshan Revolutionary Cemetery in western Beijing. This burial ground was reserved for distinguished Communists who had made important contributions to the socialist revolution.

In her study of death rituals of the early Soviet period, Catherine Merridale terms Bolshevik revolutionaries' interments "red funerals." The burials followed a routine of pomp and practices that included the announcement of the death with black-bordered obituaries in the press, giant wreaths, and honor guards.[38] Ren's funeral adhered closely to the red funeral pattern. But Ren's funeral was distinct, not because of its rituals and the massive assembly of mourners but instead because of where it was held. It is difficult to know why the CCP chose the WPCP, but the choice clearly showed that the Party never regarded the park as merely a recreational venue for citizens. It served an even more important purpose as a platform where the Party could publicly honor a dead leader who devoted his life to the socialist cause.

Mourning and recreation were inherently emotionally incompatible and socially contradictory activities. If the Party's original intention in converting the ancestral temple into a public park was to exorcise the ghosts of the feudal past, then holding a funeral there—reenacting a ritual long detested and condemned by the Communists as archaic—contradicted its initial objective in creating the park. The new Communist leaders may have thought, however, that commemorating the deceased leader in the former ancestral temple would symbolically place Ren in the new pantheon of the nation's founding fathers. Ren's elevated status would transform the WPCP from a workers' park to a secular ancestral temple in the service of the CCP. Over the ensuring years, the WPCP has been the venue for memorial services for many senior Party leaders, including, in January 1976, Zhou Enlai.

The Leading Role of the Workers

That the Working People's Cultural Palace was placed under the management of the Beijing Federation of Trade Unions indicates that, at least nominally, the site was specifically to serve workers' interests. Chinese official records reveal that the capital, which had a total urban population of 1.4 million, had 390,605 workers in 1950, of whom 186,158 (47.7 percent) were affiliated with a union.[39] The BFTU was determined to give the workers distinguished status, as shown in a 1955 internal memo, in which the federation spelled out the role of the WPCP: "The primary functions of the cultural palace were to disseminate, through lively formats, the policies of the Party and the people's government as well as those of the trade unions."[40] The BMBP added its voice: "Socialist parks must be different from the private gardens of the past," and be designed to "serve the politics of the proletariat as well as the mass of the workers, peasants, and soldiers."[41] These parks, the officials emphasized, were "one of the key places for disseminating political propaganda and offering cultural education to the masses."[42] Clearly, in these government pronouncements, the earlier declaration that public parks were created for the private recreational needs of city dwellers was overridden.

The BFTU was, however, only a front organization that oversaw the activities of the WPCP. Archival sources reveal that the agenda was actually set by the Beijing Municipal Party, which in turn was directed by even higher Party leadership. Activities in the parks, as Municipal Party officials repeatedly stressed, had to be "centrally arranged" (tongyi anpai).[43] The supporting agencies, including the BFTU and the BMBP, implemented decisions made by the Municipal Party. Clearly, the CCP's tight network of organizational control was in full force.

One of the BFTU's major propaganda tactics was the promotion of "model workers" (laodong mofan). Here again the Soviet influence was apparent. The Stakhanovite movement—named after Aleksei Stakhanov, a miner who produced fourteen times the government's prescribed quota of coal—was promoted by Stalin during the Second Five-Year Plan, in 1935, as a model of high productivity and total devotion to Soviet leadership.[44] Stakhanov was idolized by the Chinese Communists during the Yan'an era,[45] but the CCP held up its own model workers at meetings to make the propaganda work more effective and to promote its own heroes.[46]

This model-worker tradition continued after the founding of the PRC, but the authorities interpreted the term "model worker" more broadly than their Soviet counterparts did. "Model workers" referred to worker and peasant heroes, but also occasionally to "advanced producers" (xianjin shengchanzhe), which encompassed a variety of professions including, for example, technicians, mailmen, dancers, and even university professors, as seen in a 1956 list of "model workers" issued by the BFTU.[47] "Model workers" and "advanced producers" were combined into one group in China because all engaged in work that could be seen as advancing the cause of socialism.

The WPCP was an ideal place for honoring labor heroes and showcasing their achievements. This was done mainly through exhibitions, display windows, public reports, lecture series, and radio broadcasts.[48] Just inside the front gate of the WPCP, a long display window titled "Honor Roll" (*guangrongbang*) listed the names and photographs of a number of model workers and included brief accounts of their contributions (figure 7).[49] From 1953 to 1954, sixty-four labor heroes were introduced this way.[50] In a January 1955 municipal government meeting, it was decided that, in addition to model workers selected by the Propaganda Section of the BFTU, valiant soldiers would also be listed. The General Political Department of the People's Liberation Army, the department responsible for political indoctrination in the army, would make the recommendations.[51]

Worker and peasant heroes, not "advanced producers," took center stage. Their remarkable achievements were retold in grand fashion at celebratory meetings. The BFTU frequently invited workers to the WPCP to share their experiences. According to federation officials, these meetings were planted to "carry forward the cooperative spirit of communism" and "to protect state property, bear the burden of work willingly, and serve the people wholeheartedly."[52] Two such distinguished workers were Zhao Guoyou (b. 1924), a machinery factory worker

Figure 7. The Honor Roll at the Working People's Cultural Palace. Source: Photo by author, October 27, 2002.

from Shenyang, and Zhao Guilan (b. 1930), a chemical factory worker from Dalian. During their trip to participate in the Chinese People's Political Consultative Conference in June 1950, they were asked to meet their admirers at the WPCP. "When these model workers entered the Cultural Palace on the night of June 18, the audience broke into thunderous applause," reported the People's Daily.[53] The two heroes declared that without "the leadership of the Chinese Communist Party and the people's government, the proletariat would never be able to genuinely stand up."[54] Zhao Guoyou, who had just returned from the Soviet Union as a member of China's delegation of workers, gave a glowing report on "the advanced production methods in the Soviet factories and the happy lives of workers there."[55] On another occasion, labor hero Liu Yingyuan (1898–1978), director of the Shijingshan Power Plant in western Beijing, echoed the goal of the model-worker movement when he spoke about how to set new production records.[56]

The government also erected bronze statues of labor heroes in the park. A famous example was that of Shi Chuanxiang (1915–1975) (figure 8). Shi, a night-soil collector, was praised by the officials as a labor hero in the 1950s for his hard work. On October 26, 1959, he was publicly commended by President Liu Shaoqi at a meeting held at the Great Hall of the People to honor labor heroes. The president told this worker, "For the work you do as a night-soil collector, you are a true servant of the people. And as the state president, I'm also a servant of the people."[57] According to Shi's widow, he never forgot "the thrill of shaking hands with a state leader."[58]

From the beginning, therefore, the WPCP was a socialist showroom. It was an advertising tool for the Party to report regularly on advances in the railway system, the electrical industry, and iron and steel production.[59] To be sure, government declarations stressed that workers' happiness extended beyond productive factory work to include culturally enriching activities. The WPCP, for example, periodically exhibited workers' paintings to emphasize that the creative talents of the proletariat were recognized and nourished under the new socialist regime.[60] Without question, state pronouncements regarding collectivism took precedence over citizens' private interests. By the end of 1954, the WPCP had hosted sixty-seven exhibitions on various kinds of labor activity, attracting 7.07 million visitors.[61] Through these exhibitions, the People's Daily reported, "working people in the capital acquired different kinds of invaluable knowledge."[62] The workers were then encouraged to apply this knowledge to advance the socialist cause. Similarly, in 1964, the BFTU instructed the WPCP to assume yet another educational role by serving as a school for youngsters during summer vacations. The goal, the BFTU emphatically declared, was to "nurture the successors to socialism and communism."[63]

Figure 8. Bronze statue of labor hero Shi Chuanxiang, the Working People's Cultural Palace. Source: Photo by author, January 23, 2011.

Internationalism

As Marxist revolutionaries, Chinese Communists were committed to a world-wide proletarian revolution. Theoretically, at least, they believed that class rather than national interest was the foundation of a global socialist movement. Thus, the WPCP was also a site where the government could promote international socialism and an international labor movement. The BFTU therefore set up an international department to coordinate these activities.

A golden opportunity came every year during international May Day celebrations. In the 1950s, the achievements of the PRC were celebrated in annual May Day parades organized by the municipal government, with thousands of people forming spectacular processions along Chang'an Avenue in the capital.[64] This was also a perfect occasion to instill a sense of pride among Chinese workers and, more important, to demonstrate solidarity among the proletariat worldwide.

On May Day, the International Department acted as a gracious host to invite foreign labor leaders, largely from socialist countries such as the Soviet Union, Albania, North Korea, Hungary, Bulgaria, and Romania. To enhance China's international prestige, labor representatives were also invited from nonsocialist nations, including Pakistan, India, Spain, and Colombia.[65] When the foreign dignitaries arrived, the WPCP was high on their itinerary, and, as expected, their Chinese hosts accompanied them for a guided tour.[66] Every year, the WPCP's main hall was converted into a concert hall with symphonies and choruses performing favorite pieces such as "The Workers Are Empowered" and other songs praising the unity of the socialist camp.[67] The cultural palace was transformed into a global stage and diplomatic platform for forging new international comradeship as well as reaffirming old commitments. To further promote friendship, soccer matches between China and the visiting foreign countries were also staged in the Workers' Stadium in eastern Beijing.[68]

Of the sixty-seven exhibitions mounted in the WPCP by the end of 1954, twenty-five were devoted to industrial development and daily life in "brotherly countries."[69] In the 1950s, when Beijing and Moscow were on good terms, exhibitions of Soviet achievements were held regularly. As May Day approached in 1950, a photo exhibition of the Soviet Union displayed the country's economic and social accomplishments, including collective farms, industrial plants, and educational systems.[70] The Red Army's defeat of the Nazis was another popular achievement commemorated in the WPCP.[71] In the 1950s, Soviet films also became a regular attraction, entertaining workers and their families in the palace compound. These films were mostly sponsored by the Sino-Soviet Friendship Association, an organization founded in 1949.[72] Anti-imperialism exhibitions, not surprisingly, were equally prominent, as demonstrated by the 1951 exhibition "The Struggle of Vietnam" against French colonialism. Reportedly, these exhibitions attracted large audiences.[73]

Beijing's WPCP was not the only cultural palace in the nation to host foreign dignitaries; the Shanghai Workers' Cultural Palace (Shanghai gongren wenhuagong) often welcomed them as well.[74]

Political Campaigns

In the unsettling nation-building years of the PRC's first decade, the WPCP's primary tasks dealt less with external affairs and more with urgent domestic issues, including promoting the Party's political campaigns. This was spelled out by the BFTU's Propaganda Department in a document stating that the WPCP was "to coordinate its activities with various kinds of political movements."[75] In the Three-Antis and Five-Antis campaigns from 1951 to 1952, in which the Communist Party denounced bureaucratism and capitalists, respectively, the BFTU was the faithful enforcer of Party policy.[76]

The WPCP played an even more active role in two of the "three greatest mass movements" in the early 1950s: the Zhenfan campaign, the Resist America campaign, and the Aid Korea Campaign (the third being the Land Reform campaign). In these campaigns, the WPCP was a convenient location for announcing the Party's policies, as evident in a series of well-publicized exhibitions staged in its compound. In mid-1950, the Beijing Security Bureau staged an exhibition there titled "Exposing the Spy System of the Chiang Kai-shek Cliques."[77] The following year they mounted an even larger show, "The Criminal Evidence of the America-Chiang Spy System," which focused not only on the history of Kuomintang espionage and US intelligence network in China before 1949 but also on the "major counterrevolutionary cases" uncovered in 1950.[78] These exhibitions were an integral part of the larger campaign to suppress counterrevolutionaries.

After the outbreak of the Korean War in June 1950, the WPCP was again transformed into a propaganda platform, this time to support the government-initiated Resist America, Aid Korea Campaign. This operation attacked the United States in four areas: the history of US imperialist aggression in China, the US rearming of Japan, US military aid to Taiwan, and the bravery of the Korean people in resisting foreign aggression.[79] The BFTU accused the United States of "undermining peace" in Asia.[80] As in the past, the Propaganda Department of the BFTU used a variety of media—including films, radio broadcasts, photos, and posters—to denounce American involvement in the Korean War.[81] The Cultural and Educational Department, another section of the BFTU, designed anti-American pamphlets and used popular forms such as cartoons, comic dialogues, and storytelling with a clapper to disseminate these messages.[82] Anti-American films were often screened in the large open courtyard in front of the WPCP's main hall, and drew five thousand to ten thousand viewers each time.[83]

Model workers were also called into action in this cultural arena. In a speech delivered in the southern city of Guangzhou, Mayor Ye Jianying encouraged labor heroes to assume a leading role in these political campaigns. "A model worker should not only be an active participant in production," Ye said, "he should also be on constant alert, preventing counterrevolutionaries from wreaking havoc in different [government] branches."[84] Urged by the government, model workers and distinguished soldiers joined together nationwide to sign an open letter, published in the *People's Daily* in late December 1950 in support of the anti-American war effort.[85] The Chinese New Democratic Youth Corps contributed to the cause by staging basketball games at the WPCP and donating the proceeds to "pay for fighter planes and cannons" to aid the North Koreans.[86] This was part of the government-sponsored Donating Airplanes and Cannons movement, which, in the early 1950s, was developed into a nationwide anti-America movement. The WPCP mounted other political exhibitions, including one—the Liberation of Taiwan—that denounced both Chiang Kai-shek and the United States,[87] and another featuring cartoons that condemned the literary critic Hu Feng (1902–1985) as a counterrevolutionary who promoted bourgeois liberalism.[88]

This politization of public parks was evident in other parts of China as well. When Shanghai celebrated its Spring Festival in 1955, the municipal government instructed administrators of the city's Zhongshan Park, for example, to integrate its activities closely with "current political missions" targeted primarily against the American military aggression in Asia.[89]

Like many other government organizations, the WPCP was inevitably drawn into the even more tumultuous political battles of the 1960s, in which the radical Maoists fought against the pragmatists led by Liu Shaoqi. In 1964, the BFTU, which had fallen under the radicals' control, criticized WPCP staff for putting on artistic programs devoid of any content concerning "class struggle." BFTU officials berated the WPCP for pursuing a bourgeois path when they hung a large number of actors' photos on the palace walls, calling it a sign of debauched capitalist taste, and for failing to "engage in class struggle."[90] They also condemned the WPCP for putting on performances of "symphonies there that were incomprehensible even to our cadres," including works by Tchaikovsky and Beethoven. This was considered to be pursuing pure "artistry" (*yishuxing*) and forsaking political goals.[91] "We must repel the furious onslaught of bourgeois thought," the senior officials reminded staff in a strongly worded statement.[92]

In the ensuing Cultural Revolution, which shook the nation from the mid-1960s to the mid-1970s, the WPCP came under the full control of the radicals, led by the so-called Gang of Four (among them Jiang Qing [1914–1991], Mao's wife). It was a favorite site for staging large political demonstrations in support of the Maoist line.[93] For instance, on May Day 1968, the WPCP and other public parks in Beijing were turned into venues for buoyant garden parties to "highlight the politics of the proletariat and hold high the great red banner of Mao Zedong Thought," according to the newly created, radical-controlled Revolutionary Committee of the BFTU.[94]

The WPCP versus Western Parks

The party-state's domination of public spaces in China, as in its control of the capital's WPCP and other large urban parks, is best demonstrated by comparing Chinese and Western parks.

Public recreational parks date back to early European history. Such parks are only one of the many types of parks in the West. The others are national parks and heritage parks.[95] London's Hyde Park, which opened to the public in the 1630s, is a notable example of a recreational park.[96] The creation of modern-day publicly funded civic parks for leisure is, however, predominantly a Victorian enterprise, a result of the Industrial Revolution, which necessitated a public recreational landscape to improve the physical conditions of workers who were trapped in noisy, overcrowded cities.[97] Many countries, including the United States, followed suit. The best-known example is New York's Central Park.

When landscape architect Frederick Law Olmsted, with the help of his partner Calvert Vaux, designed Central Park, he had a distinct notion of what an urban park should do: it should be a communal place where people from a variety of backgrounds could congregate and socialize. It is well known that Olmsted's idea was inspired by what he saw during two visits to Birkenhead Park near Liverpool in 1850 and 1859. He was genuinely impressed by the British parks—what he called "people's gardens"—with their winding paths, open meadows, and woodland belts.[98]

In designing Central Park, Olmsted went beyond imagining an idealized countryside landscape where people could amble. He wanted a park with a unified composition, one that blended scenery with humanist social values; he especially believed that a park should not be a mere imitation of nature but must have a "human presence."[99] It should be a place for "gregarious recreation,"[100] a communal institution open to citizens of all classes, where people could enjoy a "social, neighborly, unexertive form of recreation."[101] In line with this aim, Olmsted stressed the social and psychological effect of the landscape on visitors to the park. Citizens from diverse backgrounds could assemble to converse, interact, and socialize in a relaxed, "beautiful open green space."[102] Located within a congested urban setting, a public park could thus become a lively and multifaceted venue for the uninhibited dialogue of weary city dwellers. Herein lies the fundamental notion of what Olmsted called "openness."[103]

Olmsted's Central Park is an archtypical example of a Western recreational park that belongs to the common people and is not under the control of interest groups or political parties. It truly belongs to everyone. A recreational park is thus democratic in that it promotes cultural diversity, accommodates dissonant voices, encourages community participation and unrestricted ideas, and provides a sense of inclusion for all citizens. In the words of the anthropologist Setha Low and her colleagues, "Olmsted believed that a complex web of volunteer and recreational social activity, and the communication such activity fostered, was the crucial underpinning of a democratic society."[104]

Obviously Beijing's WPCP differed markedly from its Western counterparts in that it was subject to a controlling government blueprint. A 1953 report by the BMBP affirmed that urban parks were set up to "strengthen cultural activities as well as to enhance the political atmosphere."[105] As it turned out, political considerations won out over public entertainment and cultural enhancements. The interest of the Party determined what the structure and contents of the WPCP and other major public parks should be. The municipal government and the BFTU coordinated the activities at the WPCP and removed items deemed undesirable and unsuitable from the park.

During the Cultural Revolution, the political nature of public parks became even more pronounced. The setting of a park, including the arrangement of flora, had to be carefully planned and supervised. "Flowers must serve political purposes and be used for festive celebrations," and must "represent the thriving of socialism," park officials insisted, adding that "displaying the quotations of Chairman Mao in the parks must strictly follow the orders that come from the central government."[106]

Did the WPCP operate in the interests of the working people, as the government officially claimed? How did urbanites actually view this popular park? A woodcut by Gu Yuan titled *Beijing's Working People's Cultural Palace* (figure 9) helps answer these questions.[107] Occupying center stage in this famous 1951 print are ordinary people playing chess. Nearby, men and women are reading newspapers and magazines, and two youngsters sit on the ground enjoying their storybooks. At the back, citizens are dancing in a circle in front of the main hall of the WPCP. Still others watch the myriad activities around them. The scene tells a simple story: the WPCP is a place where common folks gather for relaxation and recreation. This seemed to fulfill the government's original promise, mentioned earlier, that the WPCP was a "paradise of the working people in the capital," where common people could congregate for amusement. But this promise was often unfulfilled because the park was frequently used for large-scale, often boisterous political activities orchestrated by the government. In renaming the Imperial Ancestral Temple the Working People's Cultural Palace in 1950, the new Chinese Communist regime redefined the nature of China's public recreational parks. It can be argued that from the beginning, the WPCP, because of its important location in Tiananmen Square, was never appropriate for promoting social and entertainment activities for city residents. That its name cites it as belonging to "the working people" created a conflict between the needs of state agencies and the goal of creating a park for city residents' recreation. For the government, such a conflict seemed easily resolved by limiting people's leisure activities and turning the park's social functions into political activities. For the authoritarian CCP, the WPCP was not supposed to have recreational functions separate from political purposes. The WPCP and other major parks in China

北京市勞動人民文化宮（木刻）

古

元

Figure 9. Gu Yuan, *Beijing's Working People's Cultural Palace* (woodcut). Source: *RMRB*, April 29, 1951, 5.

thus reflected the Communist regime's primary concern with controlling public spaces to ensure social stability and political harmony. The large public spaces were actually used in an Orwellian way to closely monitor and eliminate any threats to the Party's grip on power.

Contrary to official pronouncements about the highly efficient and superior management of the city's public parks, these recreational areas were plagued with problems. Archival sources and internal memos reveal that waste, corruption, and theft were common and that the staff often were incompetent.[108] "The staff's educational level is low," park officials confessed. These troubles seem minor, however, relative to the political intrusions by various government agencies, including the BFTU. In the PRC's ceaseless political campaigns during Mao's era, park administrators were directed to toe the line and constantly be wary of potential opposition to Communist rule.

Public parks have undergone some changes. The post-Mao reforms since the late 1970s saw a clear transformation of the boundary between state and society, greater reliance being put on market forces and new social organizations that allowed individuals more access to allocated urban space.[109] Beginning in the 1980s, a calmer ambiance began to prevail at the urban parks. The frantic political rallies of the Maoist era are no longer held. In my visits to urban parks in cities such as Beijing, Shanghai, Guangzhou, Xi'an, Wuhan, Guilin, Yan'an, and others in recent years, I saw that life is much more peaceful and joyful now. These urban parks are regularly filled with retired city dwellers enjoying social dances; the elderly doing light exercises; and people singing, playing chess, practicing calligraphy, or even napping—in short, enjoying recreation and relaxation. In crowded cities such as Beijing and Shanghai, where private space is in short supply, the parks are green sanctuaries.

But this retreat of the party-state does not reflect a fundamental change in its political nature or an increased willingness to accept open criticism or challenges to its authority. People enjoy greater recreational freedom, but only if the activities pose no threat to the regime. Large, open spaces continue to be considered potentially dangerous because crowds can assemble in them and such gatherings can easily spin out of control. Indeed, one incident made the Party particularly nervous about "undesirable" gatherings in the parks.[110] In the 1980s, large urban parks, including the WPCP, became favorite places for master teachers to instruct large assemblies in *qigong*—a traditional form of breathing techniques that teach self-cultivation and personal balance, believed to be beneficial to health.[111] One of the most popular *qigong* groups was that of the Falun Gong sect. But, as mentioned in chapter 3, when the group staged a demonstration outside Zhongnanhai in April 1999 to protest the government's criticism and negative portrayals of *qigong*, the Party took swift action to clamp down on it, arresting its leaders and banning all such practices. Public parks were immediately put under close watch.

Only in rare circumstances does the government permit organized activities in the parks. During the 2008 Beijing Summer Olympic Games, under pressure from the International Olympic Committee, the government agreed to set up three parks—Purple Bamboo Park, Ritan (sun altar) Park, and World Park—as protest zones where citizens could air grievances against the government. The application procedures, on the surface, were surprisingly easy: a citizen could simply submit an application form at a local police station. In the end, the government received a total of seventy-seven applications from one hundred forty-nine people, and yet not a single demonstration actually took place.[112] Chinese officials explained that all the concerns had been "resolved" through "dialogue and communication." "Chinese culture always emphasizes the concept of harmony," they added.[113] This official script, however, hid the cruel reality of police harassment and the arrest of demonstrators. Many who dared to apply were either detained or sentenced to political reeducation. According to human rights groups, two Chinese women, one of whom was seventy years old and nearly blind, applied to protest against local authorities for forcibly evicting them from their homes. As soon as they submitted their applications, they were interrogated by police for ten hours; eventually they were ordered to undergo a year of "reeducation through labor."[114]

This was a clear breach of the promises Chinese organizers had made that there would be more openness and more respect for human rights, which had helped China win its bid to host the 2008 Games in the first place.[115] Many believed that the designated protest zones were merely a government ploy to quell recurring criticism of China's lack of free expression and, worse still, to ferret out potential troublemakers.[116] The party-state to this day never hesitates to impose control over the public, by force if necessary. In doing so, it obliterates the distinction between government policies and citizens' everyday lives; more important, the line between public and private spheres is erased. In the end, the monopoly of power by the Chinese Communist Party is ensured.

CHAPTER 7

Architecture and Ethnicity

Unity under One Roof?

When, in 1994, the people of Beijing were asked to name their favorite buildings of national style in the capital, topping the list of the fifty most nominated structures was the Cultural Palace of Nationalities (Minzu wenhuagong; CPN) (figure 10) at west Chang'an Avenue near Xidan.[1] Few people, however, looked at this celebrated building—one of the Ten Monumental Buildings constructed in 1959 to celebrate the tenth anniversary of the founding of the People's Republic of China (PRC)[2]—as an edifice that epitomized the government's controversial ethnic policies of the 1950s. Since its inception, the CPN has served multiple purposes: as an architectural icon, a structure that represents the power of the state, a national museum of ethnicity, an exhibition center of cultural relics, and a symbol of unity among national minorities in China under the leadership of the Chinese Communist Party (CCP).

In communist nations, an imposing government building is never merely a manifestation of architectural artistry. It is often a fusion of technology, art, and—most important—state policies. Constructed largely in the national style with traditional double-eaved roofs and glazed tiles, the CPN is an unambiguous political symbol of the government's ethnic policies in the early years of the PRC, a crucial period of consolidation for the CCP.

Among China's fifty-six officially designated ethnic groups, the Han people are the largest; the remaining fifty-five are all labeled "ethnic minorities." In recent years, these ethnic minority peoples, who live mostly on the nation's resource-rich and strategically important frontier lands, have become one of the fastest-growing fields of scholarly inquiry.[3] But most of these works remain largely within the bounds of specific disciplines. In this chapter, I adopt a multidisciplinary approach and argue that Chinese Communist leaders communicated their policies on ethnic minorities not only through laws and regulations but also through national architectural forms. I examine the close interaction between politics, ethnicity, architecture, and museums, especially regarding the CPN as a significant political edifice that furnishes an official narrative of

Figure 10. The Cultural Palace of Nationalities, Beijing. Source: Photo by author, October 21, 2002.

ethnicity by means of display strategies. A careful look at how the CPN was built, as well as at the items exhibited inside, reveals not only the CCP's manipulation of images of national minorities but also the difficulties the Party encountered in dealing with ethnic nationalism, regional separatism, and local identity in the early decades of the PRC.

Starting in 1949, the Party faced a dilemma in its ethnic policies; on the one hand, it attempted to impose a tight rule on the ethnic minorities; on the other, it needed to allow a certain degree of regional autonomy and the continued existence of varied local cultures. Granting autonomy, even in limited form, ran the risk of fostering local nationalism, which could give rise to the ethnic groups' calling for secession from the PRC. Whenever this contradiction could not be realistically resolved, the party-state, putting stability and security ahead of everything else, would tighten down on non-Han people. The Han-style CPN building, which ostensibly functioned primarily as a museum and exhibition center of ethnic artifacts, apparel, musical instruments, craftworks, and photographs, served the interests of the CCP as a powerful way to communicate the Party's policy of uniting ethnic minorities under Han domination. The building speaks with a single voice and differs considerably from most modern-day nongovernment Western museums, where pluralism, contested views, and sometime irreconcilable differences are commonplace.

Background

When the Communists came to power in 1949, Mao and senior Party leaders faced the daunting task of rebuilding a ravaged nation. In addition to economic ruin and social instability, ethnic tensions ranked as one of the thorniest issues demanding the new government's immediate attention. To be sure, ethnic troubles had plagued previous Chinese rulers. The Qing court dealt with them by using a combination of persuasion (such as the tribute system) and coercion (such as military campaigns against the Muslim rebellion in the nineteenth century), but met with only modest success. During the ensuing Republican era, the Kuomintang (KMT) regime attempted a policy of control through assimilation. It met strong resistance from minorities in places such as Yunnan, Xinjiang, Tibet, and Outer Mongolia.[4] The new Communist regime faced even more difficulty in dealing with ethnic groups. Xinjiang, where Soviet influence was strong, and Tibet were major concerns. The People's Liberation Army moved swiftly to occupy Xinjiang in September 1949, when Nationalist troops surrendered. A year later, the army entered Tibet. Lhasa was occupied in September 1951, and an agreement was reached with Tibetan leaders to grant the territory a significant measure of autonomy under the leadership of the central government. Each territory was later given the status of an autonomous region, a formula based on the Soviet approach to a multinational and multicultural state.[5] However, the situation remained tense and volatile in these areas.

In 1953, China's ethnic minorities, making up 5.89 percent of the total population of 577 million, were still a cause of concern for the new government.[6] In its first constitution, adopted in 1954, the PRC spelled out its basic policy toward national minorities:

The People's Republic of China is a single multinational state.

All the nationalities are equal. Discrimination against, or oppression of, any nationality, and acts which undermine the unity of the nationalities are prohibited.

All the nationalities have freedom to use and foster the growth of their spoken and written languages, and to preserve or reform their own customs or ways.

Regional autonomy applies in areas where people of national minorities live in compact communities. National autonomous areas are inalienable parts of the People's Republic of China.[7]

The government criticized traditional Han prejudices, calling it "Great Han chauvinism" (da Hanzuzhuyi)—a patronizing and degrading attitude toward ethnic minorities.[8] This erroneous perspective, the officials charged, was primarily "the result of the crimes of the reactionary rulers of the past."[9] They then asserted "a record of humiliation of our fraternal minorities."[10] Combating this prejudice became one of the government's main concerns. This new attitude was exemplified by removing the name of Xinjiang's capital city, Dihua, which means "to enlighten" in Chinese, thus blatantly displaying the assumed superiority and cultural insensitivity of the Han Chinese toward the native Uyghurs.[11] The name of the capital was changed in 1954 to Urumqi, a Mongolian word meaning "beautiful pasture."

The government adopted a series of measures to improve its relationship with the ethnic communities, including offering tuition subsidies to minority schoolchildren;[12] reducing taxes levied on mosques;[13] and providing better medical assistance to minorities in major cities, such as setting up Muslims' kitchens (Qingzhen zao) at hospitals to accommodate Muslim patients' dietary needs.[14] Guided tours were also arranged for minority leaders to visit cities such as Beijing and Shanghai, where they were sure to be impressed with modern urban life and their attitudes toward the CCP could be ferreted out. But the subsequent internal reports were unsettling. One such document cautioned, "They [the leaders] visited temples in Beijing, but they expressed doubts about the religious freedom [promised by the government]."[15]

Mao viewed the ethnic issues with utmost concern. He warned in November 1949, barely a month after the new republic was established, that "without a large number of Communist cadres drawn from minority nationalities, we cannot fundamentally solve the nationality problems and completely isolate ethnic reactionaries." In addition to training "a large number of minority cadres," he proposed establishing classes to educate Han people about ethnic issues in places such as Qinghai, Xinjiang, and Ningxia, where national minorities were concentrated.[16] A month earlier, the government had created the Nationalities Affairs Commission (Minzu shiwu weiyuanhui; NAC), currently the State Ethnic Affairs Commission, which oversaw minority affairs and mapped out strategies for improving relationships among various ethnic groups. In June 1951, the government also established the Central Institute for Nationalities, which had branches in many regions, to train specialists in ethnic affairs.[17] At the same time, local authorities were also instructed to assign a number of officials to work exclusively on minority affairs.[18]

June Dreyer rightly characterizes the PRC's ethnic policies in the early 1950s as exhibiting "moderation" and "flexibility," evident in the government's painstaking efforts to improve transportation in minority regions, eliminate derogatory place names, and, most significantly, grant legal equality to minorities.[19] Scholarly works on the government's strategies to win the hearts and minds of the ethnic minorities had until then focused mainly on legal, economic, and military methods. Another important but little explored tactic, however, was the construction of the Cultural Palace of Nationalities. Building the CPN revealed not only the government's obvious purpose of promoting its ethnic policies but also its undeclared contradictions. As mentioned, the Party allowed for a degree of regional autonomy while trying to exert tight control. It affirmed that all minorities were equal and yet pursued hard-line assimilationist measures. It granted religious freedom and yet implemented rules to limit religious practices. It proclaimed a basic respect for local traditions and yet demonstrated insensitivity to minority customs.

An Architectural Landmark

Perhaps nothing that the Party did to affirm the importance of the minorities was symbolically greater than to erect a grand building dedicated to them in the nation's capital. Such a structure would enhance the status of the minorities, affirm their rightful place as full-fledged, not marginal, members of the nation, and, most important from the standpoint of officials, demonstrate the government's genuine concern for their well-being.

Mao was credited as the first leader to propose erecting such a building. According to Zhang Ximing (1913–2007), a key official in charge of the construction of the CPN, Mao, in a 1951 Politburo meeting, suggested that "constructing a Cultural Palace of Nationalities will not only serve as a symbol of unity among various nationalities but also as an activity center for them."[20] However, Zhang Bo (1911–1999), the principal architect of the CPN, attributed the idea not to Mao but to the NAC, which recommended it the same year.[21] The original concept could even have been inspired by the Soviet Union. In the early days of the PRC, Chinese officials and scholars showed strong interest in Soviet museums.[22] In their repeated visits to Moscow and Leningrad (now St. Petersburg), they could not have failed to see the unique political role played by Soviet museums of ethnography, which propagandized the blissful relationships among the various ethnic groups that made up the Soviet Union. A notable example was the famed Museum of Ethnography in Leningrad, which became a model for the Chinese. Soviet influence was clearly apparent in borrowing the term "cultural palace" for the name of the CPN (see chapter 6).

Although the CPN project was first proposed in 1951, the dream took several years to realize. Serious planning did not begin until 1954, when Wang Feng

(1910–1998), vice chair of the NAC, requested tentative plans from Zhang Bo, chief architect at the Beijing Institute of Architectural Design and a student of renowned Tsinghua University architecture professor Liang Sicheng.[23] In September 1957, the NAC reiterated the urgent need to construct a building to serve as a place "to introduce the lifestyles of different minority nationalities through patriotic and internationalist education for the Chinese people."[24] Groundbreaking for the building was first scheduled for October 1, 1957, to commemorate the eighth anniversary of the founding of the PRC.[25] The schedule was delayed, however, because many hurdles had not been crossed, including setting on an ideal location, finalizing plans, and planning for relocating residents whose houses would have to be demolished.[26]

Several sites were proposed, including Taoranting Park, south of the city. But the NAC considered that area too far from the city center and worried that minority groups would deem the distance an affront.[27] Eventually, a spot was chosen near Xidan, west of Tiananmen Square, because of its central location in a bustling commercial district. The decision was clearly intended to send a strong signal to the minorities that they were not perceived as living at the periphery.

Zhang Bo and his team worked feverishly to develop several plans.[28] A tentative proposal was endorsed in an important NAC meeting held on September 25, 1957, chaired by Vice Premier Ulanhu (1906–1988), a Mongol Communist, and attended by Feng Jiping, the vice mayor of Beijing, along with Wang Feng, Zhang Ximing, and Zhang Bo. The central government formally approved the final plan in March 1958.[29] In the summer of 1958, when the CCP Politburo decided to build a number of major buildings—later known as the Ten Monumental Buildings, which, as noted, were to commemorate the tenth anniversary of the founding of the PRC in the following year—the CPN was incorporated into the plan as one of the ten. Full-scale construction work, however, did not actually begin until early October 1958.[30]

The CPN was officially opened in October 1959 and declared a great success. But because construction had to be rushed and completed in less than a year, poor building practices were the norm. Archival sources reveal that construction problems abounded, including shoddy electrical wiring and use of eroded reinforced concrete, which further delayed the project.[31] The hurried completion of the project plainly reflected the frenzied spirit of the Great Leap Forward, Mao's massive drive to rapidly transform China from an agrarian society into a highly industrialized nation. "This [poor construction] was brought about by the Great Leap Forward," one official claimed in an effort to fend off criticism, "[the building] was completed in just over nine months, [with workers] designing, assembling materials, and constructing it as [they] went along."[32]

When completed, nevertheless, the CPN was an imposing structure in the capital's landscape. With a floor space of 30,770 square meters, it is not the largest of the Ten Monumental Buildings,[33] but it exudes the most distinctive native air in the architectural style of the time, with a traditional north-south direction and a front gate facing south. The building complex, with its white exterior wall, has three sections: a central tower flanked by two lower wings. Seen in its entirety, the floor plan resembles the Chinese character that means "mountain" (*shan*). The thirteen-storied tower looms over neighboring buildings while joining harmoniously with the two horizontal wings. The overall design of the complex evokes reason and balance, exhibited by the parallel relationship between the grand auditorium in the east wing and the recreational hall in the west.

The central tower is visually arresting. Reaching a height of sixty-seven meters on a raised platform, it was one of the tallest structures in the city and thus a rarity in those days, even surpassing the height of Tiananmen Gate to its east in Tiananmen Square by thirty-three meters. The tower's elevation makes it appear to be perched majestically on a massive raised platform, commanding its surroundings. It has two segments, a rectangular sturdy lower section and a smaller upper extension, which is adorned with peacock-blue glazed tiles and capped by time-honored double-eaved roofs. At its crown is an observation deck, which, in the words of one Chinese commentator, was "designed specifically for visiting minorities so they can enjoy the scenery of the capital."[34] Visually, the layered formation appears to shrink upward, seemingly lifting the building up from the ground and lending it a superior presence. Viewers are invited to see the layered structure soaring upward from the base.

In designing the building, Zhang Bo drew inspiration from China's architectural past, particularly for conceiving the tower as a raised platform with curved roofs, and glazed tiles. He spoke with pride of putting a main tower on a weighty platform, giving it an indigenous feel. One was reminded, he said, of the Hall of Supreme Harmony in the former Forbidden City and the Temple of Heaven, as both sat on multilayered terraces with a height of more than ten meters.[35] The relationship between the tower and the building's two wings was one of command and subordination, the latter playing a supporting role. The spatial language that Zhang used was "height"; in his words, "height represents respect." In political monuments, tallness asserts authority and prestige, and it is also a way to overwhelm and intimidate.

The exterior of the building advertises the strong presence of the Party. Inscribed on the top of the front gate, in Mao's calligraphy, is "The Cultural Palace of Nationalities." Gracing the entryway are a pair of characters that mean "Unity" (*tuanjie*) and "Progress" (*jinbu*), which encompass the Party's ethnic stand. The

Party's influence also dominates the interior space, which is made up of six sections: a museum that houses five huge exhibition halls, a library, auditoriums, a dance hall, restaurants, and guestrooms.[36]

The central hall immediately behind the main gates conveys a buoyant sense of the promise of the new socialist regime. In the middle of the hall, a statue of Mao exudes authority. The decor is not particularly ornate, but mounted on the walls are four giant white marble reliefs with life-size figures of minority peoples. These sculptures, each representing one season, portray the life of the minorities in four locations. Living in a land of plenty, these minorities come from all walks of life: they are workers, peasants, and fishermen. All exhibit the honorable traits of industriousness, confidence, and devotion to the motherland. The boisterous scenes and festive spirit are intended to generate outpourings of patriotic fervor. They reveal, echoing the 1954 Constitution, a land in which "various nationalities in the big family of our motherland, under the leadership of the Party and Chairman Mao, are equal and united," as reported in the *People's Daily*. These artworks were the collective products of the Department of Sculpture at the Central Institute of Arts, which sent students and faculty to the minority regions to observe their lifestyles firsthand.[37] As propaganda pieces, they did not reflect the tumult of the Great Leap Forward but rather projected an image of paradise on earth.

Zhang Bo made navigating the interior of the building easier by positioning the three grand exhibition halls immediately to the north, east, and west of the central hall. Inscribed in marble on the front of the northern hall, the largest and most important, is Mao's exhortation, "Ethnic groups of China, Unite!"[38] Objects and artifacts were displayed in these three grand halls, as well as in a dozen smaller ones. Zhang Bo carefully knit these spacious rooms together so as to impart a sense of balance; for example, he made the grand auditorium on the east wing parallel in decor to the recreational hall on the west wing.

The CPN was not only a museum but also a gathering place for representatives of ethnic minority regions when they assembled in the capital for official events. It offered two dozen guestrooms. Like its counterparts in the Soviet Union, the CPN provided guests with recreational areas such as a gymnasium and a billiard room. A Muslim dining room was also installed. To accommodate the two most distinguished visitors from Tibet, the Dalai Lama and the Panchen Lama, the NAC requested two special rooms, accompanied by a lecture room, to be prepared on opposite sides of the tower. These two rooms had to be "on an equal footing," showing identical respect for the two religious leaders.[39]

The construction of the CPN was meant to strongly reinforce the CCP's authority, notwithstanding its avowed purpose of promoting unity among all nationalities. Officials constantly reminded the architects that their job was, fundamentally, a "political assignment" (*zhengzhi renwu*).[40] A 1959 official document advanced the Party's intent, declaring that the building was meant "to demonstrate that only under the leadership of the CCP can all nationalities cast off the yoke of the imperialist invasion and the domination of the domestic and foreign reactionary class."[41] Among other features of the CPN, the tower in particular "symbolizes a new spirit in which the various ethnic groups rally around the Party's Central Committee."[42] Here architecture and politics were closely interwoven.

Closely affiliated with the CPN, in spirit as well as political motivation, was the Nationality Hotel (Minzu fandian). Located immediately adjacent to the western side of the CPN, the Nationality Hotel, also designed by Zhang Bo, was another of the Ten Monumental Buildings constructed in 1959. The hotel, which had close to six hundred guestrooms and was equipped with a Muslim restaurant in addition to others, resembled the CPN in that it was erected to house ethnic minorities who visited the capital for political conventions.[43] That two of the Ten Monumental Buildings had the term "nationality" in their names indicates the enormous importance and sensitivity that the government attached to this issue.

Collecting Exhibition Materials

The CPN is primarily a national museum of ethnicity that displays a rich collection of cultural relics. Museums in the West have four key activities: collection, classification, display, and reception for the viewers. Among the four, museologists generally regard display, or what they commonly call the "strategies of display," as the most important feature of a museum.[44] The CPN, however, placed equal emphasis on display and collection. Clearly, they are intertwined. Display capability is based on what collections have been assembled in the first place, and the CPN museum collection strategy was dictated by CCP policies. Archival sources and internal government documents reveal a complicated picture of control and manipulation by Chinese Communists in assembling materials for exhibition. Officials wasted no time, even before construction began, in ordering what was needed for the exhibition halls.

On November 21, 1958, the State Council issued an important circular, "Artifacts and Books for the Exhibition at the Cultural Palace of Nationalities," outlining the general criteria for collecting artifacts:

> The main purpose of the museum and the library—the two key components of the Cultural Palace of Nationalities—is to spread the news about

the great victory of the Party's ethnic policies and the extraordinary results of its ethnicity projects in the last ten years. . . . . Through exhibited
objects and books, we educate various nationalities in matters of patriotism and internationalism in order to consolidate the unification of the
motherland, enhance the unity of the nationalities, and strengthen socialist education.[45]

The circular was sent to provinces with high concentrations of minorities, for
example, Heilongjiang, Yunnan, and Sichuan, as well as autonomous regions
such as the Xinjiang Uyghur Autonomous Region and the Ningxia Hui Autonomous Region.[46] The capital also played a leading role in this endeavor, specifically the municipal government's Bureau of Civil Affairs, which even suggested
that a vice mayor should be put in charge of the entire operation.[47] Other than
details about minority cadres,[48] little information is available about whether local ethnic minorities were involved. Overall, the operation was centrally directed, and the Party made a strong imprint on the content of the exhibits.

The State Council's circular identified a number of key exhibit materials to be
gathered in the minority regions. These were items related to the achievements
minorities had made during the period of socialist reconstruction in the new
regime: accomplishments in industry, agriculture, husbandry, and fishery; ad-
vancements in culture, education, and hygiene; the rise in their standard of living; and the production tools they used in everyday life.[49]

Targeted for collection were items related to the minorities' everyday lives, or
what the government called "production tools."[50] These were associated with the
laboring process of the minorities, and were, as the circular elaborated, "historical artifacts reflecting the diligence, courage, and great intelligence of the minority peoples as well as their history of revolutionary struggle."[51] Predictably, the
emphasis was on economic activities and culture of production, which was in
line with the Marxist assumption that labor played a determining role in shaping
the course of history. Here the minorities were viewed as workers laboring within
a specific economic system closely tied to the means of production. Utensils,
tools, costumes, and handicrafts, as well as musical instruments and folk songs,
were key items in the tapestry of their lives.

The items collected for display were not assembled to show the minorities'
aesthetic appreciation or to express their uninhibited feelings but, according to
the officials, to demonstrate their ways of experiencing the joy and hardship of
labor. Party officials never viewed the CPN as a repository of artistic mastery;
instead, they saw it as a museum documenting the lives of minorities. Not mentioned in the circular were religious items, given that Chinese Communists

viewed religion as a delusion and an impediment to production. The absence of such items directly reflected officials' uneasiness and suspicion on this issue. Although some religious scriptures and pamphlets were collected and exhibited later on, they were often labeled not as religious texts but rather as "rare books and records of the nationalities."[52]

Exhibiting the lives of the minorities was wrapped in the language of class, revolutionary struggle, and patriotism. Efforts were made to acquire "criminal evidence" of exploitation, such as land titles, indentured service, and pawned documents.[53] These records accentuated the social woes of a pre-1949 society suffering from widespread injustice and economic oppression. In the official literature, minority peoples had been victims squeezed by heartless landlords and oppressed by intrusive officials. In a memo issued by the Bureau of Civil Affairs, collectors were instructed to gather information on how "minority people were oppressed and discriminated against politically before Liberation."[54]

Minorities, nevertheless, were not regarded as merely hapless and passive victims. The Communists saw a constant struggle between the minorities and their oppressors, and so collectors were asked to find records of the minorities' "heroic resistance" against domination and discrimination. An example of such resistance was the famous Baisha Rebellion on Hainan Island in July 1943. The Li minority in Baisha County clashed with the Kuomintang, and though the insurrection was brutally suppressed, the rebels later joined the Communists in preparing future military action.[55]

Another guideline for collectors was to use the year 1949 as a divide to distinguish two worlds: the world before the Communist takeover and the world that followed. Collectors were asked to assemble evidence to "compare the living standards of minorities before and after Liberation, including increases in income and buying power, and the improvement of material life among minorities [after 1949]."[56] This historical dividing line was clearly political, because 1949, according to the official propaganda, marked a stark contrast between the present admirable Communist regime and the former corrupt Kuomintang government. In the case of Tibet, Chinese officials argued that the peasant serfs were liberated from the old oppressive religious and social system only after the Communists came to power.[57] This Manichean division between good and evil, liberation and oppression, selfless Communists and corrupt Nationalists, can be traced to the Yan'an era, when the tactic was first carefully cultivated. Later, collectors in Beijing were told to use Niujie (Oxen Street), where the Hui minority concentrated, as a case study to highlight the "enormous transformation after Liberation."[58]

The differentiation between new and old was sharpened by the even more important message that it was the CCP that provided the correct path for the people to follow. Government circulars stressed that the CCP alone had made possible these accomplishments in the minority regions. It was thus crucial, as officials insisted, to focus collection on "the revolutionary struggle of the minorities in their regions under the leadership of the CCP."[59] As a result, treasured items included newspapers, currencies, official seals, banners, slogans, leaflets, and pictorials highlighting the role of the Party in bringing peace and unity to a ruined country.[60] The Party described its historical orientation in the early 1950s as "stressing the importance of the present and slighting the past [houjin bogu]," which meant that CPN displays should not be about the past but should focus squarely on the present, namely, "the achievements of the last ten years since Liberation."[61]

Finally, collectors were instructed to follow the official line of major political campaigns in full swing at that time in China, meaning that the selected materials should be unmistakably about the "Great Leap Forward, the great developments, and the great unity after the Rectification Campaign and the Anti-Rightist Movement," as a State Council circular stated.[62] This included materials affirming the success of "socialist construction" in the minority territories, as well as evidence showing the increased number of mutual aid groups, the development of cooperatives, and the successful implementation of the People's Commune.[63]

If the construction of the CPN was, in effect, an announcement of the CCP's achievements, the collecting exercise was another way for the Party to tell the world what these achievements were about. In the CPN, the Party created a single space in which art and politics were inextricably intertwined. In his study of Soviet museums, Boris Groys argues that because of their totalitarian nature these museums created "a single, total visual space within which to efface the boundary separating art from life."[64] The Chinese used the CPN in much the same way that the Soviets used their cultural institutions, but, compared with the Soviets, the CCP wielded even more hegemonic control. Whereas the Union of Soviet Artists, as Groys argues, controlled the purchasing policies of Soviet museums,[65] the CCP directly controlled both the Chinese museums and the Chinese Writers Union, which could make no independent decisions whatsoever. In the Maoist aesthetic, no distinctions were made between art, life, and politics.

The First Exhibition

Despite my repeated attempts to find out how many objects were collected and what criteria were used to select those that were displayed in the CPN, contemporary staff at the CPN refused to disclose whether such archival information existed, or, if it did, whether outside researchers could have access to it.[66] Fortunately, archival sources about the CPN from the National Day Project Office (Guoqing gongcheng bangongshi), which the CCP established in 1958 to coordinate the construction of the Ten Monumental Buildings, are now accessible at the Beijing Municipal Archives. These documents allow scholars a glimpse into the internal processes of the establishment of the CPN. Relevant information at the Shanghai Municipal Archives on ethnic minority issues also sheds light on the CCP's general policies on minority nationalities. In addition, an important record known as the "Exhibition on Nationalities Work in the Past Ten Years" provides some details about items that were actually displayed in the CPN. The exhibits clearly, if inadvertently, revealed the contradictions in the Party's ethnic policies, including the gulf between political rhetoric and actual practice, the avoidance of sensitive issues such as religion, the downplaying of minority autonomy, and, finally, the pervasiveness of the Party's tight control at every turn.

Vice Premier Ulanhu and other dignitaries in attendance, the initial exhibition was inaugurated with fanfare on October 6, 1959, the same day the CPN was officially opened to the public, hence a double celebration with the tenth anniversary of the founding of the PRC.[67] Through charts, photographs, models, and illustrations, officials and museum staff attempted to paint a success story of the unity of nationalities in the new China.[68] The show was divided into three areas: a comprehensive hall, regional halls, and a special themes hall. The purpose of the Comprehensive Hall was not to address specific issues but to delineate Party lines and recite Mao's directive. It conveyed a panoramic view of the situation. The regional halls had fifteen exhibits on specific regions, including the Inner Mongolia Autonomous Region and the Xinjiang Uyghur Autonomous Region. The Special Themes Hall represented thirteen provinces and cities that were home to smaller minority groups.

The Comprehensive Hall undoubtedly was the heart of the exhibition, the venue where the Party spelled out its official policies and highlighted the achievements of socialist construction under the new regime. At the center of the hall was a huge banner inscribed with the familiar slogan of the Great Leap Forward, "Go all out, aim high, and achieve greater, faster, better, and more economical results in building socialism!," an indication that the current political campaign was in full swing. An official statement was also posted on the wall announcing that "the People's Republic of China is a vast socialist family in which all ethnic groups are equal, united, friendly, and cooperative." The statement was accompanied by a reminder that the constitution guaranteed equality to all nationalities. A chart showed that among 1,226 participants in the First National People's Congress held in Beijing in 1954, 178 (14.52 percent) were delegates from the minorities. Another chart showed that the minorities were only about 6 percent of China's population of 594 million in 1953, and therefore were fairly represented in the central government.[69] The establishment of autonomous regions was highlighted with commemorative photographs and press reports, a policy heralded as a wise and resounding success.

Occupying center stage were photographs of Chairman Mao, where he was often seen greeting minority leaders or surrounded by minority delegates who cheerfully attended the First National People's Congress. These photographs suggested unity among the various ethnic groups, all appearing under the same roof. An atmosphere of amity was also created with photos of senior Party officials who had been dispatched to minority regions such as Inner Mongolia and Tibet, confirming that the central government looked after ordinary minority people. At the same time, minority delegations arrived in Beijing, according to a photo caption, to "pay tribute to Chairman Mao."[70]

Rapid progress in industry and agriculture was the other main topic: the former was hailed as "advancing by leaps and bounds," and the latter said to be "enjoying bumper harvests."[71] In the Comprehensive Hall, the government constructed a myth of unfailing optimism, demanding an unwavering faith in a bright future under socialism.

Political pronouncements alone could not convey a feeling of immediacy and concreteness. The regional halls attempted to make these tangible through displays of artifacts and models. This part of the exhibition started with the Inner Mongolia Autonomous Region, the first such region to be established. They also encompassed other territories where large numbers of minorities were concentrated, including Heilongjiang, Yunnan, Qinghai, Guizhou, and the Xinjiang Uyghur Autonomous Region, the Ningxia Hui Autonomous Region, the Guangxi Tong Autonomous Region, and the Tibet Autonomous Region (which exhibit was only partially completed).

In these rooms, the contrast between the period before and after communism was made concrete and visual. For example, to demonstrate the sharp class differentiations in pre-1949 society, the gaudy, sumptuous costumes worn by the former elite were placed next to the tattered dresses of the commoners. "One side was poverty-stricken, whereas the other was dissipated and unashamed," the caption read. Comparisons between the rich and the poor went beyond dresses. Visitors were told that under socialism Yunnan minorities were able to overthrow the feudal lords, as did the Tibetans, who, with the Communists' help, eliminated the cruel serf system. Figures and statistics were used to show that the central government had given abundant economic aid and almost unlimited resources to all minority territories. A placard noted that it also helped to train "a large number of cadres that formed the core of the socialist reform and construction in the regions."[72]

Because of its strategic geographical location, Tibet drew considerable attention. Using more than two hundred photographs, thirty charts, and more than a hundred display objects, the organizers showed that Tibet had long been "an indivisible part of China." Stories of the Western powers' rapacious exploitation of the land were countered by reports of the Tibetans' "heroic anti-imperialist struggle." The effect was a boast that only after the PRC was established was Tibet "peacefully liberated" by Communist troops. The photographs and charts reminded viewers of "the arduous work done by the Party and the government in this region and the remarkable results accrued in the past eight years."[73]

As with the collection process, the displays followed closely the political campaigns in progress. The four major targeted goals of the Great Leap Forward—mechanization, electrification, irrigation, and fertilization—applied also to minority regions. An exhibit in the Xinjiang Uyghur Autonomous Regional Hall featured its newly developed petroleum industry. Although not specified in the show, this clearly referred to the Karamay oilfield, a site discovered in October 1955 in northern Xinjiang. A model of a drilling rig and samples of petroleum products in the Xinjiang room marked this exciting development. "A petroleum industry is gradually taking shape in our nation," the exhibit announced. The Xinjiang Production and Construction Corps, established in 1954, was also highlighted.[74] Organized with a military structure, this economic and paramilitary organization was designed to speed up agricultural and industrial development in this remote northwestern region. "By the autumn of 1954," according to the sinologist Colin Mackerras, "the Corps had over 200,000 members, more than 90 percent of them Han."[75]

Agricultural achievement was portrayed in the Ningxia Hui Autonomous Region Hall with a model of the Qingtongxia Dam and its irrigated areas, a major project begun in 1958 but not completed until 1978. In the Gansu Hall, posters and models declared that "in the Great Leap Forward of 1958, the minority regions in Gansu were all turned into People's Communes."[76] One placard stated that the People's Commune would "bring all ethnic groups a boundless happy future."[77] The Special Themes Hall, smaller in scale, emphasized the "close friendship that developed between scattered ethnic groups and the Han."[78]

The entire exhibition can be summarized by this statement posted in the Comprehensive Hall: "In the last ten years, all ethnic groups in the nation experienced the greatest social transformation in history. The overwhelming majority of them were liberated from the old feudal system."[79]

The Missing Elements

Since the end of the eighteenth century, and especially in the twentieth, Western museums have been hotly contested battlegrounds.[80] Although no longer supporting the aims of princes or wealthy patrons, modern museums exist within specific social circumstances and invoke particular communal values. Hence they are subject to competing interests and diverse constituencies. Exhibition culture reflects prevailing domestic and international policies and values of government as well as the influence of corporate sponsors, philanthropic organizations, and business tycoons. The artist Hans Haacke even goes as far as to argue that "every museum is perforce a political institution, no matter whether it is privately run or maintained and supervised by governmental agencies."[81] In Haacke's words, art exhibitions in the museums are "inevitably imbued with ideological significations."[82] Carol Duncan echoes this when she asserts that art museums are in fact ritual structures and ideological sites, places where "politically organized and socially institutionalized power most avidly seeks to realize its desire to appear as beautiful, natural, and legitimate."[83] Granted that Western museums are under the inevitable sway of political organizations and influenced by special interest groups, they nonetheless operate in a complex, pluralistic environment; consequently, museums' values and agendas can be challenged, debated, or even rebuked. Museums often become sites of contested interests and memories. In other words, no single, all-embracing value system can be imposed on modern Western museums. Modern museums are not, to borrow museologist Duncan Cameron's terminology, "temples," but instead "forums," where different voices are heard and argued.[84]

In China, however, state museums have one primary purpose: to serve the interests of the CCP. The CPN was not meant to be a public museum in the Western sense of the word. It was instead a state-run institution with a clear political agenda. The CPN's exhibition halls were highly controlled spaces where displayed objects told stories selected to justify Communist rule. The CPN, therefore, was not a forum but indeed a temple that celebrated the CCP's achievements in ethnic affairs.

Official media painted a picture of the CPN enjoying a warm public reception.[85] But because independent sources are unavailable, this must be read with caution. As primarily part of a sanctified temple, the exhibits disclosed little about the enormous diversity in the ethnic territories, portraying the glories and promises of these territories in an unbelievably rosy light. The deeper significance of the displays was in fact not so much in what was presented as in what was missing. These missing elements accentuate the nature and the predicament of the CCP's ethnic policies.

One important missing element was religion. Although religious items associated with the ethnic groups were not targeted for collection, they were nonetheless mentioned in the exhibit, but in a more or less negative light. For example, in the Tibetan Hall, religion was directly linked with serfs and the traditional estate system. The anthropologist Melvyn Goldstein argues that, indeed, lamas, monasteries, and government officials who were monks "derived their income overwhelmingly" from the estate system in which "hereditarily bound peasants worked their fields without pay, as corvée tax obligations."[86] Given this exclusive focus, displayed items did not touch on the Buddhist faith and spirituality that had profoundly influenced the lives of Tibetans. Nor did it portray positive images of Islam in the Xinjiang Hall.

The Xinjiang Production and Construction Corps did work for the economic betterment of the region. It also, however, acted as a vigilant military agency with a purpose of deterring domestic or international trouble. The situation in Xinjiang was complex, given strong separatist tendencies and foreign (mostly Soviet) interests there. The presence of an armed force underscored Beijing's dilemma in granting the region a large degree of autonomy while ensuring that the territory did not go astray. The ambivalent nature of the corps and conflicts between the region and the central government were not addressed in the exhibition.

Closely linked to the Construction Corps was the important problem of internal migration, which the exhibition also did not address. Of the five autonomous regions, Xinjiang experienced the largest Han migration in the first decade of the PRC. According to Mackerras, in 1953 the Han made up only 6.94 percent of the total 4.78 million in Xinjiang, but by 1964 had increased to 31.93 percent (2.32 million), relative to 54.91 percent (3.99 million) of Uyghurs.[87] This huge influx of Han Chinese had strong implications for assimilating minorities into the PRC, given that it was the government's pragmatic way of extending its control in a faraway land. The contradiction between assimilation and promised regional autonomy was overlooked in the exhibit.

Heavily emphasized in the exhibition was the central government's massive economic aid to the minority regions, which brought new schools, railways, and improved medical facilities. "Prosperity appears in every corner," a report in the Gansu section proudly announced.[88] The exhibition offered no opportunities for local voices to comment on whether the new facilities and economic ventures were sensitive to their minority cultures or whether the arrival of Han immigrants and modern enterprises diluted regional minority identities.

The exhibition, of course, did not reveal how the party-state operated behind the scenes to develop and maintain tight institutional control. For instance, in an important document issued by the Ethnic Affairs Committee of the East China Bureau in November 1953, and approved by the central authorities in Beijing, the CCP named three things that local governments had to strictly observe in dealing with Hui organizations: First, no local branches of ethnic associations could be established. China's Islam Association and the Hui Cultural Association at the capital would be the sole representatives overseeing ethnic affairs. This ensured that control would be exercised at the top. Second, local Hui organizations could only be formed when ethnic Communist cadres were the key components. Once formed, they "must be under the direction of the local government." Finally, those Hui groups already in existence had to "work under the leadership of the local government in order to prevent them from adopting a laissez-faire attitude that [if that occurred] would disadvantage [national minority] efforts."[89] The CCP prized consolidation of its power and the achievement of stability above all else in this early phase of its rule. The CPN and its exhibitions were a text carefully scripted by the Party for its purpose. What was absent in these displays were the genuine reactions of ethnic groups and their actual social, economic, and cultural conditions.

From its beginnings, the CPN was an incongruous mixture of grand architectural design, chronicle of national minorities, and exhibition center of ethnic achievements under socialism, with the overall goal of expounding the party-state policy of ethnic harmony. When I interviewed Zhang Bo, the principal architect of the CPN, in December 1994, he spoke with pride about his masterpiece. "This building project," he said, was, like the other nine of the Ten Monumental Buildings, constructed as a "political demand" (*zhengzhi yaoqiu*) from the top. It was built to celebrate the tenth anniversary of the founding of the PRC.[90] At a height of sixty-seven meters, it was one of the tallest buildings in the capital at the time and could be seen from everywhere. For Chinese Communists, the building represented the magnificent manifestation of the supremacy of the Party as well as a fruitful encounter between art and politics.

The CPN was also given a special assignment by the CCP to articulate the Party's ethnic policies. Zhang Bo, in the interview, underscored the symbolic meaning assigned to it by the Communist leaders. It was specifically designed to symbolize "the great unity of all nationalities."[91] The Nationality Hotel, situated immediate west of the CPN, reinforced the Party's respect for ethnic minorities.

The two buildings indicated that the Party gave topmost importance to ethnic minorities.

The CPN is also a political museum. As discussed, no museum, not even an art museum, is completely free of expressing a point of view, for all are cultural institutions possessing many contradictions.[92] One of these contradictions, as many art historians argue, is that between art, which is associated with pleasure and aesthetic appreciation, and artifact, which connotes instruction of its audience.[93] The Louvre is a case in point. When the Louvre was transformed from a royal palace into a public museum in 1793, the painter Jacques-Louis David was quick to suggest that it should be turned into "an imposing school" to educate people about Republican ideals.[94] But the ideological underpinnings of these Western public museums are not always imposing and confining. More important, museumgoers are not passive when they visit Western museums. They arrive with their own minds and freely interpret what they see. The relationship between the visitor and the museum is therefore negotiated, never one-dimensional. The CPN, as a government museum of national minorities, operates on a different principle: it enforces a single narrative expressing the Party line. Here, art rarely exists outside politics; aesthetic appreciation for its own sake is discouraged. The mission of the museum, as clearly spelled out in the 1958 official document "Artifacts and Books for the Exhibition at the Cultural Palace of Nationalities" mentioned earlier, was to "propagate the great victory of the Party's ethnic policies" through carefully chosen artifacts, charts, paintings, and photographs. Thus the CPN constructed an approved history of the ethnic minority regions under the guidance of the party-state.

This strategy of display was not static but instead continuously revised to reflect the reality of the Party's changing policies. After the market reforms that began in the late 1970s, exhibitions continued to underscore economic and social achievements in ethnic minority regions, but they reduced the Maoist-era rhetoric of class struggle and revolution. In 1981, for example, the CPN put on the highly publicized "Exhibition on Social and Historical Conditions in Tibet."[95] Exhibits on cultural and economic advances made by ethnic minorities, including those of the Yao and Yi, were also mounted. The items included in these exhibits were carefully selected from the CPN's vast ethnic collection of more than fifty thousand objects, the most held in one place in China.[96]

In September 1994, the staff organized a permanent display of three major topics of the ethnic minorities—apparel, musical instruments, and arts and crafts in five exhibition halls.[97] The overall theme is not about ethnic diversities and particularities but about interactions between the ethnic groups and a shared history. Whenever images of ethnic diversity were presented, they were, as Kirk

Denton points out, intended to "promote the imagination of a polity unified by a shared political ideology."[98] Such a strategy, as Marzia Varutti notes, extends to other ethnic museums in China as well, as in the case of the Museum of the Southwest University for Nationalities in Chengdu, Sichuan Province.[99] The CPN continues to reinforce the two long-standing ethnic stands of the Party: "Unity" and "Progress," the pair of characters displayed on the entryway of the CPN. Deep down, the museum affirms China as a multiethnic homeland where fifty-six groups live happily under the same roof.

Finally, the construction of the CPN in the late 1950s represented China's rapid rise in reclaiming its national greatness. After 1949, the CCP developed a national narrative that highlighted the country's past, since the late Qing dynasty, as a victim of foreign aggression. It also underscored that only the CCP—not the corrupt and inept pro-American KMT—could bring independence and peace to a land long devastated by imperialist invasions and domestic upheavals. In my interview with Zhang Bo, he emphasized that Chinese architects were more than qualified to construct a major building such as the CPN and to complete it within the time mandated by the Party. "Otherwise, the Chinese people could never raise their heads [tai buqi toulai]," he said.[100] Zhang's remark echoed Mao's famous saying, "The Chinese people have stood up!" spoken on the eve of the founding of the PRC.[101] Nationalistic fervor thus was the driving force behind the construction of the CPN (and other major buildings), much more than Marxist rhetoric. That the building was constructed in the traditional Han Chinese style (not a Soviet replica) and by a native architect (not a foreign expert) swelled national pride. It was tantamount to China's declaration of national independence at a time of increasingly strained relations between Beijing and Moscow in the late 1950s.

Indeed, the creation of the CPN encompassed the many contradictions the CCP faced in governing a vast land with myriad traditions. The contradictions included equality of ethnic groups versus domination by the Han majority, the government's promise of autonomy to ethnic groups versus its assimilative policy, freedom of religion versus an inherently negative attitude toward spiritual practices, and respect for local cultures versus tight control over independent social organizations. Physically, the Han-style architecture of the building raised doubts about whether the museum could truly represent the spirit of the many ethnic groups.

The building has experienced a number of changes over time. In the early 1960s and during the Cultural Revolution, when conflicts between Maoist radicals and moderate reformers associated with Liu Shaoqi escalated, the Maoists turned the CPN into a stage for "anti-imperialist" demonstrations and attacks against "modern revisionists."[102] In the 1980s, when China under the leadership of Deng Xiaoping was undergoing brisk economic reform, the CPN took on a new role. In addition to mounting its usual exhibitions, it also (like other state-run enterprises) sought creative commercial ways to sustain its regular operations.[103] In 1981, with the approval of the NAC, the CPN formed a company to host independent exhibitions.[104] The website of the Cultural Palace of Nationalities states that it "can provide exhibition space and equipment rental to all sectors of society to undertake a variety of exhibitions and help organizing [sic] side events, such as press conferences."[105] A number of companies took the opportunity to use this landmark building to market their products. In August 1988, for instance, a large sports products show was held. In June 1994, a camera equipment display drew large crowds.[106] These commercial enterprises seem incongruous with the serious political intent the CPN has traditionally represented. Capitalist ventures and Communist politics are indeed strange bedfellows in China.

It would be a mistake, however, to think that the political color of this iconic building has faded. The government designated March 28, 2009, as Serf Liberation Day in commemoration of the fiftieth anniversary of the takeover of Tibet. A major show titled "The Fiftieth Anniversary of Democratic Reform in Tibet" was launched on that date and given extensive publicity. That the nine Politburo members, including President Hu Jintao, separately visited the exhibition immediately prior to the opening indicates the uppermost importance the Party attached to it.[107] The CPN continues to serve as the logical platform for the government to announce new ethnic policies to the public. But, in light of the disturbances in Tibet in March 2008, in Xinjiang in July 2009, and the sending of one million Muslims in Xinjiang to reeducation camps in 2019, ethnic issues remain a volatile problem for the CCP. The contradictions embodied in the CPN make it clear that the nation's ethnic problems will not go away any time soon. The CCP is acutely aware that if it mismanages this difficult situation, the minority regions could easily erupt into chaos.

Conclusion

When the People's Liberation Army took control of Beiping in late January 1949, the Chinese Communists carefully projected themselves as not only military victors but also, and above all, as peace restorers and cultural protectors of the country. The founding of the People's Republic a few months later, in October 1949, inspired euphoric hope among the public. Many credited Mao Zedong and senior Communist leaders with restoring peace and establishing independence for their nation, a land long plagued by foreign incursions and domestic turmoil. The prevailing sentiment was a wish for the ruinous civil war between the Nationalists and the Communists to end quickly so that people could resume normal lives. They had high expectations for the Chinese Communist Party (CCP), which, unlike the corrupt and ineffective Kuomintang (KMT), was trying to look after the well-being of ordinary people. But for intellectuals such as Liang Sicheng, the establishment of a new regime meant something even more important: it marked the beginning of a long-awaited national cultural rejuvenation. He was soon disappointed, however, as the CCP quickly showed itself to be not a cultural protector but a cultural controller. Liang was soon criticized for his advocacy of traditional Chinese architectural style.

The beginning years of the PRC, from 1949 to 1953, are generally regarded by scholars as a transitional period, involving a gradual process of consolidation of power by the Communists. Guided by Mao's theory of establishing a "people's democratic dictatorship," the CCP first sought a united front with other political parties and promised freedom of thought, speech, publication, assembly, and religious belief, as stated in the interim constitution known as the Common Program.[1] This made the new regime appear both domestically and internationally democratic and accommodating rather than radically Marxist. In this book, I have argued that rather than moving gradually, the Party actually moved swiftly right after seizing power to consolidate its rule by controlling cultural activities and people's minds. The new state sought to expand its power over people's lives. From the outset of their struggle, Mao and his senior associates realized that creating a communist state required not only building a stable government in an independent nation but also, and at least as important, creating a new socialist culture. This new socialist state would need to be anchored on a permanent cultural foundation. This end was accomplished not only by persuasion and teaching but also by indoctrination and coercion.

Immediately after their military takeover, the Communists began to take control of the media through censorship, mass mobilization campaigns against certain publications, and restructuring the old media and cultural institutions. Through a number of venues, such as book publishing, newspapers, religious groups, community cultural centers, kindergarten education, public parks, and architectural style, the CCP instituted and maintained control over citizens' cultural lives. This control was important for promoting the Party's aims and making it possible to rule the nation. The Party's success cannot be attributed to any one factor, but I consider the following four the most essential for accomplishing their agenda: developing specific policies and procedures of control in the 1950s, building tight organizations, establishing a pervasive censorship system, and creating an all-encompassing propaganda network.

Control Methods Developed in the Early PRC

The CCP's cultural control methods are best understood historically. The basic patterns took shape during the Yan'an era. They evolved into a systematic pattern of policies and rules once a legitimate government, with its abundant resources and personnel, was established. The Communists acted quickly and forcefully in the early 1950s to restore order by eliminating landlords and redistributing land, while mounting mass mobilizations such as the Three-Antis and Five-Antis Campaigns of 1951–1952. The outbreak of the Korean War in June 1950 intensified the process of internal consolidation. Through the nationwide Resist America, Aid Korea Campaign, the party-state extended its influence to almost every sphere of public life.

Inspired by the Soviets and drawing from their own experience in Yan'an, Chinese Communist leaders realized that culture was too important (and dangerous) an arena to be ignored even while they were pursuing social reconstruction. They believed that they urgently needed to train a new generation of men and women through cultural means. Mao's "cultural army," mentioned in his Yan'an Talks, thus carried the task of more than merely "uniting our own ranks and defeating the enemy." It needed to transform people into willing supporters of the new socialist regime.

Basic policies and essential procedures were formulated during this early period, primarily through centralization, institutionalization, and coercion. In the cultural arena, the Communists closed down the KMT press, launched their own official media, closed churches with suspected foreign connections, arrested members of popular religious groups deemed subversive to the regime, engaged in massive Han migration to ethnic minority regions, and built museums to showcase the Party's achievements. These methods of cultural control changed overtime, but many continue to have relevance today, especially in the area of news and book censorship.

Organization

Political control was achieved through having an integrated organizational structure established by the CCP along Leninist lines. The Party with its strict organization was a far cry from the fragmented Kuomintang; Mao and his senior comrades were able to effectively exercise power from the top.

Tight organization required an efficient bureaucracy. Like the Soviets, the CCP built its strength by creating an army of loyal bureaucrats who functioned under a set of strict rules: political allegiance, centralization of supervision, differentiation of functions, clear chain of command, and secrecy. In book publishing, the three-tiered network of control—the Propaganda Department of the CCP Central Committee, the General Administration of Publications (GAP) under the State Council, and the Press and Publications Office of the Beijing Municipal Government (BPPO)—provided a multilayered check on publications and saw to it that prescribed procedures were closely followed. A tightly structured start-to-end process from manuscript submission to evaluation, editing, printing, and distribution in the book market was put in force. The GAP and BPPO ensured that no undesirable texts would enter the open market and that the approved books would help spread the socialist cause. At the municipal level, a three-tiered apparatus of cultural centers, cultural stations, and village clubs followed the same principle of coordination and control. This development of layered Party organizational structures constituted one of the most formidable achievements of the authoritarian state.

The emphasis on organization was not without its problems. The overlapping levels of command and control caused confusion in practice and gave rise to conflicts at various levels. In the case of cultural centers, many of them were hastily created, especially in the villages. Others did not function effectively due to poor leadership, lack of resources, unclear instructions from the top, and shortage of staff.

An organization can be eroded in a multitude of ways. In the 1950s, continuous political instability was one. Bureaucrats often worried about their job security or political future because they were required to undergo continuous loyalty assessment by their superiors. Mao's idea of "uniting our own ranks" involved not only unifying thought but also purging Party members considered unreliable. Because of the danger of counterrevolution, it was necessary to ferret out spies, enemies, and opposition forces hiding in the dark or concealing themselves in Party ranks. Rectification of thought had been a routine practice ever since the Yan'an era, but intensified during the formative era of the PRC. The continuous screening was commonly known as "cleaning up" (*qingli*). Beijing Mayor Peng Zhen sounded an alert in 1951 when he wrote, "Why do we have to clean up our ranks? It's because they are very complicated."[2] Continuous expulsions of suspect Party members became necessary to prevent infiltration by class enemies. A case in point was the successive dismissal of a number of staff members of the *Beijing Daily* who were said to be hiding their landlord or KMT backgrounds. The expulsions created anxiety and fear in the publication's ranks. Later, and even worse, when political doctrines were in flux in the 1960s because of political infightings at the top, the future of individual bureaucrats became precarious.

Notwithstanding these problems, the top-down Party organizational structure did result in an efficient system of discipline and order, two of the most essential ingredients for a strong organization. Cultural centers established after 1949 proved far more stable than their predecessors, the poorly coordinated and underfunded popular education centers of the KMT.

Censorship

Censorship was and is another effective Party weapon. Censorship epitomizes the conflict between the power of the state and the rights of its citizens. It also manifests the contest between control and creation. Ultimately, however, the authoritarian state wields tremendous power over what a citizen can or cannot read or write. Censorship is also an essential component of the state's monopoly on mass communications. Lenin valued censorship as a necessary tool when he shut down bourgeois newspapers immediately after the Bolsheviks took power in 1917. "To tolerate these newspapers would mean not to be a socialist," he said.[3] In Soviet-occupied Germany after World War II, authorities discovered that the biggest problem they faced was the lack of an apparatus to censor the Germans, and therefore hurriedly created a censorship agency.[4] Chinese Communists' censorship began with Mao's Yan'an Talks, which stipulated that intellectuals and artists must follow the mass line in Communist-controlled base areas. This policy became further institutionalized and legitimized when the Culture Takeover Committee (CTC) was created in January 1949 under the direction of the Beiping Military Control Commission (BMCC).

The sheer speed with which the Communists took over the print industry (books and periodicals), other media, and universities was astonishing. The CTC dismantled age-old cultural standards and replaced them with new ones. In April 1949, for example, Derk Bodde, a young American Fulbright scholar studying in Beiping, recorded in his diary his experience of the Communists' early efforts at "thought control":

> In the field of art, the Cultural Control Committee [Culture Takeover Committee] has banned the performance of fifty-seven plays belonging to the traditional repertory. Included are 23 plays that are superstitious; 14, licentious; 4, derogatory to national dignity owing to the prominence given in them to acts of foreign aggression (invasions of the Huns, Mongols, etc.); 4, catering to a "slave morality"; 5, upholding feudalistic oppression; 7, "extremely boring" or lacking a definite scenario.[5]

By mid-1949, a few months before the official founding of the PRC, the BMCC declared the occupation a big success. In the ensuing years, censorship continued unabated, even intensified. For instance, the publication and media industry virtually eliminated non-Party publications in the sensitive areas of religion and ethnicity. At the BPPO, censors vetted religious and national minority books with extreme care, basing their decisions on whether they were in line with state policies. Titles by authors who were cheerleaders of the new regime, however, were easily approved. In 1953, the Nationalities Press was established after the encouragement of Zhou Enlai to publish books that promoted harmony among all ethnic groups.[6] The same theme was also fully manifested in the construction of the Cultural Palace of Nationalities to celebrate the tenth anniversary of the founding of the PRC.

Censorship in Maoist China was a complex process that was not merely a limiting of expression of public opinions or prohibiting intellectual exchanges. As we have seen, it also involved a tense relationship between censors and authors. Censors were eager to produce a set of rules, which were only vaguely known to the public and constantly changing, to facilitate their work and justify their decisions; meanwhile, authors warily wove their way around and through the rules in order to have their work published. The career of a censor was not a smooth one in the 1950s. If a censor failed to spot hidden subversive meanings in a text, the consequences could be serious. As discussed in chapter 2, editors and writers at the *Beijing Daily* became embroiled, willingly or unwillingly, in top Party leaders' infighting about the proper course of socialism. This led to the newspaper's self-censorship as an act of self-preservation.

Today, censorship continues to be strictly enforced by the CCP. China is not the only communist state that prohibits undesirable printed and electronic media material. North Korea and Vietnam do so as well.[7] What has often been overlooked, though, is that freedom of the press is under assault in many non-communist countries as well. A Western-style free press does exist in Malaysia, Singapore, and the Philippines, but is heavily monitored.[8] In these countries, swarms of censors routinely erase articles critical of their governments, and, as one journalism scholar points out, "a sophisticated combination of legislation and ownership concentration ensured the media remained under control."[9] What distinguishes China from others, however, is that state intervention in the literary realm goes beyond newspapers, books, and television; it extends to almost all cultural arenas, including religion, parks, and museums. The Party's control of people's cultural lives can be said to be total. Among the world's twenty largest economies, China is the only one that enshrines single-party rule at the heart of its constitution. When a party wields almost unlimited power, it can assert authority over almost everything.

Propaganda

Propaganda accompanied the Chinese Communists' consolidation of power every step of the way. The effectiveness of propaganda lies in its basic strategies: promoting a cause, telling partial truths, simplifying complex issues, and playing on emotions. The sociologist Jacques Ellul adds another ingredient: repetition. Ellul writes that propaganda is "based on slow, constant impregnation. It creates convictions and compliance through imperceptible influences that are effective only by continuous repetition."[10]

All governments produce propaganda, and in large quantity. The major difference between that of an authoritarian government and a democratic one is that the former manufactures propaganda in a closed setting, imposing it on its population unilaterally and dictatorially. The situation is especially complicated in China. The Chinese term xuanchuan (propaganda) also carries a benign connotation. Xuanchuan is not what the West understands by propaganda as a rigid indoctrination of ideas or manipulation of policies. In China it is sometimes interpreted as a positive way of imparting certain points of view to its intended audience. This more positive implication makes CCP propaganda more complicated and its impact more pervasive. It suggests that propaganda is not only communicating information based on the leader's will but also imparting it for a good cause.

Chinese Communists, like their Soviet counterparts, were ingenious propagandists. Mao was a master propagandist. As mentioned, he observed as early as

1927 that slogans and cartoons had a wide impact on the peasants. This aware-ness led to creating a policy reality in the 1940s when Yan'an artists, especially those trained at the Lu Xun Academy of Art (Lu Xun yishu xueyuan) were in-structed to create new *yangge* plays and reformed New Year prints with socialist contents to denounce the Nationalists and the Japanese. These new artistic forms drew heavily from China's folk traditions and were both easily recognizable and well liked. They proved effective as propaganda tools.[11] The use of *yangge* and graphic art by cultural center staff in the 1950s no doubt was following in the steps of this trend.

In the anti-Yiguandao campaign, we see a different kind of propaganda be-ing put to use. Here, the Communists used mass mobilization to arouse public animosity against what they saw as an evil cult. In this instance, state media, public trials, films, and exhibitions were all employed. Among them, public tri-als drew the most attention. Similar to those in Stalin's Russia in the 1930s, the trial of the leaders of popular religious groups, especially Yiguandao, were or-ganized as theatrical performances for a broad audience.[12] The purpose was not only to demonstrate the crimes of the accused but also to expose the heinous nature of the group the person belonged to. A son's public denunciation of his father for associating with a popular religious sect was especially sensational. Such an open denunciation incorporated the element of suspense and enter-tainment to increase public interest (hence maximum impact). Moreover, be-cause such presentations were publicized as being legal proceedings, the verdicts had added power. Most important, a young accuser, symbolizing self-sacrifice, youthful courage, and the resolve to challenge a dark social force, represented the new socialist man who recognized his highest duty as being toward the state. These tools were designed to elicit the enthusiastic support of the people in whose name the party-state ruled. Mass mobilization aroused mass excite-ment, and the agitated populace became eager supporters of the state's agendas.

Most potent among the Chinese Communists' propaganda tools were the news outlets given that they reached a far-flung audience. The *People's Daily* and the *Beijing Daily* were the best-known weapons in the media campaign. Chinese leadership continues to put a high premium on news media propaganda in an era of electronic communications. On the morning of February 19, 2016, President Xi Jinping made a whirlwind trip—or what Chinese officials called a "research tour" (*diaoyan*)—to the headquarters of the three state-run flagship news organi-zations: the *People's Daily,* the New China News Agency, and the China Central Television (CCTV).[13] CCTV staff extended a warm welcome to Xi by posting the following words on a digital screen in the hall: "The family name of the CCTV is 'the Party.' We are absolutely loyal to the Party. Please inspect us."[14] At all three stops, Xi told the adoring media staff gathered around him, in unequivocal language,

> All news media run by the Party must work to speak for the Party's will and its propositions[,] and protect the Party's authority and unity. . . . The mission of the Party's media work is to provide guidance for the public, serve the country's overall interests, unite the general public, instill confidence and pool strength, tell right from wrong and connect China to the world.[15]

At CCTV headquarters, Xi even made a videoconference call to the station's Washington-based North America outlet, remarking to its staff, "I see that your team is an international team. I hope you can explain developments in the Chinese economy and society objectively, truthfully and comprehensively. We have to tell China's stories, promote Chinese culture and build bridges of friendship where you are."[16] Xi's statements insist on two mutually contradictory obligations for the staff, both at home and abroad: to report objectively and truthfully about domestic and international events, on the one hand, and to carry out propaganda and promote the CCP's agendas, on the other. Clearly, in the minds of top Communist leaders, "China's stories" cannot be told randomly or freely; they must be scripted by the CCP. Xi's visits indicate the urgency that he saw for using official media to paint a glowing picture of China's future at a time when the nation's economic growth was slowing down and social inequality was widening.

China's propaganda has gone global since the early 2000s. The creation of the government-funded Confucius Institute in 2004 (affiliated with the Ministry of Education), which teaches Chinese language, history, and culture courses in foreign educational institutions, projects Chinese Communists' "soft power" (borrowing a term from the political scientist Joseph Nye) worldwide.[17] These branches of the Confucius Institute, which today can be found on every continent, offer a seemingly innocuous opportunity for Beijing leaders to advance China's image as a peace-loving country, intent on working harmoniously and cooperatively with countries everywhere.[18] This initiative, however, has been met with suspicion by some foreign educators as a propaganda agency. In fact, Li Changchun (b. 1944), a high Party official, admitted in 2014 that the institutes are "an important part of China's overseas propaganda set-up."[19] It is ironic to see that Confucius, China's sixth-century BCE philosopher, who was vilified during the Maoist era as a pillar of China's feudal monarchy and society,[20] is now being honored with a cultural institute that bears his name and with an enormous statue in Tiananmen Square.[21]

The launching of the One Belt, One Road Initiative (now officially called Belt and Road Initiative) by Xi Jinping in 2013 can be read as another global propaganda drive to buttress China's image as a benevolent, rising world power.[22] The initiative is highly promoted by the Chinese government as an economic bridge to the west. It proposes to build ports, highways, and cross-border infrastructure projects (such as railways) to enrich both China's economy and its sixty plus trading partners in Central Asia, the Middle East, Europe, and Africa. Such an ambitious initiative has raised skepticism among critics, first, in regard to China's ability to raise the required $8 trillion to bring it to fruition, and, second, because establishing stable collaboration with so many countries, many of which are in political dispute with one another, is extremely difficult. Above all, many doubt China's real motives behind this plan. Is China's goal for mutual benefits, or to enhance its partners' economic dependence on Beijing, thereby bolstering Beijing's geostrategic position? Others question the moral problem of nations collaborating with a country that has a long history of human rights abuses.

Impact

Beginning in 1949, the CCP spent considerable time and energy building a network of cultural control of the Chinese people. To what extent was it effective, and did it change the course of China's cultural history? These questions are hard to answer because it is inherently difficult to assess the influence of a cultural policy that is intermingled with other government programs, including political campaigns and social and economic plans. Thanks to the partial opening up of some Chinese archives, we now know more about the thinking of the CCP's planners. But many archives remain closed to the public, especially those deemed sensitive (such as those concerning religion and ethnicity). Furthermore, government sources (such as decrees, public announcements, official reports) provide only a partial, and often misleading, picture of what actually transpired at the lower levels. The government's characteristically glowing reports must be read with caution. Finally, it is challenging to assess the thoughts of the people who were at the receiving end of policies as most of them were illiterate and left few written records. One rare find concerns readers' letters sent to the *Beijing Daily*. An archival source indicates that among the 18,492 letters received in 1959, the editors answered about 52 percent, and about 1 percent were published.[23] This source is, nevertheless, still far from perfect because the newspaper's files at the Beijing Municipal Archives hold only simple statistics, not the actual letters. We have yet to hear the full authentic voices of these readers.

Imperfect as they are, the materials I have been able to assemble shed considerable light on the question of the impact of the CCP's cultural policies. The government did achieve considerable success in some areas. For example, the ruthless campaign against Yiguandao dealt a crashing blow to all popular religious sects. By the end of the Zhenfan campaign in 1953, officials had imprisoned the sect's leaders, confiscated their property, and declared their gatherings illegal. In book publishing, bureaucrats eventually took over the entire publishing industry, enforcing strict printing guidelines and monitoring distribution channels. Although uncertainties existed for some time in regard to the private publishing houses, by early 1956 the problem was resolved when the government managed to get them under control.[24] Control of book publishing soon extended to control of all free expression and writing. This was the result of the Anti-Rightist Campaign of 1957 that purged intellectuals and politicians (such as Democratic League members) who held views contrary to those of the CCP. Liang Sicheng's passionate championing of traditional Chinese-style architecture landed him in trouble and the authorities criticizing him for endorsing "traditional revivalism" and indulging in "wastefulness" at a time of scarce national resources. The architect was forced to confess that he had committed serious errors in his work.[25]

Other areas are harder to gauge. For example, we know very little about what happened when museumgoers visited the Cultural Palace of Nationalities. Surveys and statistics are not available, and no one knows what went on in visitors' minds when they saw photographs of Mao greeting minority leaders who were cheerfully attending the First National People's Congress in 1954.

The question of impact can be examined from another angle. Officials who drew up plans could be frustrated when trying to put them into practice. Archival sources reveal a complex situation behind the scenes: censors' uneven standards in vetting books, supervisors' complaints about the shortage of qualified personnel, and kindergarten teachers' failure to adjust quickly to the new socialist curriculum. Cultural center staff were often frustrated with book borrowers more interested in popular magazines and comic books than political pamphlets. These disappointments were often recorded in their reports—realistic feedback that never appeared in print.

Despite all these imperfections, the Communists' cultural policy certainly made a big impact on people's lives, not so much by telling them what to do, but by dictating what not to do. The Chinese Communists fully understood that, to establish the Party's absolute rule, they had to first monopolize the cultural arenas and control communications. This control was secured not through persuasion but instead through indoctrination and coercion. This imposition ensured that people had few or no alternatives. The party-state, through its propaganda, delivered only one truth, not a plurality of ideas. When the party-state monopolized culture, they monopolized people's minds. The CCP's cultural control in the Maoist era was a resounding success for one simple reason: if children, beginning in preschool, were presented with an incomplete picture, they naturally would believe that it was the whole truth as they grew up.

Gone are the days of fanatic mass demonstrations staged by Red Guards in Tiananmen Square in support of Mao's call for continuous revolution. The numerous Party-led nationwide campaigns (such as the Great Leap Forward) characteristic of the early decades of the PRC are also a thing of the past. On my visits in the last decade to parks in Beijing, Shanghai, Guangzhou, and other cities, I saw people enjoying a more relaxed life. Dancing, singing, or private chatting are common scenes. China has grown to become the second largest national economy, second only to the United States, and many Chinese are rightly proud of what their country has achieved since 1949. But the nation remains a land of many sharp contradictions that collide and to some extent coexist: lofty communist ideals and profit-maximizing capitalist ventures; cosmopolitanism and traditionalism; rampant corruption and iron discipline to oppose it; official declarations of the need for rule of law and simultaneous cracking down on dissidents; and the disparagement of Confucius's moral philosophy as feudal under Mao and the current government's promotion of Confucian notions of filial piety, loyalty, and harmony. Thus far, the CCP has been able to navigate the ship of state through these waters and has been amenable to changes when needed to continue its hold on power. Some scholars call this flexible adaptability a "guerrilla policy style," a practice that operates not based on dogmatic theoretical agendas but on opportunistic pragmatism.[26] One such practice has been to harness the country's top talents by showering them with honors and fame. The nonconformist film director Zhang Yimou (b. 1950), who once created dramas portraying his country's political misrule and poverty that drew the ire of authorities, has evolved into a court artist as the director of the lavishly pro-government opening ceremony of the 2008 Beijing Olympics. Clearly, the current CCP leaders are not adherents of Mao's fanatical idealism that put "politics in command" and class struggle into action. Instead, they are followers of pragmatist Deng Xiaoping, who believed that "it doesn't matter if a cat is black or is white; so long as it catches the mouse, it's a good cat."[27]

To promote its image as a global power, China realizes that it needs more than economic and military might; perhaps even more important, it needs soft power. Through the Confucius Institute branches, performing arts, literature, music, and film, China is actively promoting its positive image abroad as a culturally rich country and generous world power eager to help others.[28] This propaganda blitz is carefully conducted by the State Council Information Office, working closely with the Propaganda Department of the CCP Central Committee. These are also the key agencies responsible for censorship; they ensure that authorized images are projected and undesirable ones suppressed.

China's current campaign to promote itself as internationally peace loving and cooperative is in sharp contrast, however, with its practice of control and censorship at home. The party-state continues to keep a close eye on cultural institutions and media, keeping a firm hold on what people can read, write, and hear. During a two-day symposium in October 2014 to commemorate Mao's 1942 Yan'an Talks—the script was made available a year later—Xi Jinping delivered a speech at the Great Hall of the People on the correct course of literature and art in today's China.[29] Despite the very different setting and seventy-two years separation in time—Mao delivered his speeches at a run-down hall in Yan'an, and Xi at a grand building in the center of the capital[30]—the parallels between the two presentations are striking. Echoing Mao's concept of "a cultural army," Xi declared that "the literary front is an important front of the Party and the people." Also like Mao, he instructed the literary world to "serve the people and socialism." Xi introduced a small twist, however: he avoided Maoist rhetoric about class struggle and instead called on writers to emphasize patriotism and national greatness. He asserted, "Among the socialist core values, the deepest, the most fundamental, and the everlasting one is patriotism."[31] The release of Xi's speech in major government-run media outlets is a reminder that, despite decades of market reform and opening up, the Communist Party line still dominates the cultural arena.

Official directives on the correct approach to writing continue to emanate from the highest levels of the government. As mentioned in chapter 5, in February 2017, the CCP Central Committee and the State Council jointly issued the "Opinions on Strengthening and Improving Ideological and Political Work in Higher Education Institutions under New Circumstance," which instructed university students to serve the Communist Party with "Comrade Xi Jinping at the core."[32] Both Xi's talk and the directive reinforce the concept that the CCP should be in charge of culture and that intellectuals and writers must not cross certain lines. Clearly, Xi's "Chinese Dream" does not permit dissenting visions.

GLOSSARY

Names, books, and periodicals that appear in the bibliography are not included.

Ai Qing 艾青
aiguozhuyi jiaoyu 爱国主义教育

baofu 包袱
Baowentang 宝文堂
Beijing nongminbao 北京农民报
Beijing wanbao 北京晚报
Beiping *fangshi* 北平方式
Beiping jiefangbao 北平解放报
Beipingshi junshi guanzhi weiyuanhui
    (BMCC) 北平市军事管制委员会
bihua 壁画
Bo Gu (Qin Bangxian) 博古 (秦邦宪)
bufa 不发

chajin 查禁
Changshiji 尝试集
Chen Hongye 陈鸿业
Chen Junlan 陈俊兰
Chen Yun 陈云
Chiang Ching-kuo 蒋经国
Chiang Kai-shek 蒋介石
Chu Anping 储安平
chuanda 传达
Cixi (Empress Dowager) 慈禧太后

da Hanzuzhuyi 大汉族主义
Da yeshou 打野兽
Dagong bao 大公报
dahui 大会
Dalai Lama 达赖喇嘛
Dang de shenghuo 党的生活
dang tianxia 党天下

Dangzhibu 党支部
dianchuanshi 点传师
diaoyan 调研
Dihua 迪化
Dongchengqu diyi wenhuaguan 东城区第一
    文化馆
dongyuan dahui 动员大会
Duzhe laixin 读者来信

Falun Gong 法轮功
Fan Changjiang 范长江
fangeming 反革命
fangxiangxing 方向性
fen 分
Feng Jinxiu 冯锦修
Fu Zuoyi 傅作义
fukua 浮夸
Fuqin, Li Dazhao 父亲, 李大钊

ganqing shi zhenshi er youlide 感情是真实而
    有力的
Gao Qingfeng 高庆丰
gongchan gongqi 共产共妻
gongren shushu 工人叔叔
Gongshang chubanshe 工商出版社
gongshenhui 公审会
Gu Yuan 古元
guangrongbang 光荣榜
guangrongpai 光荣牌
guganfenzi 骨干分子

Hai Rui baguan 海瑞罢官
He Guang 何光

heibanbao 黑板报
heibang 黑榜
hongbang 红榜
Hou Yongchang 侯永昌
houjin bogu 厚今薄古
Hu Feng 胡风
Hu Shi 胡适
Hua Junwu 华君武
huabiao 华表
huaifenzi 坏分子
Huang Zhong 黄忠
huimen daomen 会门道门

Jiang Qing 江青
Jiang Xuezhu 蒋雪珠
Jiangxi Soviet 江西苏维埃
jianju 检举
jiaoyangyuan 教养员
jichu 基础
jiduan fandong 极端反动
jieban 接办
jiedao youeryuan 街道幼儿园
Jiefangjun bao 解放军报
jijifenzi 积极分子
Jiluan wencun 季鸾文存
Jin-Cha-Ji (Shanxi-Chaher-Hebei) 晋察冀
   (山西-察哈尔-河北)
Jin-Cha-Ji ribao 晋察冀日报
Jin Ping Mei 金瓶梅
jinbu 进步
jiuping zhuang xinjiu 旧瓶装新酒
Juzan 巨赞

kefa 可发
kong Mei xinli 恐美心理
kongjiazi 空架子
kongsuhui 控诉会
kuaiban 快板
kuanda wubian 宽大无边

Lao She 老舍
laodong 劳动
laodong mofan 劳动模范
Laodong renmin wenhuagong (WPCP) 劳动
   人民文化宫
Li Changchun 李长春

Li Hua 李桦
Li Xuefeng 李雪峰
Li Ye 李野
Liang Shanbo 梁山伯
Liang Zhengjiang 梁正江
Liangyou Bookstore 良友书店
lianhuanhua 连环画
Lin Biao 林彪
Lin Yutang 林语堂
Liu Shuzhen 刘淑珍
Liu Xiangting 刘翔亭
Liu Xieyuan 刘燮元
Liu Yingyuan 刘英源
Liulichang 琉璃厂
Longhua (sect) 龙华
Lu Dingyi 陆定一
Lu Xun 鲁迅
Lu Xun yishu xueyuan 鲁迅艺术学院
Luo Cheng 罗成
Luo Lin 罗林
Luotuo Xiangzi 骆驼祥子
Lushan Conference 庐山会议

Ma Xulun 马叙伦
Mao Dun, see Shen Yanbing
Miaofeng (Mount) 妙峰山
miaohui 庙会
minzhong jiaoyuguan 民众教育馆
Minzu fandian 民族饭店
Minzu shiwu weiyuanhui 民族事务委员会

nanbatian 南霸天
Niujie 牛街
nongcun julebu 农村俱乐部

Panchen Lama 班禅喇嘛
Peng Dehuai 彭德怀
piping 批评
piping jiexian 批评界限

qiangtoucao 墙头草
Qianxian 前线
qigong 气功
Qindian 寝殿
qingli 清理
Qingming Festival 清明节

qingshi 请示
Qingtongxia 青铜峡
Qingzhen zao 清真灶
quandang banbao 全党办报
quanshi banbao 全市办报
qunzhong dahui 群众大会
qunzhong wenhua 群众文化
Qunzhong wenhuachu 群众文化处

Ren Bishi 任弼时
Ren Chengshui 任成水
Renmin datuanjie 人民大团结
renmin gongyuan 人民公园
renmin jiaoyuguan 人民教育馆
renmin wenhuaguan 人民文化馆
renshi huanjing 认识环境
Ritan 日坛

Sha Kefu 沙可夫
Shaan-Gan-Ning (Shaanxi-Gansu-Ningxia)
    陕甘宁 (陕西-甘肃-宁夏)
shan 山
Shanghai gongren wenhuagong 上海工人文
    化宫
shaodeng 少登
Shejitan 社稷坛
Shen Yu 沈予
Shen Yanbing (Mao Dun) 沈雁冰 (茅盾)
Shi Chuanxiang 時傳祥
Shi shui zhansheng le Riben qinlüezhe? 是谁
    战胜了日本侵略者?
Shijie ribao 世界日报
shijinshi 试金石
shizun 师尊
shuangchong lingdao 双重领导
Shuoshuo changchang 说说唱唱
song huodong shangmen 送活动上门
song jiaoyu shangmen 送教育上门
Su Xinqun 苏辛群
Sun Yat-sen 孙逸仙

tai buqi toulai 抬不起头来
Taimiao 太庙
Tao Xisheng 陶希圣
Tao Yuanming 陶渊明
Tian Han 田汉

Tian Zuoliang 田作良
Tiaodian 祧殿
tongsu duwu 通俗读物
tongxunwang 通讯网
tongyi anpai 统一安排
tuanjie 团结
tuguangbo 土广播
tuidao 退道

Ulanhu 乌兰夫
Urumqi 乌鲁木齐

Wang Feng 汪锋
Wang Jingwei 汪精卫
Wang Jueyi 王觉一
Wang Tingshu 王廷枢
Wang Yaping 王亚平
Wang Yitang 王揖唐
weida de qunzhong yundong 伟大的群众运
    动
wending yadao yiqie 稳定压倒一切
Weng Dujian 翁独健
Wenhua jieguan weiyuanhui (CTC) 文化接
    管委员会
wenhua yu xiuxi 文化与休息
wenhuache xiaxiang 文化车下乡
Wenhuachu 文化处
wenhuagong 文化宫
wenhuaguan 文化馆
wenhuazhan 文化站
Wu Han 吴晗
Wu Jifu 吴吉福
Wusetu 五色土
Wushi niandai chubanshe 五十年代出版社

xiachangzu 下厂组
Xianban 仙班
Xiangdian 享殿
xiangsheng 相声
xianjin shengchanzhe 先进生产者
Xiao Ming 肖明
Xichengqu wenhua zhongxin (Xichengqu
    wenhuaguan) 西城区文化中心 (西城区文
    化馆)
xiejiao 邪教
Xin xiangsheng 新相声

Notes

Introduction

1. Lin Zhu, *Dajiang de kunhuo* (The puzzlement of a great architect) (Beijing: Zuojia chubanshe, 1991), 85.

2. Lin Zhu, *Dajiang de kunhuo*, 85–86.

3. For details of this conflict, see Chang-tai Hung, *Mao's New World: Political Culture in the Early People's Republic* (Ithaca, N.Y.: Cornell University Press, 2011), 23–72.

4. Liang Sicheng, *Liang Sicheng quanji* (Complete works of Liang Sicheng), 9 vols. (Beijing: Zhongguo jianzhu gongcheng chubanshe, 2001), 5:268–269.

5. Isaiah Berlin, *Against the Current: Essays in the History of Ideas,* ed. Henry Hardy (Princeton, N.J.: Princeton University Press, 2001), 321.

6. Song Yongyi, ed., *Zhongguo fanyou yundong shujuku, 1957–* (The Chinese Anti-Rightist Campaign Database, 1957–) (Hong Kong: Universities Service Centre for China Studies, Chinese University of Hong Kong, 2009); Roderick MacFarquhar, *The Origins of the Cultural Revolution,* vol. 1, *Contradictions among the People, 1956–1957* (New York: Columbia University Press, 1974), 167–310; Zhang Yihe, *Zuihou de guizu* (The last aristocrats) (Hong Kong: Oxford University Press, 2004); and Merle Goldman, *China's Intellectuals: Advise and Dissent* (Cambridge, Mass.: Harvard University Press, 1981), 1–17.

7. Mao Zedong, "Talks at the Yenan Forum on Literature and Art," in *Selected Works of Mao Tse-tung,* 5 vols. (Peking: Foreign Languages Press, 1967–1977), 3:69.

8. Zhongguo gongchandang Beijingshi weiyuanhui bangongting, "Wenhua jieguan weiyuanhui ge danwei renyuan mingdan" (List of names in various units of the CTC), Beijing Municipal Archives (BMA), 1-6-277.

9. See *Beiping heping jiefang qianhou* (Before and after the peaceful liberation of Beiping; BPHJQ), ed. Beijingshi dang'anguan (Beijing: Beijing chubanshe, 1998), 87.

10. Shanghaishi dang'anguan, ed., *Shanghai jiefang* (The liberation of Shanghai), 3 vols. (Beijing: Zhongguo dang'an chubanshe, 2009), 2:267–270, 371–413; Nanjingshi dang'anguan, ed., *Nanjing jiefang* (The liberation of Nanjing), 2 vols. (Beijing: Zhongguo dang'an chubanshe, 2009), 1:169–172, 183–189, 301–314; Gansusheng dang'anguan, ed., *Lanzhou jiefang* (The liberation of Lanzhou) (Beijing: Zhongguo dang'an chubanshe, 2009), 95–97, 114–123, 125–126. The Military Control Commission did not set up culture takeover committees in every city the Communists captured, but controlling cultural activities was always a top priority. The committee's name was slightly different in each city. In Nanjing, it was called the Culture and Education Takeover Division (Wenjiao xitong jieguanbu), and in Shanghai the Culture and Education Committee (Wenhua jiaoyu weiyuanhui).

11. Anne-Marie Brady, *Marketing Dictatorship: Propaganda and Thought Work in Contemporary China* (Lanham, Md.: Rowman and Littlefield, 2008); and Hung, *Mao's New World.*

12. Jeremy Brown and Paul G. Pickowicz, eds., *Dilemmas of Victory: The Early Years of the People's Republic of China* (Cambridge, Mass.: Harvard University Press, 2007).

13. For works on 1949 as a critical divide, see, for example, William C. Kirby, "Continuity and Change in Modern China: Economic Planning on the Mainland and on Taiwan, 1943–1958," *Australian Journal of Chinese Affairs* 20 (July 1990): 121–141.

14. Brown and Pickowicz, *Dilemmas of Victory.*

15. Julia C. Strauss, "Paternalist Terror: The Campaign to Suppress Counterrevolutionaries and Regime Consolidation in the People's Republic of China, 1950–1953," *Comparative Studies in Society and History* 44, no. 1 (January 2002): 80–105; Yang Kuisong, "Reconsidering the Campaign to Suppress Counterrevolutionaries," *China Quarterly* 193 (March 2008): 102–121; and Patricia Thornton, *Disciplining the State: Virtue, Violence, and State-Making in Modern China* (Cambridge, Mass.: Harvard University Asia Center, 2007).

16. Joseph Esherick, *Ancestral Leaves: A Family Journey through Chinese History* (Berkeley: University of California Press, 2011); Gail Hershatter, *The Gender of Memory: Rural Women and China's Collective Past* (Berkeley: University of California Press, 2011); Neil J. Diamant, *Revolutionizing the Family: Politics, Love, and Divorce in Urban and Rural China, 1949–1968* (Berkeley: University of California Press, 2000); and Janet Y. Chen, *Guilty of Indigence: The Urban Poor in China, 1900–1953* (Princeton, N.J.: Princeton University Press, 2012).

17. Thomas S. Mullaney, *Coming to Terms with the Nation: Ethnic Classification in Modern China* (Berkeley: University of California Press, 2011); Tsering Woeser and Wang Lixiong, *Voices from Tibet: Selected Essays and Reportage,* ed. and trans. Violet Law (Hong Kong: Hong Kong University Press, 2014); Rian Thum, *The Sacred Routes of Uyghur History* (Cambridge, Mass.: Harvard University Press, 2014); David Brophy, *Uyghur Nation: Reform and Revolution on the Russia-China Frontier* (Cambridge, Mass.: Harvard University Press, 2016); and Tom Cliff, *Oil and Water: Being Han in Xinjiang* (Chicago: University of Chicago Press, 2016).

18. Vincent Goossaert and David A. Palmer, *The Religious Question in Modern China* (Chicago: University of Chicago Press, 2011); Paul P. Mariani, *Church Militant: Bishop Kung and Catholic Resistance in Communist China* (Cambridge, Mass.: Harvard University Press, 2011); and David Ownby, *Falun Gong and the Future of China* (New York: Oxford University Press, 2008).

19. Wang Jun, *Beijing Record: A Physical and Political History of Planning Modern Beijing* (Singapore: World Scientific, 2011); and Shuishan Yu, *Chang'an Avenue and the Modernization of Chinese Architecture* (Seattle: University of Washington Press, 2013).

20. Brady, *Marketing Dictatorship;* Barbara Mittler, *A Continuous Revolution: Making Sense of Cultural Revolution Culture* (Cambridge, Mass.: Harvard University Asia Center, 2012); Nicolai Volland, "The Control of the Media in the People's Republic of China" (PhD diss., University of Heidelberg, 2003); and David Shambaugh, "China's Propaganda: Institutions, Processes and Efficacy," *China Journal* 57 (January 2007): 25–58.

21. Gu Mingyuan, *Zhongguo jiaoyu de wenhua jichu* (Cultural foundations of Chinese education) (Taiyuan: Shanxi jiaoyu chubanshe, 2004); and Margaret Mih Tillman, *Raising China's Revolutionaries: Modernizing Childhood for Cosmopolitan Nationalists and Liberated Comrades, 1920s–1950s* (New York: Columbia University Press, 2018).

22. Cynthia Brokaw and Christopher A. Reed, eds., *From Woodblocks to the Internet: Chinese Publishing and Print Culture in Transition, circa 1800 to 2008* (Leiden: Brill, 2010);

Jennifer Altehenger, *Legal Lessons: Popularizing Laws in the People's Republic of China, 1949–1989* (Cambridge, Mass.: Harvard University Asia Center, 2018); Wang Jianjun, *Zhongguo jindai jiaokeshu fazhan yanjiu* (A study of the development of modern Chinese textbooks) (Guangzhou: Guangdong jiaoyu chubanshe, 1996); and Ying Du, "Shanghaiing the Press Gang: The Maoist Regimentation of the Shanghai Popular Publishing Industry in the Early PRC (1949–1956)," *Modern Chinese Literature and Culture* 26, no. 2 (Fall 2014): 89–141.

23. Sun Xupei, *Kanke zhilu: Xinwen ziyou zai Zhongguo* (A bumpy road: Freedom of the press in China) (Taipei: Juliu tushu gufen youxian gongsi, 2013); and Park Coble, *China's War Reporters: The Legacy of Resistance against Japan* (Cambridge, Mass.: Harvard University Press, 2015).

24. Kirk Denton, *Exhibiting the Past: Historical Memory and the Politics of Museums in Postsocialist China* (Honolulu: University of Hawai'i Press, 2014); Denise Y. Ho, *Curating Revolution: Politics on Display in Mao's China* (Cambridge: Cambridge University Press, 2018); and Marzia Varutti, *Museums in China: The Politics of Representation after Mao* (Woodbridge, UK: Boydell Press, 2014).

25. Perry Link, *The Uses of Literature: Life in the Socialist Chinese Literary System* (Princeton, N.J.: Princeton University Press, 2000); Xiaobing Tang, *Visual Culture in Contemporary China: Paradigms and Shifts* (Cambridge: Cambridge University Press, 2015); and Melissa Chiu and Shengtian Zheng, eds., *Art and China's Revolution* (New Haven, Conn.: Yale University Press, 2008).

26. Jeremy Brown and Matthew D. Johnson, eds., *Maoism at the Grassroots: Everyday Life in China's Era of High Socialism* (Cambridge, Mass.: Harvard University Press, 2015).

27. Michel de Certeau, *The Practice of Everyday Life,* trans. Steven Rendall (Berkeley: University of California Press, 1984); and James C. Scott, *Weapons of the Weak: Everyday Forms of Peasant Resistance* (New Haven, Conn.: Yale University Press, 1985).

28. E. P. Thompson, "History from Below," *Times Literary Supplement,* April 7, 1966, 279–281.

29. Strauss, "Paternalist Terror"; and Yang Kuisong, "Reconsidering the Campaign."

30. Peter Burke, *Varieties of Cultural History* (Ithaca, N.Y.: Cornell University Press, 1997), 1.

31. François Furet, *Interpreting the French Revolution,* trans. Elborg Forster (Cambridge: Cambridge University Press, 1981); and Clifford Geertz, *The Interpretation of Cultures* (New York: Basic Books, 1973).

32. Jacob Burckhardt, *The Civilization of the Renaissance in Italy,* 2 vols., intro. Benjamin Nelson and Charles Trinkaus (New York: Harper & Row, 1958).

33. Hannah Arendt, *The Origins of Totalitarianism* (New York: World Publishing, 1958), 474.

34. Sheila Fitzpatrick, "New Perspectives on Stalinism," *Russian Review* 45, no. 4 (October 1986): 357–373; see also Michael Geyer and Sheila Fitzpatrick, eds., *Beyond Totalitarianism: Stalinism and Nazism Compared* (Cambridge: Cambridge University Press, 2009), 1–37, 266–301.

35. Brown and Johnson, *Maoism at the Grassroots.*

36. Robert Darnton, *Censors at Work: How States Shaped Literature* (New York: W. W. Norton, 2014), 17.

37. See Herman Ermolaev, *Censorship in Soviet Literature: 1917–1991* (Lanham, Md.: Rowman and Littlefield, 1997); and Harold Swayze, *Political Control of Literature in the USSR, 1946–1959* (Cambridge, Mass.: Harvard University Press, 1962).

38. Gao Hua, *Hongtaiyang shi zenyang shengqi de: Yan'an zhengfeng yundong de lailong qumai* (How did the sun rise? The origin and development of the Yan'an Rectification

Movement) (Hong Kong: Chinese University Press, 2000); and Chang-tai Hung, *War and Popular Culture: Resistance in Modern China, 1937–1945* (Berkeley: University of California Press, 1994).

39. See *Shehuizhuyi shiqi Zhonggong Beijing dangshi jishi* (Chronicles of the history of the CCP in Beijing during the socialist period; *SHZY*), ed. Zhonggong Beijing shiwei dangshi yanjiushi, 4 vols. (Beijing: Renmin chubanshe, 1994–1998), 1:30–33; see also *Beiping jiefang* (The liberation of Beiping; *BPJF*), ed. Beijingshi dang'anguan, 2 vols. (Beijing: Zhongguo dang'an chubanshe, 2009), 1:417–418; and *Zhonghua renmin gongheguo chuban shiliao* (Historical materials relating to publications in the People's Republic of China; *ZRGCS*), ed. Zhongguo chuban kexue yanjiusuo and Zhongyang dang'anguan (Beijing: Zhongguo shuji chubanshe, 1995), 20–21.

40. Michael Schudson, *Discovering the News: A Social History of American Newspapers* (New York: Basic Books, 1978), 5–6, 9–10.

41. Jeffrey Brooks, *Thank You, Comrade Stalin! Soviet Public Culture from Revolution to Cold War* (Princeton, N.J.: Princeton University Press, 2000), 3.

42. Karl Marx, *Critique of Hegel's "Philosophy of Right,"* ed. with intro. and notes Joseph O'Malley (Cambridge: Cambridge University Press, 1970), 131; and "A Contribution to the Critique of Hegel's Philosophy of Right," in *Early Writings*, intro. Lucio Colletti, trans. Rodney Livingstone and Gregor Benton (London: Penguin, 1992), 244.

43. Quoted in Carl J. Friedrich and Zbigniew K. Brzezinski, *Totalitarian Dictatorship and Autocracy*, 2nd rev. ed. (New York: Praeger, 1966), 300.

44. Lynne Viola, *Peasant Rebels under Stalin: Collectivization and the Culture of Peasant Resistance* (New York: Oxford University Press, 1996), 38–44.

45. John Lagerwey, *China: A Religious State* (Hong Kong: Hong Kong University Press, 2010), 1.

46. "Dai Xinwen zongshu, Chuban zongshu zhuanfa yibufen Jidujiao renshi de xuanyan de xuanchuan tongbao" (A circular of the declaration of some Christian believers transmitted by the General Administration of the Press and the GAP), BMA, 8-2-187. On related official documents, see *Jianguo yilai zhongyao wenxian xuanbian* (Selected important documents after the founding of the nation; *JYZW*), ed. Zhonggong zhongyang wenxian yanjiushi, 20 vols. (Beijing: Zhongyang wenxian chubanshe, 1992–1998), 1:510–515.

47. Ma Xisha and Han Bingfang, *Zhongguo minjian zongjiaoshi* (History of Chinese folk religions) (Shanghai: Shanghai renmin chubanshe, 1992).

48. J. J. M. de Groot, *Sectarianism and Religious Persecution in China*, 2 vols. (Taipei: Literature House, 1963).

49. Zhongguo shehui kexueyuan lishi yanjiusuo Qingshishi, ziliaoshi, ed., *Qing zhongqi wusheng Bailianjiao qiyi ziliao* (Materials on the White Lotus Rebellion in five provinces in the mid-Qing dynasty), 5 vols. (Nanjing: Jiangsu renmin chubanshe, 1981). On related subjects, see Susan Naquin, *Millenarian Rebellion in China: The Eight Trigrams Uprising of 1813* (New Haven, Conn.: Yale University Press, 1976).

50. Mao Zedong, "Guanyu gonghui gongzuo de fangzhen" (On the policy of the labor unions), in *Mao Zedong wenji* (Collected writings of Mao Zedong), 8 vols. (Beijing: Renmin chubanshe, 1996), 5:327.

51. Mao Zedong, "Guanyu zhenya fangeming" (On the suppression of counterrevolutionaries), in *Mao Zedong wenji*, 6:117.

52. Luo Ruiqing, *Lun renmin gong'an gongzuo* (On the people's public security work) (Beijing: Qunzhong chubanshe, 1994), 98.

53. Mao Zedong, "Zhenya fangeming bixu shixing dang de qunzhong luxian" (In launching the Campaign to Suppress Counterrevolutionaries we must implement the Party's mass line), in *Mao Zedong wenji,* 6:162.

54. Mark Selden, *The Yenan Way in Revolutionary China* (Cambridge, Mass.: Harvard University Press, 1971); and *China in Revolution: The Yenan Way Revisited* (Armonk, N.Y.: M. E. Sharpe, 1995).

55. Mao Zedong, "Talks at the Yenan Forum on Literature and Art," in *Selected Works,* 3:81.

56. Raymond A. Bauer, *The New Man in Soviet Psychology* (Cambridge, Mass.: Harvard University Press, 1952), 13–102; Lisa A. Kirschenbaum, *Small Comrades: Revolutionizing Childhood in Soviet Russia, 1917–1932* (New York: Routledge, 2001), 8–32; and Sheila Fitzpatrick, *Everyday Stalinism: Ordinary Life in Extraordinary Times: Soviet Russia in the 1930s* (New York: Oxford University Press, 1999), 76.

57. Mao Zedong, "Rectify the Party's Style of Work," in *Selected Works,* 3:49–50.

58. Karl Marx, "Enquête ouvrière," in *Karl Marx: Selecting Writings in Sociology and Social Philosophy,* ed. T. B. Bottomore and Maximilien Rubel (New York: McGraw-Hill, 1956), 203.

59. PRC, *The Common Program and Other Documents of the First Plenary Session of the Chinese People's Political Consultative Conference* (Peking: Foreign Languages Press, 1950), 2.

60. PRC, *The Constitution of the People's Republic of China* (Peking: Foreign Languages Press, 1954), 9.

61. *Renmin ribao (People's daily; RMRB),* September 8, 1959, 3.

62. Colin Mackerras, *China's Minority: Integration and Modernization in the Twentieth Century* (Hong Kong: Oxford University Press, 1994); Melvyn C. Goldstein, *A History of Modern Tibet,* vol. 3, *The Storm Clouds Descend, 1955–1957* (Berkeley: University of California Press, 2014); Wang Lixiong, *Tianzang: Xizang de mingyun* (Sky burial: The destiny of Tibet) (Taipei: Dakuai wenhua chuban gufen youxian gongsi, 2009), esp. 117–267, 433–459; and Wang Lixiong, *Wo de Xiyu, ni de Dongtu* (My West China, your East Turkestan) (Taipei: Dakuai wenhua chuban gufen youxian gongsi, 2007), esp. 89–261.

Chapter 1: Policing Books in Beijing

1. Ye Jianying, "Beipingshi junshi guanzhi weiyuanhui chengli bugao" (Proclamation of the establishment of the BMCC), in *BPHJQ,* 84; see also BMA, 1–6-273; 1–6-280; and 1–12-19.

2. *SHZY,* 1:24.

3. See *BPHJQ,* 101.

4. *SHZY,* 1:135.

5. *SHZY,* 1:52.

6. Mao Zedong, "On the People's Democratic Dictatorship," in *Selected Works,* 4:411–424.

7. James Z. Gao, *The Communist Takeover of Hangzhou: The Transformation of City and Cadre, 1949–1954* (Honolulu: University of Hawai'i Press, 2004), 247.

8. Julia C. Strauss, "Paternalist Terror"; and Yang Kuisong, "Reconsidering the Campaign."

9. Cynthia J. Brokaw and Kai-wing Chow, eds., *Printing and Book Culture in Late Imperial China* (Berkeley: University of California Press, 2005); Brokaw and Reed, eds., *From Woodblocks to the Internet;* Christopher A. Reed, *Gutenberg in Shanghai: Chinese Print Capitalism,*

1876–1937 (Vancouver: UBC Press, 2004); Wang Jianjun, *Zhongguo jindai jiaokeshu,* 191–300; and Robert Culp, "'China–The Land and Its People': Fashioning Identity in Secondary School History Textbooks, 1911–37," *Twentieth-Century China* 26, no. 2 (April 2001): 17–62.

10. Nicolai Volland provides a succinct account of the reform of the New China Bookstore after 1949 in "Books for New China: Xinhua shudian and the Transformation of Chinese Book Publishing," chap. 5 in "The Control of the Media" (PhD diss., University of Heidelberg, 2003), 243–291.

11. Brooks, *Thank You, Comrade Stalin!,* 3–18.

12. I use Robert Darnton's definition. See *Censors at Work: How States Shaped Literature* (New York: W. W. Norton, 2014), 235.

13. Plato, *The Republic,* vol. 1, bk. 2, trans. Paul Shorey (Cambridge, Mass.: Harvard University Press, 1937), 177.

14. Darnton, *Censors at Work,* 21–86, esp. 58.

15. Olaf Peters, ed., *Degenerate Art: The Attack on Modern Art in Nazi Germany 1937* (Munich: Prestel, 2014), 90–257; and Peter Adam, *Art of the Third Reich* (New York: Harry N. Abrams, 1992), 120–127.

16. W. E. Mosse, *Alexander II and the Modernization of Russia,* rev. ed. (New York: Collier, 1958), 24–25; for a later period of censorship under Nicholas I, see Jeffrey Brooks, *How Russia Learned to Read: Literacy and Popular Literature, 1861–1917* (Princeton, N.J.: Princeton University Press, 1985), 299–300.

17. Swayze, *Political Control of Literature.*

18. Sima Qian, "Rulin liezhuan" (Biographies of the Confucian scholars), in *Shiji* (Records of the Grand Historian), 10 vols. (Beijing: Zhonghua shuju, 1987), 10:3116.

19. R. Kent Guy, *The Emperor's Four Treasures: Scholars and the State in the Late Ch'ien-lung Era* (Cambridge, Mass.: Council on East Asian Studies, Harvard University, 1987).

20. Lee-hsia Hsu Ting, *Government Control of the Press in Modern China, 1900–1949* (Cambridge, Mass.: East Asian Research Center, Harvard University, 1974), 79–186.

21. For a brief account of the history of publishing during the Yan'an period, see Zhou Baochang, "Xinhua shudian zai Yan'an chuchuang shiqi" (The initial stages of Yan'an's New China Bookstore), *Chuban shiliao* 2 (December 1983): 1–4; Song Yulin, "Huiyi Yan'an Xinhua shudian" (Remembering Yan'an's New China Bookstore), *Chuban shiliao* 2 (December 1983): 5–7; Liu Ni, ed., *Qingliangshan jiyi* (Remembering Mount Qingliang) (Xi'an: Sanqin chubanshe, 2011); Volland, "Control of the Media," 73–241; and Christopher Reed, "Advancing the (Gutenberg) Revolution: The Origins and Development of Chinese Print Communism, 1921–1947," in *From Woodblocks to the Internet,* ed. Brokaw and Reed, 275–311.

22. Zhou Baochang, "Xinhua shudian zai Yan'an"; Song Yulin, "Huiyi Yan'an Xinhua shudian"; and Liu Ni, ed., *Qingliangshan jiyi.*

23. Zhonggong zhongyang xuanchuanbu bangongting and Zhongyang dang'anguan bianyanbu, eds., *Zhongguo gongchandang xuanchuan gongzuo wenxian xuanbian, 1937–1949* (Selected documents concerning the propaganda work of the Chinese Communist Central Committee, 1937–1949) (Beijing: Xuexi chubanshe, 1996), 367.

24. Zhongguo shehui kexueyuan xinwen yanjiusuo, ed., *Zhongguo gongchandang xinwen gongzuo wenjian huibian* (Collection of CCP documents related to work in the various journalistic media), 3 vols. (Beijing: Xinhua chubanshe, 1980), 1:86–88.

25. Mao, "Talks at the Yenan Forum," in *Selected Works,* 3:69–98.

26. Hung, *War and Popular Culture,* 246.

27. Dangdai Zhongguo congshu bianjibu, ed., *Dangdai Zhongguo de chuban shiye* (The publishing industry in contemporary China), 3 vols. (Beijing: Dangdai Zhongguo chubanshe, 1993), 1:52.

28. V. I. Lenin, *What Is to Be Done? Burning Questions of Our Movement* (New York: International Publishers, 1969).

29. "Ye Jianying guanyu Junguanhui wenti de baogao yaodian" (Essential points in the report of the BMCC by Ye Jianying), in *BPJF*, 1:198–200.

30. PRC, *Common Program*, 3.

31. *BPJF*, 1:422–423.

32. Lenin, *What Is to Be Done?*, 156.

33. Anne Applebaum, *Iron Curtain: The Crushing of Eastern Europe, 1944–1956* (New York: Doubleday, 2012), 174–191.

34. *BPJF*, 1:434–435. Fan was later persecuted as a "capitalist roader" during the Cultural Revolution and committed suicide in 1970.

35. *SHZY*, 1:11.

36. *BPJF*, 1:400, 404.

37. Zhongguo gongchandang Beijingshi weiyuanhui bangongting, "Wenhua jieguan weiyuanhui," BMA, 1–6-277. The other three departments were Garrison Headquarters, the Municipal Government, and the Commodity Control Commission (see *BPHJQ*, 84–87).

38. *BPHJQ*, 87.

39. Qian Junrui, "Zizhuan" (Autobiography), in Qian, *Qian Junrui xuanji* (Selected writings of Qian Junrui) (Taiyuan: Shanxi jingji chubanshe, 1986), 7.

40. Zhongguo gongchandang Beijingshi, "Wenhua jieguan weiyuanhui," BMA, 1–6-277.

41. *ZRGCS*, 20–21; and *SHZY*, 1:30–33.

42. *SHZY*, 1:135–138.

43. The GAP ended in November 1954. Its responsibilities were taken over by the Ministry of Culture.

44. Hu Yuzhi, *Wo de huiyi* (My memoirs) (Nanjing: Jiangsu renmin chubanshe, 1990), 26.

45. Zhu Shunzuo, *Hu Yuzhi* (Hu Yuzhi) (Shijiazhuang: Huashan wenyi chubanshe, 1999), 257.

46. BPPO, "Beijingshi renmin zhengfu xinwenchu yewu yu zuzhi qingkuang" (The structure and work of the BPPO), BMA, 8–1-1. The office was initially called the Press Office under the administration of the BMCC. It was renamed the Press and Publications Office of the Beijing Municipal Government in January 1950. The office was incorporated into the Cultural Bureau of the Municipal Government in 1955. See Beijingshi difangzhi bianzuan weiyuanhui, ed., *Beijingzhi: Xinwen chuban guangbo dianshi juan: Chubanzhi* (The history of Beijing: News, publications, and television: The history of publications) (Beijing: Beijing chubanshe, 2005), 579–580.

47. BPPO, "Xinwenke yijiusijiu gongzuo zongjie" (Summary report of the work done by the News Section in 1949), BMA, 8–1-13.

48. For propaganda work in general, see Shambaugh, "China's Propaganda," 26; and Brady, *Marketing Dictatorship*.

49. See the letter of the Ministry of Culture to the BPPO. See BPPO, "Hanfu Wenhuabu Shen buzhang de jianyi" (A reply to Minister Shen's suggestions), BMA, 8–2-421.

50. Chen Qingquan and Song Guangwei, *Lu Dingyi zhuan* (Biography of Lu Dingyi) (Beijing: Zhonggong dangshi chubanshe, 1999), 373–385; see also Hu Qiaomu zhuan bianxiezu,

ed., *Hu Qiaomu shuxinji* (Collected letters of Hu Qiaomu) (Beijing: Renmin chubanshe, 2002), 32–34, 36–44, 41–42.

51. BPPO, "Guanzhi guowai jinkou chubanwu diyici huiyi jilu" (Minutes of the first meeting on controlling imported publications), BMA, 8-2-706.

52. For an excellent account of the transformation of the New China Bookstore into the central publishing house after 1949, see Volland, "Control of the Media," 243–291.

53. See *ZRGCS*, 219–220.

54. Hu Yuzhi, *Hu Yuzhi wenji* (Collected writings of Hu Yuzhi), 6 vols. (Beijing: Shenghuo, dushu, xinzhi sanlian shudian, 1996), 5:293–294.

55. Quoted in Fei Xiaotong et al., eds., *Hu Yuzhi yinxiangji* (Impressions of Hu Yuzhi), rev. ed. (Beijing: Zhongguo youyi chuban gongsi, 1996), 140.

56. Fei, *Hu Yuzhi yinxiangji*, 140.

57. BMA, 8-2-754.

58. BPPO, "Benchu guanyu xinwen guanli gongzuo de chubu fang'an" (The preliminary plan of the news management work of the BPPO), BMA, 8-2-40.

59. BPPO, "Benchu guanyu xinwen," BMA, 8-2-40.

60. *SHZY*, 1:94.

61. *BPJF*, 1:422.

62. Frederic Wakeman Jr., "'Cleanup': The New Order in Shanghai," in *Dilemmas of Victory: The Early Years of the People's Republic of China*, ed. Jeremy Brown and Paul G. Pickowicz (Cambridge, Mass.: Harvard University Press, 2007), 46.

63. See BPPO, "Gezhong kanwu shenqing dengji chuli qingkuangbiao" (List of ways of handling the application for registration of various types of periodicals), BMA, 8-1-2.

64. "Shiwei jiguan youguan gexiang gongzuo de tongzhi ji Beijing shiwei junguanhui daihaobiao" (Circular on the work done by various departments in the Municipal Party and the code names in the BMCC), BMA, 40-2-2.

65. BMA, 8-1-7; see also 8-1-1; 8-1-27; 8-2-291; and 8-2-326.

66. BMA, 8-1-7.

67. *BPJF*, 1:448.

68. BPPO, "Dui Wenhua gongyingshe chubanwu de shendu baogao" (Report on reviewing the publications of the Cultural Supply Publishing House), BMA, 8-2-226.

69. BPPO, "Benchu jinji chuli jiu fandong shukan gongzuo jihua" (The BPPO's urgent plan on how to handle reactionary books and periodicals), BMA, 8-2-780.

70. BMA, 8-2-776.

71. BMA, 8-2-293.

72. BPPO, "Benchu diaocha fandongshu ji fanbanshu fenxi qingkuang gongzuo zongjie baogao" (The BPPO's summary report of the investigation of reactionary and reprinted books), BMA, 8-2-789.

73. BPPO, "Benchu jinji chuli," BMA, 8-2-780.

74. BMA, 8-2-296.

75. BMA, 8-1-88.

76. BPPO, "Benchu jinji chuli," BMA, 8-2-780.

77. BPPO, "Hanfu Wenhuabu Shen buzhang," BMA, 8-2-421.

78. For an example of short reports, see BPPO, "Dui Baowentang chubanwu de shencha jilubiao" (Review lists of books published by Baowentang Publishing House), BMA, 8-2-227. For a longer report, see BPPO, "Dui Dazhong shudian chubanwu de shendu baogao ji shencha jilubiao" (Review report and lists of books published by the Mass Bookstore), BMA, 8-2-453.

79. See BPPO, "Dui Baowentang chubanwu," BMA, 8-2-227.

80. BPPO, "Xin lianhuanhua shencha jilubiao" (Review list of the new serial picture stories), BMA, 8-2-159.

81. BPPO, "Benchu diaocha fandongshu," BMA, 8-2-789.

82. "Zhongyang renmin zhengfu Wenhuabu guanyu diaocha chuli huangse shukan de gexiang zhishi tongzhi" (Instructions of the Ministry of Culture of the Central People's Government on the investigation and handling of pornographic books and periodicals), BMA, 8-2-508.

83. BMA, 8-2-776.

84. BPPO, "Benchu diaocha fandongshu," BMA, 8-2-789.

85. BMA, 8-2-241.

86. BMA, 8-2-293.

87. "Chuban zongshu guanyu dangqian chajin jiushu zhong de yixie guiding" (Rules on censoring existing old publications by the GAP), BMA, 8-2-757.

88. BPPO, "Chuli 'Xinshenghuo yundong' deng shisi zhong fandongshu xiang Chuban zongshu baogao ji pifu" (Report to and reply from the GAP concerning our handling of the fourteen books on the New Life Movement and other issues), BMA, 8-2-417.

89. BPPO, "Chuli Dongdan, Dong'an shichang shutan shoumai fandong shuji jingguo baogao" (Report on handling the sale of reactionary books at Dongdan and Dong'an markets), BMA, 8-2-426.

90. BMA, 8-2-776.

91. Quoted in Jerome B. Grieder, *Hu Shih and the Chinese Renaissance: Liberalism in the Chinese Revolution, 1917–1937* (Cambridge, Mass.: Harvard University Press, 1970), 321. For the national campaign against Hu Shi in the mid-1950s, see *Hu Shi sixiang pipan* (A critique of Hu Shi's thought), 8 vols. (Beijing: Sanlian shudian, 1955–1956).

92. BPPO, "Benchu diaocha fandongshu," BMA, 8-2-789.

93. Mao, "On the People's Democratic Dictatorship," in *Selected Works*, 4:415.

94. BMA, 8-2-231.

95. BPPO, "Xin lianhuanhua shencha jilubiao," BMA, 8-2-159.

96. BPPO, "Xin lianhuanhua shencha jilubiao," BMA, 8-2-159.

97. BPPO, "Dui Baowentang chubanwu," BMA, 8-2-227.

98. BPPO, "Dui Wushi niandai chubanshe de shendu baogao ji shencha jilubiao" (Review report and lists of books published by the Fifties Publishing House), BMA, 8-2-454.

99. BMA, 8-2-159; 8-2-227; and 8-2-453.

100. See, for example, Hu Jiwei, *Qingchun suiyue: Hu Jiwei zishu* (Youthful days: The autobiography of Hu Jiwei) (Zhengzhou: Henan renmin chubanshe, 1999), 323.

101. BPPO, "Hanfu Wenhuabu Shen buzhang," BMA, 8-2-421 (Hitler); and BPPO, "Benchu jinji chuli," BMA, 8-2-780 (Trotsky).

102. BMA, 8-2-249; and BPPO, "Dui Wushi niandai chubanshe," BMA, 8-2-454.

103. BPPO, "Guanzhi guowai jinkou," BMA, 8-2-706.

104. BPPO, "Guanzhi guowai jinkou," BMA, 8-2-706; and BPPO, "Chuli Dongdan," BMA, 8-2-426.

105. "*Renmin ribao* dinggou jinkou chubanwu de han" (Letter of the *People's Daily* concerning imported publications), BMA, 8-2-641.

106. BPPO, "Guanyu ke zhun Yanjing daxue jinkou *Yindu zhixing* deng liangshu de baogao" (Report on the permission to import *A Passage to India* and the other book proposed by Yenching University), BMA, 8-2-629.

107. For Mao Zedong's general view of modern Chinese history, see his "On New Democracy," in *Selected Works*, 2:339–384.

108. BMA, 8-2-143.

109. BMA, 8-2-427; 8-2-429; 8-2-442; 8-2-508; 8-2-509; and 22-12-523.

110. BPPO, "Qudi jiulishu qingkuang" (On banning old almanacs), BMA, 8-2-256.

111. Hung, *War and Popular Culture*, 221–269.

112. Hung, *Mao's New World*, 182–209.

113. BMA, 8-2-151.

114. BPPO, "Benchu guanyu chuli jiu lianhuanhua de qingkuang baogao" (Report on the handling of old serial picture booklets), BMA, 8-1-73.

115. BMA, 8-2-778.

116. BPPO, "Benchu guanyu chuli jiu lianhuanhua," BMA, 8-1-73.

117. *SHZY*, 1:205–206.

118. Zhongguo renmin zhengzhi xieshang huiyi Beijingshi weiyuanhui wenshi ziliao weiyuanhui, ed. *Zhou Enlai yu Beijing* (Zhou Enlai and Beijing) (Beijing: Zhongyang wenxian chubanshe, 1998), see frontispiece photographs.

119. BPPO, "Beijingshi tongsu duwu shencha jilubiao" (Review lists of popular readings in Beijing), BMA, 8-2-250.

120. BPPO, "Tuijian benshi youliang tongsu duwu yilanbiao" (A list of excellent popular books recommended by the city), BMA, 8-2-423.

121. "Zhongyang renmin zhengfu Wenhuabu," BMA, 8-2-508.

122. More than eighteen thousand Soviet experts in many fields are estimated to have come to China in the 1950s. See Shen Zhihua, *Sulian zhuanjia zai Zhongguo* (Soviet experts in China) (Beijing: Zhongguo guoji guangbo chubanshe, 2003), 4, 408.

123. BMA, 8-2-265.

124. On private book publishing, see BMA, 8-2-511.

125. BMA, 8-1-110; 8-2-137; and 8-2-670.

126. Hu Yuzhi, *Hu Yuzhi wenji*, 5:414–431.

127. Fei, *Hu Yuzhi yinxiangji*, 139, 147.

128. Fei, *Hu Yuzhi yinxiangji*, 138–145.

129. BMA, 8-1-110.

130. Dangdai Zhongguo congshu bianjibu, *Dangdai Zhongguo*, 1:56.

131. BPPO, "Hanfu Wenhuabu Shen buzhang," BMA, 8-2-421.

132. See, for example, BMA, 8-2-429; and 8-2-433.

133. BPPO, "Shimin Zhang Beiye jianju jiulishu de laixin ji benchu diaocha baogao" (Citizen Zhang Beiye's letter informing against old almanacs and the BPPO's report of the investigation), BMA, 8-2-257.

134. BMA, 8-2-14.

135. *RMRB*, November 6, 1951, 3.

136. Hu Qiaomu zhuan bianxiezu, *Hu Qiaomu shuxinji*, 38.

137. Friedrich and Brzezinski, *Totalitarian Dictatorship and Autocracy*, 205–218.

138. Quoted in Yuan Ying, *Fengyun ceji: Wo zai Renmin ribao fukan de suiyue* (Sideline reports: My years working at the *People's Daily* literary supplement) (Beijing: Zhongguo dang'an chubanshe, 2006), 58; see also *SHZY*, 1:146.

139. Quoted in Yuan Ying, *Fengyun ceji*, 58.

140. BPPO, "Guanzhi guowai jinkou," BMA, 8-2-706.

141. For general national policies and regulations on publication, see *ZRGCS*.

142. Hu Yuzhi, *Hu Yuzhi wenji*, 5:425.

143. BPPO, "Guanzhi guowai jinkou," BMA, 8-2-706.

144. BMA, 8-2-754.

145. Zhou Yingpeng, "Liangxiao shenghui xi kongqian: Yi xin Zhongguo chenglihou 'Diyijie quanguo chuban huiyi'" (An unprecedented grand meeting: Remembering the First National Conference on Publishing after the establishment of a new China), http://www.pep .com.cn/cbck/200909x/201012/t20101227_993513.htm (accessed February 6, 2016).

146. BMA, 8-2-509.

147. Hu Yuzhi, *Hu Yuzhi wenji*, 5:426–427.

148. "Chuban zongshu guanyu chajin huo chuli shukan de zhishi" (Instructions of the GAP on banning or regulating books and periodicals), BMA, 8-2-753.

149. Leszek Kołakowski, *Main Currents of Marxism: Its Origins, Growth, and Dissolution*, 3 vols., trans. P. S. Falla (Oxford: Clarendon Press, 1978), 3:7.

150. Applebaum, *Iron Curtain*; Norman Naimark and Leonid Gibianskii, eds., *The Establishment of Communist Regimes in Eastern Europe, 1944-1949* (Boulder, Colo.: Westview, 1997).

151. Fei, *Hu Yuzhi yinxiangji*, 433–446.

152. Fei, *Hu Yuzhi yinxiangji*, 235–239.

153. Roy Medvedev, ed., *The Samizdat Register* (New York: W. W. Norton, 1977); *The Samizdat Register II* (New York: W. W. Norton, 1981); and Andrei Sinyavsky, "Samizdat and the Rebirth of Literature," *Index on Censorship* 9, no. 4 (1980): 8–13.

154. Darnton, *Censors at Work*, 178–179.

155. For a list of China's underground journals in the 1970s, see Claude Widor, *The Samizdat Press in China's Provinces, 1979–1981: An Annotated Guide* (Stanford, Calif.: Hoover Institution Press, Stanford University, 1987). For a discussion of contemporary underground journals, see Link, *Uses of Literature*, 138–142; Ian Johnson, "China's Brave Underground Journal," *New York Review of Books*, December 4, 2014, 52–53; "China's Brave Underground Journal II," *New York Review of Books*, December 18, 2014, 70–72; and Bei Ling, "Bei Ling: The State of Underground Literature in China," October 13, 2009, https://www.igfm.de/bei-ling.

156. "Guowuyuan guanyu yanli daji feifa chuban huodong de tongzhi" (Notice of the State Council on severely striking down illegal publishing activities), July 6, 1987, http://www .people.com.cn/electric/flfg/d4/870706.html.

Chapter 2. Censorship and Purges at a Municipal Newspaper

1. "Mao zhuxi wei *Beijing ribao* xie de baotou" (The masthead of the *Beijing Daily* written by Chairman Mao), BMA, 114-1-11. Mao rewrote the masthead in 1964.

2. Quoted in Brooks, *Thank You, Comrade Stalin!*, 3.

3. Patricia Stranahan, *Molding the Medium: The Chinese Communist Party and the Liberation Daily* (Armonk, N.Y.: M. E. Sharpe, 1990); and Hung, *War and Popular Culture*, 221–269.

4. "Zhongyang guanyu zhongshi yunyong *Dagong bao* de tongzhi deng" (Directive from the CCP Central Committee on emphasizing the importance of *Dagong bao*, and other directives), BMA, 43-1-22; and "Guanyu baoshe qian Jing jihua he jianzao dalou gei Guowuyuan de baogao" (Report to the State Council on the relocation of *Dagong bao* and construction of office buildings), BMA, 43-1-23.

5. Brooks, *Thank You, Comrade Stalin!*, 6.

6. "*Beijing ribao* gongzuo tiaoli (cao'an)" (The working rules at the *Beijing Daily* [draft]), BMA, 114-1-160.

7. On the *Liberation Daily*, see Stranahan, *Molding the Medium*.

8. *"Beijing ribao* bianji chuban fangzhen (cao'an)" (Editorial guidelines at the *Beijing Daily* [draft]), BMA, 114-1-15; see also 114-1-3; 114-1-4.

9. BMA, 114-1-15.

10. BMA, 114-1-119; and 114-1-160.

11. "Chuangkanci" (Inaugural editorial), *Beijing ribao* (*BJRB*), October 1, 1952, 1.

12. Schudson, *Discovering the News*, 6.

13. Angus Roxburgh, *Pravda: Inside the Soviet News Machine* (New York: George Braziller, 1987), 25–26; see also Brooks, *Thank You, Comrade Stalin!*, 19.

14. Hu Jiwei, *Qingchun suiyue*, 322–323.

15. Roxburgh, *Pravda*, 26, 61, 76–79.

16. See *BJRB*, October 1, 1952, 4.

17. Deng Tuo, *Deng Tuo wenji* (Selected writings of Deng Tuo), 4 vols. (Beijing: Beijing chubanshe, 1986), 1:282–284.

18. Hu Jiwei, *Qingchun suiyue*, 323.

19. Hung, *War and Popular Culture*, 221–269.

20. Sheila Fitzpatrick, "Signals from Below: Soviet Letters of Denunciation of the 1930s," in *Accusatory Practices: Denunciation in Modern European History, 1789–1989*, ed. Sheila Fitzpatrick and Robert Gellately (Chicago: University of Chicago Press, 1997), 89.

21. "Benbao you yanzhong zhengzhi lishi wenti renyuan qingkuang" (*Beijing Daily* staff who have serious past political problems), BMA, 114-1-127.

22. Fan Jin, "Huainian yu jinyi: Huiyi Shiwei lingdao dui *Beijing ribao* de guanhuai" (Reminiscences and respect: Recalling the care given to the *Beijing Daily* by the Municipal Party leadership), *Xinwen yu chuanbo yanjiu* 1 (1983): 48–58; for an English biography of Deng Tuo, see Timothy Cheek, *Propaganda and Culture in Mao's China: Deng Tuo and the Intelligentsia* (Oxford: Clarendon Press, 1997).

23. Zhou You, "Jianchi weiwuzhuyi, jianchi shishiqiushi: jinian *Beijing ribao* chuangkan sanshi zhounian" (Upholding materialism and insisting on seeking truth from facts: Commemorating the thirtieth anniversary of the founding of the *Beijing Daily*), *Xinwen yu chuanbo yanjiu* 1 (1983): 59–67.

24. *Beijing ribao sanshinian* (Thirty years of the *Beijing Daily*) (n.p., n.d.), 213.

25. "*Beijing ribao* bianzhi renshu chubu yijian" (Preliminary suggestion for staff size of the *Beijing Daily*), BMA, 114-1-127.

26. See, for example, *BJRB*, October 1, 1952, 4.

27. Cited in Roxburgh, *Pravda*, 17.

28. BMA, 114-1-15; see also 114-1-160.

29. *BJRB*, October 22, 1952, 3.

30. *BJRB*, June 15, 1954, 1.

31. *BJRB*, May 1, 1957, 1.

32. *BJRB*, July 31, 1958, 1.

33. See, for example, *BJRB*, November 7, 1952, 1–2; and November 7, 1958, 1–4.

34. *BJRB*, March 9, 1952, 1.

35. *BJRB*, November 23, 1958, 1.

36. *BJRB*, July 19, 1958, 1.

37. *BJRB*, March 27, 1954, 1; and May 28, 1958, 1.

38. *BJRB*, October 22, 1952, 4; October 26, 1952, 4; and November 14, 1952, 4.

39. *"Beijing ribao* banmian gexin jihua (cao'an)" (Plan for the rearrangement of the layout of the *Beijing Daily* [draft]), BMA, 114-1-40.

40. In 1952, the cost per issue was 600 yuan in renminbi (people's currency) under the first currency system issued by the CCP's People's Bank of China on December 1, 1948 (see *BJRB*, October 1, 1952). In 1955, the bank issued a new series of renminbi notes that replaced the old ones at a rate of one new renminbi to ten thousand old. Hence 600 yuan became 6 fen.

41. Li Weiyi, *Zhongguo gongzi zhidu* (China's wage system) (Beijing: Zhongguo laodong chubanshe, 1991), 96; for the wage system in the 1950s, see also Yan Zhongqin, *Dangdai Zhongguo de zhigong gongzi fuli he shehui baoxian* (Wages, welfare, and social insurance of workers in contemporary China) (Beijing: Dangdai Zhongguo chubanshe, 2009), 41.

42. BMA, 114-1-22.

43. BMA, 114-1-80.

44. BMA, 114-1-159.

45. BMA, 114-1-159.

46. BMA, 114-1-80.

47. "Gaijin *Beijing wanbao* de chubu yijian" (Preliminary views on improving the *Beijing Evening News*), BMA, 114-1-120.

48. For example, the lead article in the March 19, 1961, issue tells about a model country mailman, Ren Chengshui, a devoted Communist Party member in Fangshan County, southwest of Beijing. See *Beijing wanbao*, March 19, 1961, 1.

49. BMA, 114-1-121; and 114-1-204.

50. *"Beijing ribao* dangzongzhi huiyi jilu" (Minutes of the General Party Branch meeting at the *Beijing Daily*), BMA, 114-1-25; see also 114-1-171.

51. Zhonggong Beijing shiwei Liu Ren zhuan bianxiezu, ed., *Liu Ren zhuan* (The biography of Liu Ren) (Beijing: Beijing chubanshe, 2000), 422.

52. Stranahan, *Molding the Medium*, 168.

53. BMA, 114-1-179.

54. BMA, 114-1-237.

55. See Peng Zhen's hand-written comments on a New Year editorial of the *Beijing Daily*, BMA, 114-1-225.

56. Fan Jin, "Huainian yu jingyi," 49.

57. "Bianwei kuoda huiyi" (Meeting of the expanded editorial committee), BMA, 114-1-176.

58. Roxburgh, *Pravda*; and Brooks, *Thank You, Comrade Stalin!*.

59. BMA, 114-1-160.

60. BMA, 114-1-130; see also 114-1-160; and 114-1-229.

61. BMA, 114-1-130.

62. BMA, 114-1-160. The document does not indicate where they were sent.

63. BMA, 114-1-130.

64. BMA, 114-1-130.

65. "Benbao jiguan dangweihui huiyi jilu" (Minutes of the Party Branch at the *Beijing Daily*), BMA, 114-1-233.

66. BMA, 114-1-125.

67. *RMRB*, July 3, 1955, 1.

68. Chen Yung-fa, *Yan'an de yinying* (Yan'an's shadows) (Taipei: Institute of Modern History, Academia Sinica, 1990), 1–186.

69. "Benbao guanyu ganbu wenti de zongjie, baogao, qingkuang deng" (Report on the final findings of the cadre problems at the *Beijing Daily*), BMA, 114-1-43.

70. BMA, 114-1-43.

71. Fan Jin, "Guanyu piping yu ziwo piping deng wenti de fayan" (Talk on criticism and self-criticism and other questions), BMA, 114-1-39.

72. "Benbao dangyuan qingkuang tongji baobiao" (Report on the survey of Party members at the *Beijing Daily*), BMA, 114-1-90.

73. "Benbao xuanchuan baodao jiancha" (An examination of the propaganda work at the *Beijing Daily*), BMA, 114-1-68.

74. BMA, 114-1-127.

75. "Beijing shiwei guanyu gaijin *Beijing ribao* gongzuo de jueyi (cao'an)" (Decisions of the Beijing Municipal Party on how to improve the quality of the *Beijing Daily* [draft]), BMA, 114-1-37.

76. "*Beijing ribao* guanyu fagao, shengao he gaigao chengxu zanxing guiding" (Temporary rules for publishing, reviewing, and revising articles at the *Beijing Daily*), BMA, 114-1-98.

77. "Benbao bianweihui huiyi jilu" (Minutes of the editorial committee meetings at the *Beijing Daily*), BMA, 114-1-158; see also "Bianwei kuoda huiyi," BMA, 114-1-176.

78. "Benbao guanyu xuanchuan baodao zhong baomi jiancha ji gaijin yijian" (Suggestions on how to improve reports that concern confidential information at the *Beijing Daily*), BMA, 114-1-122.

79. BMA, 114-1-158.

80. "*Beijing ribao* qingkuang jieshao (cao'gao)" (An introduction to the *Beijing Daily* [draft]), BMA, 114-1-56.

81. BMA, 114-1-37 ; see also 114-1-22; and 114-1-56.

82. *BJRB*, October 1, 1952, 4.

83. See "Letters to the Editor," *BJRB*, October 2, 1952, 2; see also "Yijiuwujiunian laixin gongzuo zongjie" (Summary of the readers' letters received in 1959), BMA, 114-1-97.

84. BMA, 114-1-97.

85. *BJRB*, January 7, 1953, 2.

86. BMA, 114-1-22.

87. BMA, 114-1-97.

88. BMA, 114-1-159.

89. *BJRB*, January 7, 1953, 2.

90. BMA, 114-1-97.

91. BMA, 114-1-159.

92. BMA, 114-1-22.

93. Sheila Fitzpatrick, "Supplicants and Citizens: Public Letter-Writing in Soviet Russia in the 1930s," *Slavic Review* 55, no. 1 (Spring 1996): 78–105.

94. *BJRB*, January 7, 1953, 2.

95. BMA, 114-1-97.

96. *BJRB*, October 1, 1952, 4. The editors noted that letters started coming in even before the first issue of the *Beijing Daily* when readers learned about its imminent publication.

97. *BJRB*, March 9, 1954, 2.

98. *BJRB*, January 11, 1953, 2.

99. *BJRB*, January 6, 1955, 2.

100. *BJRB*, January 12, 1953, 2.

101. *BJRB*, January 9, 1953, 2.

102. *BJRB*, January 12, 1953, 2.

103. *BJRB*, March 12, 1953, 2.

104. *BJRB*, June 9, 1957, 2.

105. Julian Chang, "'The Mechanics of State Propaganda: The People's Republic of China and the Soviet Union in the 1950s," in *New Perspectives on State Socialism in China*, ed. Timothy Cheek and Tony Saich (Armonk, N.Y.: M. E. Sharpe, 1997), 110.

106. Quoted in Roderick MacFarquhar and John K. Fairbank, eds., *Cambridge History of China*, vol. 15 (Cambridge: Cambridge University Press, 1991), 71.

107. *BJRB*, October 2, 1958, 1.

108. *BJRB*, August 30, 1959, 1.

109. *BJRB*, October 23, 1958, 1; and Zhonggong Beijing shiwei Liu Ren zhuan bianxiezu, *Liu Ren zhuan*, 391.

110. BMA, 114-1-139; 114-1-140; and 114-1-141.

111. Deng Tuo's essays first appeared in the *Beijing Evening News* on March 19, 1961. See Ma Nancun, "Shengming de sanfen zhi yi" (One third of life), *Beijing wanbao*, March 19, 1961, 3. For a discussion of Deng's writings in the *Beijing Evening News*, see Cheek, *Propaganda and Culture*, 240–254.

112. *BJRB*, May 29, 1966, 3.

113. Peng Zhen, *Peng Zhen wenxuan, 1941–1990* (Selected writings of Peng Zhen, 1941–1990) (Beijing: Renmin chubanshe, 1991), 313, 316.

114. Song Liansheng, *Deng Tuo de hou shinian* (The last ten years of Deng Tuo) (Wuhan: Hubei renmin chubanshe, 2010), 90.

115. BMA, 114-1-120.

116. "Benbao zongbianji huiyi jilu" (Minutes of the chief editors' meeting at the *Beijing Daily*), BMA, 114-1-177.

117. "Benbao bianweihui huiyi jilu" (Minutes of the editorial committee meetings at the *Beijing Daily*), BMA, 114-1-200.

118. *JYZW*, 1:190–193.

119. "Daxue Zhuxi zhuzuo, gaijin baozhi gongzuo" (Learn Chairman Mao's writings, and improve the quality of the newspaper), BMA, 114-1-221.

120. BMA, 114-1-200.

121. BMA, 114-1-233.

122. "Benbao zongbianji huiyi jilu" (Minutes of the chief editors' meeting at the *Beijing Daily*), BMA, 114-1-199.

123. "Bianwei kuodahui taolun Mao zhu de wenti" (How to study the writings of Chairman Mao discussed at the expanded editorial committee meeting), BMA, 114-1-216; and 114-1-185.

124. BMA, 114-1-200.

125. BMA, 114-1-216.

126. BMA, 114-1-201.

127. BMA, 114-1-200; and 114-1-221.

128. BMA, 114-1-200.

129. "Zhongyang he Shiwei lingdao tongzhi dui baozhi gongzuo de zhishi" (Instructions on the work of the newspapers by the leaders at the Central Committee and the Municipal Party), BMA, 114-1-198.

130. BMA, 114-1-200.

131. *BJRB*, June 4, 1966, 1.

132. *BJRB*, June 7, 1966, 4; July 19, 1966, 5; BMA 114-1-155; and 114-1-234.

133. *BJRB*, April 5, 1966, 2–3.

134. See Stranahan, *Molding the Medium*, 166.

135. Beijingshi difangzhi bianzuan weiyuanhui, ed., *Beijingzhi: Xinwen chuban guangbo dianshi juan: Baoye, tongxunshezhi* (The history of Beijing: News, publications, and television: The history of newspapers and news agencies) (Beijing: Beijing chubanshe, 2006), 151.

136. Fan's son, Yu Zhengsheng (b. 1945), was the chairman of the Chinese People's Consultative Conference from 2013 to 2018.

137. Beijingshi difangzhi bianzuan weiyuanhui, *Beijingzhi*, 266, 284. These 1993 numbers are the only official figures that I can find thus far.

138. Fang Hanqi, ed., *Zhongguo xinwen shiye tongshi* (General history of Chinese journalism), 3 vols. (Beijing: Zhongguo renmin daxue chubanshe, 1992-1999), 3:434.

139. Sun Xupei, "Sanshinian xinwen lifa licheng yu sikao" (The path of news legislation in the past thirty years and my reflections), *Yanhuang chunqiu* 2 (2012): 4–5; see also Sun Xupei, *Kanke zhilu*, 359–416.

Chapter 3. The Attack on a Popular Religious Sect

1. *RMRB*, January 22, 1949, 2.

2. "Xibeiju guanyu kaizhan fandui Yiguandao huodong de gongzuo zhishi" (Directive of the Northwest China Bureau on the initiation of the anti-Yiguandao campaign), *Dang de wenxian* 4 (1996): 11–13.

3. Prasenjit Duara, "Knowledge and Power in the Discourse of Modernity: The Campaigns against Popular Religion in Early Twentieth-Century China," *Journal of Asian Studies* 50, no. 1 (February 1991): 67–83; Rebecca Nedostup, *Superstitious Regimes: Religion and the Politics of Chinese Modernity* (Cambridge, Mass.: Harvard University Asia Center, 2009), 67–149; and Shuk-wah Poon, *Negotiating Religion in Modern China: State and Common People in Guangzhou, 1900-1937* (Hong Kong: Chinese University Press, 2011), 67–91.

4. Marx, *Critique of Hegel.*

5. John Anderson, *Religion, State and Politics in the Soviet Union and Successor States* (Cambridge: Cambridge University Press, 1994), 1–5; Sheila Fitzpatrick, *Stalin's Peasants: Resistance and Survival in the Russian Village after Collectivization* (New York: Oxford University Press, 1994), 59–65; and Viola, *Peasant Rebels under Stalin*, 38–44.

6. For a brief account, see Goossaert and Palmer, *The Religious Question*, 138–404; on the CCP's attack on the Catholic Church, see James T. Myer, *Enemies without Guns: The Catholic Church in the People's Republic of China* (New York: Paragon, 1991), 83–226.

7. Jan Kiely, "The Communist Dismantling of Temple and Monastic Buddhism in Suzhou," in *Recovering Buddhism in Modern China*, ed. Jan Kiely and J. Brooks Jessup (New York: Columbia University Press, 2016), 216–253.

8. Holmes Welch, *Buddhism under Mao* (Cambridge, Mass.: Harvard University Press, 1972), 42–83.

9. Mariani, *Church Militant*, 109–168.

10. Kenneth G. Lieberthal, *Revolution and Tradition in Tientsin, 1949-1952* (Stanford, Calif.: Stanford University Press, 1980).

11. Prasenjit Duara, *Sovereignty and Authenticity: Manchukuo and the East Asian Modern* (Lanham, Md.: Rowman and Littlefield, 2003), 87–129; David Ownby, "Recent Chinese Scholarship on the History of 'Redemptive Societies,'" *Chinese Studies in History* 44, nos. 1–2 (Fall 2010/Winter 2010–2011): 3–9; and S. A. Smith, "Redemptive Religious Societies and the Communist State, 1949 to the 1980s," in *Maoism at the Grassroots*, ed. Brown and Johnson, 340–364.

12. de Groot, *Sectarianism and Religious Persecution*.

13. C. K. Yang, *Religion in Chinese Society: A Study of Contemporary Social Functions of Religion and Some of Their Historical Factors* (Berkeley: University of California Press, 1961).

14. Daniel Overmyer, *Folk Buddhist Religion: Dissenting Sects in Late Traditional China* (Cambridge, Mass.: Harvard University Press, 1976), 38–52; for other millenarian rebellions, such as the Eight Trigrams, see Naquin, *Millenarian Rebellion in China*.

15. PRC, *Common Program*, 4.

16. "Zhonghua renmin gongheguo chengzhi fangeming tiaoli" (PRC rules for punishing the counterrevolutionaries), *RMRB*, February 22, 1951, 1.

17. "Zhonggong zhongyang guanyu zhenya fangeming huodong de zhishi" (Directive on the suppression of counterrevolutionary activities by the Central Committee of the CCP), in *JYZW*, 1:420–423.

18. *RMRB*, July 24, 1950, 1.

19. Mao Zedong, "Guanyu zhenya fangeming" (On the suppression of counterrevolutionaries), in *Mao Zedong wenji*, 6:119.

20. Ma and Han, *Zhongguo minjian zongjiaoshi*, 1150–1167.

21. For a brief history of Yiguandao, see Li Shiyu, *Xiandai huabei mimi zongjiao* (Secret religions in modern North China) (Shanghai: Shanghai wenyi chubanshe, 1990), 32–130; Ma and Han, *Zhongguo minjian zongjiaoshi*, 1092–1167; Fu Zhong, *Yiguandao fazhanshi* (The development of Yiguandao) (Taibei xian: Zhengyi shanshu chubanshe, 1999), 1–296; Zhongwei Lu, "Huidaomen in the Republican Period," *Chinese Studies in History* 44, nos. 1–2 (Fall 2010/Winter 2010–2011): 10–37; and Joseph Bosco, "Yiguan Dao: 'Heterodoxy' and Popular Religion in Taiwan," in *The Other Taiwan: 1945 to the Present*, ed. Murray A. Rubinstein (Armonk, N.Y.: M. E. Sharpe, 1994), 423–444.

22. David K. Jordan and Daniel L. Overmyer, *The Flying Phoenix: Aspects of Chinese Sectarianism in Taiwan* (Princeton, N.J.: Princeton University Press, 1986), 213–218; see also Overmyer, *Folk Buddhist Religion*, 106.

23. Li Shiyu, *Xiandai huabei*, 45–55.

24. For a brief biography of Zhang Tianran, see Li Shiyu, *Xiandai huabei*, 48–50; see also Jordan and Overmyer, *Flying Phoenix*, 213–217.

25. Song Guangyu, "Yiguandao de zuotian, jintian he mingtian" (The past, present, and future of Yiguandao), *Lianhe yuekan* 10 (May 1982): 75.

26. See the Shanghai municipal government's pre-1949 orders to ban Yiguandao, Shanghai Municipal Archives (SMA), Q6-10-413; and Q155-4-33.

27. "Jianjue qudi Yiguandao" (Determine to ban Yiguandao), *RMRB*, December 20, 1950, 1.

28. Song Guangyu, "Yiguandao de zuotian," 75.

29. *Neibu cankao* (Internal references; *NBCK*), September 25, 1950, 145.

30. Qinggeltu, "Jianguo chuqi Suiyuan diqu qudi Yiguandao de douzheng" (The banning of Yiguandao in the Suiyuan areas during the early People's Republic), *Neimenggu daxue xuebao* 33, no. 3 (May 2001): 45.

31. "Jingjiao qudi Yiguandao gongzuo zongjie" (Summary report on the banning of Yiguandao in the suburbs of Beijing), BMA, 1-14-165.

32. "Xibeiju guanyu kaizhan," 11.

33. Feng Jiping, "Jixu gaijin shoudu de shehui zhixu" (Continue to improve the public order in the capital), in *Beijingshi zhongyao wenxian xuanbian, 1951* (Selected important documents of Beijing, 1951; *BZWX 1951*), ed. Beijingshi dang'anguan and Zhonggong Beijing shiwei dangshi yanjiushi (Beijing: Zhongguo dang'an chubanshe, 2001), 55.

34. *NBCK*, September 25, 1950, 145.

35. "Jingjiao qudi Yiguandao," BMA, 1-14-165.

36. "Beijingshi gong'anju guanyu qudi Yiguandao gongzuo de qingkuang ji jingyan jiaoxun de baogao" (Report on the experience and lessons of the suppression of Yiguandao by the Public Security Bureau, Beijing), in *BZWX 1951*, 262.

37. "Jingjiao qudi Yiguandao," BMA, 1-14-165.

38. "Jingjiao qudi Yiguandao," BMA, 1-14-165.

39. Gao, *Communist Takeover of Hangzhou*, 142.

40. "Jingjiao qudi Yiguandao," BMA, 1-14-165; and Lieberthal, *Revolution and Tradition*, 108–109.

41. "Zhonggong zhongyang pizhuan Zhongyang gong'anbu 'Guanyu quanguo gong'an huiyi de baogao'" (Report on the national conference on public security, issued by the Ministry of the Public Security and transmitted by the Central Committee of the Party), in *JYZW*, 1:444.

42. Luo Ruiqing, *Lun renmin gong'an gongzuo* (On the people's public security work) (Beijing: Qunzhong chubanshe, 1994), 147.

43. Mao Zedong, *Jianguo yilai Mao Zedong wengao* (Mao Zedong's manuscripts since the founding of the PRC), 13 vols. (Beijing: Zhongyang wenxian chubanshe, 1988), 2:71.

44. *BZWX 1951*, 259–260.

45. "Cuihui fandong tongzhi, jianli renmin zhengquan" (Smash reactionary rule, establish the people's regime), in *Beijingshi zhongyao wenxian xuanbian, 1950* (Selected important documents of Beijing, 1950; *BZWX 1950*), ed. Beijingshi dang'anguan and Zhonggong Beijing shiwei dangshi yanjiushi (Beijing: Zhongguo dang'an chubanshe, 2001), 130.

46. "Beijingshi renmin zhengfu bugao, yanli qudi Yiguandao" (Proclamation of the Beijing People's Government to sternly suppress Yiguandao), *RMRB*, December 19, 1950, 4.

47. "Jingjiao qudi Yiguandao," BMA, 1-14-165.

48. *BZWX 1951*, 260.

49. Mao, "Guanyu zhenya fangeming," in *Mao Zedong wenji*, 6:121.

50. Mao, "Guanyu zhenya fangeming," in *Mao Zedong wenji*, 6:117.

51. "Kaizhan zhenya fangeming qunzhong yundong de xuanchuan yaodian" (Key propaganda issues in launching the suppression of the counterrevolutionary mass movement), SMA, A22-1-14.

52. *RMRB*, March 7, 1951, 1.

53. Luo Ruiqing, "Zhonggong zhongyang zhuanfa Luo Ruiqing guanyu qudi fandong huidaomen qingkuang de baogao" (Luo Ruiqing's report concerning the suppression of reactionary sects, transmitted by the Central Committee of the CCP), *Dang de wenxian* 4 (1996): 18.

54. Quoted in Guo Yuqiang, "Jianguo qianhou qudi Yiguandao de douzheng" (Struggle in the banning of Yiguandao before and after the founding of the nation), *Zhonggong dangshi ziliao* 60 (December 1996): 129.

55. "Beijingshi renmin zhengfu bugao."

56. "Yancheng huebuquan de huidaomen shoue" (Severely punish obdurate and irre-deemable sect leaders), *RMRB*, January 19, 1951, 1; see also *Guangming ribao* (Enlightenment daily; *GMRB*), January 19, 1951, 3.

57. *RMRB*, January 19, 1951, 1.

58. *GMRB*, February 19, 1951, 1.

59. *GMRB*, March 26, 1951, 1.

60. *NBCK*, August 31, 1951, 107.

61. *GMRB*, January 19, 1951, 3.

62. *GMRB*, May 23, 1951, 1–6.

63. "Jianjue qudi Yiguandao," *RMRB*, December 20, 1950, 1.

64. Guo Yuqiang, "Jianguo qianhou," 126.

65. Luo Ruiqing, "Sannianlai zhenya fangeming gongzuo de weida chengjiu" (The great achievements of the Zhenfan campaign in the past three years), *RMRB*, September 29, 1952, 2.

66. Luo, *Lun renmin gong'an gongzuo*, 145–149.

67. Luo Ruiqing, "Qudi fandong huidaomen gongzuo chujian chengxiao" (The initial suc-cess of the suppression of reactionary sects), in *Lun renmin gong'an gongzuo*, 169–173; see also Guo Yuqiang, "Jianguo qianhou," 124.

68. Yang Kuisong, "Reconsidering the Campaign," 120.

69. Luo, *Lun renmin gong'an gongzuo*, 98.

70. *GMRB*, May 15, 1951, 1; and October 1, 1951, 2.

71. Luo, "Sannianlai zhenya fangeming."

72. Lewis H. Siegelbaum, *Stakhanovism and the Politics of Productivity in the USSR, 1935–1941* (Cambridge: Cambridge University Press, 1988).

73. Julia Strauss, "Morality, Coercion and State Building by Campaign in the Early PRC: Regime Consolidation and After, 1949–1956," *China Quarterly* 188 (December 2006): 898.

74. Mao, "Guanyu zhenya fangeming," 120.

75. Liu Shaoqi, "Guanyu kaizhan fandui Yiguandao huodong gei Xibeiju de xin" (A letter to the Northwest Bureau concerning the launch of the anti-Yiguandao activities), *Dang de wenxian* 4 (1996): 10.

76. *NBCK*, June 26, 1950, 97.

77. *GMRB*, March 26, 1951, 1.

78. Luo, "Zhonggong zhongyang zhuanfa," 19.

79. "Jingjiao qudi Yiguandao," BMA, 1-14-165.

80. "Jingjiao qudi Yiguandao," BMA, 1-14-165; see also *GMRB*, June 9, 1950, 4.

81. Gao, *Communist Takeover of Hangzhou*, 42–68.

82. *BZWX 1951*, 260.

83. "Zhenya fangeming xuanchuan gongzuo de xiaojie" (Summary of the propaganda campaign to suppress counterrevolutionaries), SMA, A22-1-14; and "Guanyu quanmian qudi fandong huidaomen gongzuo zhong xuanchuan gongzuo de tongzhi" (Circular of the propa-ganda work in the all-out suppression of counterrevolutionary sects), SMA, A22-1-93.

84. *BZWX 1951*, 260.

85. Peng Zhen, "Gong'an gongzuo yao yikao qunzhong" (Public security work relies on the masses), in *Peng Zhen wenxuan*, 253.

86. David Holm, *Art and Ideology in Revolutionary China* (Oxford: Clarendon Press, 1991).

87. "Xibeiju guanyu kaizhan," *Dang de wenxian,* 12; see also *Beijingshi zhongyao wenxian xuanbian, 1948.12–1949* (Selected important documents of Beijing, 1948.12–1949; *BZWX 1948.12–1949*), ed. Beijingshi dang'anguan and Zhonggong Beijing shiwei dangshi yanjiushi (Beijing: Zhongguo dang'an chubanshe, 2001), 739.

88. *BZWX 1948.12–1949,* 737.

89. Hung, *War and Popular Culture,* 221–269.

90. *Yiguan hairendao* (A reactionary sect), a film produced by Zhongyang dianyinju, Beijing dianying zhipianchang (Beijing Film Studio, the Central Film Bureau), 1952.

91. Fang Cheng, *Dianchuanshi* (Yiguandao instructor), *RMRB,* August 4, 1955, 2.

92. Tian Zuoliang, *Xianban* (The class of the immortals), *RMRB,* May 9–12, 1951, 3.

93. "Guanyu benshi guanche zhenya fangeming yundong de xuanchuan gongzuo tongzhi" (Proclamation of the city's implementation of propaganda work to suppress counterrevolutionaries), SMA, A22-1-93.

94. *GMRB,* May 17, 1951, 1.

95. *RMRB,* December 26, 1950, 3.

96. Geng Zhizhong, "Wo zenyang tuichule Yiguandao" (How I withdrew from Yiguandao), *RMRB,* December 24, 1950, 3.

97. Geng Zhizhong, "Wo zenyang tuichule Yiguandao."

98. Zhongguo geming bowuguan, ed., *Jiefangqu zhanlanhui ziliao* (Materials on the exhibitions held in the liberated areas) (Beijing: Wenwu chubanshe, 1988), preface, 1.

99. "Ji Yiguandao zuizheng zhanlan" (On the exhibition of the criminal evidence against Yiguandao), *RMRB,* March 3, 1951, 3.

100. *GMRB,* January 18, 1951, 3; and *RMRB,* March 3, 1951, 3.

101. "Ji Yiguandao zuizheng zhanlan," *RMRB,* March 3, 1951, 3.

102. Shanghaishi renmin zhengfu gong'anju, "Qudi fandong huidaomen xuanchuan gongzuo shouce" (Propaganda handbook for banning reactionary sects), SMA, A22-1-93.

103. Qinggeltu, "Jianguo chuqi," 47.

104. For some names of public trials, see *Xinhua yuebao* (New China monthly; *XHYB*) 4, no. 1 (May 25, 1951): 19–21; see also *GMRB,* March 27, 1950, 4.

105. Elizabeth A. Wood, *Performing Justice: Agitation Trials in Early Soviet Russia* (Ithaca, N.Y.: Cornell University Press, 2005); and Sheila Fitzpatrick, *Tear Off the Masks! Identity and Imposture in Twentieth-Century Russia* (Princeton, N.J.: Princeton University Press, 2005), 203–239; on public trials in the history of modern Europe, see Sheila Fitzpatrick and Robert Gellately, eds., *Accusatory Practices: Denunciation in Modern European History, 1789–1989* (Chicago: University of Chicago Press, 1997).

106. *GMRB,* March 25, 1951, 1; and *XHYB* 4, no. 1 (May 25, 1951): 19.

107. "Guanyu benshi guanche zhenya fangeming," SMA, A22-1-93.

108. "Zhenya fangeming xuanchuan," SMA, A22-1-14.

109. *XHYB* 3, no. 6 (April 25, 1951): illustrations.

110. *GMRB,* January 18, 1951, 3; and May 18, 1951, 1.

111. *GMRB,* May 18, 1951, 1.

112. *GMRB,* May 22, 1951, 1.

113. *GMRB,* May 22, 1951, 1; and May 23, 1951, 2.

114. Robert Conquest, *The Harvest of Sorrow: Soviet Collectivization and the Terror-Famine* (New York: Oxford University Press, 1986), 295; and Fitzpatrick, *Tear Off the Masks!,* 203–239.

115. *XHYB* 4, no. 1 (May 25, 1951): 19.

116. *GMRB*, May 22, 1951, 1.

117. "Weishenme yao qudi fandong huidaomen" (Why reactionary sects must be outlawed), SMA, A22-1-93.

118. "Weishenme yao qudi fandong huidaomen," SMA, A22-1-93.

119. Feng Shaoqian, "Wo jianju le yeye" (I report my grandfather's offenses to the authorities), *RMRB*, April 17, 1951, 3.

120. *XHYB* 4, no. 1 (May 25, 1951): 19.

121. *NBCK*, June 20, 1951, 64.

122. Yang Kuisong, "Reconsidering the Campaign," 113.

123. Luo, "Zhonggong zhongyang zhuanfa," 19.

124. *NBCK*, April 12, 1951, 67–68.

125. *NBCK*, June 25, 1951, 85.

126. *NBCK*, June 20, 1951, 64.

127. *NBCK*, June 12, 1954, 68.

128. Shiwei yanjiushi, "Gongye wenti zuotanhui jiyao: (21) Jiefang yilai, gongchang li kaizhan le neixie qunzhong yundong?" (Summary of a forum on industrial issues: (No. 21) What mass movements have been conducted in factories since the Liberation?" BMA, 1-9-585.

129. *XHYB* 7 (1954): 25.

130. Guo Yuqiang, "Jianguo qianhou," 134–135.

131. Fu Zhong, *Yiguandao fazhanshi*; Yunfeng Lu, *The Transformation of Yiguan Dao in Taiwan: Adapting to a Changing Religious Economy* (Lanham, Md.: Rowman and Littlefield, 2008), 146–151; Bosco, "Yiguan Dao"; Robert P. Weller, *Alternate Civilities: Democracy and Culture in China and Taiwan* (Boulder, Colo.: Westview, 1999), 92–93; and Goossaert and Palmer, *Religious Question in Modern China*, 356–357.

132. Yunfeng Lu, *Transformation of Yiguan Dao*, 59–60.

133. Ownby, *Falun Gong*, 23–44, 161–227; and Maria Hsia Chang, *Falun Gong: The Ends of Days* (New Haven, Conn.: Yale University Press, 2004), 32–59, 96–123.

134. Yang, *Religion in Chinese Society*, 231.

135. Ian Johnson, *The Souls of China: The Return of Religion after Mao* (New York: Pantheon Books, 2017), 16–32, 73–93, 125–151, 195–215, 301–332.

136. Goossaert and Palmer, *Religious Question in Modern China*, 191.

137. Pitman B. Potter, "Belief in Control: Regulation of Religion in China," *China Quarterly* 174 (June 2003): 317–337.

138. Nancy N. Chen, *Breathing Spaces: Qigong, Psychiatry, and Healing in China* (New York: Columbia University Press, 2003), 170–179.

Chapter 4. Building Cultural Centers at the Grassroots

1. "Beijing de wenhuaguan" (Beijing's cultural centers), BMA, 1-12-870. "*Qunzhong*" (mass) and "*wenhua*" (culture) are familiar words in Chinese, but this combination has been used as a term with specific political implications only since the founding of the People's Republic of China. See Beijingshi dang'anguan, ed., *Beijing dang'an shiliao, 2012, no. 2: Dang'an zhong de Beijing wenhua* (Beijing archival sources, 2012, no. 2: Beijing cultures in the archives) (Beijing: Xinhua chubanshe, 2012), 151.

2. Peter Kenez, *The Birth of the Propaganda State: Soviet Methods of Mass Mobilization, 1917–1929* (Cambridge: Cambridge University Press, 1985).

3. Brady, *Marketing Dictatorship*; Michael Schoenhals, *Doing Things with Words in Chinese Politics: Five Studies* (Berkeley: Institute of East Asian Studies, University of California, 1992); Cheek, *Propaganda and Culture;* Julian Chang, "The Mechanics of State Propaganda"; Volland, "The Control of the Media"; and Shambaugh, "China's Propaganda."

4. See John K. Fairbank and Kwang-ching Liu, eds., *The Cambridge History of China,* vol. 11 (Cambridge: Cambridge University Press, 1980), 375–415.

5. Zhou Huimei, *Minzhong jiaoyuguan yu Zhongguo shehui bianqian* (Popular education centers and changes in Chinese society) (Taipei: Xiuwei zixun keji gufen youxian gongsi, 2013), 83.

6. Zhou Huimei, *Minzhong jiaoyuguan,* 84–85.

7. Zhou Huimei, *Minzhong jiaoyuguan,* 96–100.

8. Zhou Huimei, *Minzhong jiaoyuguan,* 107.

9. Kenez, *Birth of the Propaganda State,* 56–57, 72.

10. Stephen Lovell, "Broadcasting Bolshevik: The Radio Voice of Soviet Culture, 1920s–1950s," *Journal of Contemporary History* 48, no. 1 (January 2013): 82.

11. Olga Boitsova, "Photographs in Contemporary Russian Rural and Urban Interiors," in *Material Culture in Russia and the USSR: Things, Values, Identities,* ed. Gram H. Roberts (London: Bloomsbury Academic, 2017), 72–82; and Kenez, *Birth of the Propaganda State,* 134–137.

12. Kenez, *Birth of the Propaganda State,* 136–139; see also Jeremy E. Taylor, "The Sinification of Soviet Agitational Theatre: 'Living Newspapers' in Mao's China," *Journal of the British Association for Chinese Studies* 2 (July 2013): 27–50.

13. See *Jiefang ribao* (Liberation daily; *JFRB*), November 17, 1941, 1; and March 5, 1942, 2.

14. *RMRB,* February 26, 1949, 3.

15. BMA, 1-12-18.

16. "Beijing de wenhuaguan," BMA, 1-12-870.

17. "Beijing de wenhuaguan," BMA, 1-12-870.

18. Mao, *Selected Works,* 4:415.

19. "Beijing de wenhuaguan," BMA, 1-12-870.

20. "Beijing de wenhuaguan," BMA, 1-12-870.

21. Beijingshi gongnong yeyu jiaoyuju, "Benju guanyu wenhuaguan, shubao yuelanshi gongzuo de gaikuo, zongjie" (The bureau's outline and summary of the activities at the cultural centers' newspaper reading rooms), BMA, 152-1-52.

22. BMA, 152-1-157.

23. "Beijing de wenhuaguan," BMA, 1-12-870; see also 164-1-175.

24. "Beijing de wenhuaguan," BMA, 1-12-870.

25. "Beijing de wenhuaguan," BMA, 1-12-870.

26. *RMRB,* November 3, 1980, 2.

27. "Guanyu bianzhi yijiuwuwunian wenhua shiye jianshe jihuashi" (The plan for cultural activities in 1955), BMA, 11-2-226.

28. *RMRB,* May 13, 1958, 7.

29. "Beijing de wenhuaguan," BMA, 1-12-870.

30. Quoted in Kenez, *Birth of the Propaganda State,* 8–9.

31. "Shehui wenhuake (Wenhuaguan bufen) zongjie" (Summary report of the Social and Cultural Section concerning the cultural center), BMA, 11-2-189; see also "Beijing de wenhuaguan," BMA, 1-12-870.

32. Kenez, *Birth of the Propaganda State,* 134–140.

33. BMA, 152-1-52.

34. "Beijing de wenhuaguan," BMA, 1–12-870.

35. "Beijing de wenhuaguan," BMA, 1–12-870.

36. "Wenhuachu guanyu sannianlai wenhua gongzuo jiancha, wenyi gongzuo huiyi ji yijiuwuernian gongzuo zongjie baogao" (Summary report of the Cultural Department on the cultural work accomplished in the past three years, the working conference on literature and art, and the work completed in 1952), BMA, 11–2-148.

37. "Wenhuachu guanyu sannianlai," BMA, 11–2-148.

38. BMA, 11–1-139; and 164–1-163.

39. Beijingshi renmin zhengfu wenhua shiye guanlichu, "He Zhenlibao jizhe de tanhua" (Talk with a reporter from *Pravda*), BMA, 11–2-160.

40. "Beijing de wenhuaguan," BMA, 1–12-870; see also 11–2-148; and *RMRB*, November 6, 1950, 2.

41. A 1960 official report divided the first decade of the cultural centers into four phases: 1949 to 1952; 1953 to June 1955; July 1955 to the end of 1956; and 1957 to 1959. See "Beijing de wenhuaguan," BMA, 1–12-870.

42. "Beijing de wenhuaguan," BMA, 1–12-870.

43. BMA, 11–2-148.

44. PRC, *Common Program*, 2.

45. BMA, 11–2-189.

46. BMA, 11–2-148.

47. BMA, 11–1-117.

48. Beijingshi wenhuaju, "Guanyu fenli wenhua, chuban, dianying sangeju de zuzhi jigou renyuan bianzhi de qingshi" (Ask for instructions concerning the organization of the staff in the three separate bureaus of Culture, Publications, and Film), BMA, 1–24-14; see also "Beijingshi diyi wenhuaguan de diaocha baogao" (An investigative report of the No. 1 Cultural Center of Beijing), BMA, 11–1-118.

49. BMA, 11–2-148.

50. "Beijing de wenhuaguan," BMA, 1–12-870.

51. Beijingshi wenhuaju, "Beijingshi wenhua shiye yuanjing guihua cao'an" (Draft of Beijing's plan for future cultural activities), BMA, 164–1-163.

52. *JYZW*, 8:56–57.

53. "Beijing de wenhuaguan," BMA, 1–12-870.

54. "Beijing de wenhuaguan," BMA, 1–12-870.

55. *JYZW*, 5:247–251.

56. Gongqingtuan Beijingshi weiyuanhui, "Guanyu wenjiaoguan de jieshuoci" (Guidelines from the Culture and Education Center), BMA, 100–3-473.

57. "Shiwei xuanchuanbu guanyu Beijingshi fazhan xuanchuanwang de qingkuang" (Report of the Beijing Municipal Propaganda Department on the development of the propaganda network in the city), BMA 1–12-96.

58. All quotes and facts in this paragraph are from "Beijing de wenhuaguan," BMA 1–12-870.

59. BMA, 152-1-52.

60. "Beijing de wenhuaguan," BMA, 1–12-870.

61. "Beijing de wenhuaguan," BMA, 1–12-870.

Notes to Pages 93–97

. "Liantiebu heibanbao zai shehuizhuyi jingsai zhong weishenme shoudao qunzhong de huanying" (Why the bulletin boards in the iron-smelting section became so popular during the socialist competition), BMA 1–12-272.

63. "Shiwei xuanchuanbu guanyu zhaokai xuanchuanyuan daibiao huiyi de jihua" (Plan for the meeting of representatives of the Municipal Propaganda Department), BMA 1–12-110.

64. "Beijing de wenhuaguan," BMA, 1–12-870.

65. "Beijing de wenhuaguan," BMA, 1–12-870.

66. "Beijing de wenhuaguan," BMA, 1–12-870.

67. "Beijing de wenhuaguan," BMA, 1–12-870; see also 1–12-223.

68. "Guanyu xuanchuan gudong gongzuo de baogao" (Report on propaganda and agitation), BMA, 101–1–334; see also 1–12-272.

69. BMA, 1–12-272.

70. BMA, 1–12-223.

71. Richard Stites, *Russian Popular Culture: Entertainment and Society since 1900* (Cambridge: Cambridge University Press, 1992), 41, 53–54.

72. Hung, *War and Popular Culture*, 221–269.

73. Mao, *Selected Works*, 3:69–98.

74. "Beijing de wenhuaguan," BMA, 1–12-870.

75. "Beijing de wenhuaguan," BMA, 1–12-870.

76. Guo Moruo and Zhou Yang, eds., *Hongqi geyao* (Songs of the Red Flag) (Beijing: Renmin wenxue chubanshe, 1979).

77. "Beijing de wenhuaguan," BMA, 1–12-870.

78. "Beijing de wenhuaguan," BMA, 1–12-870.

79. "Beijing de wenhuaguan," BMA, 1–12-870.

80. Clifford Geertz, *Negara: The Theatre State in Nineteenth-Century Bali* (Princeton, N.J.: Princeton University Press, 1980); see also Victor Turner, ed., *Celebration: Studies in Festivity and Ritual* (Washington, D.C.: Smithsonian Institution Press, 1982).

81. "Wenhuabu guanyu jiaqiang nongcun chunjie wenhua yishu gongzuo de zhishi" (Instructions for strengthening cultural and artistic activities in villages during the Spring Festival, issued by the Ministry of Culture), BMA, 8–2-20.

82. BMA, 1–5-272.

83. "Beijing de wenhuaguan," BMA, 1–12-870.

84. "Beijing de wenhuaguan," BMA, 1–12-870.

85. "Beijing de wenhuaguan," BMA, 1–12-870.

86. "Beijing de wenhuaguan," BMA, 1–12-870.

87. Quoted in Victoria E. Bonnell, *Iconography of Power: Soviet Political Posters under Lenin and Stalin* (Berkeley: University of California Press, 1997), 4–5.

88. Mao, "Report on an Investigation of the Peasant Movement in Hunan," in *Selected Works*, 1:48.

89. Hung, *War and Popular Culture*, 221–269.

90. "Xuanchuanhua: youxiao de xuanchuan wuqi" (Propaganda pictorials, an effective weapon of propaganda), BMA, 1–12-223.

91. "Beijing de wenhuaguan," BMA, 1–12-870.

92. BMA, 101–1–334.

93. "Beijing de wenhuaguan," BMA, 1–12-870.

94. Bonnell, *Iconography of Power*, 10.

95. BMA, 1–12-223.

96. "Diyishe shencha xin lianhuanhua mingdan" (List of serial picture story books for review by the First Association), BMA, 8–2-154.

97. BMA, 152–1-52.

98. "Beijing de wenhuaguan," BMA, 1–12-870.

99. Lovell, "Broadcasting Bolshevik," 80.

100. "Beijingzhi: Guangbo tongxunshe chubanbian" (Annals of Beijing: The history of broadcasting and the news agency), BMA, 1–12-863.

101. "Guanyu jieban Beijing renmin guangbo diantai wenti de qingshi baogao" (Report on taking over the Beijing People's Radio Station), BMA, 1–12-442.

102. BMA, 1–12-863; see also *SHZY*, 2:210–211.

103. BMA, 1–12-863.

104. "Yijiuwujiunian Guangbochu gongzuo zongjie (caogao)" (Summary of the work of the Broadcasting Bureau in 1959 [draft]), BMA, 164–1-234.

105. BMA, 1–12-863.

106. "Beijing de wenhuaguan," BMA, 1–12-870.

107. BMA, 1–12-863.

108. "Beijing de wenhuaguan," BMA, 1–12-870.

109. "Beijing de wenhuaguan," BMA, 1–12-870.

110. "Guanyu jiaoqu dianhua, guangbowang touzi xiaoguo jiancha baogao" (Report on the benefits of telephones and broadcasting networks in Beijing's outlying areas), BMA, 1–14-396.

111. "Guanyu jiaoqu dianhua," BMA, 1–14-396.

112. "Beijing de wenhuaguan," BMA, 1–12-870.

113. "Beijing de wenhuaguan," BMA, 1–12-870.

114. "Beijing de wenhuaguan," BMA, 1–12-870.

115. "Beijing de wenhuaguan," BMA, 1–12-870.

116. "Beijing de wenhuaguan," BMA, 1–12-870; see also *RMRB*, September 19, 1950, 6; and January 24, 1954, 3.

117. BMA, 11–1-117.

118. *RMRB*, June 15, 1957, 7.

119. *RMRB*, June 15, 1957, 7.

120. BMA, 1–24-14.

121. BMA, 11–1-139.

122. "Beijing de wenhuaguan," BMA, 1–12-870.

123. See Gao, *Communist Takeover of Hangzhou*.

124. Staff increased in the late 1950s. For example, in the Chaoyang Cultural Center, the number reached twenty-two in 1959, compared to only four in 1951. See "Beijing de wenhuaguan," BMA, 1–12-870.

125. "Beijing de wenhuaguan," BMA, 1–12-870.

126. BMA, 11–2-148.

127. BMA, 1–12-650; 11–1-139; and 11–2-148.

128. BMA, 11–1-139.

129. Kenez, *Birth of the Propaganda State*, 54, 257.

130. "Wenhuachu gongzuo zhoubao" (Weekly bulletin of the work of the Cultural Department), BMA, 11–2-157.

131. "Beijing de wenhuaguan," BMA, 1-12-870.

132. "Benshi ge wenhuaguan, zhanganbu peibeibiao he xuexi jihua" (The personnel arrangement of the cadres at various cultural centers and cultural stations in Beijing and their study plan), BMA, 11-2-77.

133. BMA, 1-12-363.

134. BMA, 1-12-650.

135. "Guanyu jiaoqu nongcun zhishiqingnian muqian de sixiang, xuexi qingkuang he wenti" (On the present ideology and study conditions of educated youths in rural areas near Beijing), BMA, 1-12-521.

136. BMA, 1-12-363.

137. Beijingshi wenhuaju, "Haidianqu nongcun wenhua gongzuo diaocha cailiao" (Investigation documents on the cultural work in the villages of Haidian District), BMA, 164-1-242.

138. Beijingshi wenhuaju, "Haidianqu nongcun," BMA, 164-1-242; see also *RMRB*, January 27, 1950, 3.

139. Beijingshi shiwei wenhuabu, "Benju dangwei guanyu yijiuwuliunian benshi jiaoqu nongcun wenhua gongzuo qingkuang ji jinhou gaijin de baogao" (Report of the Party Committee of the Cultural Bureau on the conditions of rural cultural work in the outlying areas of Beijing in 1956 and its future improvement), BMA, 164-1-9.

140. "Beijingshi wenhuaju guanyu nongcun wenhua gongzuo de qingkuang ji jinhou gaijin yijian de baogao (cao'an)" (Report of the Cultural Bureau of the City of Beijing on the conditions of rural cultural work and its future improvement [draft]), BMA, 164-1-4.

141. "Guanyu Dayuejin yilai jiceng wenhua gongzuo de jiantao baogao" (Review of the cultural activities at the grassroots level since the Great Leap Forward), BMA, 164-1-46.

142. "Xuanchuanbu yijiuliusannian shangbannian gongzuo xiaojie" (Brief summary of the work done in the first six months of 1963 by the Propaganda Department), BMA, 101-1-1170.

143. BMA, 1-12-363; and 84-2-339.

144. "Guanyu jinyibu gaizao minjian zhiye xiqu jutuan de fang'an" (Plan for further reforming the professional folk opera troupes), BMA, 164-1-15.

145. A 2013 article in Chinese touches very briefly on Shanghai's cultural centers. See Xiao Wenming, "Guojia chujiao de xiandu zhi zai kaocha: yi xin Zhongguo chengli chuqi Shanghai de wenhua gaizao wei gean" (A reinvestigation of the limitations of the official outreach program: A case study of cultural reform in Shanghai in the early years of the People's Republic), *Kaifang shidai* 3 (2013): 130–152.

146. See *RMRB*, April 27, 1950, 6; June 27, 1950, 3; and January 24, 1954, 3.

147. *RMRB*, April 27, 1950, 6.

148. *RMRB*, May 17, 1950, 3; June 21, 1951, 3; and April 2, 1952, 6.

149. Jacques Ellul, *Propaganda: The Formation of Men's Attitudes*, trans. Konrad Kellen and Jean Lerner (New York: Vintage Books, 1973), 18.

150. Li Li, "Xinshiqi zuohao xianji wenhuaguan gongzuo de jidian sikao" (On how to better manage the county-level cultural centers in the new era), *Dazhong wenyi* 14 (2012): 199; and Wang Jiangzheng, "Qianxi wenhuaguan zai qunzhong wenhua shijian zhong de zhineng yu fahui" (A brief analysis of the function and development of the cultural centers in promoting mass culture), *Dazhong wenyi* 2 (2016): 21.

151. The average monthly salary for a worker at the Guangzhou Cultural Center in South China in 2017 was 2,662 yuan ($394), whereas that of a university graduate in the same year was 4,854 yuan ($719). See "Wenhuaguan de gongzi" (Cultural center salaries), https://www

.kanzhun.com/gsx1599688.html (accessed February 10, 2019); and "2017 nian Zhongguo daxue biyesheng de qixin gongbule, han shuo, boshi" (Starting salaries of university graduates, including master's degree and PhD graduates, in 2017), https://chinaqna.com/a/14973 (accessed February 10, 2019).

152. Dong Futeng, "Xinshiqi wenhuaguan rencai duiwu jianshe yu guanli yanjiu" (The recruitment of talent and management issues in cultural centers in the new era), *Dazhong wenyi* 2 (2016): 9.

153. "Yidai, yilu zai woguan yanchu" (The staging of the opera *One Belt, One Road* at our cultural center), http://dcwhg.bjdch.gov.cn/n3363374/n3373107/n3373108/n3373109/c3571655/content.html (accessed February 17, 2017).

154. "Guangdongsheng wenhuaguan dangzhibu kaizhan zhuti dangri xuexi huodong" (Studying important [Party] decisions on the special day set aside for organization activities launched by the Party Branch of the Cultural Center of Guangdong Province), http://www.gdsqyg.com/agdzxdt/workinginfo?id=2018122623760481 (accessed January 9, 2019).

Chapter 5. Turning Chinese Children Red

1. Beijingshi jiaoyuju youjiaoke, "Yijiuwulingnian diyi xueqi geyuan zibian jiaocai" (Teacher-prepared teaching materials in kindergartens for the first semester of 1950), BMA, 153-4-2440.

2. Lynn Mally, *Culture of the Future: The Proletkult Movement in Revolutionary Russia* (Berkeley: University of California Press, 1990), 180.

3. Lin Yü-sheng, *The Crisis of Chinese Consciousness: Radical Antitraditionalism in the May Fourth Era* (Madison: University of Wisconsin Press, 1979), 116–121.

4. Gu, *Zhongguo jiaoyu de wenhua jichu*; Suzanne Pepper, *Radicalism and Education Reform in 20th-Century China: The Search for an Ideal Development Model* (Cambridge: Cambridge University Press, 1996); and Ruth Hayhoe, *China's Universities, 1895–1995: A Century of Cultural Conflict* (New York: Garland, 1996).

5. A notable work on kindergartens is Tillman's *Raising China's Revolutionaries*.

6. The Chinese terms *youzhiyuan* and *youeryuan*, both meaning kindergarten, were used interchangeably in the 1950s to refer to early childhood education from three to seven years of age. See Beijingshi jiaoyuju youjiaoke, "Guanyu taolun youzhiyuan zanxing guicheng (cao'an) de tongzhi" (Circular on the discussion about the temporary kindergarten regulations [draft]), BMA, 153-4-2441.

7. He Dongchang, ed., *Dangdai zhongguo jiaoyu* (Contemporary Chinese education), 2 vols. (Beijing: Dangdai zhongguo chubanshe, 1996), 1:41–51.

8. An example is Tillman's *Raising China's Revolutionaries*, which gives too little attention to Soviet influence in China's education.

9. Sheila Fitzpatrick, *The Commissariat of Enlightenment: Soviet Organization of Education and the Arts under Lunacharsky, October, 1917–1921* (Cambridge: Cambridge University Press, 1970); *Education and Social Mobility in the Soviet Union, 1921–1934* (Cambridge: Cambridge University Press, 1979); and Mally, *Culture of the Future*.

10. Kirschenbaum, *Small Comrades*, 13.

11. Catriona Kelly, *Children's World: Growing Up in Russia, 1890–1991* (New Haven, Conn.: Yale University Press, 2007), 61–129; see also Kirschenbaum, *Small Comrades*, 35–37.

12. Kirschenbaum, *Small Comrades*, 88–159.

13. On the concept of the "new man," see Miin-ling Yu, *Xingsu "Xinren": Zhonggong xuan-chuan yu Sulian jingyan* (Shaping the "new man": CCP propaganda and Soviet experiences) (Taipei: Institute of Modern History, Academia Sinica, 2015); and Yinhong Cheng, *Creating the "New Man": From Enlightenment Ideals to Socialist Realities* (Honolulu: University of Hawai'i Press, 2009).

14. Fred I. Greenstein, *Children and Politics*, rev. ed. (New Haven, Conn.: Yale University Press, 1969), 80–81; and Richard W. Wilson, *Learning to Be Chinese: The Political Socialization of Children in Taiwan* (Cambridge, Mass.: MIT Press, 1970), 51, 58.

15. Chen Lifu, *Chengbai zhijian* (The memoirs of Chen Lifu) (Taipei: Zhengzhong shuju, 1994), 205–332; and John Israel, *Lianda: A Chinese University in War and Revolution* (Stanford, Calif.: Stanford University Press, 1998), 95–117.

16. Chen Lifu, *Chengbai zhijian*.

17. Pepper, *Radicalism and Education Reform*, 118–154.

18. See Yu, *Xingsu "Xinren*,*"* 45–123; Gu, *Zhongguo jiaoyu de wenhua jichu*, 227–255; and Kirschenbaum, *Small Comrades*.

19. Gu Mingyuan, "Lun Sulian jiaoyu lilun dui Zhongguo jiaoyu de yingxiang" (Influence of the Soviet Union's educational theories on Chinese education), *Beijing shifan daxue xuebao (shehui kexueban)* 1 (2004): 5–13; and interview with Gu Mingyuan, January 17, 2012, Beijing Normal University.

20. Beijingshi jiaoyuju, "Jiaoyuju jieguan gongzuo jihua cao'an" (Draft of the Education Bureau's plans for taking over [the control of schools]), BMA, 153-1-2.

21. PRC, *Common Program*, 16–17.

22. "Beijingshi zhongzhuan, zhongxiaoxue he youeryuan jiaoyu fazhan gaikuang: cankao ziliao" (Reference documents concerning the general situation of educational development in Beijing's technical secondary schools, secondary and primary schools, and kindergartens), BMA, 147-3-32; see also 153-4-2426.

23. Mao, "On New Democracy," in *Selected Works*, 2:339–84.

24. Beijingshi jiaoyuju, "Jiaoyuju jieguan gongzuo," BMA, 153-1-2.

25. BMA, 11-1-76.

26. Zhonghua renmin gongheguo jiaoyubu jihua caiwusi, ed., *Zhongguo jiaoyu chengjiu: tongji ziliao, 1949–1983* (Achievements in education in China: Statistics, 1949–1983) (Beijing: Renmin jiaoyu chubanshe, 1984), 229.

27. BMA, 11-1-75.

28. BMA, 153-1-718.

29. BMA, 153-4-2441.

30. BMA, 153-4-2464.

31. Beijingshi jiaoyuju, "Zuzhi jiedao youeryuan (youerban) cankao banfa" (Methods for organizing street kindergartens), BMA, 153-1-755; see also 153-1-752; and 153-1-756.

32. Beijingshi jiaoyuju, "Gongzuo zhong cunzai de wenti ji jiejue wenti de yijian" (Existing problems in education and suggestions for their solution), BMA, 1-23-16.

33. BMA, 8-2-694.

34. Beijingshi renmin zhengfu wenhua jiaoyu weiyuanhui, "Sixiao jieban gongzuo jian-bao" (A brief report on taking management control of the private primary schools), BMA, 11-1-70.

35. BMA, 11-1-45; for a list of publication regulations issued by the Beijing Municipal Education Bureau in 1954, see 153-4-32.

36. BMA, 1-6-960.

37. Qian Junrui, "Dangqian jiaoyu jianshe de fangzhen" (Guiding principles for building contemporary education), *Renmin jiaoyu* (People's education; *RMJY*) 1, no. 1 (May 1950): 10.

38. Cao Fu, "Duwei pipan yinlun" (An introduction to Dewey criticism), *RMJY* 1, no. 6 (October 1950), 21–28; and *RMJY* 2, no.1 (November 1950), 22–29.

39. For a number of critical articles opposing Chen Heqin, see *RMJY* 1 (January 1952).

40. Chen Heqin, "Wo dui 'Huojiaoyu' de zai jiantao" (My second self-criticism of "Live Education"), *RMJY* 4 (April 1952): 8–10; for a detailed account of official criticism of Chen Heqin, see Tillman, *Raising China's Revolutionaries*, 160–186.

41. Mao, "On the People's Democratic Dictatorship," in *Selected Works*, 4:415.

42. BMA, 153-1-718; 153-4-1384; 153-4-2384; 151-4-2444; see also He Dongchang, *Dangdai zhongguo jiaoyu*, 43.

43. Shen Zhihua, *Sulian zhuanjia zai Zhongguo*, 4, 407, 408.

44. Gu Mingyuan, "Lun Sulian jiaoyu lilun," 6; and interview with Gu Mingyuan, January 17, 2012, Beijing Normal University.

45. I. A. Kairov, *Jiaoyuxue* (Educational pedagogy), trans. Shen Ying and Nan Zhishan, et al., 2 vols. (Beijing: Renmin jiaoyu chubanshe, 1952), 1:11, 39.

46. Galina's full name has yet to be confirmed. The archival documents at Beijing Normal University Archives that I had consulted did not give a clear answer. It was handwritten in Cyrillic but with two question marks following it. See "Woxiao zengpin renshi jihua" (Plans for hiring additional personnel at our university), Beijing Normal University Archives (BNUA), President's Office, 26 (1951); and "Woxiao shisan ge xi jiaoxue dagang baobu wengao" (Records of the teaching programs of thirteen departments at our university), BNUA, President's Office, 38 (1951).

47. For a brief account of the work done by Soviet education experts at Beijing Normal University in the 1950s, see Beijing shifan daxue xiaoshi bianxiezu, ed., *Beijing shifan daxue xiaoshi, 1902–1982* (History of Beijing Normal University, 1902–1982) (Beijing: Beijing shifan daxue chubanshe, 1982), 140–156; see also Yan Fang, "Sulian zhuanjia dui Beijing shifan daxue jiaoyu gaige de yingxiang" (The influence of Soviet experts on the education reforms at Beijing Normal University), *Gaoxiao jiaoyu guanli* 5, no. 3 (May 2011): 57–61.

48. Beijingshi jiaoyuju youjiaoke, "Yijiuwulingniandu diyi xueqi gongzuo zongjie ge shili youeryuan" (A summary report on municipal kindergartens in the first semester of 1950), BMA, 153-4-2436; see also 153-4-2438.

49. BMA, 153-4-2441.

50. BMA, 153-4-2441; 153-4-2088; and 153-4-2438.

51. Galina, "Sulian ertong daode pinzhi de jiaoyu" (Education for moral character in Soviet children), *RMJY* 2, no. 3 (January 1951): 41–49; and "Sulian de youer jiaoyu" (Kindergarten education in the Soviet Union), *RMJY* 6 (June 1952): 31–36.

52. Galina, *Sulian youer jiaoyu jiangzuo* (Lectures on kindergarten education in the Soviet Union) (Beijing: Renmin jiaoyu chubanshe, 1953), 8.

53. Joseph J. Tobin, David Y. H. Wu, and Dana H. Davidson, *Preschool in Three Cultures: Japan, China, and the United States* (New Haven, Conn.: Yale University Press, 1989).

54. Beijingshi jiaoyuju youjiaoke, "Youeryuan jiaocai" (Kindergarten teaching material), BMA, 153-4-2461; see also 153-4-2384; and 153-4-2440.

55. *Dingzheng xinzhuan guowen jiaokeshu* (Newly revised Chinese language and literature textbook), vol. 6 (n.p., n.d.).

56. Galina, *Sulian youer jiaoyu jiangzuo*, 38.
57. Galina, *Sulian youer jiaoyu jiangzuo*, 36, 38–39, 43.
58. BMA, 153-4-2461.
59. BMA, 153-4-2441.
60. Tobin, *Preschool in Three Cultures*, 96–97.
61. Galina, "Sulian de youer jiaoyu," 35.
62. BMA, 153-4-2461.
63. Galina, "Sulian ertong daode pinzhi," 44–45.
64. BMA, 153-4-2436; and 153-4-2088.
65. BMA, 153-4-2088.
66. BMA, 153-4-2088; 153-4-2436; and 153-4-2461.
67. BMA, 153-4-2436; 153-4-2438; see also 153-4-2444.
68. Kairov, *Jiaoyuxue*, 1:177–180; and Galina, *Sulian youer jiaoyu jiangzuo*, 53–54.
69. Galina, *Sulian youer jiaoyu jiangzuo*, 14, 53.
70. Fitzpatrick, *Education and Social Mobility*, 27; see also BMA, 153-4-2162.
71. Galina, *Sulian youer jiaoyu jiangzuo*, 4.
72. "Furen daxue fushu youzhiyuan xueqi gongzuo zongjie" (A summary report of the semester work at Furen University's affiliated kindergarten), BMA, 153-4-2438; see also 153-4-2436.
73. BMA, 153-4-2444.
74. BMA, 153-4-2438.
75. BMA, 147-3-33.
76. Kairov, *Jiaoyuxue*, 2:103–116.
77. Galina, *Sulian youer jiaoyu jiangzuo*, 5, 53.
78. BMA, 153-4-2438; and 153-4-2441.
79. Beijingshi jiaoyuju, "Beijingshi shiernian lai youer jiaoyu gongzuo ji Beijingshi tigao youeryuan jiaoyu zhiliang de gongzuo qingkuang" (On kindergarten education in Beijing during the past twelve years and the work done to improve its quality), BMA, 153-4-2545.
80. BMA, 147-3-32; and 153-1-749.
81. Beijing Normal University Kindergarten, "Pictures of Events in the Kindergarten's History," http://bnuk.english.bnu.edu.cn/about_bnuk/history_bnuk/37913.htm (accessed January 8, 2019).
82. Liu Yu, ed., *Chuxiao guoyu* (Chinese language and literature for the lower primary school) (n.p.: Xinhua shudian, n.d.); and Jin-Cha-Ji bianqu xingzheng weiyuanhui jiaoyuting, ed., *Guoyu keben* (Chinese language and literature textbook) (n.p., 1948).
83. BMA, 153-4-2438; and 153-4-2461.
84. BMA, 153-4-2427.
85. BMA, 153-4-2426.
86. BMA, 153-4-2440.
87. Beijingshi jiaoyuju youjiaoke, "Yijiusijiunian diyi xueqi gongzuo zongjie ge sili youeryuan" (A summary report on private kindergartens in the first semester of 1949), BMA, 153-4-2426.
88. BMA, 153-4-2436.
89. BMA, 153-5-117.
90. BMA, 153-4-2088; and 153-4-2426.
91. Greenstein, *Children and Politics*, 74.

92. Galina, "Sulian ertong daode pinzhi," 44.

93. BMA, 153-4-2461.

94. BMA, 153-4-2461.

95. BMA, 153-4-2436.

96. BMA, 153-4-2438.

97. BMA, 153-4-2438.

98. Beijing Normal University Kindergarten, "Pictures of Events."

99. BMA, 153-4-2438.

100. BMA, 153-4-2436.

101. BMA, 153-4-2436.

102. BMA, 153-4-2436; 153-4-2438; and 153-4-2444.

103. BMA, 153-4-2444.

104. Clifford Geertz, "Centers, Kings, and Charisma: Reflections on the Symbolics of Power," in *Local Knowledge: Further Essays in Interpretive Anthropology* (New York: Basic Books, 1983), 121–146; and Geertz, *Negara*.

105. Kirschenbaum, *Small Comrades,* 123–128, 158.

106. BMA, 153-4-2444.

107. BMA, 153-4-2461.

108. BMA, 11-2-319.

109. BMA, 153-4-2440.

110. BMA, 153-4-2436.

111. *Chuji xiaoxue keben yuwen dierce jiaoxue cankaoshu* (Teaching references for Chinese language and literature in primary schools, vol. 2) (Beijing: Renmin jiaoyu chubanshe, 1955), 74.

112. BMA, 153-4-2567.

113. Wilson, *Learning to Be Chinese,* 77–85.

114. "Deng Xiaoping yeye zhishu" (Grandpa Deng Xiaoping plants a tree), in *Yuwen: Yinianji, xiace* (Chinese: Grade 1, vol. 2), ed. Kecheng jiaocai yanjiusuo and Xiaoxue yuwen kecheng jiaocai yanjiu kaifa zhongxin (Beijing: Renmin jiaoyu chubanshe, 2001), 9–11.

115. "Deng Xiaoping yeye zhishu" (Grandpa Deng Xiaoping plants a tree), http://www.pep.com.cn/xiaoyu/jiaoshi/tbjx/jiaocan/tb1x/201103/t20110311_1026957.htm (accessed June 8, 2013).

116. BMA, 153-4-2438; and 147-3-32.

117. BMA, 153-4-2440.

118. BMA, 153-4-2444.

119. BMA, 153-4-2436.

120. "Furen daxue fushu youzhiyuan," BMA, 153-4-2438.

121. BMA, 153-4-2461.

122. BMA, 153-4-2438.

123. BMA, 153-4-2438.

124. BMA, 153-4-2468.

125. Zhonghua renmin gongheguo jiaoyubu jihua caiwusi, ed., *Zhongguo jiaoyu chengjiu,* 229; and He Dongchang, *Dangdai Zhongguo jiaoyu,* 57.

126. See Lu Lezhen, ed., *Youer daode qimeng de lilun yu shijian* (The theory and practice of the moral enlightenment of kindergartners) (Fuzhou: Fujian jiaoyu chubanshe, 1999), esp. 153–260; see also He Dongchang, *Dangdai Zhongguo jiaoyu,* 165–174.

127. BMA, 1–6-960; and 153–4-2444.

128. BMA 11–1-70.

129. BMA, 153–4-2490.

130. BMA, 11–1-1; and 11–1-50.

131. BMA, 147–3-5; 153–4-2436; and 153–4-2444.

132. BMA, 153–4-2436.

133. BMA, 11–1-94.

134. BMA, 153–4-2444.

135. BMA, 11–1-94.

136. BMA, 11–1-94.

137. BMA, 153–4-2444.

138. BMA, 153–4-2436.

139. BMA, 153–4-2426.

140. BMA, 153–4-2436.

141. Greenstein, *Children and Politics,* 74.

142. BMA, 153–4-2436.

143. BMA, 153–4-2436.

144. Li Shufang, "Sulian zhuanjia Gelina" (Galina, the Soviet expert), *BJRB,* November 5, 1952, 4.

145. Suzanne Pepper, *China's Education Reform in the 1980s: Policies, Issues, and Historical Perspectives* (Berkeley: Institute of East Asian Studies, University of California, 1990), 38.

146. Greenstein, *Children and Politics,* 45–46.

147. Wilson, *Learning to Be Chinese,* 48, 79, 114–115.

148. Tang Shu and Sun Qiying, eds., *Youeryuan kecheng jiben lilun he zhengti gaige* (Fundamental theories and comprehensive reform of the kindergarten curriculum) (Nanjing: Nanjing shifan daxue chubanshe, 2010), 3–10.

149. Tang Shu, ed., *Youeryuan kecheng yanjiu yu shijian* (Study and practice of the kindergarten curriculum) (Nanjing: Nanjing shifan daxue chubanshe, 2000), 64.

150. Quoted in Jian Liu and Changyun Kang, "Reflection in Action: Ongoing K–12 Curriculum Reform in China," in *Education Reform in China: Changing Concepts, Contexts and Practices,* ed. Janette Ryan (London: Routledge, 2011), 35.

151. Liu and Kang, "Reflection in Action," 21–40.

152. Zhonghua renmin gongheguo jiaoyubu, ed., *Youeryuan jiaoyu zhidao gangyao (shixing)* (Essential guide to kindergarten education [a trial run]) (Beijing: Beijing shifan daxue chubanshe, 2001), 1, 5.

153. Zhonggong zhongyang, Guowuyuan (The CCP Central Committee and the State Council), "Guanyu jiaqiang he gaijin xin xingshi xia gaoxiao sixiang zhengzhi gongzuo de yijian" (Opinions on strengthening and improving ideological and political work in higher education institutions under new circumstances), *RMRB,* February 28, 2017, 1–2; see also Ministry of Education of the PRC, "Review of China's Education Reform in 2017," http://en.moe.gov.cn/News/Top_News/201801/t20180130_326023.html (accessed January 6, 2019).

154. Zhonggong zhongyang, Guowuyuan, "Guanyu jiaqiang he gaijin," *RMRB,* February 28, 2017, 1–2.

Chapter 6. A Political Park

1. Gongyuan guanli weiyuanhui mishushi, "Benhui yijiuwusannian gongzuo jihua yao-dian" (The committee's major plans for 1953), BMA, 98-1-101.

2. The "Beijing's First-Rank Municipal Park" sign was later taken down for reasons unknown.

3. Jia Fulin, *Taimiao tanyou* (A history of the Imperial Ancestral Temple) (Beijing: Wenwu chubanshe, 2005), 1–37.

4. *GMRB,* April 7, 1950, 4.

5. PRC, *Constitution of the People's Republic of China,* 9.

6. *GMRB,* May 1, 1950, 4.

7. *RMRB,* May 1, 1950, 3.

8. Zhang Xinchen, "Beijing laodong renmin de leyuan: Beijingshi Laodong renmin wenhuagong" (The paradise of Beijing's working people: Beijing's WPCP), *RMRB,* July 19, 1953, 3.

9. "Quanguo laodong mofan" (National model workers), BMA, 101-1-1299.

10. Beijingshi zonggonghui xuanchuanbu, "Beijingshi Laodong renmin wenhuagong gongzuo zonghe baogao (caogao)" (Comprehensive report on the work done at Beijing's WPCP [draft]), BMA, 101-1-502; see also 2-16-366 on the WPCP; for related information, see *GMRB,* April 30, 1950, 1; *RMRB,* May 1, 1950, 3; and May 5, 1950, 1.

11. Beijingshi zonggonghui xuanchuanbu, "Beijingshi laodong renmin wenhuagong," BMA, 101-1-502; see also *RMRB,* July 19, 1953, 3.

12. *RMRB,* August 11, 1957, 4; and Beijingshi zonggonghui xuanchuanbu, "Beijingshi laodong renmin wenhuagong," BMA, 101-1-502.

13. Zhang Xinchen, "Beijing laodong renmin."

14. Beijingshi zonggonghui xuanchuanbu, "Beijingshi Laodong renmin wenhuagong," BMA, 101-1-502.

15. *RMRB,* September 8, 1957, 4.

16. BMA, 101-1-214.

17. "Guangzhoushi gongren wenhuagong kaiban yilai de chubu gongzuo zongjie" (Summary of the preliminary work performed at the Guangzhou Working People's Cultural Palace since its inception), GMA, 92-0-84; see also *RMRB,* January 8, 1953, 1; and February 9, 1957, 2.

18. *RMRB,* February 9, 1957, 2. On the construction of Shanghai's cultural palaces, see also SMA, C1-2-1387; C1-2-2135; and C1-2-4255.

19. SMA, C1-2-580.

20. *GMRB,* January 8, 1953, 1; and February 9, 1957, 2.

21. Tong Jun, *Jiangnan yuanlin zhi* (History of gardens in Jiangnan), 2nd ed. (Beijing: Zhongguo jianzhu gongye chubanshe, 1984), 21.

22. Xiong Yuezhi, "Wan Qing Shanghai siyuan kaifang yu gonggong kongjian de tuozhan" (The opening of private parks and the extension of the public sphere in late Qing Shanghai), *Xueshu yuekan* no. 8 (1998): 73–81.

23. Lewis H. Siegelbaum, "The Shaping of Soviet Workers' Leisure: Workers' Clubs and Palaces of Culture in the 1930s," *International Labor and Working-Class History* 56 (Fall 1999): 79.

24. Siegelbaum, "The Shaping," 78.

25. John Hatch, "Hangouts and Hangovers: State, Class and Culture in Moscow's Workers' Club Movement, 1925–1928," *Russian Review* 53, no. 1 (January 1994): 98.

222 Notes to Pages 136-140

26. S. Frederick Starr, *Melnikov: Solo Architect in a Mass Society* (Princeton, N.J.: Princeton University Press, 1978), 134–142.

27. Peter Hayden, *Russian Parks and Gardens* (London: Frances Lincoln, 2005), 7, 22–39, 46–50.

28. Karl Marx, *Marx's Grundrisse*, ed. David McLellan (London: Macmillan, 1971), 148.

29. Marx, *Marx's Grundrisse*, 142.

30. See Vera Adamovna Gitsevich's lithograph, *For the Proletarian Park of Culture and Leisure* (1932), https://www.bowdoin.edu/art-museum/exhibitions/2017/soviet-propoganda-posters .html (accessed March 31, 2020)

31. Rosalinde Sartori, "Stalinism and Carnival: Organisation and Aesthetics of Political Holidays," in *The Culture of the Stalin Period*, ed. Hans Günther (New York: St. Martin's Press, 1990), 41–77; and Fitzpatrick, *Everyday Stalinism*, 94–95.

32. Mao Dun, *Sulian jianwenlu* (What I saw and heard in the Soviet Union) (Shanghai: Kaiming shudian, 1948), 20, 210.

33. BMA, 98-1-157; 98-1-373; and SMA, B172-1-174-1.

34. Beijingshi yuanlinchu mishushi, "Benchu yijiuwusinian gongzuo zongjie" (Summary of the work done by the BMBP in 1954), BMA, 98-1-157.

35. *RMRB*, October 28, 1950, 1.

36. Ren Yuanyuan, ed., *Jinian Ren Bishi* (In memory of Ren Bishi) (Beijing: Wenwu chubanshe, 1986), photo no. 295.

37. Ren, *Jinian Ren Bishi*, photos nos. 301 and 302.

38. Catherine Merridale, *Night of Stone: Death and Memory in Twentieth-Century Russia* (New York: Penguin Books, 2000), 83–84.

39. *BZWX 1950*, 40.

40. Beijingshi zonggonghui xuanchuanbu, "Beijingshi Laodong renmin wenhuagong," BMA, 101-1-502.

41. Beijingshi yuanlinju, "Guanyu gongyuan gongzuo zhong ruogan daiyou fangxiang luxianxing wenti de diaocha baogao" (A report concerning the direction of some of the work in public parks), BMA, 98-2-410.

42. Beijingshi yuanlinchu mishushi, "Benchu yijiuwusinian gongzuo zongjie," BMA, 98-1-157.

43. "Guanyu zai shoudu ge gongyuan nei sheli laodong mofan ji zhandou yingxiong shiji tupian huiyi de jilu" (Record of the meeting on displaying photos of model workers and heroic soldiers in the capital's public parks), BMA, 153-1-1238.

44. Siegelbaum, *Stakhanovism*.

45. See *JFRB*, September 29, 1942, 2; and December 19, 1943, 1.

46. Zhongguo geming bowuguan, *Jiefangqu zhanlanhui ziliao*, 1–23, 30–38, 126–135, 205–210, 260–262.

47. "Quanguo laodong mofan," BMA, 101-1-1299.

48. Beijingshi zonggonghui xuanchuanbu, "Beijingshi Laodong renmin wenhuagong," BMA, 101-1-502.

49. Beijingshi zonggonghui xuanchuanbu, "Beijingshi Laodong renmin wenhuagong," BMA, 101-1-502; see also *RMRB*, July 19, 1953, 3; and May 1, 1980, 4.

50. Beijingshi zonggonghui xuanchuanbu, "Beijingshi Laodong renmin wenhuagong," BMA, 101-1-502.

51. "Guanyu zai shoudu ge gongyuan," BMA, 153-1-1238.

52. BMA, 101-1-799.

53. *RMRB*, June 21, 1950, 3.

54. *RMRB*, June 21, 1950, 3.

55. *RMRB*, June 26, 1950, 3.

56. *RMRB*, June 26, 1950, 3.

57. Zhonggong zhongyang wenxian yanjiushi, ed., *Liu Shaoqi nianpu, 1898–1969* (Chronological biography of Liu Shaoqi, 1898–1969), 2 vols. (Beijing: Zhongyang wenxian chubanshe, 1996), 2:466.

58. *People's Daily Online*, "An Honorable Night-soil Collector and His Family," September 10, 1999, http://en.people.cn/50years/celebrities/19990910C105.html.

59. Beijingshi zonggonghui xuanchuanbu, "Beijingshi Laodong renmin wenhuagong," BMA, 101-1-502.

60. *GMRB*, July 15, 1951, 3.

61. Beijingshi zonggonghui xuanchuanbu, "Beijingshi Laodong renmin wenhuagong," BMA, 101-1-502.

62. Zhang Xinchen, "Beijing laodong renmin."

63. BMA, 101-1-1256.

64. Chang-tai Hung, "Mao's Parades: State Spectacles in China in the 1950s," *China Quarterly* 190 (June 2007): 411–431.

65. BMA, 101-1-691; 101-1-1095; 101-1-1181; and *RMRB*, May 2, 1962, 4.

66. BMA, 101-1-163.

67. *RMRB*, May 2, 1982, 5.

68. BMA, 101-1-214.

69. Beijingshi zonggonghui xuanchuanbu, "Beijingshi Laodong renmin wenhuagong," BMA, 101-1-502.

70. *RMRB*, April 29, 1950, 4; and May 1, 1950, 3.

71. *RMRB*, June 22, 1950, 3.

72. *RMRB*, May 12, 1950, 3.

73. Zhang Xinchen, "Beijing laodong renmin"; see also *RMRB*, September 6, 1951, 4.

74. SMA, H1-11-8-47; H1-11-9-16; H1-11-10-15; H1-11-13-53; and H1-12-3-110.

75. Beijingshi zonggonghui xuanchuanbu, "Beijingshi Laodong renmin wenhuagong," BMA, 101-1-502.

76. BMA, 101-1-346.

77. *RMRB*, June 14, 1950, 3.

78. *RMRB*, April 18, 1951, 1.

79. BMA, 101-1-314.

80. Beijingshi zonggonghui wenjiaobu, "Kang-Mei yuan-Chao xuanchuan gongzuo de zhishi" (Instruction on the propaganda work concerning the Resist America, Aid Korea Campaign), BMA, 101-1-296.

81. *GMRB*, April 29, 1951, 3.

82. BMA, 101-1-297.

83. Beijingshi zonggonghui xuanchuanbu, "Beijingshi Laodong renmin wenhuagong," BMA, 101-1-502.

84. "Ye shizhang zai Guangzhoushi diyici gong-nong-bing laodong mofan dahui shang de zhishi" (Mayor Ye's instructions at the first model workers meeting of workers, peasants, and soldiers in Guangzhou), GMA, 92-0-2.

85. *RMRB*, December 19, 1950, 2.

86. *GMRB*, October 8, 1951, 3.

87. Beijingshi zonggonghui xuanchuanbu, "Beijingshi Laodong renmin wenhuagong," BMA, 101-1-502.

88. *RMRB*, August 10, 1955, 3.

89. Shanghaishi wenhuaju, "Shanghai Zhongshan gongyuan wenhuaguan 1955 nian chunjie huodong jihua" (Plans for the Cultural Center at Shanghai's Zhongshan Park during the 1955 Spring Festival), SMA, B172-4-429-42.

90. BMA, 101-1-214.

91. BMA, 101-1-214.

92. "Beijingshi yuanlinju yijiuliusannian gongzuo zongjie" (Summary of the work done in 1963 by the BMBP), BMA, 98-1-547.

93. See *RMRB*, April 30, 1974, 4; and May 2, 1975, 4.

94. Beijingshi yuanlinju geming lingdao xiaozu, "Guanyu Wuyi youyuan huodong qingkuang de huibao" (Report on the May Day garden parties), BMA, 98-2-48.

95. In the United States, Ellis Island is an example of a heritage park, Yellowstone of a national park.

96. Hazel Conway, *People's Parks: The Design and Development of Victorian Parks in Britain* (Cambridge: Cambridge University Press, 1991), 12.

97. George F. Chadwick, *The Park and the Town: Public Landscape in the 19th and 20th Centuries* (London: Architectural Press, 1966), 19.

98. Frederick Law Olmsted, "The People's Park at Birkenhead, near Liverpool," in *The Papers of Frederick Law Olmsted*, Supplementary Series, ed. Charles E. Beveridge and Carolyn F. Hoffman (Baltimore, Md.: Johns Hopkins University Press, 1997), 1:69–78.

99. Frederick Law Olmsted, "Preliminary Report to the Commissioners for Laying Out a Park in Brooklyn, New York," in *The Papers of Frederick Law Olmsted*, Supplementary Series, 1:87.

100. Frederick Law Olmsted, "Public Parks and the Enlargement of Towns," in *The Papers of Frederick Law Olmsted*, Supplementary Series, 1:185.

101. Olmsted, "Public Parks and the Enlargement of Towns," 1:187.

102. Frederick Law Olmsted, "The Greensward Plan: 1858," in *The Papers of Frederick Law Olmsted: Creating Central Park, 1857–1861*, ed. Charles E. Beveridge and David Schuyler (Baltimore, Md.: Johns Hopkins University Press, 1983), 3:151.

103. Olmsted, "Public Parks and the Enlargement of Towns," 1:190.

104. Setha Low, Dana Taplin, and Suzanne Scheld, *Rethinking Urban Parks: Public Space and Cultural Diversity* (Austin: University of Texas Press, 2005), 210.

105. Gongyuan guanli weiyuanhui mishushi, "Benhui yijiuwusannian gongzuo jihua yaodian," BMA, 98-1-101.

106. Beijingshi yuanlinju bangongshi, "Ju dangwei yanjiu pi-Lin pi-Kong ruhe jiehe yuanyi fangzhen, guwei jinyong wenti de jilu" (Records of an investigation concerning how to integrate the Anti-Lin Biao and Anti-Confucius campaigns with the landscaping as well as the issue of Using the Past to Serve the Present), BMA, 98-2-369.

107. *RMRB*, April 29, 1951, 5.

108. Gongyuan guanli weiyuanhui mishushi, "Benhui yijiuwusannian gongzuo jihua yaodian," BMA, 98-1-101; see also 98-1-119; and 101-1-502.

109. Deborah S. Davis, "Introduction: Urban China," in *Urban Spaces in Contemporary China: The Potential for Autonomy and Community in Post-Mao China,* ed. Deborah S. Davis et al. (Washington, D.C.: Woodrow Wilson Center Press, 1995), 1–19.

110. "Beijing Laodong renmin wenhuagong de Falun Gong xiaoxueyuan liangongdian, Zhongguo, Beijing" (Junior followers practicing Falun Gong at the WPCP, Beijing, China). https://www.flickr.com/photos/49183068@N06/galleries/72157624068125013 (accessed March 31, 2020).

111. Chen, *Breathing Spaces,* 170–179.

112. Andrew Jacobs, "A Would-Be Demonstrator Is Detained in China after Seeking a Protest Permit," *New York Times,* August 19, 2008, A6.

113. Geoffrey York, "IOC Criticizes Beijing over Unused Protest Zones," *Globe and Mail,* August 21, 2008, A9.

114. York, "IOC Criticizes Beijing."

115. Minky Worden, ed., *China's Great Leap: The Beijing Games and Olympian Human Rights Challenges* (New York: Seven Stories Press, 2008), 26.

116. York, "IOC Criticizes Beijing."

Chapter 7. Architecture and Ethnicity

1. "Minzu wenhuagong" (Cultural Palace of Nationalities), http://cpon.cn (accessed March 30, 2020).

2. For a discussion of the Ten Monumental Buildings, see Hung, *Mao's New World,* 51–72.

3. Among the many notable names in the field are June Teufel Dreyer, Dru C. Gladney, Melvyn C. Goldstein, Stevan Harrell, and Colin Mackerras. Recent works on this subject include Mullaney, *Coming to Terms with the Nation;* Woeser and Wang, *Voices from Tibet;* Thum, *Sacred Routes of Uyghur History;* Brophy, *Uyghur Nation;* and Cliff, *Oil and Water.*

4. For a brief history of China's pre-1949 ethnic issues, see Colin Mackerras, *China's Minorities: Integration and Modernization in the Twentieth Century* (Hong Kong: Oxford University Press, 1994), 21–136; June Teufel Dreyer, *China's Forty Millions: Minority Nationalities and National Integration in the People's Republic of China* (Cambridge, Mass.: Harvard University Press, 1976), 7–41; and Melvyn C. Goldstein, *A History of Modern Tibet, 1913–1951: The Demise of the Lamaist State* (Berkeley: University of California Press, 1989).

5. Dreyer, *China's Forty Millions,* 263.

6. Guojia minzu shiwu weiyuanhui "Zhongguo minzu gongzuo wushinian" bianji weiyuanhui, ed., *Zhongguo minzu gongzuo wushinian* (Fifty years of nationalities work in China) (Beijing: Minzu chubanshe, 1999), 725.

7. PRC, *Constitution of the People's Republic of China,* 9–10.

8. *NBCK,* October 20, 1953, 212–213.

9. Shanghaishi minzu shiwu weiyuanhui, "Ge minzu zongjiao xinyang fengsu xiguan shenghuo fuli bufen" (On religious beliefs, customs, and welfare benefits of various minority groups), SMA, B21-1-5.

10. Shanghaishi minzu shiwu weiyuanhui, "Shanghaishi minzu gongzuo qingkuang baogao (caogao)" (Report of the work on ethnic minorities in Shanghai [draft]), SMA, B21-1-8-1.

11. *NBCK,* September 18, 1952, 309.

12. Shanghaishi minzu shiwu weiyuanhui, "Minzu gongzuo youguan guiding" (Rules concerning the works of ethnic minorities), SMA, B21-1-42-9.

13. Shanghaishi minzu shiwu weiyuanhui, "Shanghaishi minzu gongzuo," SMA, B21-1-8-1.

14. Shanghaishi minzu shiwu weiyuanhui, "Youguan shaoshu minzu zhaogu de zanxing banfa" (Temporary measures on giving special consideration to ethnic minorities), SMA, B21-2-16.

15. Shanghaishi xiongdi minzu zhaodai weiyuanhui, "Zhaodai Qinghaisheng ge minzu canguantuan zonghe jianbao" (A summary report on entertaining the ethnic groups of Qinghai Province), SMA, B21-2-65.

16. Mao Zedong, "Guanyu daliang xishou he peiyang shaoshu minzu ganbu de dianbao" (Telegram on recruiting and training a large number of national minority cadres), in *Jianguo yilai Mao Zedong wengao*, 1:138.

17. Minzu tushuguan, ed., *Zhonghua renmin gongheguo minzu gongzuo dashiji, 1949–1983* (Chronicle of nationalities work of the PRC, 1949–1983) (Beijing: Minzu chubanshe, 1984), esp. 102–110, 545–568.

18. Shanghaishi minzu shiwu weiyuanhui, "Guanyu quhua tiaozheng hou dui gequ minzu gongzuo ganbu peibei de yijian" (Views on the allocation of cadres for the ethnic minority works after the redrawing of district lines), SMA, B21-1-17-1.

19. Dreyer, *China's Forty Millions*, 136.

20. Zhang Ximing, "Minzu wenhuagong choujian shimo" (The story of the construction of the CPN), *Zhongguo minzubao*, February 24, 2006, 7.

21. Zhang Bo, *Wo de jianzhu chuangzuo daolu* (My career as an architect) (Beijing: Zhongguo jianzhu gongye chubanshe, 1994), 118.

22. *Wenwu cankao ziliao* 10 (October 30, 1950): 66–77; 4 (May 30, 1953): 29–42; 4 (April 30, 1954): 95–100; 5 (May 30, 1954): 81–85; and 6 (June 30, 1954): 86–94.

23. Zhang Bo, *Wo de jianzhu*, 118.

24. "Minzu wenhuagong chubu fang'an shuoming" (The preliminary plan of the CPN), BMA, 47-1-10.

25. "Guanyu xiujian Minzu wenhuagong de huiyi jiyao" (Minutes of the meetings on the construction of the CPN), BMA, 47-1-10.

26. "Guanyu xiujian Minzu wenhuagong," BMA, 47-1-10.

27. Zhang Bo, *Wo de jianzhu*, 118.

28. Zhang Bo, *Wo de jianzhu*, 139.

29. "Guanyu xiujian Minzu wenhuagong," BMA, 47-1-10.

30. "Minzu wenhuagong gongcheng de jiben qingkuang" (The basic conditions concerning the construction of the CPN), BMA, 47-1-92; and Zhang Bo, *Wo de jianzhu*, 139–140.

31. "Minzu wenhuagong gongcheng jijian dang'an zhengli gongzuo zongjie" (Summary of putting in order the archives of the construction of the CPN), BMA, 44-1-99.

32. "Minzu wenhuagong gongcheng," BMA, 44-1-99.

33. The largest building is the Great Hall of the People, which has a floor space of 171,800 square meters.

34. Shi Ping, "Xingjian zhong de Minzu wenhuagong" (The CPN under construction), *Minzu tuanjie* 16 (January 1959), 16.

35. Zhang Bo, *Wo de jianzhu*, 128.

36. *RMRB*, April 16, 1958, 1; September 8, 1959, 3; and October 7, 1959, 4.

37. *RMRB*, September 8, 1959, 3.

38. *RMRB*, September 8, 1959, 3.

39. Zhang Bo, *Wo de jianzhu*, 132.

40. Guoqing gongcheng bangongshi, "Minzu wenhuagong shigong qingkuang" (The CPN under construction), BMA, 125-1-1219.

41. "Minzu wenhuagong" (The Cultural Palace of Nationalities), *Jianzhu xuebao* 9–10 (October 1959): 47.

42. Guoqing gongcheng bangongshi, "Minzu wenhuagong" (The Cultural Palace of Nationalities), BMA, 125-1-1219.

43. "Minzu fandian gongcheng de jiben qingkuang" (Basic conditions of the Nationality Hotel project), BMA, 47-1-92.

44. Daniel J. Sherman and Irit Rogoff, eds., *Museum Culture: Histories, Discourses, Spectacles* (Minneapolis: University of Minnesota Press, 1994), x–xii, 233, 239.

45. "Guowuyuan guanyu souji Minzu wenhuagong suoxu zhanpin he tushu de tongzhi" (Circular of the State Council on collecting the exhibited artifacts and books in the CPN), BMA, 196-2-676.

46. "Guowuyuan guanyu souji," BMA, 196-2-676.

47. Beijingshi Minzhengju and Beijingshi Wenhuaju, "Beijingshi wei Minzu wenhuagong souji zhanpin, tushu he jinxing yuzhan gongzuo jihua" (Beijing Municipal Government's plan for collecting exhibit items and books and preparing for the preliminary exhibition at the CPN), BMA, 196-2-676.

48. Beijingshi Minzhengju, "Souji Minzu wenhuagong suoxu zhanpin he tushu de jihua tigang" (Outlines of collecting exhibit items and books for the CPN), BMA, 196-2-676.

49. "Guowuyuan guanyu souji," BMA, 196-2-676.

50. Beijingshi Minzhengju, "Souji Minzu wenhuagong," BMA, 196-2-676.

51. Beijingshi Minzhengju, "Souji Minzu wenhuagong," BMA, 196-2-676.

52. *RMRB*, January 3, 1982, 8.

53. Beijingshi Minzhengju, "Souji Minzu wenhuagong," BMA, 196-2-676.

54. Beijingshi Minzhengju, "Wei Minzu wenhuagong souji zhanpin he tushu de jihua tigang" (General plan for collecting exhibit items and books for the CPN), BMA, 196-2-676.

55. Beijingshi Minzhengju, "Souji Minzu wenhuagong," BMA, 196-2-676.

56. "Guowuyuan guanyu souji," BMA, 196-2-676.

57. "Diquguan" (Regional halls), in *Minzu wenhuagong luocheng he shinianlai minzu gongzuo zhanlan* (The completion of the CPN and the exhibition on nationalities work in the last ten years) (Beijing: n.p, n.d.).

58. Beijingshi Minzhengju, "Guanyu Beijingshi wei Minzu wenhuagong minzu gongzuo zhanlan buchong he xiugai zhanpin gongzuo de qingshi" (The city of Beijing's request for instructions concerning the addition to and revision of the exhibits at the CPN), BMA, 2-16-60.

59. Beijingshi Minzhengju, "Souji Minzu wenhuagong," BMA, 196-2-676.

60. Beijingshi Minzhengju, "Souji Minzu wenhuagong," BMA, 196-2-676.

61. Beijingshi Mingzhengju, "Guanyu wei Minzu wenhuagong souji zhanpin tushu he jinxing yuzhan gongzuo jihua de qingshi" (Request for instructions concerning the collection of the exhibits and the plan for the preparation of the preview at the CPN), BMA, 196-2-676.

62. "Guowuyuan guanyu souji," BMA, 196-2-676.

63. Beijingshi Minzhengju, "Souji Minzu wenhuagong," BMA, 196-2-676.

64. Boris Groys, "The Struggle against the Museum; or, The Display of Art in Totalitarian Space," in *Museum Culture*, ed. Sherman and Rogoff, 144.

65. Groys, "Struggle against the Museum," 159.

66. For example, during my first visit to the office of the CPN on October 21, 2002, the staff mentioned that the Cultural Palace's internal archives "have yet to be sorted out," but no one elaborated on what this meant or indicated what materials, if any, are held there.

67. *RMRB*, October 7, 1959, 4.

68. The exhibition was covered by major newspapers such as the *People's Daily* (see, for example, *RMRB*, October 7, 1959, 4). An illustrated pamphlet was issued to document the event. See *Minzu wenhuagong luocheng*.

69. "Zongheguan" (The Comprehensive Hall), in *Minzu wenhuagong luocheng*. China's total population in 1953 was later revised downward to 577 million.

70. "Zongheguan," in *Minzu wenhuagong luocheng*.

71. "Zongheguan," in *Minzu wenhuagong luocheng*.

72. "Diquguan," in *Minzu wenhuagong luocheng*.

73. "Diquguan," in *Minzu wenhuagong luocheng*.

74. "Diquguan," in *Minzu wenhuagong luocheng*.

75. Mackerras, *China's Minorities*, 252. For an ethnographic account of the way of life associated with the Xinjiang Production and Construction Corps, see Cliff, *Oil and Water*, 50–179.

76. "Diquguan," in *Minzu wenhuagong luocheng*.

77. "Zongheguan," in *Minzu wenhuagong luocheng*.

78. "Zhuantiguan" (Special Themes Hall), in *Minzu wenhuagong luocheng*.

79. "Zongheguan," in *Minzu wenhuagong luocheng*.

80. Andrew McClellan, *Inventing the Louvre: Art, Politics, and the Origins of the Modern Museum in Eighteenth-Century Paris* (Berkeley: University of California Press, 1994).

81. Brian Wallis, ed., *Hans Haacke, Unfinished Business* (New York: New Museum of Contemporary Art, 1986), 66.

82. Pierre Bourdieu and Hans Haacke, *Free Exchange* (Stanford, Calif.: Stanford University Press, 1995), 85.

83. Carol Duncan, *Civilizing Rituals: Inside Public Art Museums* (London: Routledge, 1995), 6.

84. Duncan F. Cameron, "The Museum: A Temple or the Forum," in *Reinventing the Museum: Historical and Contemporary Perspectives on the Paradigm Shift*, ed. Gail Anderson (Walnut Creek, Calif.: AltaMira Press, 2004), 61–73.

85. *RMRB*, October 7, 1959, 4.

86. Melvyn C. Goldstein, *A History of Modern Tibet*, vol. 2, *The Calm before the Storm, 1951–1955* (Berkeley: University of California Press, 2007), 457.

87. Mackerras, *China's Minorities*, 253.

88. "Diquguan," in *Minzu wenhuagong luocheng*.

89. Huadong xingzheng weiyuanhui minzu shiwu weiyuanhui, "Guanyu Huimin yaoqiu zuzhi Huimin tuanti difang zuzhi wenti de dafu" (Response to the issue concerning the Hui people's request to establish local Hui organizations), SMA, B21-2-16.

90. Interview with Zhang Bo, December 14, 1994, Beijing.

91. Interview with Zhang Bo, December 14, 1994, Beijing; and Zhang Bo, *Wo de jianzhu*, 118.

92. Tony Bennett, *The Birth of the Museum: History, Theory, Politics* (London: Routledge, 1995); and Duncan, *Civilizing Rituals*.

93. Sherman and Rogoff, *Museum Culture*, xii.

94. McClellan, *Inventing the Louvre*, 91–92.

95. Minzu wenhuagong bowuguan, ed., *Minzu bowuguan de lilun yu shijian* (Theory and practice of the ethnology museum) (Beijing: Minzu chubanshe, 1999), 5.

96. Minzu wenhuagong bowuguan, *Minzu bowuguan*, 5–7.

97. "Minzu wenhuagong" (Cultural Palace of Nationalities).

98. Denton, *Exhibiting the Past*, 199.

99. Varutti, *Museums in China*, 145–158.

100. Interview with Zhang Bo, December 14, 1994, Beijing.

101. Mao, "The Chinese People Have Stood Up!" in *Selected Works*, 5:16–17.

102. Beijingshi Minzhengju, "Guanyu Beijingshi wei Minzu wenhuagong," BMA, 2-16-60.

103. Minzu wenhuagong bowuguan, *Minzu bowuguan*, 334–335.

104. Minzu wenhuagong bowuguan, *Minzu bowuguan*, 24.

105. "Minzu wenhuagong" (Cultural Palace of Nationalities).

106. *RMRB*, August 15, 1988, 3; and June 27, 1994, 3.

107. Xinhuanet, "Hu Jintao deng dang he guojia lingdaoren canguan 'Xizang minzhu gaige wushinian daxing zhanlan'" (Hu Jintao and other Party and state leaders visited the large exhibition titled *The Fiftieth Anniversary of Democratic Reform in Tibet*), March 28, 2009, http://news.xinhuanet.com/politics/2009-03/28/content_11087844.htm.

Conclusion

1. PRC, "Article 5," in *Common Program*, 3.

2. Peng Zhen, *Peng Zhen wenxuan*, 215.

3. Jeffrey Brooks, *Thank You, Comrade Stalin!*, 4.

4. Naimark and Gibianskii, eds., *The Establishment of Communist Regimes*, 218.

5. Derk Bodde, *Peking Diary: A Year of Revolution* (New York: Henry Schuman, 1950), 142.

6. Dangdai Zhongguo congshu bianjibu, *Dangdai Zhongguo*, 1:636; see Minzu tushuguan, *Zhonghua renmin gongheguo minzu gongzuo dashiji*, 448.

7. See Jane Portal, *Art under Control in North Korea* (London: Reaktion Books, 2005), 7–30, 53–104; and Bill Hayton, *Vietnam: Rising Dragon* (New Haven, Conn.: Yale University Press, 2010), 135–158.

8. Louise Williams and Roland Rich, eds., *Losing Control: Freedom of the Press in Asia* (Canberra: Australian National University E Press, 2013), 1–15, 115–137, 147–189.

9. Louise Williams, "Censors at Work, Censors out of Work," in *Losing Control*, ed. Williams and Rich, 2.

10. Ellul, *Propaganda*, 17–18.

11. Hung, *War and Popular Culture*, 221–269.

12. Wood, *Performing Justice*; and Fitzpatrick, "Signals from Below."

13. *People's Daily Online*, "President Xi Jinping makes research tour to *People's Daily*," February 19, 2016, http://en.people.cn/n3/2016/0219/c90000-9018740.html.

14. "Xi Jinping dao zhongyang dianshitai diaoyan" (Xi Jinping makes research tour to China Central Television), http://news.cntv.cn/special/xjpmtdy/special.shtml (accessed February 20, 2016).

15. *China Daily*, "China's Xi underscores CPC's leadership in news reporting," February 20, 2016, http://www.chinadaily.com.cn/china/2016-02/20/content_23564276.htm.

16. Edward Wong, "Xi Jinping's News Alert: Chinese Media Must Serve the Party," *New York Times*, February 23, 2016, http://www.nytimes.com/2016/02/23/world/asia/china-media-policy-xi-jinping.html.

17. Joseph S. Nye Jr., *Soft Power: The Means to Success in World Politics* (New York: Public Affairs, 2004).

18. On the Confucius institutes, see, for example, Kenneth King, *China's Aid and Soft Power in Africa: The Case of Education and Training* (Woodbridge, UK: Boydell & Brewer, James Currey, 2003), 1–67, 144–212; and Ying Zhou and Sabrina Luk, "Establishing Confucius Institutes: A Tool for Promoting China's Soft Power?" *Journal of Contemporary China* 25, no. 100 (March 2016): 628–642.

19. "A Message from Confucius: New Ways of Projecting Soft Power," *The Economist*, October 22, 2009, 10.

20. Joseph R. Levenson, "The Role of Confucius in Communist China," *China Quarterly* 12 (October–December 1962): 1–18.

21. A bronze statue of Confucius was set up in early 2011 on the northern side of the National Museum of China in Tiananmen Square, facing East Chang'an Avenue. I saw the statue there during my January 2011 trip to Beijing. After little more than three months, however, the statue was moved to a less prestigious location in a courtyard inside the National Museum. No official explanation for the statue's relocation was offered. It is possible that how to properly evaluate China's most famous philosopher remains a subject of contention among top leaders.

22. On the One Belt, One Road Initiative, see, for example, Simeon Djankov and Sean Miner, eds., *China's Belt and Road Initiative Motives: Scope, and Challenges* (Washington, D.C.: Peterson Institute for International Economics, 2016); Anoushiravan Ehteshami and Niv Horesh, eds., *China's Presence in the Middle East: The Implications of the One Belt, One Road Initiative* (Abingdon, UK: Routledge, 2018); and Flynt Leverett and Wu Bingbing, "The New Silk Road and China's Evolving Grand Strategy," *China Journal* 77 (January 2017): 110–132.

23. BMA, 114-1-97.

24. Dangdai Zhongguo congshu bianjibu, *Dangdai Zhongguo*, 1:56.

25. Liang Sicheng, *Liang Sicheng quanji*, 5:268.

26. Sebastian Heilmann and Elizabeth J. Perry, eds., *Mao's Invisible Hand: The Political Foundations of Adaptive Governance* (Cambridge, Mass.: Harvard University Asia Center, 2011), 1–29.

27. Roderick MacFarquhar and Michael Schoenhals, *Mao's Last Revolution* (Cambridge, Mass.: Belknap Press of Harvard University Press, 2006), 69.

28. David Shambaugh, "China's Soft-Power Push," *Foreign Affairs* 94, no. 4 (July–August 2015): 99–107.

29. Xi Jinping, "Zai Wenyi gongzuo zuotanhui shang de jianghua" (Talk at the Forum on Literature and Art), October 15, 2014, http://www.xinhuanet.com/politics/2015–10/14/c_1116825558.htm.

30. In June 2014, when I visited the hall in Yan'an where Mao delivered his talks in 1942—the Central Office of the CCP Central Committee, known as the Airplane Building because of its shape—I found it sparsely decorated, with only a few photos, including two of *yangge* dances.

31. Xi Jinping, "Zai Wenyi gongzuo zuotanhui shang de jianghua."

32. Zhonggong zhongyang, Guowuyuan, "Guanyu jiaqiang he gaijin," *RMRB*, February 28, 2017, 1–2.

Bibliography

Archives

Beijing shifan daxue dang'anguan 北京师范大学档案馆 (Beijing Normal University Archives) (BNUA)
Beijingshi dang'anguan 北京市档案馆 (Beijing Municipal Archives) (BMA)
Guangzhoushi dang'anguan 广州市档案馆 (Guangzhou Municipal Archives) (GMA)
Shanghaishi dang'anguan 上海市档案馆 (Shanghai Municipal Archives) (SMA)

Newspapers and Journals

Beijing ribao 北京日报 *(Beijing daily) (BJRB)*
Guangming ribao 光明日报 *(Enlightenment daily) (GMRB)*
Jiefang ribao 解放日报 *(Liberation daily) (JFRB)*
Neibu cankao 内部参考 *(Internal references) (NBCK)*
Renmin jiaoyu 人民教育 *(People's education) (RMJY)*
Renmin ribao 人民日报 *(People's daily) (RMRB)*
Xinhua yuebao 新华月报 *(New China monthly) (XHYB)*

Books and Articles

Adam, Peter. *Art of the Third Reich.* New York: Harry N. Abrams, 1992.

Altehenger, Jennifer. *Legal Lessons: Popularizing Laws in the People's Republic of China, 1949–1989.* Cambridge, Mass.: Harvard University Asia Center, 2018.

Anderson, John. *Religion, State and Politics in the Soviet Union and Successor States.* Cambridge: Cambridge University Press, 1994.

Applebaum, Ann. *Iron Curtain: The Crushing of Eastern Europe, 1944–1956.* New York: Doubleday, 2012.

Arendt, Hannah. *The Origins of Totalitarianism.* New York: World Publishing, 1958.

Bauer, Raymond A. *The New Man in Soviet Psychology.* Cambridge, Mass.: Harvard University Press, 1952.

Bei Ling. "Bei Ling: The State of Underground Literature in China." October 13, 2009. http://www.igfm.de/bei-ling.

"Beijing de wenhuaguan" 北京的文化馆 (Beijing's cultural centers). BMA, 1-12-870.

"Beijing Laodong renmin wenhuagong de Falun Gong xiaoxueyuan liangongdian, Zhongguo, Beijing" (Junior followers practicing Falun Gong at the WPCP, Beijing, China). 北京劳动人民文化宫的法轮功小学员炼功点, 中国, 北京. Accessed February 17, 2017. https://www.flickr.com/photos/49183068@N06/galleries/721576 24068125013.

Beijing Normal University Kindergarten. "Pictures of Events in the Kindergarten's History." Accessed April 8, 2020. http://bnuk.english.bnu.edu.cn/about_bnuk/history_bnuk/37913.htm.

"*Beijing ribao* banmian gexin jihua (cao'an)" 北京日报版面革新计划 (草案) (Plan for the rearrangement of the layout of the *Beijing Daily* [draft]). BMA, 114-1-40.

"*Beijing ribao* bianji chuban fangzhen (cao'an)" 北京日报编辑出版方针 (草案) (Editorial guidelines at the *Beijing Daily* [draft]). BMA, 114-1-15.

"*Beijing ribao* bianzhi renshu chubu yijian" 北京日报编制人数初步意见 (Preliminary suggestion for staff size of the *Beijing Daily*). BMA, 114-1-127.

"*Beijing ribao* dangzongzhi huiyi jilu" 北京日报党总支会议记录 (Minutes of the General Party Branch meeting at the *Beijing Daily*). BMA, 114-1-25.

"*Beijing ribao* gongzuo tiaoli (cao'an)" 北京日报工作条例 (草案) (The working rules at the *Beijing Daily* [draft]). BMA, 114-1-160.

"*Beijing ribao* guanyu fagao, shengao he gaigao chengxu zanxing guiding" 北京日报关于发稿、审稿和改稿程序暂行规定 (Temporary rules for publishing, reviewing, and revising articles at the *Beijing Daily*). BMA, 114-1-98.

"*Beijing ribao* qingkuang jieshao (cao'gao)" 北京日报情况介绍 (草稿) (An introduction to the *Beijing Daily* [draft]). BMA, 114-1-56.

Beijing ribao sanshinian 北京日报三十年 (Thirty years of the *Beijing Daily*). n.p., n.d.

Beijing shifan daxue xiaoshi bianxiezu 北京师范大学校史编写组, ed. *Beijing shifan daxue xiaoshi, 1902–1982* 北京师范大学校史, 1902–1982 (History of Beijing Normal University, 1902–1982). Beijing: Beijing shifan daxue chubanshe, 1982.

"Beijing shiwei guanyu gaijin *Beijing ribao* gongzuo de jueyi (cao'an)" 北京市委关于改进北京日报工作的决议 (草稿) (Decisions of the Beijing Municipal Party on how to improve the quality of the *Beijing Daily* [draft]). BMA, 114-1-37.

Beijingshi dang'anguan 北京市档案馆, ed. *Beijing dang'an shiliao, 2012, 2: Dang'an zhong de Beijing wenhua* 北京档案史料, 2012, 2: 档案中的北京文化 (Beijing archival sources, 2012, 2: Beijing cultures in the archives). Beijing: Xinhua chubanshe, 2012.

Beijingshi difangzhi bianzuan weiyuanhui 北京市地方志编纂委员会, ed. *Beijingzhi: Xinwen chuban guangbo dianshi juan: Baoye, tongxunshezhi* 北京志: 新闻出版广播电视卷: 报业、通讯社志 (The history of Beijing: News, publications, and television: The history of newspapers and news agencies). Beijing: Beijing chubanshe, 2006.

——, ed. *Beijingzhi: Xinwen chuban guangbo dianshi juan: Chubanzhi* 北京志: 新闻出版广播电视卷: 出版志 (The history of Beijing: News, publications, and television: The history of publications). Beijing: Beijing chubanshe, 2005.

"Beijingshi diyi wenhuaguan de diaocha baogao" 北京市第一文化馆的调查报告 (An investigative report of the No. 1 Cultural Center of Beijing). BMA, 11-1-118.

"Beijingshi gong'anju guanyu qudi Yiguandao gongzuo de qingkuang ji jingyan jiaoxun de baogao" 北京市公安局关于取缔一贯道工作的情况及经验教训的报告 (Report on the experience and lessons of the suppression of Yiguandao by the Public Security Bureau, Beijing), in *BZWX 1951*, 259–267.

Beijingshi gongnong yeyu jiaoyuju 北京市工农业余教育局. "Benju guanyu wenhuaguan, shubao yuelanshi gongzuo de gaikuo, zongjie" 本局关于文化馆、书报阅览室工作的概括、总结 (The bureau's outline and summary of the activities at the cultural centers' newspaper reading room). BMA, 152–1-52.

Beijingshi jiaoyuju 北京市教育局. "Beijingshi shiernian lai youer jiaoyu gongzuo ji Beijingshi tigao youeryuan jiaoyu zhiliang de gongzuo qingkuang" 北京市十二年来幼儿教育工作及北京市提高幼儿园教育质量的工作情况 (On kindergarten education in Beijing during the past twelve years and the work done to improve its quality). BMA, 153–4-2545.

———. "Gongzuo zhong cunzai de wenti ji jiejue wenti de yijian" 工作中存在的问题及解决问题的意见 (Existing problems in education and suggestions for their solution). BMA, 1–23-16.

———. "Jiaoyuju jieguan gongzuo jihua cao'an" 教育局接管工作计划草案 (Draft on the Education Bureau's plans for taking over [the control of schools]). BMA, 153–1-2.

———. "Zuzhi jiedao youeryuan (youerban) cankao banfa" 组织街道幼儿园 (幼儿班) 参考办法 (Methods for organizing street kindergartens). BMA, 153–1-755.

Beijingshi jiaoyuju youjiaoke 北京市教育局幼教科. "Guanyu taolun youzhiyuan zanxing guicheng (cao'an) de tongzhi" 关于讨论幼稚园暂行规程(草案)的通知 (Circular on the discussion about the temporary kindergarten regulations [draft]). BMA, 153–4-2441.

———. "Yijiusijiunian diyi xueqi gongzuo zongjie ge sili youeryuan" 一九四九年第一学期工作总结各私立幼儿园 (A summary report on private kindergartens in the first semester of 1949). BMA, 153–4-2426.

———. "Yijiuwulingnian diyi xueqi geyuan zibian jiaocai" 一九五0年第一学期各园自编教材 (Teacher-prepared teaching materials in kindergartens for the first semester of 1950). BMA, 153–4-2440.

———. "Yijiuwulingniandu diyi xueqi gongzuo zongjie ge shili youeryuan" 一九五0年度第一学期工作总结各市立幼儿园 (A summary report on municipal kindergartens in the first semester of 1950). BMA, 153–4-2436.

———. "Youeryuan jiaocai" 幼儿园教材 (Kindergarten teaching material). BMA, 153–4-2461.

Beijingshi Minzhengju 北京市民政局. "Guanyu Beijingshi wei Minzu wenhuagong minzu gongzuo zhanlan buchong he xiugai zhanpin gongzuo de qingshi" 关于北京市为民族文化宫民族工作展览补充和修改展品工作的请示 (The city of Beijing's request for instructions concerning the addition to and revision of the exhibits at the CPN). BMA, 2–16-60.

———. "Guanyu wei Minzu wenhuagong souji zhanpin tushu he jinxing yuzhan gongzuo jihua de qingshi" 关于为民族文化宫搜集展品图书和进行预展工作计划的请示 (Request for instructions concerning the collection of the exhibits and the plan for the preparation of the preview at the CPN). BMA, 196–2-676.

———. "Souji Minzu wenhuagong suoxu zhanpin he tushu de jihua tigang" 搜集民族文化宫所需展品和图书的计划提纲 (Outlines of collecting exhibit items and books for the CPN). BMA, 196–2-676.

———. "Wei Minzu wenhuagong souji zhanpin he tushu de jihua tigang" 为民族文化宫搜集展品和图书的计划提纲 (General plan for collecting exhibit items and books for the CPN). BMA, 196-2-676.

———, and Beijingshi Wenhuaju 北京市文化局. "Beijingshi wei Minzu wenhuagong souji zhanpin, tushu he jinxing yuzhan gongzuo jihua" 北京市为民族文化宫搜集展品, 图书和进行预展工作计划 (Beijing Municipal Government's plan for collecting exhibit items and books and preparing for the preliminary exhibition at the CPN). BMA, 196-2-676.

"Beijingshi renmin zhengfu bugao, yanli qudi Yiguandao" 北京市人民政府布告, 严厉取缔一贯道 (Proclamation of the Beijing People's Government to sternly suppress Yiguandao). RMRB, December 19, 1950, 4.

Beijingshi renmin zhengfu wenhua jiaoyu weiyuanhui 北京市人民政府文化教育委员会. "Sixiao jieban gongzuo jianbao" 私小接办工作简报 (A brief report on taking management control of the private primary schools). BMA, 11-1-70.

Beijingshi renmin zhengfu wenhua shiye guanlichu 北京市人民政府文化事业管理处. "He Zhenlibao jizhe de tanhua" 和真理报记者的谈话 (Talk with a reporter from Pravda). BMA, 11-2-160.

Beijingshi renmin zhengfu xinwen chubanchu (BPPO) 北京市人民政府新闻出版处. "Beijingshi renmin zhengfu xinwenchu yewu yu zuzhi qingkuang" 北京市人民政府新闻处业务与组织情况 (The structure and work of the BPPO). BMA, 8-1-1.

———. "Beijingshi tongsu duwu shencha jilubiao" 北京市通俗读物审查记录表 (Review lists of popular readings in Beijing). BMA, 8-2-250.

———. "Benchu diaocha fandongshu ji fanbanshu fenxi qingkuang gongzuo zongjie baogao" 本处调查反动书及翻版书分析情况工作总结报告 (The BPPO's summary report of the investigation of reactionary and reprinted books). BMA, 8-2-789.

———. "Benchu guanyu chuli jiu lianhuanhua de qingkuang baogao" 本处关于处理旧连环画的情况报告 (Report on the handling of old serial picture booklets). BMA, 8-1-73.

———. "Benchu guanyu xinwen guanli gongzuo de chubu fang'an" 本处关于新闻管理工作的初步方案 (The preliminary plan of the news management work of the BPPO). BMA, 8-2-40.

———. "Benchu jinji chuli jiu fandong shukan gongzuo jihua" 本处紧急处理旧反动书刊工作计划 (The BPPO's urgent plan on how to handle reactionary books and periodicals). BMA, 8-2-780.

———. "Chuli Dongdan, Dong'an shichang shutan shoumai fandong shuji jingguo baogao" 处理东单、东安市场书摊售卖反动书籍经过报告 (Report on handling the sale of reactionary books at Dongdan and Dong'an markets). BMA, 8-2-426.

———. "Chuli 'Xinshenghuo yundong' deng shisi zhong fandongshu xiang Chuban zongshu baogao ji pifu" 处理 "新生活运动" 等十四种反动书向出版总署报告及批复 (Report to and reply from the GAP concerning our handling of the fourteen books on the New Life Movement and other issues). BMA, 8-2-417.

———. "Dui Baowentang chubanwu de shencha jilubiao" 对宝文堂出版物的审查记录表 (Review lists of books published by Baowentang Publishing House). BMA, 8-2-227.

———. "Dui Dazhong shudian chubanwu de shendu baogao ji shencha jilubiao" 对大众
书店出版社出版物的审读报告及审查记录表 (Review report and lists of books
published by the Mass Bookstore). BMA, 8–2-453.

———. "Dui Wenhua gongyingshe chubanwu de shendu baogao" 对文化供应社出版物
的审读报告 (Report on reviewing the publications of the Cultural Supply Publishing House). BMA, 8–2-226.

———. "Dui Wushi niandai chubanshe de shendu baogao ji shencha jilubiao" 对五十年代
出版社的审读报告及审查记录表 (Review report and lists of books published by the
Fifties Publishing House). BMA, 8–2-454.

———. "Gezhong kanwu shenqing dengji chuli qingkuangbiao" 各种刊物申请登记处理
情况表 (List of ways of handling the application for registration of various types of
the periodicals). BMA, 8–1-2.

———. "Guanyu ke zhun Yanjing daxue jinkou Yindu zhixing deng liangshu de baogao"
关于可准燕京大学进口 "印度之行" 等两书的报告 (Report on the permission to
import A Passage to India and the other book proposed by Yenching University).
BMA, 8–2-629.

———. "Guanzhi guowai jinkou chubanwu diyici huiyi jilu" 管制国外进口出版物第一次
会议记录 (Minutes of the first meeting on controlling imported publications). BMA,
8–2-706.

———. "Hanfu Wenhuabu Shen buzhang de jianyi" 函复文化部沈部长的建议 (A reply
to Minister Shen's suggestions). BMA, 8–2-421.

———. "Qudi jiulishu qingkuang" 取缔旧历书情况 (On banning old almanacs). BMA,
8–2-256.

———. "Shimin Zhang Beiye jianju jiulishu de laixin ji benchu diaocha baogao" 市民张北
野检举旧历书的来信及本处调查报告 (Citizen Zhang Beiye's letter informing
against old almanacs and the BPPO's report of the investigation). BMA, 8–2-257.

———. "Tuijian benshi youliang tongsu duwu yilanbiao" 推荐本市优良通俗读物一览表
(A list of excellent popular books recommended by the city). BMA, 8–2-423.

———. "Xin lianhuanhua shencha jilubiao" 新连环画审查记录表 (Review lists of the
new serial picture stories). BMA, 8–2-159.

———. "Xinwenke yijiusijiu gongzuo zongjie" 新闻科一九四九工作总结 (Summary report of the work done by the News Section in 1949). BMA, 8–1-13.

Beijingshi shiwei wenhuabu 北京市市委文化部. "Benju dangwei guanyu yijiuwuliunian
benshi jiaoqu nongcun wenhua gongzuo qingkuang ji jinhou gaijin de baogao" 本局
党委关于一九五六年本市郊区农村文化工作情况及今后改进的报告 (Report of
the Party Committee of the Cultural Bureau on the conditions of rural cultural
work in the outlying areas of Beijing in 1956 and its future improvement). BMA,
164–1-9.

Beijingshi wenhuaju 北京市文化局. "Beijingshi wenhua shiye yuanjing guihua cao'an"
北京市文化事业远景规划草案 (Draft of Beijing's plan for future cultural activities). BMA, 164–1-163.

———. "Guanyu fenli wenhua, chuban, dianying sangeju de zuzhi jigou renyuan bianzhi
de qingshi" 关于分立文化、出版、电影三个局的组织机构人员编制的请示 (Ask for

instructions concerning the organization of the staff in the three separate bureaus of Culture, Publications, and Film). BMA, 1-24-14.

———. "Haidianqu nongcun wenhua gongzuo diaocha cailiao" 海淀区农村文化工作调查材料 (Investigation documents on the cultural work in the villages of Haidian District). BMA, 164-1-242.

"Beijingshi wenhuaju guanyu nongcun wenhua gongzuo de qingkuang ji jinhou gaijin yijian de baogao (cao'an)" 北京市文化局关于农村文化工作的情况及今后改进意见的报告 (草案) (Report of the Cultural Bureau of the City of Beijing on the conditions of rural cultural work and its future improvement [draft]). BMA, 164-1-4.

Beijingshi yuanlinchu mishushi 北京市园林处秘书室. "Benchu yijiuwusinian gongzuo zongjie" 本处1954年工作总结 (Summary of the work done by the BMBP in 1954). BMA, 98-1-157.

Beijingshi yuanlinju 北京市园林局. "Guanyu gongyuan gongzuo zhong ruogan daiyou fangxiang luxianxing wenti de diaocha baogao" 关于公园工作中若干带有方向路线性问题的调查报告 (A report concerning the direction of some of the work in public parks). BMA, 98-2-410.

Beijingshi yuanlinju bangongshi 北京市园林局办公室. "Ju dangwei yanjiu pi-Lin pi-Kong ruhe jiehe yuanyi fangzhen, guwei jinyong wenti de jilu" 局党委研究批林批孔如何结合园艺方针、古为今用问题的记录 (Records of an investigation concerning how to integrate the Anti-Lin Biao and Anti-Confucius campaigns with the gardening work as well as the issue of Using the Past to Serve the Present). BMA, 98-2-369.

Beijingshi yuanlinju geming lingdao xiaozu 北京市园林局革命领导小组. "Guanyu Wuyi youyuan huodong qingkuang de huibao" 关于五一游园活动情况的汇报 (Report on the May Day garden parties). BMA, 98-2-48.

"Beijingshi yuanlinju yijiuliusannian gongzuo zongjie" 北京市园林局一九六三年工作总结 (Summary of the work done in 1963 by the BMBP). BMA, 98-1-547.

"Beijingshi zhongzhuan, zhongxiaoxue he youeryuan jiaoyu fazhan gaikuang: cankao ziliao" 北京市中专、中小学和幼儿园教育发展概况: 参考资料 (Reference documents concerning the general situation of educational development in Beijing's technical secondary schools, secondary and primary schools, and kindergartens). BMA, 147-3-32.

Beijingshi zonggonghui wenjiaobu 北京市总工会文教部. "Kang-Mei yuan-Chao xuanchuan gongzuo de zhishi" 抗美援朝宣传工作的指示 (Instruction on the propaganda work concerning the Resist America, Aid Korea Campaign). BMA, 101-1-296.

Beijingshi zonggonghui xuanchuanbu 北京市总工会宣传部. "Beijingshi Laodong renmin wenhuagong gongzuo zonghe baogao (caogao)" 北京市劳动人民文化宫工作综合报告 (草稿) (Comprehensive report on the work done at Beijing's WPCP [draft]). BMA, 101-1-502.

"Beijingzhi: Guangbo tongxunshe chubanbian" 北京誌: 广播通讯社出版篇 (Annals of Beijing: The history of broadcasting and the news agency). BMA, 1-12-863.

"Benbao bianweihui huiyi jilu" 本报编委会会议记录 (Minutes of the editorial committee meetings at the Beijing Daily). BMA, 114-1-158.

"Benbao bianweihui huiyi jilu" 本报编委会会议记录 (Minutes of the editorial committee meetings at the *Beijing Daily*). BMA, 114–1-200.

"Benbao dangyuan qingkuang tongji baobiao" 本报党员情况统计报表 (Report on the survey of Party members at the *Beijing Daily*). BMA, 114–1-90.

"Benbao guanyu ganbu wenti de zongjie, baogao, qingkuang deng" 本报关于干部问题的总结、报告、情况等 (Report on the final findings of the cadre problems at the *Beijing Daily*). BMA, 114–1-43.

"Benbao guanyu xuanchuan baodao zhong baomi jiancha ji gaijin yijian" 本报关于宣传报道中保密检查及改进意见 (Suggestions on how to improve reports that concern confidential information at the *Beijing Daily*). BMA, 114–1-122.

"Benbao jiguan dangweihui huiyi jilu" 本报机关党委会会议记录 (Minutes of the Party Branch at the *Beijing Daily*). BMA, 114–1-233.

"Benbao xuanchuan baodao jiancha" 本报宣传报道检查 (An examination of the propaganda work at the *Beijing Daily*). BMA, 114–1-68.

"Benbao you yanzhong zhengzhi lishi wenti renyuan qingkuang" 本报有严重政治历史问题人员情况 (*Beijing Daily* staff who have serious past political problems). BMA, 114–1-127.

"Benbao zongbianji huiyi jilu" 本报总编辑会议记录 (Minutes of the chief editors' meeting at the *Beijing Daily*). BMA, 114–1-177.

"Benbao zongbianji huiyi jilu" 本报总编辑会议记录 (Minutes of the chief editors' meeting at the *Beijing Daily*). BMA, 114–1-199.

Bennett, Tony. *The Birth of the Museum: History, Theory, Politics.* London: Routledge, 1995.

"Benshi ge wenhuaguan, zhanganbu peibeibiao he xuexi jihua" 本市各文化馆、站干部配备表和学习计划 (The personnel arrangement of the cadres at various cultural centers and cultural stations in Beijing and their study plan). BMA, 11–2-77.

Berlin, Isaiah. *Against the Current: Essays in the History of Ideas.* Edited by Henry Hardy. Princeton, N.J.: Princeton University Press, 2001.

"Bianwei kuoda huiyi" 编委扩大会议 (Meeting of the expanded editorial committee). BMA, 114–1-176.

"Bianwei kuodahui taolun Mao zhu de wenti" 编委扩大会讨论毛著的问题 (How to study the writings of Chairman Mao discussed at the expanded editorial committee meeting). BMA, 114–1-216.

Bodde, Derk. *Peking Diary: A Year of Revolution.* New York: Henry Schuman, 1950.

Boitsova, Olga. "Photographs in Contemporary Russian Rural and Urban Interiors." In *Material Culture in Russia and the USSR: Things, Values, Identities,* edited by Gram H. Roberts, 71–99. London: Bloomsbury Academic, 2017.

Bonnell, Victoria E. *Iconography of Power: Soviet Political Posters under Lenin and Stalin.* Berkeley: University of California Press, 1997.

Bosco, Joseph. "Yiguan Dao: 'Heterodoxy' and Popular Religion in Taiwan." In *The Other Taiwan: 1945 to the Present,* edited by Murray A. Rubinstein, 423–444. Armonk, N.Y.: M. E. Sharpe, 1994.

Bourdieu, Pierre, and Hans Haacke. *Free Exchange.* Stanford, Calif.: Stanford University Press, 1995.

BPHJQ. Beiping heping jiefang qianhou 北平和平解放前后 (Before and after the peaceful liberation of Beiping). Edited by Beijingshi dang'anguan 北京市档案馆. Beijing: Beijing chubanshe, 1998.

BPJF. Beiping jiefang 北平解放 (The liberation of Beiping). 2 vols. Edited by Beijingshi dang'anguan 北京市档案馆. Beijing: Zhongguo dang'an chubanshe, 2009.

Brady, Anne-Marie. *Marketing Dictatorship: Propaganda and Thought Work in Contemporary China*. Lanham, Md.: Rowman and Littlefield, 2008.

Brokaw, Cynthia J., and Christopher A. Reed, eds. *From Woodblocks to the Internet: Chinese Publishing and Print Culture in Transition, circa 1800 to 2008*. Leiden: Brill, 2010.

———, and Kai-wing Chow, eds. *Printing and Book Culture in Late Imperial China*. Berkeley: University of California Press, 2005.

Brooks, Jeffrey. *How Russia Learned to Read: Literacy and Popular Literature, 1861–1917*. Princeton, N.J.: Princeton University Press, 1985.

———. *Thank You, Comrade Stalin! Soviet Public Culture from Revolution to Cold War*. Princeton, N.J.: Princeton University Press, 2000.

Brophy, David. *Uyghur Nation: Reform and Revolution on the Russia-China Frontier*. Cambridge, Mass.: Harvard University Press, 2016.

Brown, Jeremy, and Matthew D. Johnson, eds. *Maoism at the Grassroots: Everyday Life in China's Era of High Socialism*. Cambridge, Mass.: Harvard University Press, 2015.

———, and Paul G. Pickowicz, eds. *Dilemmas of Victory: The Early Years of the People's Republic of China*. Cambridge, Mass.: Harvard University Press, 2007.

Burckhardt, Jacob. *The Civilization of the Renaissance in Italy*, 2 vols. Introduced by Benjamin Nelson and Charles Trinkaus. New York: Harper & Row, 1958.

Burke, Peter. *Varieties of Cultural History*. Ithaca, N.Y.: Cornell University Press, 1997.

BZWX 1948.12–1949. Beijingshi zhongyao wenxian xuanbian, 1948.12–1949 北京市重要文献选编, 1948.12–1949 (Selected important documents of Beijing, December 1948–1949). Edited by Beijingshi dang'anguan 北京市档案馆 and Zhonggong Beijing shiwei dangshi yanjiushi 中共北京市委党史研究室. Beijing: Zhongguo dang'an chubanshe, 2001.

BZWX 1950. Beijingshi zhongyao wenxian xuanbian, 1950 北京市重要文献选编, 1950 (Selected important documents of Beijing, 1950). Edited by Beijingshi dang'anguan 北京市档案馆 and Zhonggong Beijing shiwei dangshi yanjiushi 中共北京市委党史研究室. Beijing: Zhongguo dang'an chubanshe, 2001.

BZWX 1951. Beijingshi zhongyao wenxian xuanbian, 1951 北京市重要文献选编, 1951 (Selected important documents of Beijing, 1951). Edited by Beijingshi dang'anguan 北京市档案馆 and Zhonggong Beijing shiwei dangshi yanjiushi 中共北京市委党史研究室. Beijing: Zhongguo dang'an chubanshe, 2001.

Cameron, Duncan F. "The Museum: A Temple or the Forum." In *Reinventing the Museum: Historical and Contemporary Perspectives on the Paradigm Shift*, edited by Gail Anderson, 61–73. Walnut Creek, Calif.: AltaMira Press, 2004.

Cao Fu 曹孚. "Duwei pipan yinlun" 杜威批判引论 (An introduction to Dewey criticism). *RMJY* 1, no. 6 (October 1950): 21–28; 2, no.1 (November 1950): 22–29.

Chadwick, George F. *The Park and the Town: Public Landscape in the 19th and 20th Centuries*. London: The Architectural Press, 1966.

Chang, Julian. "The Mechanics of State Propaganda: The People's Republic of China and the Soviet Union in the 1950s." In Cheek and Saich, *New Perspectives on State Socialism in China*, 76–124.

Chang, Maria Hsia. *Falun Gong: The Ends of Days*. New Haven, Conn.: Yale University Press, 2004.

Cheek, Timothy. *Propaganda and Culture in Mao's China: Deng Tuo and the Intelligentsia*. Oxford: Clarendon Press, 1997.

———, and Tony Saich, eds. *New Perspectives on State Socialism in China*. Armonk, N.Y.: M. E. Sharpe, 1997.

Chen Heqin 陈鹤琴. "Wo dui 'Huojiaoyu' de zai jiantao" 我对 "活教育" 的再检讨 (My second self-criticism of "Live Education"). *RMJY* 4 (April 1952): 8–10.

Chen, Janet Y. *Guilty of Indigence: The Urban Poor in China, 1900–1953*. Princeton, N.J.: Princeton University Press, 2012.

Chen Lifu 陈立夫. *Chengbai zhijian* 成败之鉴 (The memoirs of Chen Lifu). Taipei: Zhengzhong shuju, 1994.

Chen, Nancy N. *Breathing Spaces: Qigong, Psychiatry, and Healing in China*. New York: Columbia University Press, 2003.

Chen Qingquan 陈清泉 and Song Guangwei 宋广渭. *Lu Dingyi zhuan* 陆定一传 (Biography of Lu Dingyi). Beijing: Zhonggong dangshi chubanshe, 1999.

Chen Yung-fa 陈永发. *Yan'an de yinying* 延安的阴影 (Yan'an's shadows). Taipei: Institute of Modern History, Academia Sinica, 1990.

Cheng, Yinhong. *Creating the "New Man": From Enlightenment Ideals to Socialist Realities*. Honolulu: University of Hawai'i Press, 2009.

China Daily. "China's Xi underscores CPC's leadership in news reporting." February 20, 2016. http://www.chinadaily.com.cn/china/2016-02/20/content_23564276.htm.

Chiu, Melissa, and Shengtian Zheng, eds. *Art and China's Revolution*. New Haven, Conn.: Yale University Press, 2008.

"Chuban zongshu guanyu chajin huo chuli shukan de zhishi" 出版总署关于查禁或处理书刊的指示 (Instructions of the GAP on banning or regulating books and periodicals). BMA, 8-2-753.

"Chuban zongshu guanyu dangqian chajin jiushu zhong de yixie guiding" 出版总署关于当前查禁旧书中的一些规定 (Rules on censoring existing old publications by the GAP). BMA, 8-2-757.

Chuji xiaoxue keben yuwen dierce jiaoxue cankaoshu 初级小学课本语文第二册教学参考书 (Teaching references for Chinese language and literature in primary schools, vol. 2). Beijing: Renmin jiaoyu chubanshe, 1955.

Cliff, Tom. *Oil and Water: Being Han in Xinjiang*. Chicago: University of Chicago Press, 2016.

Coble, Park. *China's War Reporters: The Legacy of Resistance against Japan*. Cambridge, Mass.: Harvard University Press, 2015.

Conquest, Robert. *The Harvest of Sorrow: Soviet Collectivization and the Terror-Famine*. New York: Oxford University Press, 1986.

Conway, Hazel. *People's Parks: The Design and Development of Victorian Parks in Britain.* Cambridge: Cambridge University Press, 1991.

"Cuihui fandong tongzhi, jianli renmin zhengquan" 摧毁反动统治, 建立人民政权 (Smash reactionary rule, establish the people's regime). In *BZWX 1950*, 127–32.

Culp, Robert. "'China–The Land and Its People': Fashioning Identity in Secondary School History of Textbooks, 1911–37." *Twentieth-Century China* 26, no. 2 (April 2001): 17–62.

"Dai Xinwen zongshu, Chuban zongshu zhuanfa yibufen Jidujiao renshi de xuanyan de xuanchuan tongbao" 代新闻总署、出版总署转发一部分基督教人士的宣言的宣传通报 (A circular of the declaration of some Christian believers transmitted by the General Administration of the Press and the GAP). BMA, 8-2-187.

Dangdai Zhongguo congshu bianjibu 当代中国丛书编辑部, ed. *Dangdai Zhongguo de chuban shiye* 当代中国的出版事业 (The publishing industry in contemporary China). 3 vols. Beijing: Dangdai Zhongguo chubanshe, 1993.

Darnton, Robert. *Censors at Work: How States Shaped Literature.* New York: W. W. Norton, 2014.

Davis, Deborah S., Richard Kraus, Barry Naughton, and Elizabeth J. Perry, eds. *Urban Spaces in Contemporary China: The Potential for Autonomy and Community in Post-Mao China.* Washington, D.C.: Woodrow Wilson Center Press, 1995.

"Daxue Zhuxi zhuzuo, gaijin baozhi gongzuo" 大学主席著作, 改进报纸工作 (Learn Chairman Mao's writings, and improve the quality of the newspaper). BMA, 114-1-221.

de Certeau, Michel. *The Practice of Everyday Life.* Translated by Steven Rendall. Berkeley: University of California Press, 1984.

de Groot, J. J. M. *Sectarianism and Religious Persecution in China.* 2 vols. Taipei: Literature House, 1963. First published 1903.

Deng Tuo 邓拓. *Deng Tuo wenji* 邓拓文集 (Selected writings of Deng Tuo). 4 vols. Beijing: Beijing chubanshe, 1986.

"Deng Xiaoping yeye zhishu" 邓小平爷爷植树 (Grandpa Deng Xiaoping plants a tree). Accessed June 8, 2013. http://www.pep.com.cn/xiaoyu/jiaoshi/tbjx/jiaocan/tb1x/201103/t20110311_1026957.htm.

Denton, Kirk A. *Exhibiting the Past: Historical Memory and the Politics of Museums in Postsocialist China.* Honolulu: University of Hawai'i Press, 2014.

Diamant, Neil J. *Revolutionizing the Family: Politics, Love, and Divorce in Urban and Rural China, 1949–1968.* Berkeley: University of California Press, 2000.

Dingzheng xinzhuan guowen jiaokeshu 订正新撰国文教科书 (Newly revised Chinese language and literature textbook), vol. 6. n.p., n.d.

"Diyishe shencha xin lianhuanhua mingdan" 第一社审查新连环画名单 (List of serial picture story books for review by the First Association). BMA, 8-2-154.

Djankov, Simeon, and Sean Miner, eds. *China's Belt and Road Initiative Motives: Scope, and Challenges.* Washington, D.C.: Peterson Institute for International Economics, 2016.

Dong Futeng 董夫腾. "Xinshiqi wenhuaguan rencai duiwu jianshe yu guanli yanjiu" 新时期文化馆人才队伍建设与管理研究 (The recruitment of talent and management issues in cultural centers in the new era). *Dazhong wenyi* 2 (2016): 9.

Dreyer, June Teufel. *China's Forty Millions: Minority Nationalities and National Integration in the People's Republic of China*. Cambridge, Mass.: Harvard University Press, 1976.

Du, Ying. "Shanghaiing the Press Gang: The Maoist Regimentation of the Shanghai Popular Publishing Industry in the Early PRC (1949–1956)." *Modern Chinese Literature and Culture* 26, no. 2 (Fall 2014): 89–141.

Duara, Prasenjit. "Knowledge and Power in the Discourse of Modernity: The Campaigns against Popular Religion in Early Twentieth-Century China." *Journal of Asian Studies* 50, no. 1 (February 1991): 67–83.

———. *Sovereignty and Authenticity: Manchukuo and the East Asian Modern*. Lanham, Md.: Rowman and Littlefield, 2003.

Duncan, Carol. *Civilizing Rituals: Inside Public Art Museum*. London: Routledge, 1995.

Ehteshami, Anoushiravan, and Niv Horesh, eds. *China's Presence in the Middle East: The Implications of the One Belt, One Road Initiative*. Abingdon, UK: Routledge, 2018.

Ellul, Jacques. *Propaganda: The Formation of Men's Attitudes*. Translated by Konrad Kellen and Jean Lerner. New York: Vintage Books, 1973.

"2017 nian Zhongguo daxue biyesheng de qixin gongbule, han shuo, boshi" 2017年中国大学毕业生的起薪公布了,含硕、博士 (Starting salaries of university graduates, including master's degree and PhD graduates, in 2017). Accessed February 10, 2019. https://chinaqna.com/a/14973.

Ermolaev, Herman. *Censorship in Soviet Literature: 1917–1991*. Lanham, Md.: Rowman and Littlefield, 1997.

Esherick, Joseph. *Ancestral Leaves: A Family Journey through Chinese History*. Berkeley: University of California Press, 2011.

Fairbank, John K., and Kwang-ching Liu, eds. *The Cambridge History of China*. Vol. 11. Cambridge: Cambridge University Press, 1980.

Fan Jin 范瑾. "Guanyu piping yu ziwo piping deng wenti de fayan" 关于批评与自我批评等问题的发言 (Talk on criticism and self-criticism and other questions). BMA, 114-1-39.

———. "Huainian yu jinyi: Huiyi Shiwei lingdao dui *Beijing ribao* de guanhuai" 怀念与敬意: 回忆市委领导对北京日报的关怀 (Reminiscences and respect: Recalling the care given to the *Beijing Daily* by the Municipal Party leadership). *Xinwen yu chuanbo yanjiu* 1 (1983): 48–58.

Fang Cheng 方成. *Dianchuanshi* 点传师 (Yiguandao instructor). *RMRB*, August 4, 1955, 2.

Fang Hanqi 方汉奇, ed. *Zhongguo xinwen shiye tongshi* 中国新闻事业通史 (General history of Chinese journalism), 3 vols. Beijing: Zhongguo renmin daxue chubanshe, 1992–1999.

Fei Xiaotong 费孝通等, et al. *Hu Yuzhi yinxiangji* 胡愈之印象记 (Impressions of Hu Yuzhi). Rev. ed. Beijing: Zhongguo youyi chuban gongsi, 1996.

Feng Jiping 冯基平. "Jixu gaijin shoudu de shehui zhixu" 继续改进首都的社会秩序 (Continue to improve the public order in the capital). In *BZWX 1951*, 54–62.

Feng Shaoqian 冯绍谦. "Wo jianju le yeye" 我检举了爷爷 (I report my grandfather's offenses to the authorities). *RMRB*, April 17, 1951, 3.

Fitzpatrick, Sheila. *The Commissariat of Enlightenment: Soviet Organization of Education and the Arts under Lunacharsky, October, 1917-1921.* Cambridge: Cambridge University Press, 1970.

———. *Education and Social Mobility in the Soviet Union, 1921-1934.* Cambridge: Cambridge University Press, 1979.

———. *Everyday Stalinism: Ordinary Life in Extraordinary Times: Soviet Russia in the 1930s.* New York: Oxford University Press, 1999.

———. "New Perspectives on Stalinism." *Russian Review* 45, no. 4 (October 1986): 357–373.

———. "Signals from Below: Soviet Letters of Denunciation of the 1930s." In Fitzpatrick and Gellately, *Accusatory Practices,* 85–120.

———. *Stalin's Peasants: Resistance and Survival in the Russian Village after Collectivization.* New York: Oxford University Press, 1994.

———. "Supplicants and Citizens: Public Letter-Writing in Soviet Russia in the 1930s." *Slavic Review* 55, no. 1 (Spring 1996): 78–105.

———. *Tear Off the Masks! Identity and Imposture in Twentieth-Century Russia.* Princeton, N.J.: Princeton University Press, 2005.

———, and Robert Gellately, eds. *Accusatory Practices: Denunciation in Modern European History, 1789-1989.* Chicago: University of Chicago Press, 1997.

Friedrich, Carl J., and Zbigniew K. Brzezinski. *Totalitarian Dictatorship and Autocracy.* 2nd rev. ed. New York: Praeger, 1966.

Fu Zhong 孚中. *Yiguandao fazhanshi* 一贯道发展史 (The development of Yiguandao). Taibei xian: Zhengyi shanshu chubanshe, 1999.

"Furen daxue fushu youzhiyuan xueqi gongzuo zongjie" 辅仁大学附属幼稚园学期工作总结 (A summary report of the semester work at Furen University's affiliated kindergarten). BMA, 153-4-2438.

Furet, François. *Interpreting the French Revolution.* Translated by Elborg Forster. Cambridge: Cambridge University Press, 1981.

"Gaijin *Beijing wanbao* de chubu yijian" 改进北京晚报的初步意见 (Preliminary views on improving the *Beijing Evening News*). BMA, 114-1-120.

Galina 戈林娜. "Sulian de youer jiaoyu" 苏联的幼儿教育 (Kindergarten education in the Soviet Union). *RMJY* 6, (June 1952): 31–36.

———. "Sulian ertong daode pinzhi de jiaoyu" 苏联儿童道德品质的教育 (Education for moral character in Soviet children). *RMJY* 2, no. 3 (January 1951): 41–49.

———. *Sulian youer jiaoyu jiangzuo* 苏联幼儿教育讲座 (Lectures on kindergarten education in the Soviet Union). Beijing: Renmin jiaoyu chubanshe, 1953.

Gansusheng dang'anguan 甘肃省档案馆, ed. *Lanzhou jiefang* 兰州解放 (The liberation of Lanzhou). Beijing: Zhongguo dang'an chubanshe, 2009.

Gao Hua 高华. *Hongtaiyang shi zenyang shengqi de: Yan'an zhengfeng yundong de lailong qumai* 红太阳是怎样升起的: 延安整风运动的来龙去脉 (How did the sun rise? The origin and development of the Yan'an Rectification Movement). Hong Kong: Chinese University Press, 2000.

Gao, James Z. *The Communist Takeover of Hangzhou: The Transformation of City and Cadre, 1949-1954.* Honolulu: University of Hawai'i Press, 2004.

Geertz, Clifford. "Centers, Kings, and Charisma: Reflections on the Symbolics of Power." In *Local Knowledge: Further Essays in Interpretive Anthropology*, 121–146. New York: Basic Books, 1983.

———. *The Interpretation of Cultures*. New York: Basic Books, 1973.

———. *Negara: The Theatre State in Nineteenth-Century Bali*. Princeton, N.J.: Princeton University Press, 1980.

Geng Zhizhong 耿志忠. "Wo zenyang tuichule Yiguandao" 我怎样退出了一贯道 (How I withdrew from Yiguandao). *RMRB*, December 24, 1950, 3.

Geyer, Michael, and Sheila Fitzpatrick, eds. *Beyond Totalitarianism: Stalinism and Nazism Compared*. Cambridge: Cambridge University Press, 2009.

Goldman, Merle. *China's Intellectuals: Advise and Dissent*. Cambridge, Mass.: Harvard University Press, 1981.

Goldstein, Melvyn C. *A History of Modern Tibet, 1951–1955: The Demise of the Lamaist State*. Berkeley: University of California Press, 1989.

———. *A History of Modern Tibet*. Vol. 2, *The Calm before the Storm, 1951–1955*. Berkeley: University of California Press, 2007.

———. *A History of Modern Tibet*. Vol. 3, *The Storm Clouds Descend, 1955–1957*. Berkeley: University of California Press, 2014.

Gongqingtuan Beijingshi weiyuanhui 共青团北京市委员会. "Guanyu wenjiaoguan de jieshuoci" 关于文教馆的解说词 (Guidelines from the Culture and Education Center). BMA, 100-3-473.

Gongyuan guanli weiyuanhui mishushi 公园管理委员会秘书室. "Benhui yijiuwusannian gongzuo jihua yaodian" 本会一九五三年工作计划要点 (The committee's major plans for 1953). BMA, 98-1-101.

Goossaert, Vincent, and David A. Palmer. *The Religious Question in Modern China*. Chicago: University of Chicago Press, 2011.

Greenstein, Fred I. *Children and Politics*. Rev. ed. New Haven, Conn.: Yale University Press, 1969.

Grieder, Jerome B. *Hu Shih and the Chinese Renaissance: Liberalism in the Chinese Revolution, 1917–1937*. Cambridge, Mass.: Harvard University Press, 1970.

Groys, Boris. "The Struggle against the Museum; or, The Display of Art in Totalitarian Space." In Sherman and Rogoff, *Museum Culture*, 144–162.

Gu Mingyuan 顾明远. "Lun Sulian jiaoyu lilun dui Zhongguo jiaoyu de yingxiang" 论苏联教育理论对中国教育的影响 (Influence of the Soviet Union's educational theories on Chinese education). *Beijing shifan daxue xuebao (shehui kexueban)* 1 (2004): 5–13.

———. *Zhongguo jiaoyu de wenhua jichu* 中国教育的文化基础 (Cultural foundations of Chinese education). Taiyuan: Shanxi jiaoyu chubanshe, 2004.

"Guangdongsheng wenhuaguan dangzhibu kaizhan zhuti dangri xuexi huodong" 广东省文化馆党支部开展主题党日学习活动 (Studying important [Party] decisions on the special day set aside for organization activities launched by the Party Branch of the Cultural Center of Guangdong Province). Accessed January 9, 2019. http://www.gdsqyg.com/agdzxdt/workinginfo?id=2018122623760481.

"Guangzhoushi gongren wenhuagong kaiban yilai de chubu gongzuo zongjie" 广州市工人文化宫开办以来的初步工作总结 (Summary of the preliminary works performed at the Guangzhou Working People's Cultural Palace since its inception). GMA, 92-0-84.

"Guanyu baoshe qian Jing jihua he jianzao dalou gei Guowuyuan de baogao" 关于报社迁京计划和建造大楼给国务院的报告 (Report to the State Council on the relocation of *Dagong bao* and construction of office buildings). BMA, 43-1-23.

"Guanyu benshi guanche zhenya fangeming yundong de xuanchuan gongzuo tongzhi" 关于本市贯彻镇压反革命运动的宣传工作通知 (Proclamation of the city's implementation of propaganda work to suppress counterrevolutionaries). SMA, A22-1-93.

"Guanyu bianzhi yijiuwuwunian wenhua shiye jianshe jihuashi" 关于编制一九五五年文化事业建设计划事 (The plan for the cultural activities in 1955). BMA, 11-2-226.

"Guanyu Dayuejin yilai jiceng wenhua gongzuo de jiantao baogao" 关于大跃进以来基层文化工作的检讨报告 (Review of the cultural activities at the grassroots level since the Great Leap Forward). BMA, 164-1-46.

"Guanyu jiaoqu dianhua, guangbowang touzi xiaoguo jiancha baogao" 关于郊区电话、广播网投资效果检查报告 (Report on the benefits of telephones and broadcasting network in Beijing's outlying areas). BMA, 1-14-396.

"Guanyu jiaoqu nongcun zhishiqingnian muqian de sixiang, xuexi qingkuang he wenti" 关于郊区农村知识青年目前的思想、学习情况和问题 (On the present ideology and study conditions of educated youths in rural areas near Beijing). BMA, 1-12-521.

"Guanyu jieban Beijing renmin guangbo diantai wenti de qingshi baogao" 关于接办北京人民广播电台问题的请示报告 (Report on taking over the Beijing People's Radio Station). BMA, 1-12-442.

"Guanyu jinyibu gaizao minjian zhiye xiqu jutuan de fang'an" 关于进一步改造民间职业戏曲剧团的方案 (Plan for further reforming the professional folk opera troupes). BMA, 164-1-15.

"Guanyu quanmian qudi fandong huidaomen gongzuo zhong xuanchuan gongzuo de tongzhi" 关于全面取缔反动会道门工作中宣传工作的通知 (Circular of the propaganda work in the all-out suppression of counterrevolutionary sects). SMA, A22-1-93.

"Guanyu xiujian Minzu wenhuagong de huiyi jiyao" 关于修建民族文化宫的会议记要 (Minutes of the meetings on the construction of the CPN). BMA, 47-1-10.

"Guanyu xuanchuan gudong gongzuo de baogao" 关于宣传鼓动工作的报告 (Report on propaganda and agitation). BMA, 101-1-334.

"Guanyu zai shoudu ge gongyuan nei sheli laodong mofan ji zhandou yingxiong shiji tupian huiyi de jilu" 关于在首都各公园内设立劳动模范及战斗英雄事迹图片会议的记录 (Record of the meeting on displaying photos of model workers and heroic soldiers in the capital's public parks). BMA, 153-1-1238.

Guo Moruo 郭沫若, and Zhou Yang 周扬, eds. *Hongqi geyao* 红旗歌谣 (Songs of the Red Flag). Beijing: Renmin wenxue chubanshe, 1979.

Guo Yuqiang 郭玉强. "Jianguo qianhou qudi Yiguandao de douzheng" 建国前后取缔一贯道的斗争 (Struggle in the banning of Yiguandao before and after the founding of the nation). *Zhonggong dangshi ziliao* 60 (December 1996): 114–135.

Guojia minzu shiwu weiyuanhui "Zhongguo minzu gongzuo wushinian" bianji weiyuanhui 国家民族事务委员会 "中国民族工作五十年" 编辑委员会, ed. *Zhongguo minzu gongzuo wushinian* 中国民族工作五十年 (Fifty years of nationalities work in China). Beijing: Minzu chubanshe, 1999.

Guoqing gongcheng bangongshi 国庆工程办公室. "Minzu wenhuagong" 民族文化宫 (The CPN). BMA, 125-1-1219.

——. "Minzu wenhuagong shigong qingkuang" 民族文化宫施工情况 (The CPN under construction). BMA, 125-1-1219.

"Guowuyuan guanyu souji Minzu wenhuagong suoxu zhanpin he tushu de tongzhi" 国务院关于搜集民族文化宫所需展品和图书的通知 (Circular of the State Council on collecting the exhibited artifacts and books in the CPN). BMA, 196-2-676.

"Guowuyuan guanyu yanli daji feifa chuban huodong de tongzhi" 国务院关于严厉打击非法出版活动的通知 (Notice of the State Council on severely striking down illegal publishing activities). July 6, 1987. http://www.people.com.cn/electric/flfg/d4/870706.html.

Guy, R. Kent. *The Emperor's Four Treasures: Scholars and the State in the Late Ch'ien-lung Era.* Cambridge, Mass.: Council on East Asian Studies, Harvard University, 1987.

Hatch, John. "Hangouts and Hangovers: State, Class and Culture in Moscow's Workers' Club Movement, 1925–1928," *Russian Review* 53, no. 1 (January 1994): 97–117.

Hayden, Peter. *Russian Parks and Gardens.* London: Frances Lincoln, 2005.

Hayhoe, Ruth. *China's Universities, 1895–1995: A Century of Cultural Conflict.* New York: Garland, 1996.

Hayton, Bill. *Vietnam: Rising Dragon.* New Haven, Conn.: Yale University Press, 2010.

He Dongchang 何东昌, ed. *Dangdai zhongguo jiaoyu* 当代中国教育 (Contemporary Chinese education). 2 vols. Beijing: Dangdai zhongguo chubanshe, 1996.

Heilmann, Sebastian, and Elizabeth J. Perry, eds. *Mao's Invisible Hand: The Political Foundations of Adaptive Governance.* Cambridge, Mass.: Harvard University Asia Center, Harvard University, 2011.

Hershatter, Gail. *The Gender of Memory: Rural Women and China's Collective Past.* Berkeley: University of California Press, 2011.

Ho, Denise Y. *Curating Revolution: Politics on Display in Mao's China.* Cambridge: Cambridge University Press, 2018.

Holm, David. *Art and Ideology in Revolutionary China.* Oxford: Clarendon, 1991.

Hu Jiwei 胡绩伟. *Qingchun suiyue: Hu Jiwei zishu* 青春岁月: 胡绩伟自述 (Youthful days: The autobiography of Hu Jiwei). Zhengzhou: Henan renmin chubanshe, 1999.

Hu Qiaomu zhuan bianxiezu 胡乔木传编写组, ed. *Hu Qiaomu shuxinji* 胡乔木书信集 (Collected letters of Hu Qiaomu). Beijing: Renmin chubanshe, 2002.

Hu Shi sixiang pipan 胡适思想批判 (A critique of Hu Shi's thought). 8 vols. Beijing: Sanlian shudian, 1955–1956.

Hu Yuzhi 胡愈之. *Hu Yuzhi wenji* 胡愈之文集 (Collected writings of Hu Yuzhi). 6 vols. Beijing: Shenghuo, dushu, xinzhi sanlian shudian, 1996.

———. *Wo de huiyi* 我的回忆 (My memoirs). Nanjing: Jiangsu renmin chubanshe, 1990.

Huadong xingzheng weiyuanhui minzu shiwu weiyuanhui 华东行政委员会民族事务委员会. "Guanyu Huimin yaoqiu zuzhi Huimin tuanti difang zuzhi wenti de dafu" 关于回民要求组织回民团体地方组织问题的答复 (Response to the issue concerning the Hui people's request to establish local Hui organizations). SMA, B21-2-16.

Hung, Chang-tai. *Mao's New World: Political Culture in the Early People's Republic.* Ithaca, N.Y.: Cornell University Press, 2011.

———. "Mao's Parades: State Spectacles in China in the 1950s." *China Quarterly* 190 (June 2007): 411–431.

———. *War and Popular Culture: Resistance in Modern China, 1937–1945.* Berkeley: University of California Press, 1994.

Israel, John. *Lianda: A Chinese University in War and Revolution.* Stanford, Calif.: Stanford University Press, 1998.

Jacobs, Andrew. "A Would-Be Demonstrator Is Detained in China after Seeking a Protest Permit." *New York Times,* August 19, 2008, A6.

"Ji Yiguandao zuizheng zhanlan" 记一贯道罪证展览 (On the exhibition of the criminal evidence against Yiguandao). *RMRB,* March 3, 1951, 3.

Jia Fulin贾福林. *Taimiao tanyou* 太庙探幽 (A history of the Imperial Ancestral Temple). Beijing: Wenwu chubanshe, 2005.

"Jianjue qudi Yiguandao" 坚决取缔一贯道 (Determine to ban Yiguandao). *RMRB,* December 20, 1950, 1.

Jin-Cha-Ji bianqu xingzheng weiyuanhui jiaoyuting 晋察冀边区行政委员会教育厅, ed. *Guoyu keben* 国语课本 (Chinese language and literature textbook). n.p., 1948.

"Jingjiao qudi Yiguandao gongzuo zongjie" 京郊取缔一贯道工作总结 (Summary report on the banning of Yiguandao in the suburbs of Beijing). BMA, 1-14-165.

Johnson, Ian. "China's Brave Underground Journal." *New York Review of Books,* December 4, 2014, 52–53.

———. "China's Brave Underground Journal II." *New York Review of Books,* December 18, 2014, 70–72.

———. *The Souls of China: The Return of Religion after Mao.* New York: Pantheon Books, 2017.

Jordan, David K., and Daniel L. Overmyer. *The Flying Phoenix: Aspects of Chinese Sectarianism in Taiwan.* Princeton, N.J.: Princeton University Press, 1986.

JYZW. Jianguo yilai zhongyao wenxian xuanbian 建国以来重要文献选编 (Selected important documents after the founding of the nation). Edited by Zhonggong zhongyang wenxian yanjiushi 中共中央文献研究室. 20 vols. Beijing: Zhongyang wenxian chubanshe, 1992–1998.

Kairov, I. A. 凯洛夫. *Jiaoyuxue* 教育学 (Educational pedagogy). Translated by Shen Ying 沈颖 and Nan Zhishan 南致善, et al. 2 vols. Beijing: Renmin jiaoyu chubanshe, 1952. First published 1951.

"Kaizhan zhenya fangeming qunzhong yundong de xuanchuan yaodian" 开展镇压反革命群众运动的宣传要点 (Key propaganda issues in launching the suppression of the counterrevolutionary mass movement). SMA, A22-1-14.

Kecheng jiaocai yanjiusuo 课程教材研究所 and Xiaoxue yuwen kecheng jiaocai yanjiu kaifa zhongxin 小学语文课程教材研究开发中心, eds. *Yuwen: Yinianji, xiace* 语文: 一年级，下册 (Chinese: Grade one, vol. 2). Beijing: Renmin jiaoyu chubanshe, 2001.

Kelly, Catriona. *Children's World: Growing Up in Russia, 1890–1991.* New Haven, Conn.: Yale University Press, 2007.

Kenez, Peter. *The Birth of the Propaganda State: Soviet Methods of Mass Mobilization, 1917–1929.* Cambridge: Cambridge University Press, 1985.

Kiely, Jan. "The Communist Dismantling of Temple and Monastic Buddhism in Suzhou." In *Recovering Buddhism in Modern China,* edited by Jan Kiely and J. Brooks Jessup, 216–253. New York: Columbia University Press, 2016.

King, Kenneth. *China's Aid and Soft Power in Africa: The Case of Education and Training.* Woodbridge, UK: Boydell & Brewer, James Currey, 2003.

Kirby, William C. "Continuity and Change in Modern China: Economic Planning on the Mainland and on Taiwan, 1943–1958." *Australian Journal of Chinese Affairs* 20 (July 1990): 121–141.

Kirschenbaum, Lisa A. *Small Comrades: Revolutionizing Childhood in Soviet Russia, 1917–1932.* New York: Routledge, 2001.

Kołakowski, Leszek. *Main Currents of Marxism: Its Origins, Growth, and Dissolution.* 3 vols. Translated by P. S. Falla. Oxford: Clarendon Press, 1978.

Lagerwey, John. *China: A Religious State.* Hong Kong: Hong Kong University Press, 2010.

Lenin, V. I. *What Is to Be Done? Burning Questions of Our Movement.* New York: International Publishers, 1969.

Levenson, Joseph R. "The Role of Confucius in Communist China." *China Quarterly* 12 (October–December 1962): 1–18.

Leverett, Flynt, and Wu Bingbing. "The New Silk Road and China's Evolving Grand Strategy." *China Journal* 77 (January 2017): 110–132.

Li Li 李莉. "Xinshiqi zuohao xianji wenhuaguan gongzuo de jidian sikao" 新时期做好县级文化馆工作的几点思考 (On how to better manage the county-level cultural centers in the new era). *Dazhong wenyi* 14 (2012): 199.

Li Shiyu 李世瑜. *Xiandai huabei mimi zongjiao* 现代华北秘密宗教 (Secret religions in modern North China). Shanghai: Shanghai wenyi chubanshe, 1990. First published 1948.

Li Shufang 黎淑芳. "Sulian zhuanjia Gelina" 苏联专家戈丽娜 (Galina, the Soviet expert). *BJRB,* November 5, 1952, 4.

Li Weiyi 李唯一. *Zhongguo gongzi zhidu* 中国工资制度 (China's wage system). Beijing: Zhongguo laodong chubanshe, 1991.

Liang Sicheng 梁思成. *Liang Sicheng quanji* 梁思成全集 (Complete works of Liang Sicheng). 9 vols. Beijing: Zhongguo jianzhu gongye chubanshe, 2001.

"Liantiebu heibanbao zai shehuizhuyi jingsai zhong weishenme shoudao qunzhong de huanying" 炼铁部黑板报在社会主义竞赛中为什么受到群众的欢迎 (Why the newsboards in the iron-smelting section became so popular during the socialist competition). BMA, 1-12-272.

Lieberthal, Kenneth G. *Revolution and Tradition in Tientsin, 1949–1952.* Stanford, Calif.: Stanford University Press, 1980.

Lin, Yü-sheng. *The Crisis of Chinese Consciousness: Radical Antitraditionalism in the May Fourth Era*. Madison: University of Wisconsin Press, 1979.

Lin Zhu 林洙. *Dajiang de kunhuo* 大匠的困惑 (The puzzlement of a great architect). Beijing: Zuojia chubanshe, 1991.

Link, Perry. *The Uses of Literature: Life in the Socialist Chinese Literary System*. Princeton, N.J.: Princeton University Press, 2000.

Liu, Jian, and Changyun Kang. "Reflection in Action: Ongoing K–12 Curriculum Reform in China." In *Education Reform in China: Changing Concepts, Contexts and Practices*, edited by Janette Ryan, 21–40. London: Routledge, 2011.

Liu Ni 刘妮, ed. *Qingliangshan jiyi* 清凉山记忆 (Remembering Mount Qingliang). Xi'an: Sanqin chubanshe, 2011.

Liu Shaoqi 刘少奇. "Guanyu kaizhan fandui Yiguandao huodong gei Xibeiju de xin" 关于开展反对一贯道活动给西北局的信 (A letter to the Northwest Bureau concerning the launch of the anti-Yiguandao activities). *Dang de wenxian* 4 (1996): 10–11.

Liu Yu 刘御, ed. *Chuxiao guoyu* 初小国语 (Chinese language and literature for the lower primary school). n.p.: Xinhua shudian, n.d.

Lovell, Stephen. "Broadcasting Bolshevik: The Radio Voice of Soviet Culture, 1920s–1950s." *Journal of Contemporary History* 48, no. 1 (January 2013): 78–97.

Low, Setha, Dana Taplin, and Suzanne Scheld. *Rethinking Urban Parks: Public Space and Cultural Diversity*. Austin: University of Texas Press, 2005.

Lu Lezhen 卢乐珍, ed. *Youer daode qimeng de lilun yu shijian* 幼儿道德启蒙的理论与实践 (The theory and practice of the moral enlightenment of kindergartners). Fuzhou: Fujian jiaoyu chubanshe, 1999.

Lu, Yunfeng. *The Transformation of Yiguan Dao in Taiwan: Adapting to a Changing Religious Economy*. Lanham, Md.: Rowman and Littlefield, 2008.

Lu, Zhongwei. "Huidaomen in the Republican Period." *Chinese Studies in History* 44, nos. 1–2 (Fall 2010/Winter 2010–2011): 10–37.

Luo Ruiqing 罗瑞卿. *Lun renmin gong'an gongzuo* 论人民公安工作 (On the people's public security work). Beijing: Qunzhong chubanshe, 1994.

———. "Qudi fandong huidaomen gongzuo chujian chengxiao" 取缔反动会道门工作初见成效 (The initial success of the suppression of reactionary sects), in *Lun renmin gong'an gongzuo*, 169–173.

———. "Sannianlai zhenya fangeming gongzuo de weida chengjiu" 三年来镇压反革命工作的伟大成就 (The great achievements of the Zhenfan campaign in the past three years). *RMRB*, September 29, 1952, 2.

———. "Zhonggong zhongyang zhuanfa Luo Ruiqing guanyu qudi fandong huidaomen qingkuang de baogao" 中共中央转发罗瑞卿关于取缔反动会道门情况的报告 (Luo Ruiqing's report concerning the suppression of reactionary sects, transmitted by the Central Committee of the CCP). *Dang de wenxian* 4 (1996): 18–20.

Ma Nancun 马南邨 (Deng Tuo 邓拓). "Shengming de sanfen zhi yi" 生命的三分之一 (One third of life). *Beijing wanbao*, March 19, 1961, 3.

Ma Xisha 马西沙, and Han Bingfang 韩秉方. *Zhongguo minjian zongjiaoshi* 中国民间宗教史 (History of Chinese folk religions). Shanghai: Shanghai renmin chubanshe, 1992.

MacFarquhar, Roderick. *The Origins of the Cultural Revolution.* Vol. 1, *Contradictions among the People, 1956–1957.* New York: Columbia University Press, 1974.

———, and John K. Fairbank, eds. *The Cambridge History of China.* Vol. 15. Cambridge: Cambridge University Press, 1991.

———, and Michael Schoenhals. *Mao's Last Revolution.* Cambridge, Mass.: Belknap Press of Harvard University Press, 2006.

Mackerras, Colin. *China's Minorities: Integration and Modernization in the Twentieth Century.* Hong Kong: Oxford University Press, 1994.

Mally, Lynn. *Culture of the Future: The Proletkult Movement in Revolutionary Russia.* Berkeley: University of California Press, 1990.

Mao Dun 茅盾. *Sulian jianwenlu* 苏联见闻录 (What I saw and heard in the Soviet Union). Shanghai: Kaiming shudian, 1948.

Mao Zedong (Mao Tse-tung) 毛泽东. *Jianguo yilai Mao Zedong wengao* 建国以来毛泽东文稿 (Mao Zedong's manuscripts since the founding of the PRC). 13 vols. Beijing: Zhongyang wenxian chubanshe, 1987–1998.

———. *Mao Zedong wenji* 毛泽东文集 (Collected writings of Mao Zedong). Edited by Zhonggong zhongyang wenxian yanjiushi 中共中央文献研究室. 8 vols. Beijing: Renmin chubanshe, 1993–1999.

———. *Selected Works of Mao Tse-tung.* 5 vols. Peking: Foreign Languages Press, 1967–1977.

"Mao zhuxi wei *Beijing ribao* xie de baotou" 毛主席为北京日报写的报头 (The masthead of the *Beijing Daily* written by Chairman Mao). BMA, 114-1-11.

Mariani, Paul P. *Church Militant: Bishop Kung and Catholic Resistance in Communist China.* Cambridge, Mass: Harvard University Press, 2011.

Marx, Karl. "A Contribution to the Critique of Hegel's Philosophy of Right." In *Early Writings.* Introduction by Lucio Colletti. Translated by Rodney Livingstone and Gregor Benton. London: Penguin, 1992.

———. *Critique of Hegel's "Philosophy of Right."* Edited with introduction and notes by Joseph O'Malley. Cambridge: Cambridge University Press, 1970.

———. "Enquête ouvrière." In *Karl Marx: Selecting Writings in Sociology and Social Philosophy,* edited by T. B. Bottomore and Maximilien Rubel. New York: McGraw-Hill, 1956.

———. *Marx's Grundrisse.* Edited by David McLellan. London: Macmillan, 1971.

McClellan, Andrew. *Inventing the Louvre: Art, Politics, and the Origins of the Modern Museum in Eighteenth-Century Paris.* Berkeley: University of California Press, 1994.

Medvedev, Roy, ed. *The Samizdat Register.* New York: W. W. Norton, 1977.

———. *The Samizdat Register II.* New York: W. W. Norton, 1981.

Merridale, Cathereine. *Night of Stone: Death and Memory in Twentieth-Century Russia.* New York: Penguin Books, 2000.

"A Message from Confucius: New Ways of Projecting Soft Power." *The Economist,* October 22, 2009, 10.

Ministry of Education of the PRC. "Review of China's Education Reform in 2017." Accessed January 6, 2019. http://en.moe.gov.cn/News/Top_News/201801/t20180130_326023.html.

"Minzu fandian gongcheng de jiben qingkuang" 民族饭店工程的基本情况 (Basic conditions of the Nationality Hotel project). BMA, 47-1-92.

Minzu tushuguan 民族图书馆, ed. *Zhonghua renmin gongheguo minzu gongzuo dashiji, 1949-1983* 中华人民共和国民族工作大事记, 1949-1983 (Chronicle of nationalities work of the PRC, 1949-1983). Beijing: Minzu chubanshe, 1984.

"Minzu wenhuagong" 民族文化宫 (Cultural Palace of Nationalities). *Jianzhu xuebao* 9-10 (October 1959): 47-51.

"Minzu wenhuagong" 民族文化宫 (Cultural Palace of Nationalities). Accessed March 30, 2020. http://www.cpon.cn.

Minzu wenhuagong bowuguan 民族文化宫博物馆, ed. *Minzu bowuguan de lilun yu shijian* 民族博物馆的理论与实践 (Theory and practice of the ethnology museum). Beijing: Minzu chubanshe, 1999.

"Minzu wenhuagong chubu fang'an shuoming" 民族文化宫初步方案说明 (Preliminary plan of the CPN). BMA, 47-1-10.

"Minzu wenhuagong gongcheng de jiben qingkuang" 民族文化宫工程的基本情况 (The basic conditions concerning the construction of the CPN). BMA, 47-1-92.

"Minzu wenhuagong gongcheng jijian dang'an zhengli gongzuo zongjie" 民族文化宫工程基建档案整理工作总结 (Summary of putting in order the archives of the construction of the CPN). BMA, 44-1-99.

Minzu wenhuagong luocheng he shinianlai minzu gongzuo zhanlan 民族文化宫落成和十年来民族工作展览 (The completion of the CPN and the "Exhibition on Nationalities Work in the Past Ten Years"). Beijing: n.p, nd.

Mittler, Barbara. *A Continuous Revolution: Making Sense of Cultural Revolution Culture.* Cambridge, Mass.: Harvard University Asia Center, 2012.

Mosse, W. E. *Alexander II and the Modernization of Russia.* Rev. ed. New York: Collier, 1958.

Mullaney, Thomas S. *Coming to Terms with the Nation: Ethnic Classification in Modern China.* Berkeley: University of California Press, 2011.

Myer, James T. *Enemies without Guns: The Catholic Church in the People's Republic of China.* New York: Paragon, 1991.

Naimark, Norman, and Leonid Gibianskii, eds. *The Establishment of Communist Regimes in Eastern Europe, 1944-1949.* Boulder, Colo.: Westview, 1997.

Nanjingshi dang'anguan 南京市档案馆, ed. Nanjing jiefang 南京解放 (The liberation of Nanjing). 2 vols. Beijing: Zhongguo dang'an chubanshe, 2009.

Naquin, Susan. *Millenarian Rebellion in China: The Eight Trigrams Uprising of 1813.* New Haven, Conn.: Yale University Press, 1976.

Nedostup, Rebecca. *Superstitious Regimes: Religion and the Politics of Chinese Modernity.* Cambridge, Mass.: Harvard University Asia Center, 2009.

Nye, Joseph S., Jr. *Soft Power: The Means to Success in World Politics.* New York: Public Affairs, 2004.

Olmsted, Frederick Law. "The Greensward Plan: 1858." In *The Papers of Frederick Law Olmsted: Creating Central Park, 1857-1861,* edited by Charles E. Beveridge and David Schuyler, vol. 3, 117-187. Baltimore, Md.: Johns Hopkins University Press, 1983.

———. *The Papers of Frederick Law Olmsted,* Supplementary Series. Edited by Charles E. Beveridge and Carolyn F. Hoffman, vol. 1. Baltimore, Md.: Johns Hopkins University Press, 1997.

———. "The People's Park at Birkenhead, near Liverpool." In *The Papers of Frederick Law Olmsted,* Supplementary Series, 1:69–78.

———. "Preliminary Report to the Commissioners for Laying Out a Park in Brooklyn, New York." In *The Papers of Frederick Law Olmsted,* Supplementary Series, 1:79–111.

———. "Public Parks and the Enlargement of Towns." In *The Papers of Frederick Law Olmsted,* Supplementary Series, 1:171–205.

Overmyer, Daniel. *Folk Buddhist Religion: Dissenting Sects in Late Traditional China.* Cambridge, Mass.: Harvard University Press, 1976.

Ownby, David. *Falun Gong and the Future of China.* New York: Oxford University Press, 2008.

———. "Recent Chinese Scholarship on the History of 'Redemptive Societies.'" *Chinese Studies in History* 44, nos. 1–2 (Fall 2010/Winter 2010–2011): 3–9.

Peng Zhen 彭真. "Gong'an gongzuo yao yikao qunzhong" 公安工作要依靠群众 (Public security work relies on the masses). In *Peng Zhen wenxuan, 1941–1990,* 253–254.

———. *Peng Zhen wenxuan, 1941–1990* 彭真文选, 1941–1990 (Selected writings of Peng Zhen, 1941–1990). Beijing: Renmin chubanshe, 1991.

People's Daily Online. "An Honorable Night-soil Collector and His Family." September 10, 1999. http://en.people.cn/50years/celebrities/19990910C105.html.

———. "President Xi Jinping makes research tour to *People's Daily.*" February 19, 2016. http://en.people.cn/n3/2016/0219/c90000-9018740.html.

People's Republic of China (PRC). *The Common Program and Other Documents of the First Plenary Session of the Chinese People's Political Consultative Conference.* Peking: Foreign Languages Press, 1950.

———. *The Constitution of the People's Republic of China.* Peking: Foreign Languages Press, 1954.

Pepper, Suzanne. *China's Education Reform in the 1980s: Policies, Issues, and Historical Perspectives.* Berkeley: Institute of East Asian Studies, University of California, 1990.

———. *Radicalism and Education Reform in 20th-Century China: The Search for an Ideal Development Model.* Cambridge: Cambridge University Press, 1996.

Peters, Olaf, ed. *Degenerate Art: The Attack on Modern Art in Nazi Germany 1937.* Munich: Prestel, 2014.

Plato. *The Republic,* vol. 1, bk. 2. Translated by Paul Shorey. Cambridge, Mass.: Harvard University Press, 1937.

Poon, Shuk-wah. *Negotiating Religion in Modern China: State and Common People in Guangzhou, 1900–1937.* Hong Kong: Chinese University Press, 2011.

Portal, Jane. *Art under Control in North Korea.* London: Reaktion Books, 2005.

Potter, Pitman B. "Belief in Control: Regulation of Religion in China." *China Quarterly* 174 (June 2003): 317–337.

Qian Junrui 钱俊瑞. "Dangqian jiaoyu jianshe de fangzhen" 当前教育建设的方针 (Guiding principles for building contemporary education). *RMJY* 1, no. 1 (May 1950): 10–16.

———. *Qian Junrui xuanji* 钱俊瑞选集 (Selected writings of Qian Junrui). Taiyuan: Shanxi jingji chubanshe, 1986.

Qinggeltu 庆格勒图. "Jianguo chuqi Suiyuan diqu qudi Yiguandao de douzheng" 建国初期绥远地区取缔一贯道的斗争 (The banning of Yiguandao in the Suiyuan areas during the early People's Republic). *Neimenggu daxue xuebao* 33, no. 3 (May 2001): 43–48.

"Quanguo laodong mofan" 全国劳动模范 (National model workers). BMA, 101-1-1299.

Reed, Christopher A. "Advancing the (Gutenberg) Revolution: The Origins and Development of Chinese Print Communism, 1921–1947." In Brokaw and Reed, *From Woodblocks to the Internet*, 275–311.

———. *Gutenberg in Shanghai: Chinese Print Capitalism, 1876–1937.* Vancouver: UBC Press, 2004.

Ren Yuanyuan 任远远, ed. *Jinian Ren Bishi* 纪念任弼时 (In memory of Ren Bishi). Beijing: Wenwu chubanshe, 1986.

"*Renmin ribao* dinggou jinkou chubanwu de han" 人民日报订购进口出版物的函 (Letter of the *People's Daily* concerning imported publications). BMA, 8-2-641.

Roxburgh, Angus. *Pravda: Inside the Soviet News Machine.* New York: George Braziller, 1987.

Ryan, Janette, ed. *China's Higher Education Reform and Internationalisation.* London: Routledge, 2011.

Sartori, Rosalinde. "Stalinism and Carnival: Organisation and Aesthetics of Political Holidays." In *The Culture of the Stalin Period,* edited by Hans Günther, 41–77. New York: St. Martin's Press, 1990.

Schoenhals, Michael. *Doing Things with Words in Chinese Politics: Five Studies.* Berkeley: Institute of East Asian Studies, University of California, 1992.

Schudson, Michael. *Discovering the News: A Social History of American Newspapers.* New York: Basic Books, 1978.

Scott, James C. *Weapons of the Weak: Everyday Forms of Peasant Resistance.* New Haven, Conn.: Yale University Press, 1985.

Selden, Mark. *China in Revolution: The Yenan Way Revisited.* Armonk, N.Y.: M. E. Sharpe, 1995.

———. *The Yenan Way in Revolutionary China.* Cambridge, Mass.: Harvard University Press, 1971.

Shambaugh, David. "China's Propaganda: Institutions, Processes and Efficacy." *China Journal* 57 (January 2007): 25–58.

———. "China's Soft-Power Push." *Foreign Affairs* 94, no. 4 (July-August 2015): 99–107.

Shanghaishi dang'anguan 上海市档案馆, ed. *Shanghai jiefang* 上海解放 (The liberation of Shanghai). 3 vols. Beijing: Zhongguo dang'an chubanshe, 2009.

Shanghaishi minzu shiwu weiyuanhui 上海市民族事务委员会. "Ge minzu zongjiao xinyang fengsu xiguan shenghuo fuli bufen" 各民族宗教信仰风俗习惯生活福利部分 (On religious beliefs, customs, and welfare benefits of various minority groups). SMA, B21-1-5.

———. "Guanyu quhua tiaozheng hou dui gequ minzu gongzuo ganbu peibei de yijian" 关于区划调整后对各区民族工作干部配备的意见 (Views on the allocation of cadres for the ethnic minority works after the redrawing of district lines). SMA, B21-1-17-1.

———. "Minzu gongzuo youguan guiding" 民族工作有关规定 (Rules concerning the works of ethnic minorities). SMA, B21-1-42-9.

———. "Shanghaishi minzu gongzuo qingkuang baogao (caogao)" 上海市民族工作情况报告 (草稿) (Report of the work on ethnic minorities in Shanghai [draft]). SMA, B21-1-8-1.

———. "Youguan shaoshu minzu zhaogu de zanxing banfa" 有关少数民族照顾的暂行办法 (Temporary measures on giving special consideration to ethnic minorities). SMA, B21-2-16.

Shanghaishi renmin zhengfu gong'anju 上海市人民政府公安局. "Qudi fandong huidaomen xuanchuan gongzuo shouce" 取缔反动会道门宣传工作手册 (Propaganda handbook to ban reactionary sects). SMA, A22-1-93.

Shanghaishi wenhuaju 上海市文化局. "Shanghai Zhongshan gongyuan wenhuaguan 1955 nian chunjie huodong jihua 上海中山公园文化馆1955年春节活动计划 (Plans for the Cultural Center at Shanghai's Zhongshan Park during the 1955 Spring Festival). SMA, B172-4-429-42.

Shanghaishi xiongdi minzu zhaodai weiyuanhui 上海市兄弟民族招待委员会. "Zhaodai Qinghaisheng ge minzu canguantuan zonghe jianbao" 招待青海省各民族参观团综合简报 (A summary report on entertaining the ethnic groups of Qinghai Province). SMA, B21-2-65.

"Shehui wenhuake (Wenhuaguan bufen) zongjie" 社会文化科 (文化馆部分) 总结 (Summary report of the Social and Cultural Section concerning the cultural center). BMA, 11-2-189.

Shen Zhihua 沈志华. Sulian zhuanjia zai Zhongguo 苏联专家在中国 (Soviet experts in China). Beijing: Zhongguo guoji guangbo chubanshe, 2003.

Sherman, Daniel J., and Irit Rogoff, eds. Museum Culture: Histories, Discourses, Spectacles. Minneapolis: University of Minnesota Press, 1994.

Shi Ping 石坪. "Xingjian zhong de Minzu wenhuagong" 兴建中的民族文化宫 (The CPN under construction). Minzu tuanjie 16 (January 1959): 16.

"Shiwei jiguan youguan gexiang gongzuo de tongzhi ji Beijing shiwei junguanhui daihaobiao" 市委机关有关各项工作的通知及北京市委军管会代号表 (Circular on the work done by various departments in the Municipal Party and the code names in the BMCC). BMA, 40-2-2.

"Shiwei xuanchuanbu guanyu Beijingshi fazhan xuanchuanwang de qingkuang" 市委宣传部关于北京市发展宣传网的情况 (Report of the Beijing Municipal Propaganda Department on the development of the propaganda network in the city). BMA, 1-12-96.

"Shiwei xuanchuanbu guanyu zhaokai xuanchuanyuan daibiao huiyi de jihua" 市委宣传部关于召开宣传员代表会议的计划 (Plan for the meeting of representatives of the Municipal Propaganda Department). BMA, 1-12-110.

Shiwei yanjiushi 市委研究室. "Gongye wenti zuotanhui jiyao: (21) Jiefang yilai, gongchang li kaizhan le neixie qunzhong yundong?" 工业问题座谈会纪要: (二十一) 解放以来、工厂里开展了哪些群众运动? (Summary of a forum on industrial issues: (No. 21) What mass movements have been conducted in factories since the Liberation?" BMA, 1-9-585.

SHZY. Shehuizhuyi shiqi Zhonggong Beijing dangshi jishi 社会主义时期中共北京党史纪
事 (Chronicles of the history of the CCP in Beijing during the socialist period). Edited by Zhonggong Beijing shiwei dangshi yanjiushi 中共北京市委党史研究室.
4 vols. Beijing: Renmin chubanshe, 1994–1998.

Siegelbaum, Lewis H. "The Shaping of Soviet Workers' Leisure: Workers' Clubs and Palaces of Culture in the 1930s." *International Labor and Working-Class History* 56
(Fall 1999): 78–92.

———. *Stakhanovism and the Politics of Productivity in the USSR, 1935–1941.* Cambridge:
Cambridge University Press, 1988.

Sima Qian 司马迁. *Shiji* 史记 (Records of the Grand Historian). 10 vols. Beijing: Zhonghua shuju, 1987.

Sinyavsky, Andrei. "Samizdat and the Rebirth of Literature." *Index on Censorship* 9, no. 4
(1980): 8–13.

Smith, S. A. "Redemptive Religious Societies and the Communist State, 1949 to the
1980s." In Brown and Johnson, *Maoism at the Grassroots,* 340–364.

Song Guangyu 宋光宇. "Yiguandao de zuotian, jintian he mingtian" 一贯道的昨天、今天
和明天 (The past, present, and future of Yiguandao). *Lianhe yuekan* 10 (May 1982):
72–79.

Song Liansheng 宋连生. *Deng Tuo de hou shinian* 邓拓的后十年 (The last ten years of
Deng Tuo). Wuhan: Hubei renmin chubanshe, 2010.

Song Yongyi 宋永毅, ed. *Zhongguo fanyou yundong shujuku, 1957–* 中国反右运动数据
库, 1957–(The Chinese Anti-Rightist Campaign Database, 1957–). Hong Kong: Universities Service Centre for China Studies, Chinese University of Hong Kong, 2009.

Song Yulin 宋玉麟. "Huiyi Yan'an Xinhua shudian" 回忆延安新华书店 (Remembering
Yan'an's New China Bookstore), *Chuban shiliao* 2 (December 1983): 5–7.

Starr, S. Frederick. *Melnikov: Solo Architect in a Mass Society.* Princeton, N.J.: Princeton
University Press, 1978.

Stites, Richard. *Russian Popular Culture: Entertainment and Society since 1900.* Cambridge: Cambridge University Press, 1992.

Stranahan, Patricia. *Molding the Medium: The Chinese Communist Party and the Liberation Daily.* Armonk, N.Y.: M. E. Sharpe, 1990.

Strauss, Julia C. "Morality, Coercion and State Building by Campaign in the Early PRC:
Regime Consolidation and After, 1949–1956." *China Quarterly* 188 (December
2006): 891–912.

———. "Paternalist Terror: The Campaign to Suppress Counterrevolutionaries and Regime Consolidation in the People's Republic of China, 1950–1953." *Comparative
Studies in Society and History* 44, no. 1 (January 2002): 80–105.

Sun Xupei 孙旭培. *Kanke zhilu: Xinwen ziyou zai Zhongguo* 坎坷之路: 新闻自由在中国
(A bumpy road: Freedom of the press in China). Taipei: Juliu tushu gufen youxian
gongsi, 2013.

———. "Sanshinian xinwen lifa licheng yu sikao" 三十年新闻立法历程与思考 (The path
of news legislation in the past thirty years and my reflections). *Yanhuang chunqiu* 2
(2012): 1–7.

Swayze, Harold. *Political Control of Literature in the USSR, 1946–1959.* Cambridge, Mass.: Harvard University Press, 1962.

Tang Shu 唐淑, ed. *Youeryuan kecheng yanjiu yu shijian* 幼儿园课程研究与实践 (Study and practice of the kindergarten curriculum). Nanjing: Nanjing shifan daxue chubanshe, 2000.

———, and Sun Qiying 孙起英, eds. *Youeryuan kecheng jiben lilun he zhengti gaige* 幼儿园课程基本理论和整体改革 (Fundamental theories and comprehensive reform of the kindergarten curriculum). Nanjing: Nanjing shifan daxue chubanshe, 2010.

Tang, Xiaobing. *Visual Culture in Contemporary China: Paradigms and Shifts.* Cambridge: Cambridge University Press, 2015.

Taylor, Jeremy E. "The Sinification of Soviet Agitational Theatre: 'Living Newspapers' in Mao's China." *Journal of the British Association for Chinese Studies* 2 (July 2013): 27–50.

Thompson, E. P. "History from Below." *Times Literary Supplement,* April 7, 1966, 279–281.

Thornton, Patricia. *Disciplining the State: Virtue, Violence, and State-Making in Modern China.* Cambridge, Mass.: Harvard University Asia Center, 2007.

Thum, Rian. *The Sacred Routes of Uyghur History.* Cambridge, Mass.: Harvard University Press, 2014.

Tian Zuoliang 田作良. *Xianban* 仙班 (The class of the immortals). *RMRB,* May 9–12, 1951, 3.

Tillman, Margaret Mih. *Raising China's Revolutionaries: Modernizing Childhood for Cosmopolitan Nationalists and Liberated Comrades, 1920s–1950s.* New York: Columbia University Press, 2018.

Ting, Lee-hsia Hsu. *Government Control of the Press in Modern China, 1900–1949.* Cambridge, Mass.: East Asian Research Center, Harvard University, 1974.

Tobin, Joseph J., David Y. H. Wu, and Dana H. Davidson. *Preschool in Three Cultures: Japan, China, and the United States.* New Haven, Conn.: Yale University Press, 1989.

Tong Jun 童寯. *Jiangnan yuanlin zhi* 江南园林志 (History of gardens in Jiangnan), 2nd ed. Beijing: Zhongguo jianzhu gongye chubanshe, 1984.

Turner, Victor, ed. *Celebration: Studies in Festivity and Ritual.* Washington, D.C.: Smithsonian Institution Press, 1982.

Varutti, Marzia. *Museums in China: The Politics of Representation after Mao.* Woodbridge, UK: Boydell Press, 2014.

Viola, Lynne. *Peasant Rebels under Stalin: Collectivization and the Culture of Peasant Resistance.* New York: Oxford University Press, 1996.

Volland, Nicolai. "The Control of the Media in the People's Republic of China." PhD diss., University of Heidelberg, 2003.

Wakeman, Frederic, Jr. "'Cleanup': The New Order in Shanghai." In Brown and Pickowicz, *Dilemmas of Victory,* 21–58.

Wallis, Brian, ed. *Hans Haacke, Unfinished Business.* New York: New Museum of Contemporary Art, 1986.

Wang Jianjun 王建军. *Zhongguo jindai jiaokeshu fazhan yanjiu* 中国近代教科书发展研究 (A study of the development of modern Chinese textbooks). Guangzhou: Guangdong jiaoyu chubanshe, 1996.

Wang Jiangzheng 王建政. "Qianxi wenhuaguan zai qunzhong wenhua shijian zhong de zhineng yu fahui" 浅析文化馆在群众文化实践中的职能与发挥 (A brief analysis of the function and development of the cultural centers in promoting mass culture). *Dazhong wenyi* 2 (2016): 21.

Wang Jun. *Beijing Record: A Physical and Political History of Planning Modern Beijing.* Singapore: World Scientific, 2011.

Wang Lixiong 王力雄. *Tianzang: Xizang de mingyun* 天葬: 西藏的命运 (Sky burial: The destiny of Tibet). Taipei: Dakuai wenhua chuban gufen youxian gongsi, 2009.

———. *Wo de Xiyu, ni de Dongtu* 我的西域, 你的东土 (My West China, your East Turkestan). Taipei: Dakuai wenhua chuban gufen youxian gongsi, 2007.

"Weishenme yao qudi fandong huidaomen" 为什么要取缔反动会道门 (Why reactionary sects must be outlawed). SMA, A22–1-93.

Welch, Holmes. *Buddhism under Mao.* Cambridge, Mass.: Harvard University Press, 1972.

Weller, Robert P. *Alternate Civilities: Democracy and Culture in China and Taiwan.* Boulder, Colo.: Westview, 1999.

"Wenhuabu guanyu jiaqiang nongcun chunjie wenhua yishu gongzuo de zhishi" 文化部关于加强农村春节文化艺术工作的指示 (Instructions for strengthening cultural and artistic activities in villages during the Spring Festival, issued by the Ministry of Culture). BMA, 8–2-20.

"Wenhuachu gongzuo zhoubao" 文化处工作周报 (Weekly bulletin of the work of the Cultural Department). BMA, 11–2-157.

"Wenhuachu guanyu sannianlai wenhua gongzuo jiancha, wenyi gongzuo huiyi ji yijiuwuernian gongzuo zongjie baogao" 文化处关于三年来文化工作检查、文艺工作会议及1952年工作总结报告 (Summary report of the Cultural Department on the cultural work accomplished in the past three years, the working conference on literature and art, and the work completed in 1952). BMA, 11–2-148.

"Wenhuaguan de gongzi" 文化馆的工资 (Cultural center salaries). Accessed February 10, 2019. https://www.kanzhun.com/gsx1599688.html.

Widor, Claude. *The Samizdat Press in China's Provinces, 1979–1981: An Annotated Guide.* Stanford, Calif: Hoover Institution Press, Stanford University, 1987.

Williams, Louise. "Censors at Work, Censors out of Work." In *Losing Control: Freedom of the Press in Asia,* edited by Louise Williams and Roland Rich, 1–15. Canberra: Australian National University E Press, 2013.

Wilson, Richard W. *Learning to Be Chinese: The Political Socialization of Children in Taiwan.* Cambridge, Mass.: MIT Press, 1970.

Woeser, Tsering, and Wang Lixiong. *Voices from Tibet: Selected Essays and Reportage.* Edited and translated by Violet Law. Hong Kong: Hong Kong University Press, 2014.

Wong, Edward. "Xi Jinping's News Alert: Chinese Media Must Serve the Party." *New York Times,* February 23, 2016. http://www.nytimes.com/2016/02/23/world/asia/china-media-policy-xi-jinping.html.

Wood, Elizabeth A. *Performing Justice: Agitation Trials in Early Soviet Russia.* Ithaca, N.Y.: Cornell University Press, 2005.

Worden, Minky, ed. *China's Great Leap: The Beijing Games and Olympian Human Rights Challenges*. New York: Seven Stories Press, 2008.

"Woxiao shisan ge xi jiaoxue dagang baobu wengao" 我校十三个系教学大纲报部文稿 (Records of the teaching programs of thirteen departments at our university). BNUA, President's Office, 38 (1951).

"Woxiao zengpin renshi jihua" 我校增聘人士计划 (Plans for hiring additional personnel at our university). BNUA, President's Office, 26 (1951).

Xi Jinping 习近平. "Zai Wenyi gongzuo zuotanhui shang de jianghua" 在文艺工作座谈会上的讲话 (Talk at the Forum on Literature and Art). October 15, 2014. http://www.xinhuanet.com/politics/2015-10/14/c_1116825558.htm.

"Xi Jinping dao zhongyang dianshitai diaoyan" 习近平到中央电视台调研 (Xi Jinping makes research tour to China Central Television). Accessed February 20, 2016. http://news.cntv.cn/special/xjpmtdy/index.shtml.

Xiao Wenming 肖文明. "Guojia chujiao de xiandu zhi zai kaocha: yi xin Zhongguo chengli chuqi Shanghai de wenhua gaizao wei gean" 国家触角的限度之再考察: 以新中国成立初期上海的文化改造为个案 (A reinvestigation of the limitations of the official outreach program: A case study of cultural reform in Shanghai in the early years of the People's Republic). *Kaifang shidai* 3 (2013): 130–152.

Xibeiju guanyu kaizhan fandui Yiguandao huodong de gongzuo zhishi" 西北局关于开展反对一贯道活动的工作指示 (Directive of the Northwest China Bureau on the initiation of the anti-Yiguandao campaign). *Dang de wenxian* 4 (1996): 11–13.

Xinhuanet. "Hu Jintao deng dang he guojia lingdaoren canguan 'Xizang minzhu gaige wushinian daxing zhanlan'" 胡锦涛等党和国家领导人参观"西藏民主改革50年大型展览" (Hu Jintao and other Party and state leaders visited the large exhibition titled *The Fiftieth Anniversary of Democratic Reform in Tibet*). March 28, 2009.

Xiong Yuezhi 熊月之. "Wan Qing Shanghai siyuan kaifang yu gonggong kongjian de tuozhan" 晚请上海私园开放与公共空间的拓展 (The opening of private parks and the extension of the public sphere in late Qing Shanghai). *Xueshu yuekan* no. 8 (1998): 73–81.

"Xuanchuanbu yijiuliusannian shangbannian gongzuo xiaojie" 宣传部1963年上半年工作小结 (Brief summary of the work done in the first six months of 1963 by the Propaganda Department). BMA, 101-1-1170.

"Xuanchuanhua: youxiao de xuanchuan wuqi" 宣传画: 有效的宣传武器 (Propaganda pictorials: an effective weapon of propaganda). BMA, 1-12-223.

Yan Fang 颜芳. "Sulian zhuanjia dui Beijing shifan daxue jiaoyu gaige de yingxiang" 苏联专家对北京师范大学教育改革的影响 (The influence of Soviet experts on the education reforms at the Beijing Normal University). *Gaoxiao jiaoyu guanli* 5, no. 3 (May 2011): 57–61.

Yan Zhongqin 严仲勤. *Dangdai Zhongguo de zhigong gongzi fuli he shehui baoxian* 当代中国的职工工资福利和社会保险 (Wages, welfare, and social insurance of workers in contemporary China). Beijing: Dangdai Zhongguo chubanshe, 2009.

"Yancheng huebuquan de huidaomen shoue" 严惩怙恶不悛的会道门首恶 (Severely punish obdurate and irredeemable sect leaders). *RMRB*, January 19, 1951, 1.

Yang, C. K. *Religion in Chinese Society: A Study of Contemporary Social Functions of Religion and Some of Their Historical Factors*. Berkeley: University of California Press, 1961.

Yang Kuisong, "Reconsidering the Campaign to Suppress Counterrevolutionaries." *China Quarterly* 193 (March 2008): 102–121.

Ye Jianying 叶剑英. "Beipingshi junshi guanzhi weiyuanhui chengli bugao" 北平市军事管制委员会成立布告 (Proclamation of the establishment of the BMCC). In *BPHJQ*, 84–87.

"Ye Jianying guanyu Junguanhui wenti de baogao yaodian" 叶剑英关于军管会问题的报告要点 (Essential points in the report of the BMCC by Ye Jianying). In *BPJF*, 1:198–200.

"Ye shizhang zai Guangzhoushi diyici gong-nong-bing laodong mofan dahui shang de zhishi" 叶市长在第一次工农兵劳动模范大会上的指示 (Mayor Ye's instructions at the first model workers meeting of workers, peasants, and soldiers in Guangzhou). GMA, 92–0-2.

"Yidai, yilu zai woguan yanchu" 一带一路在我馆演出 (The staging of the opera *One Belt, One Road* at our cultural center). Accessed February 17, 2017. http://dcwhg .bjdch.gov.cn/n3363374/n3373107/n3373108/n3373109/c3571655/content.html.

Yiguan hairendao 一贯害人道 (A reactionary sect). A film produced by Zhongyang dianyingju, Beijing dianying zhipianchang 中央电影局, 北京电影制片厂. Beijing Film Studio, Central Film Bureau, 1952.

"Yijiuwujiunian laixin gongzuo zongjie" 1959 年来信工作总结 (Summary of the readers' letters received in 1959). BMA, 114–1-97.

"Yijiuwujiunian Guangbochu gongzuo zongjie (caogao)" 1959 年广播处工作总结 (草稿) (Summary of the work of the Broadcasting Bureau in 1959 [draft]). BMA, 164–1-234.

York, Geoffrey. "IOC Criticizes Beijing over Unused Protest Zones." *Globe and Mail*, August 21, 2008, A9.

Yu Miin-ling 余敏玲. *Xingsu "Xinren": Zhonggong xuanchuan yu Sulian jingyan* 形塑 "新人": 中共宣传与苏联经验 (Shaping the "new man": CCP propaganda and Soviet experiences). Taipei: Institute of Modern History, Academia Sinica, 2015.

Yu, Shuishan. *Chang'an Avenue and the Modernization of Chinese Architecture*. Seattle: University of Washington Press, 2013.

Yuan Ying 袁鹰. *Fengyun ceji: Wo zai Renmin ribao fukan de suiyue* 风云侧记: 我在人民日报副刊的岁月 (Sideline reports: My years working at the literary supplement of the *People's Daily*). Beijing: Zhongguo dang'an chubanshe, 2006.

Zhang Bo 张镈. *Wo de jianzhu chuangzuo daolu* 我的建筑创作道路 (My career as an architect). Beijing: Zhongguo jianzhu gongye chubanshe, 1994.

Zhang Ximing 张西铭. "Minzu wenhuagong choujian shimo" 民族文化宫筹建始末 (The story of the construction of the CPN). *Zhongguo minzubao*, February 24, 2006, 7.

Zhang Xinchen 张新辰. "Beijing laodong renmin de leyuan: Beijingshi Laodong renmin wenhuagong" 北京劳动人民的乐园: 北京市劳动人民文化宫 (The paradise of Beijing's working people: Beijing's WPCP). *RMRB*, July 19, 1953, 3.

Zhang Yihe 章诒和. *Zuihou de guizu* 最后的贵族 (The last aristocrats). Hong Kong: Oxford University Press, 2004.

"Zhenya fangeming xuanchuan gongzuo de xiaojie" 镇压反革命宣传工作的小结 (Summary of the propaganda campaign to suppress counterrevolutionaries). SMA, A22–1-14.

Zhonggong Beijing shiwei Liu Ren zhuan bianxiezu 中共北京市委刘仁传编写组, ed. *Liu Ren zhuan* 刘仁传 (The biography of Liu Ren). Beijing: Beijing chubanshe, 2000.

"Zhonggong zhongyang guanyu zhenya fangeming huodong de zhishi" 中共中央关于镇压反革命活动的指示 (Directive on the suppression of counterrevolutionary activities by the Central Committee of the CCP). In *JYZW*, 1:420–423.

Zhonggong zhongyang, Guowuyuan 中共中央、国务院 (The CCP Central Committee and the State Council). "Guanyu jiaqiang he gaijin xin xingshi xia gaoxiao sixiang zhengzhi gongzuo de yijian" 关于加强和改进新形势下高校思想政治工作的意见 (Opinions on strengthening and improving ideological and political work in higher education institutions under new circumstances). *RMRB*, February 28, 2017, 1–2.

"Zhonggong zhongyang pizhuan Zhongyang gong'anbu 'Guanyu quanguo gong'an huiyi de baogao'" 中共中央批转中央公安部"关于全国公安会议的报告" (Report on the national conference on public security, Ministry of the Public Security and transmitted by the Central Committee of the Party). In *JYZW*, 1:441–446.

Zhonggong zhongyang wenxian yanjiushi中共中央文献研究室, ed. *Liu Shaoqi nianpu, 1898–1969* 刘少奇年谱, 1898–1969 (Chronological biography of Liu Shaoqi, 1898–1969). 2 vols. Beijing: Zhongyang wenxian chubanshe, 1996.

Zhonggong zhongyang xuanchuanbu bangongting 中共中央宣传部办公厅 and Zhongyang dang'anguan bianyanbu 中央档案馆编研部, eds. *Zhongguo gongchandang xuanchuan gongzuo wenxian xuanbian, 1937–1949* 中国共产党宣传工作文献选编, 1937–1949 (Selected documents concerning the propaganda work of the Chinese Communist Central Committee, 1937–1949). Beijing: Xuexi chubanshe, 1996.

Zhongguo geming bowuguan 中国革命博物馆, ed. *Jiefangqu zhanlanhui ziliao* 解放区展览会资料 (Materials on the exhibitions in the liberated areas). Beijing: Wenwu chubanshe, 1988.

Zhongguo gongchandang Beijingshi weiyuanhui bangongting 中国共产党北京市委员会办公厅. "Wenhua jieguan weiyuanhui ge danwei renyuan mingdan" 文化接管委员会各单位人员名单 (List of names in various units of the CTC). BMA, 1-6-277.

Zhongguo renmin zhengzhi xieshang huiyi Beijingshi weiyuanhui wenshi ziliao weiyuanhui 中国人民政治协商会议北京市委员会文史资料委员会, ed. *Zhou Enlai yu Beijing* 周恩来与北京 (Zhou Enlai and Beijing). Beijing: Zhongyang wenxian chubanshe, 1998.

Zhongguo shehui kexueyuan lishi yanjiusuo Qingshishi, ziliaoshi 中国社会科学院历史研究所清史室、资料室, ed. *Qing zhongqi wusheng Bailianjiao qiyi ziliao* 清中期五省白莲教起义资料 (Materials on the White Lotus Rebellion in five provinces in the mid-Qing dynasty). 5 vols. Nanjing: Jiangsu renmin chubanshe, 1981.

Zhongguo shehui kexueyuan xinwen yanjiusuo 中国社会科学院新闻研究所, ed. *Zhongguo gongchangdang xinwen gongzuo wenjian huibian* 中国共产党新闻工作文件汇编 (Collection of CCP documents related to work in the various journalistic media). 3 vols. Beijing: Xinhua chubanshe, 1980.

"Zhonghua renmin gongheguo chengzhi fangeming tiaoli" 中华人民共和国惩治反革命条例 (PRC rules for punishing the counterrevolutionaries). *RMRB*, February 22, 1951, 1.

Zhonghua renmin gongheguo jiaoyubu 中华人民共合国教育部. *Youeryuan jiaoyu zhi-dao gangyao (shixing)* 幼儿园教育指导纲要 (试行) (Essential guide to kindergarten education [a trial run]). Beijing: Beijing shifan daxue chubanshe, 2001.

Zhonghua renmin gongheguo jiaoyubu jihua caiwusi 中华人民共和国教育部计划财务司, ed. *Zhongguo jiaoyu chengjiu: tongji ziliao, 1949–1983* 中国教育成就: 统计资料, 1949–1983 (Achievement of education in China: Statistics, 1949–1983). Beijing: Renmin jiaoyu chubanshe, 1984.

"Zhongyang guanyu zhongshi yunyong *Dagong bao* de tongzhi deng" 中央关于重视运用大公报的通知等 (Directive from the CCP Central Committee on emphasizing the importance of *Dagong bao*, and other directives). BMA, 43–1-22.

"Zhongyang he Shiwei lingdao tongzhi dui baozhi gongzuo de zhishi" 中央和市委领导同志对报纸工作的指示 (Instructions on the work of the newspapers by the leaders at the Central Committee and the Municipal Party). BMA, 114–1-198.

"Zhongyang renmin zhengfu Wenhuabu guanyu diaocha chuli huangse shukan de gexiang zhishi tongzhi" 中央人民政府文化部关于调查处理黄色书刊的各项指示通知 (Instructions of the Ministry of Culture of the Central People's Government on the investigation and handling of pornographic books and periodicals). BMA, 8–2-508.

Zhou Baochang 周保昌. "Xinhua shudian zai Yan'an chuchuang shiqi" 新华书店在延安初创时期 (The initial stages of Yan'an's New China Bookstore). *Chuban shiliao* 2 (December 1983): 1–4.

Zhou Huimei 周慧梅. *Minzhong jiaoyuguan yu Zhongguo shehui bianqian* 民众教育馆与中国社会变迁 (Popular education centers and changes in Chinese society). Taipei: Xiuwei zixun keji gufen youxian gongsi, 2013.

Zhou, Ying, and Sabrina Luk. "Establishing Confucius Institutes: A Tool for Promoting China's Soft Power?" *Journal of Contemporary China* 25, no. 100 (March 2016): 628–642.

Zhou Yingpeng 周应鹏. "Liangxiao shenghui xi kongqian: Yi xin Zhongguo chenglihou 'Diyijie quanguo chuban huiyi'" 良宵盛会喜空前: 忆新中国成立后 "第一届全国出版会议" (An unprecedented grand meeting: Remembering the First National Conference on Publishing after the establishment of a new China). Accessed February 6, 2016. http://www.pep.com.cn/cbck/200909x/201012/t20101227_993513.htm.

Zhou You 周游. "Jianchi weiwuzhuyi, jianchi shishiqiushi: jinian *Beijing ribao* chuangkan sanshi zhounian" 坚持唯物主义, 坚持实事求是: 纪念北京日报创刊三十周年 (Upholding materialism and insisting on seeking truth from facts: Commemorating the thirtieth anniversary of the founding of the *Beijing Daily*). *Xinwen yu chuanbo yanjiu* 1 (1983): 59–67.

Zhu Shunzuo 朱顺佐. *Hu Yuzhi* 胡愈之 (Hu Yuzhi). Shijiazhuang: Huashan wenyi chubanshe, 1999.

ZRGCS. Zhonghua renmin gongheguo chuban shiliao 中华人民共和国出版史料 (Historical materials relating to publications in the People's Republic of China). Edited by Zhongguo chuban kexue yanjiusuo 中国出版科学研究所 and Zhongyang dang'anguan 中央档案馆. Beijing: Zhongguo shuji chubanshe, 1995.

INDEX

Bold page numbers refer to figures or tables.

ABOUT THE AUTHOR

CHANG-TAI HUNG is chair professor of humanities emeritus at the Hong Kong University of Science and Technology. He is the author of *Going to the People: Chinese Intellectuals and Folk Literature, 1918–1937*; *War and Popular Culture: Resistance in Modern China, 1937–1945*; and *Mao's New World: Political Culture in the Early People's Republic.*

Made in the USA
Monee, IL
22 August 2022

12223503R00173